GREAT DISASTERS

GREAT DISASTERS

*Dramatic True Stories of
Nature's Awesome Powers*

The Reader's Digest Association, Inc.
Pleasantville, New York • Montreal

GREAT DISASTERS

Editor: Kaari Ward
Senior Art Editor: Robert M. Grant
Senior Editor: James Cassidy
Associate Editor: Joseph Gonzalez
Research Editor: Shirley Miller
Research Associate: Susan Yannella
Associate Art Editor: Marisa Gentile
Associate Picture Editor: Richard Pasqual
Editorial Assistant: Dolores Damm

Contributors _____

Writers: Robert C. Alberts, Charles C. Bricker, Jr.,
Robert M. Brown, Thomas Christopher,
Josh Eppinger, Martha Fay,
Charles Flowers, Mark Gasper,
Arthur John, Judson Mead,
Wendy Murphy, Donald Pfarrer,
Carl Proujan, Thomas L. Robinson,
Richard Sudhalter, Bryce Walker

Researcher: Jozefa Stuart
Picture Researcher: Natalie Goldstein
Copy Editor: Susan Converse Winslow
Indexer: Sydney Wolfe Cohen

READER'S DIGEST GENERAL BOOKS

Editor in Chief: John A. Pope, Jr.
Managing Editor: Jane Polley
Art Director: David Trooper
Group Editors: Norman B. Mack, Susan J. Wernert
Joseph L. Gardner (International)
Joel Musler (Art)
Chief of Research: Monica Borrowman
Copy Chief: Edward W. Atkinson
Picture Editor: Robert J. Woodward
Rights and Permissions: Pat Colomban
Head Librarian: Jo Manning

*Downtown Galveston at the height of the great
hurricane of 1900 (page 156).*

The acknowledgments and credits that appear on pages
319–320 are hereby made a part of this copyright page.

Library of Congress Cataloging in Publication Data

Great disasters.

At head of title: Reader's digest.
Includes index.
1. Natural disasters.   I. Reader's Digest
Association.
GB5014.G74 1989 904'.5   88-26504
ISBN 0-89577-321-X

Printed in the United States of America

CONTENTS

Foreword

Enveloped in wispy *clouds, the blue earth stands in contrast to the desolate, lifeless moon.*

OUR PLANET EARTH is a restless, violent place. Since time immemorial we have been plagued by great natural disasters—earthquakes, volcanic eruptions, floods, megastorms—that strike without warning and leave havoc and destruction in their wake.

GREAT DISASTERS tells the stories of the most dramatic of these calamities, moving chronologically from prehistoric times to the present, with a final chapter that looks at what the future may hold. Throughout the book, special features and commissioned drawings explain the natural forces behind the disasters.

We know far more today about how our planet works than our ancestors did, and yet we are nearly as powerless as they were against the forces of nature. Although we have made great strides in recent decades in tracking world weather, monitoring seismic rumblings deep underground, and otherwise keeping our finger on the earth's pulse, predicting disasters is still an infant science. From the moment of the first registered tremor at Mount St. Helens on March 20, 1980, scientists were certain that a major eruption was soon to come—but they could not say exactly when. As David A. Johnston of the U.S. Geological Survey put it: "This mountain is a powder keg, and the fuse is lit, but we don't know how long the fuse is." When the mountain finally erupted some eight weeks later, Johnston was a victim of the blast. Even the experts were stunned by the violence of the explosion, which far surpassed the destructive force of any nuclear weapon built by man.

Each year at least 20,000 people worldwide lose their lives in natural disasters; in some years the death toll is much higher. The profound human tragedy is compounded by the massive destruction of property—houses, schools, dams, factories, sometimes whole towns. The end result can be economic and social chaos. Yet amid the devastation and suffering there often emerge dramatic accounts of extraordinary individual courage, of heroic rescues, and of "miracle babies" born safe and sound against all odds. These serve as testimony to the power of the human spirit—a power as great as any wielded by nature.

Sometimes the catastrophes have a positive effect on the stricken areas. Shantytowns washed out by mud slides are rebuilt so that they will defy the next deluge; earthquake-resistant buildings rise from the rubble, making use of hard-earned knowledge that will save lives in future quakes. Burned-out forests are reborn from the ashes, stronger and healthier than those they have replaced, and farmlands on riverbanks are enriched by the fertile silt deposited by floodwaters.

Earthquakes and volcanic eruptions and floods and fires are an inevitable part of the natural cycle of destruction and renewal. GREAT DISASTERS helps us to understand and respect the awesome powers of nature and to see how their imprint has sometimes altered the course of human history for the better.

Survivors take refuge *in an open field on the outskirts of Chicago, as the city is consumed by flames (page 127). While newspapers across the U.S. were reporting on the 1871 catastrophe, Chicagoans were optimistically declaring that their city would rise again.*

DISASTERS SINCE THE DAWN OF TIME

Death of the Dinosaurs

Their 160-million-year reign comes to an abrupt end

LIKE MAMMALS TODAY, dinosaurs were a diverse group. They came in many different shapes and sizes and fitted into virtually every niche of the natural world. There were enormous beasts more than 80 feet long, the largest creatures ever to roam the earth, but there were also small dinosaurs no bigger than a raven. Some, like the triceratops, ambled along on all fours, while others, like the 40-foot-long tyrannosaur, moved on two hind feet, their short forelimbs dangling in the air. Not all these creatures were slow and ponderous, though that is how they have been depicted in popular legend. Some dinosaurs tiptoed rapidly on long, slender legs, like large birds. There were meat-eating dinosaurs with sharp, curved teeth, plant-eating ones with simple peg-shaped teeth, and a few with no teeth at all, which meant that their diet probably consisted of soft foods such as fruits, insects, and eggs. None of the different species existed for the entire 160 million years, but the dinosaurs' ability to change, adapt, and proliferate made them the most numerous land creatures of their time.

They evolved from primitive reptiles related to crocodiles sometime in the Triassic period, which ended about 200 million years ago. During the next chapter of earth history, known as the Jurassic period, dinosaurs emerged as undisputed masters of the animal kingdom, rulers of all they surveyed. They continued to produce wave after wave of new species for about another 70 million years, until the close of the Cretaceous period.

Throughout this vast time span, which was part of the Mesozoic era, the planet enjoyed a generally mild climate. There were no sharply defined seasons, and high average temperatures gave rise to lush and varied vegetation. At first the dinosaurs' habitat was a single landmass that scientists call Pangaea, or "all earth," but in time this supercontinent split up into the separate continents. The gradual dispersion seems to have posed no problem to the dinosaurs, whose skeletons have been found embedded in the sedimentary rock formations of every continent except Antarctica.

Sixty-five million years ago something terrible happened that caused the worldwide extinction of dinosaurs.

After millions of years of successful evolution, *all* the dinosaurs disappeared, seemingly at once. In layer after layer of Cretaceous rock, there are rich fossil accumulations, and then, suddenly, nothing at all. So, too, the plesiosaurs and mosasaurs (marine rep-

The Age of Reptiles, represented in a mural by Rudolph Zallinger, spanned more than 300 million years in earth history. This detail from the painting covers the last 200 million years (from right to left), to the end of the Creta-

tiles), the pterosaurs (flying reptiles), the ammonites (an ancient type of flat, spiral shellfish), and the chalk-forming plankton at the surface of the sea vanished from the face of the earth. Even the creatures that survived—certain mammals, birds, and a few reptiles—show evidence of being greatly reduced in numbers.

Just why the dinosaurs and so many lesser animals died out suddenly and without warning remains one of the most intriguing puzzles in modern paleontology. In the late 18th century, Baron Georges Cuvier of France theorized that the earth had suffered several natural catastrophes after the Creation and that these were responsible for repeated mass extinctions. The idea that certain animals had existed in the distant past and then vanished from the face of the earth was a fairly new theory, with few adherents and far-reaching implications. Before natural historians could even formally acknowledge the extinction of any other form of life, they had first to give up a fundamental religious precept: that God in His wisdom had populated the earth with all its creatures at the beginning, and for all time. Such a God would not allow any species to perish. Clues such as dinosaur bones and other fossils were variously dismissed as mistakes that God cast aside before the Creation, as the works of Mother Nature in a playful mood, or as tricks of the Devil.

Daring Cuvier, however, was on the right track. His work with fossils had already made him something of a celebrity. When the French scientist was given an extraordinarily large set of jawbones to examine in order to determine their origin, he declared that they belonged to a very ancient marine lizard that had

passed into extinction. This idea, and the discovery of yet another marine fossil that Cuvier claimed was a flying reptile, paved the way for the identification of the first dinosaur bones in Sussex, England, in the 1820's—and to the creation of the word *dinosaur*, which means terrible lizard. Since that remarkable find, scientists have offered many ingenious theories explaining their sudden disappearance.

Did dinosaurs die out because they were just too stupid to get along in their world?

One theory was that dinosaurs were slow and dumb, and were outwitted by smarter, more aggressive mammals that were their competitors. However, extensive studies show otherwise. In spite of their remarkably small brains, not only did the dinosaurs survive for an exceedingly long time, they were also one of the most versatile groups of animals that ever existed. And based on measurements of their brain cavities, they were no less intelligent than the reptiles that survived.

Another notion that found brief popularity has been playfully called dinosaur eggstermination. Given that dinosaur young were hatched from eggs, some theorists have wondered if something went awry in the egg-laying stage. Two explanations have been put forward. One holds that some other animals developed an appetite for the eggs and devoured them faster than the dinosaurs could produce new ones, thereby exhausting the supply for good. The other is that environmental stress caused the females to produce

ceous period, when the dinosaurs died out. During this time, dinosaurs had come to outnumber the earlier rep-

tiles, while grasses, flowering plants, and hardwood forests superseded primitive ferns and conifers.

extremely thin-shelled eggs, thus not only depriving embryos of sufficient calcium to build their skeletons but offering them very fragile housing to boot.

The environmental stress might have been caused by overpopulation or climatic changes, says Heinrich Erben, of the Institute of Paleontology at Bonn University. Since female birds undergoing stress are known to produce excess hormones that lead to thin eggshells, why not the dinosaur?

Changes in diet have also been implicated in the dinosaurs' disappearance. The dominant plant life on earth had once consisted of nonflowering plants, such as ferns, and cone-bearing plants, such as pine trees. The herbivorous dinosaurs feasted on this greenery, eating as much as a ton a day. But during the Creta-

ceous period, a new class of plants, the angiosperms, began to appear. They included many of the flowering deciduous trees and shrubs, leafy plants, palms, cereal grasses, bamboo, sugarcane, and such flowers as asters, dahlias, and dandelions.

Possibly the dinosaurs developed as hearty an appetite for the angiosperms as they had for the ferns and conifers. At least one paleontologist has proposed that the new food was indigestible in large quantities, and that the dinosaurs died of constipation. Another has theorized that the angiosperms caused a slow kind of poisoning or drug intoxication because they contained potent alkaloids, including strychnine and morphine. Most mammals avoid bitter tastes, and the most harmful alkaloids are very bitter; the mammals'

DISCOVERING DINOSAUR BONES

Accidental discoveries do happen. In 1822 an Englishwoman out for a stroll made one of the earliest fossil finds—some shiny teeth embedded in rocks to be used for road repairs. In 1878 coal miners in Belgium, working at a depth of more than 1,000 feet, came upon a remarkable group of skeletons. But present-day discoveries are nearly always the result of deliberate searches by paleontologists—scientists who study fossil remains.

Dinosaur fossils, like other fossils, are found only in sedimentary rock, formed when sediments are compressed by the weight of deposits that harden into rock over long periods of time. Although muscles and the other soft parts of animals and plants decay, the bones and other hard structures are preserved. Since most dinosaurs were land dwellers, sedimentary rock laid down at the bottom of the sea—the source of many a fossil—is not a prime source of dinosaur finds. Rocks that originated from river-borne sediments are. For example, dozens of skeletons have been unearthed in Utah's Dinosaur National Monument from a cliff face that was once a sandbank in a river. Currents swept dinosaur carcasses to the bank, where they were covered by sediments and preserved for future fossil hunters.

Extracting fossilized skeletons from rock is an intricate art. Although fossils are made of stone, they shatter easily, and special techniques must be employed. At the site, scientists first remove as much of the surrounding rock as possible, using jackhammers, picks, chisels, and even delicate brushes. Careful notes are made of the fossils' measurements and position, and before being moved, the bones are coated with one or more protective substances, such as shellac, plaster of paris, or polyurethane. If the fossils are to be put on display, several years' work may be required to construct a complete skeleton. Matching up the bones is like completing an intricate jigsaw puzzle—and without all of the pieces present.

Gigantic dinosaur bones are embedded in rock, tilted by earth movements, at Dinosaur National Monument, Utah.

rather highly evolved livers can detoxify the milder poisons. Is it possible that dinosaurs had not developed either sophisticated taste buds or livers and thus poisoned themselves into extinction?

In support of their argument, the alkaloid theorists point out that many dinosaur skeletons have been found in highly contorted positions, as if the animals went to their death in the kind of nervous spasm and convulsions that poisons produce. But the opinion of most experts is that the dinosaurs, however they died, underwent the same skeletal distortion that other animals experience as rigor mortis sets in. It only looks more dramatic in those dinosaurs with extraordinarily long neck muscles, which were subject to greater than average shrinkage.

Changes in the earth's climate, too, have been blamed for the demise of dinosaurs.

As the Mesozoic era drew to a close, the earth's climate was changing. In North America and Europe the land was rising and the great inland seas were disappearing; ocean currents and wind patterns were shifting too. Lush, swampy regions that supported some of the largest plant-eating dinosaur species were gradually being replaced by regions in which deciduous trees and grasses predominated, where the climate was cooler, drier, and more subject to seasonal variation. Many species of dinosaurs were doubtless affected, particularly those living in areas farthest from the equator. Still, the changes were generally so slow—taking millions of years and thousands of generations—that the animals could in all likelihood have migrated to more favorable areas before their populations diminished substantially. And climatic change alone cannot explain the dinosaurs' disappearance from the regions where tropical conditions continued to prevail long after the mass extinction.

A contrary explanation is offered by a theory involving a greenhouse effect caused by worldwide volcanic action. Theorists propose that hundreds of volcanoes were active almost simultaneously at the end of the Mesozoic era, and that their constant explosions saturated the earth's atmosphere with carbon dioxide, the product of combustion, and trapped the radiant heat from the sun. The result was a sharp rise in temperatures that disrupted the food chain at every level. This may also have inhibited the male dinosaurs' ability to produce sperm, or it may have produced hyperthermia and infertility in the females.

If volcanic action did not create a greenhouse effect, say others, it might have yielded enough chlorine gas temporarily to destroy the upper atmosphere's ozone

Two survivors *from the time of the dinosaurs are the American opossum and the ginko tree. Because the opossum (top, left) has changed so little since the Cretaceous period, it is sometimes referred to as a "living fossil." The fossilized ginko leaves (above) are not very different from those of the modern ginko (top, right).*

layer. Since the ozone layer shields the earth against excess ultraviolet radiation, its depletion would have exposed the earth's inhabitants to severe burning. Bare-skinned animals such as dinosaurs, and sea creatures that also lived partly on land, would have been subjected to heavier doses of radiation than furry mammals, feathered birds, burrowing animals, and bottom-dwelling marine life, resulting in selective extinction.

As one after another of these earth-oriented theories has failed to win decisive acceptance among scientists, more and more attention has shifted toward the possibility that some sort of cosmic catastrophe was involved. Here the paleontologists are joined in their speculations by astronomers, geologists, and geophysicists. These scholars, too, have yet to reach a consensus on what exactly killed off the dinosaurs, but some of their ideas seem to offer a real promise of solving the mystery once and for all.

One of these theories has to do with the death of a star. Whenever a dying star explodes, it releases an enormous amount of cosmic radiation. In our galaxy

such an explosion, or supernova, takes place on an average of once every 50 years, but it is usually too distant to cause any harm. However, about once every 50 million years a supernova occurs close enough to the earth to deliver a radiation dosage of perhaps 500 roentgens (nearly 17,000 times greater than the normal upper atmospheric levels). Statistically then, there would have been more than enough time for a supernova to wreak havoc in our galaxy.

The ground-level radiation might have been sufficient to kill the dinosaurs or induce a slow, cancerous death. It might very well have rendered the dinosaurs sterile or caused dramatic mutations in their offspring, making them doomed misfits in their environment. And such an explosion also might have altered the heat-retaining capacity of the atmosphere, so that the earth would have been plunged briefly into winter, and dinosaurs, with little or no insulating mechanism, would have been among the most severely affected.

The theory that keeps gaining momentum, however, involves a collision between the earth and an asteroid or comet. In 1979 geologist Walter Alvarez, of the University of California at Berkeley, announced a new and intriguing extinction hypothesis. In the Apennine Mountains of northern Italy, while carrying out routine samplings of limestone sediments dating from the Cretaceous and subsequent Tertiary eras, Alvarez had found a reddish-gray layer of clay less than an inch thick.

Uncertain about what he had uncovered, he brought the samples home to his father, Nobel Prize winning physicist Luis Alvarez. Chemical analysis showed that the clay held uncharacteristically high levels of the heavy metal iridium, which is found in high concentrations in meteorites and other cosmic materials. The clay was also barren of fossils, though the layers of limestone immediately below and above were rich in specimens.

The iridium, father and son reasoned, had to have come from outer space. The most plausible agent was an asteroid, one of those thousands of small planetary bodies that orbit the sun in a belt between Jupiter and Mars. Traveling at a speed of 45,000 miles per hour when the collision occurred, the errant asteroid, estimated to have been at least 6 miles in diameter, would have blasted out a huge crater in the earth's surface. Until recently no evidence of such a crater existed, but in June 1987, two Canadians announced a spectacular find: an undersea crater 28 miles wide. Situated on the continental shelf 125 miles southeast of Nova Scotia, the crater was found to contain rich deposits of iridium.

As a result of this powerful collision, the

The collision of an asteroid or a meteorite with the earth has been blamed by some scientists for the dinosaurs' death. This impending catastrophe is depicted in the drawing above. At right is an artist's impression of the terrifying moment of impact. A Tyrannosaurus rex, one of the most powerful of creatures, seems startled by the fiery explosion. The collision would have produced an impenetrable cloud of steam and dust, thus blotting out the life-giving sun.

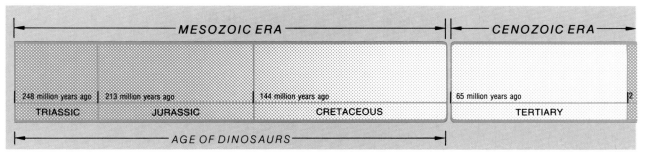

MESOZOIC ERA				CENOZOIC ERA
248 million years ago	213 million years ago	144 million years ago	65 million years ago	2
TRIASSIC	JURASSIC	CRETACEOUS		TERTIARY

AGE OF DINOSAURS

In the Mesozoic era *the earth was inhabited by reptiles, birds, and certain mammals. At the Cretaceous-Tertiary boundary, after the dinosaurs and other dominant reptiles* *became extinct, mammals began to emerge as the dominant life form. Man, however, did not arrive on the scene until a mere 2 million years ago.*

Alvarezes concluded, a cloud of dusty debris had girdled the globe, blotting out the life-giving rays of the sun and plunging the planet into darkness for several months. This caused temperatures to fall sharply, as much as 80° F in inland regions, freezing some animals and plants outright and temporarily interrupting the growth of the remaining plants. The herbivorous creatures that managed to survive the cold died for lack of food. The carnivorous dinosaurs succumbed to starvation soon after, since they depended upon a continuing supply of plant-eating creatures as their source of food.

In 1983 paleontologists of the University of Chicago charted the extinction records of some 3,500 families of marine organisms during the past 250 million years. They found that mass extinctions seem to occur with notable regularity every 26 million years. The next step was to find some cosmic phenomenon that could account for a cyclical pattern on so vast a time frame. This was a task for the astronomers and astrophysicists, and in 1984 two research teams, working independently, came up with almost identical theories.

The central figure in both theories was a mysterious sister star of the sun, variously dubbed Nemesis and Death Star. (The majority of stars in our galaxy are paired, and the fact that a companion star to our sun has not yet been sighted does not by any means rule out the possibility.) This sister star, say the theory's proponents, is perhaps one-tenth the sun's mass and travels an elongated orbit that is completed every 26 million years. At one point in its long journey, the Death Star enters a cloud of interstellar debris that exists on the outermost margins of the solar system. This penetration causes a gravitational disturbance, loosing a spectacular comet shower of perhaps a billion comets at one time. It is statistically probable that during this event from 10 to 200 of the intergallactic missiles would come crashing to earth.

Now, comets are presumed to have less mass than asteroids. Much of what makes them spectacular to see is gases, but some comets are thought to have rocky cores that could blast small craters on earth and leave the same type of iridium deposits as a colliding asteroid. So Walter Alvarez promptly set out to compare the formation dates of the 13 small comet-scaled craters on earth that have been thoroughly analyzed with the 26-million-year orbit of the Death Star and the 26-million-year cycle of mass extinctions. Surprisingly, the pattern held: each crater had been formed at a time that roughly matched the occurrence of each of the mass extinctions.

Scientists find an increasing number of clues that the earth was struck by a comet or asteroid.

In 1987 researchers at the United States Geological Survey in Denver, Colorado, announced that they had found strong evidence to support the Alvarezes' theory that a huge asteroid or comet had collided with the earth 65 million years ago. The geologists analyzed microscopic particles of quartz found in 65-million-year-old sediments from eight widely separated sites around the world. These quartz deposits contained structural cracks associated with a single cataclysmic impact. More specifically, the fractures were of a type that could only be produced by sudden impacts exceeding 1.3 million pounds per square inch, and not by the lesser pressures created by volcanic eruptions. Finally, the crystals were embedded in the same sediment layers that contained abnormally high amounts of iridium.

Whether the comet-collision theory will someday be generally accepted, or whether still other ideas are to replace or modify it, no one can yet say. But one thing seems certain: when the answers are found, they will have implications that go far beyond the margins of the dinosaurs' past—they will extend to matters of man's future too.

15

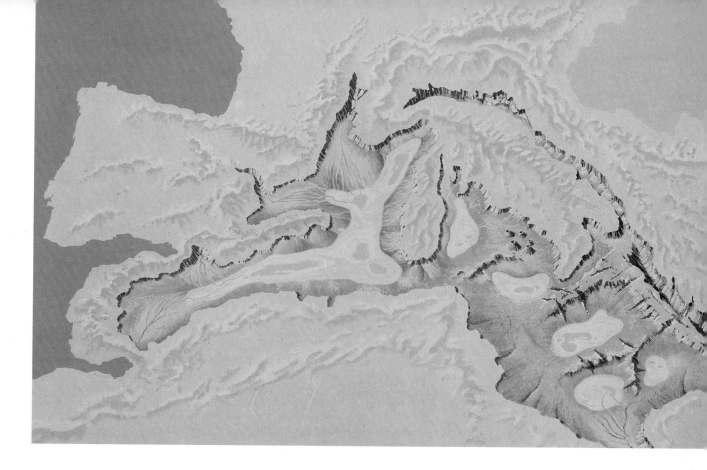

The Mediterranean Vanishes

World's largest inland sea dries up

I T IS ALMOST impossible to imagine, but the Mediterranean Sea basin was once a harsh, searing desert plunging thousands of feet below present sea level. Six million years ago, toward the end of the Miocene epoch, the Mediterranean was fed primarily by Atlantic waters flowing through narrows that cut across Spain and North Africa—predecessors of today's Strait of Gibraltar. But within a mere tick of the geologic clock, a collision of drifting continents severed the Atlantic lifeline, causing the Mediterranean to evaporate and all life within it to perish.

For hundreds of millions of years the African continental plate has been drifting north and intermittently knocking into Eurasia. For a time in the late Miocene, the grinding together of Africa and Europe pushed up the barrier between the Atlantic and the Mediterranean. Natural dams eventually formed in the shallow connecting passages between the two seas, and the Atlantic "faucets" were shut off. Without inflow from the Atlantic to replenish water lost through evaporation, the Mediterranean began to dry up at an extraordinary rate. Year by year the level of the sea fell, and the remaining waters grew ever more salty. In this increasingly hostile marine environment, bottom-

dwelling creatures were the first to become extinct. Fish and other marine animals that could not find refuge in lakes and rivers struggled for survival and lost. What had been a vast blue sea teeming with life was rapidly turning into a salt lake capable of supporting nothing but a few hardy dwarf species of mollusks.

Under a relentless sun the dying sea continued to evaporate, leaving behind a scorched desert basin.

As desert replaced the sea, vast quantities of salt left behind by the vanishing waters formed deposits thousands of feet thick in the basin's deepest parts. Within perhaps just a few millennia, the mighty Mediterranean dwindled into a series of salt-encrusted pools surrounded by sand dunes and parched salt flats.

In this newly created no-man's-land, islands were transformed into lofty mountains and plateaus, and previously submerged volcanoes towered over a desiccated landscape. Rivers that had once flowed peaceably into the Mediterranean gained new strength as

16

The appearance of the dried-out Mediterranean basin is recreated in this artist's rendering (left). Salt-encrusted pools punctuate the desert terrain. The Nile, Rhone, and other rivers that empty into the basin have carved out deep new gorges. Today, the salt flats around a brine pool in Ethiopia's Danakil Depression (above)—itself a desiccated arm of the Red Sea—give a vivid impression of what the Mediterranean desert may have looked like some 6 million years ago.

they plummeted thousands of feet into the desert basin. The Nile, the Rhone, and other resurgent rivers carved out spectacular gorges. As the rivers cut through to the exposed sea floor, they deposited gravel and other debris in their wake and, in all likelihood, gave rise to green oases along their banks.

A dried-up sea bed may even have provided a path to Europe for African animals. Small, three-toed ancestors of the horse entered what is now Spain, probably by way of a Gibraltar land bridge, and hippopotamuses wound up on the island of Cyprus.

The creation of a desert in place of a sea had an enormous impact on the global environment. Rainfall levels in Europe and Africa declined dramatically. In this drier, warmer climate, the forests of central Europe were replaced by savannas, and scientists have found evidence that palm trees flourished in Switzerland. In Africa, too, less rain led to the reduction of forests and the spread of savannas. As a result, arboreal creatures were forced to abandon the trees and adapt not only to life on the grasslands but, in some cases, to life on two legs.

Yet, however dry the Mediterranean basin may once have been, the fact remains that it is now filled with water—nearly 1 million cubic miles of it. How, then, was the sea restored, and how was the evidence of its former disappearance discovered under all that water?

The first clues that something had gone terribly wrong in the late Miocene Mediterranean came from fossils found in Italy in 1833. They revealed that 6 million years ago the marine life of the Mediterranean

had, for reasons then unknown, disappeared in a biological cataclysm. But according to the same fossil records, about a million years later, at the beginning of the Pliocene epoch, the Mediterranean was once again stocked with native species that had returned from the Atlantic as well as with newly introduced Atlantic species.

Late in the 19th century, a search for groundwater under the Valence plain in southern France revealed the existence of a deep gorge beneath the bottom of the Rhone River. The gorge was eventually found to extend nearly 200 miles, from Lyons to the Rhone Delta, and to contain Pliocene marine sediments covered by the sands and gravels of the Rhone's bed. But at the time of its discovery, and for decades afterward, scientists could offer no satisfactory explanation for the gorge's existence. Equally puzzling was the discovery in the mid-1960's of a similar but even more spectacular gorge underlying the Nile Valley for 750 miles, from Aswan to Cairo. Like its Rhone counterpart, the Nile gorge was filled with Pliocene sediments topped by alluvial debris.

A startling new clue turned up during an exploration of the Mediterranean floor by the oceanographic research vessel *Chain* in 1961. The ship was equipped with a continuous seismic-profiling (CSP) device, a sort of super echo sounder that could record sound waves bouncing back not only from the sea floor but from any hard material that might lie underneath the floor's soft sedimentary surface. In a sense, the seismic-profiling device could see into the Mediterranean

17

The Strait of Gibraltar (above) is the channel through which water from the Atlantic Ocean feeds the Mediterranean Sea and keeps it from evaporating. After opening and closing several times during the late Miocene epoch, the Atlantic "faucets" opened for the last time about 5 million years ago, and the world's greatest waterfall (left) began to refill the Mediterranean basin.

Water level today

5 million years ago

floor, and what it found there were enormous column-shaped structures, miles in diameter and hundreds to thousands of feet high, poking like fingers into the sea-floor sediment.

To scientists studying the *Chain* expedition's findings, among them Dr. William B. F. Ryan of the Lamont-Doherty Geological Observatory of Columbia University, these buried structures looked very much like the salt domes commonly found along the Gulf Coast of the United States. Salt domes are masses of salt forced up by subterranean pressures into overlying sediment layers; they come from deep beds of rock salt that geologists believe were formed by the evaporation of ancient coastal lagoons or shallow seas. But if salt domes originated in shallow-water salt deposits, what were they doing under the deepest parts of the Mediterranean basin? And if these were indeed salt domes, how did all that salt get into the Mediterranean floor in the first place?

The mystery deepened later in the 1960's with the discovery—again thanks to seismic profiling—of a

hard rock layer several hundred feet below the entire Mediterranean bottom. What puzzled experts about this feature was that ocean-floor sediments are usually soft oozes consisting of the remains of marine microorganisms. A layer of material hard enough to reflect acoustic signals from deep within the sedimentary floor seemed out of place and inexplicable.

The explanation finally came late in the summer of 1970 when the deep-sea drilling ship *Glomar Challenger* embarked on a two-month cruise of the Mediterranean with Dr. Ryan and Dr. Kenneth J. Hsü, of the Geological Institute in Zurich, Switzerland, on board as co-chief scientists. Able to drill several thousand feet into the sea floor through depths as great as 20,000 feet, the *Glomar Challenger* would help to unlock some of the Mediterranean's deepest secrets.

On the evening of August 23, the ship's crew began drilling about 100 miles southeast of Barcelona, Spain. By the following morning they had delivered the first of many surprises: gravel. Not only was it unusual to find gravel in the sea, but this sample was especially peculiar—it contained no minerals that could identify it as having been washed down from the nearby Spanish coast. Instead, the gravel seemed to have originated in a dried-up sea floor.

Later on the 24th, material brought up from the top of the hard layer under the sea floor was identified as anhydrite, one of a class of minerals called evaporites, residues left behind when brine pools evaporate. Here was a truly amazing find, for anhydrite can form only in temperatures above 95° F, a condition that could never have existed at the cold bottom of a deep-water Mediterranean. Evidently, the sea must once have been hot enough and shallow enough to allow anhydrite to form.

Six weeks of drilling in sites all over the Mediterranean basin enabled Hsü and Ryan to confirm that the mysterious hard layer was composed throughout of evaporites dating from the late Miocene epoch. In addition to anhydrite and alluvial gravel, some of the core samples turned up the fossil remains of blue-green algae, minute plant organisms that require sunlight, and therefore shallow water, to grow.

A final probe of the sea floor yielded a key to the Mediterranean's past.

As the *Glomar Challenger* headed home in October, one last borehole in a site about 80 miles west of Sardinia produced the clincher: rock salt. Because rock salt is the most soluble of the evaporites and thus the last to precipitate out of a brine, the *Glomar* scientists had been looking for it in the lowest parts of the sea floor, where the last dregs of a drying Mediterranean would have accumulated. And here, 10,000 feet down, in the central, deepest part of what must have been a vast evaporating pan, was the sought-after salt in a deposit thousands of feet thick. To Hsü and Ryan the conclusion seemed inescapable: cut off from the Atlantic Ocean by tectonic forces, the Mediterranean had evaporated under the late Miocene sun.

Now all the pieces of the puzzle began falling rapidly into place. The drying out of the Mediterranean Sea accounted for the vanished marine life, the buried river gorges, the "misplaced" salt domes, and the hard layer under the sea floor. The fact that the hard layer was sandwiched between layers of deep-water marine sediments proved that the Mediterranean had been a deep sea before, and not just after, its dry period. And as if the discovery of a Mediterranean desert were not surprising enough, the thickness of the evaporite layer and the existence of marine sediments within it indicated that the sea had dried out and flooded not once but many times during the late Miocene epoch as the floodgates between the Atlantic and the Mediterranean were repeatedly closed and opened.

Both the fossil records and the sediment at the bottom of the Nile and Rhone gorges date that last opening at the beginning of the Pliocene epoch, some 5 million years ago. "One can picture the desiccated Mediterranean as a giant bathtub, with the Strait of Gibraltar as the faucet," suggests Hsü. As the land parted, "seawater roared in from the Atlantic through the strait in a gigantic waterfall." To compensate for evaporative losses, Atlantic water must have poured into the Mediterranean basin at the astonishing rate of 10,000 cubic miles per year, in cascades 1,000 times the size of Niagara Falls. And even at that rate, it probably took a century to refill the empty "tub."

Today the African continental plate continues its northward drift into the Eurasian plate, and the Mediterranean loses more water by evaporation than it takes in from all sources other than the Atlantic Ocean. Could the sea dry up and turn into a vast desert once again? It is not likely to happen anytime soon. But according to Hsü, if the Strait of Gibraltar *were* to dam up, it would take only 1,000 or so years under present conditions for the Mediterranean to vanish as completely as it did 6 million years ago.

The floating drill rig Glomar Challenger *could sink up to four miles of pipe from her 142-foot derrick and probe deep into the sea floor. During a two-month exploration of the Mediterranean in 1970, the ship provided crucial evidence of the sea's desert phase.*

Indelible Imprint of the Ice Age

Worldwide cold alters the very nature of life on earth

IMAGINE A SUMMER DAY, 15,000 years ago. On a coastline along the North Pacific, where the Bering Sea will eventually rise to separate Siberia from Alaska, a group of men and women are butchering and skinning seals. Summer flowers nod between the rocks; the temperature is in the 50's. Beyond the beach a rough, low-lying landscape stretches more than 600 miles north to the Arctic Ocean, its vegetation too sparse to support more than occasional herds of musk oxen and smaller animals. It is the sea that provides the means of survival, and the seal hunters remain close to the bountiful shore as they make their way eastward, from Asia into North America.

Such a scene may have been familiar to the ancestors of the modern Eskimo tribes that inhabit the North American Arctic. They lived so long ago that it is difficult to imagine the time span in terms of generations. Yet the world they knew was similar to ours; they used language, built shelters, played music, painted pictures, and even wore jewelry. But their world was also colder—much colder. A mild maritime climate may have allowed flowers to blossom and birds to sing along that North Pacific coast, but elsewhere the realities of life were starkly different.

Vast areas of the earth's surface lay frozen beneath a crushing mantle of ice.

Immense sheets of ice had pushed down from the Arctic to blanket much of North America, so thick that even the top of 6,288-foot Mount Washington in present-day New Hampshire was submerged. In the west, another ice sheet reached out from the northern Rockies into the Aleutian Islands; ahead of the seal hunters, lobes of this sheet blocked passage along the coast. Northern Europe, including most of the British Isles, was buried. In the Southern Hemisphere, glaciers spilled down from the Andes and the mountains of New Zealand; Antarctica's ice sheets rode far into the sea.

In all, some 18 million cubic miles of water formed the ice covering the planet—three times the present amount. With so much water locked up as ice, sea level on average was more than 425 feet lower than it is now, increasing the world's land area by 8 percent. Where the Bering Strait is today, Asia and North America were joined by a land bridge (named Beringia by modern geographers), across which the seal hunters traveled.

All this was the result of a climatic change that began much earlier, when temperatures all over the globe turned a few degrees cooler and snow began to stay year-round over large areas of both hemispheres. This snow cover accumulated and spread, millennium after millennium, until it lay compressed in ice sheets sprawling across continents. In the Northern Hemisphere, the ice had made a great advance by 65,000 years ago, before retreating briefly into Canada and Scandinavia. Then around 18,000 years ago, it surged forward again, covering an even larger area than before, reaching as far south as southern Illinois.

Ice sheets and mountain glaciers leave impressive evidence of their movements. When glaciers are near the melting point, ice thousands of feet deep spreads out under its own weight, scraping the surface of the

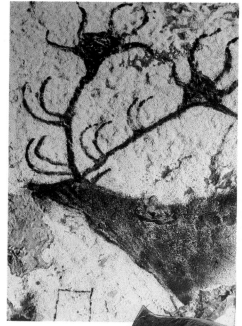

Ice age artists *recorded the life of hunting societies with an almost playful flair that suggests it was more than a constant, brutal struggle for survival. Left, this elegant deer was painted on a wall of Lascaux Cave, in France, more than 15,000 years ago. The amiable horse head below was carved on a small piece of bone.*

Vast slabs of ice *like Alaska's 40-mile-long Columbia Glacier once blanketed much of the Northern Hemisphere.*

land, carrying away debris in an icy glue. It carves parallel grooves in the bedrock as it drags its tremendous weight downhill. It breaks off rock outcrops as large as trucks and shoves them dozens of miles away, sometimes leaving one enormous stone perched precariously on a remote ledge. It flows down river valleys and scoops their V-shapes into U's, and where these glaciated valleys meet the sea the ice cuts deep fjords.

By 15,000 years ago the world's vegetation zones had shifted hundreds of miles closer to the equator. In the south of England, giant deer browsed in the chilly summer on the mosses and lichens of a harsh, treeless tundra that stretched across Europe as far as southern Russia. South of the tundra, a wide swath of cool, arid grassland reached east from the Atlantic far into Asia. Clumps of trees survived here and there, but the forests had retreated south of the Alps and Pyrenees. In North America a narrow band of tundra at the margin of the ice gave way to a forest of spruce and fir.

Even far from the ice, much of the world was inhospitable: the global climate was not only cooler but drier. In the latitudes between 30° north and 30° south, deserts covered nearly half the land, an area five times greater than today. The belt of tropical rain forests that girdles the globe had shrunk toward the equator, to less than a few hundred miles across in

some places. Much of what is now Colombian mountain forest in South America was cool grassland. In Africa, sand dunes rolled across large areas where the rain forests of Zaire flourish today.

The world's landscape is radically reshaped by every ice age, but during this last one there was an additional change to the face of the earth: a wave of extinctions that swept away most of the largest mammals. "We live in a zoologically impoverished world," the noted zoologist Alfred Wallace wrote more than a century ago, "from which all the hugest, and fiercest, and strangest forms have recently disappeared." So recently, indeed, that we have pictures of some left by early artists on cave walls.

Among the victims were such wonders as the elephant-like mammoth, of which the largest in North America was up to 14 feet tall at the shoulder, with great incurved tusks; the fearsome saber-toothed cat; a kangaroo almost 12 feet tall; the giant beaver, 9 feet long and as heavy as a modern black bear; and a ground sloth that weighed more than three tons and stood 20 feet tall when it reared up on its hind legs, braced by a thick tail, to browse in the trees.

What happened to these fantastic creatures is a mystery. The extinctions occurred in a relatively brief period, all over the world, in a variety of climatic

21

conditions. The wave of death was selective, taking large animals but sparing most small ones, scouring the land but leaving marine mammals largely undisturbed. There were other extinctions during earlier ice ages, but when they created ecological gaps, new animals evolved to fill them. This time, the species that perished were not replaced. Large animals died out worldwide. Europe was depopulated of about half its large species over a 20,000-year period, and North America lost even more. On only one continent, Africa, did any of these giants survive.

What could have caused these mass deaths? Most likely each was the result of a different combination of factors, including changes in climate and habitat, competition among species for the same diminished food supply, and disruptions of the balance between predators and prey. Africa is the only continent where animals were free to roam north and south across the equator to find favorable habitats. Finally, there was at least one factor unique to the last ice age, exploding with vitality while many of the most impressive creatures of the animal kingdom were disappearing: man.

By 150,000 years ago, Neanderthal man had evolved sufficiently to adapt to life in the bitter cold winters of glacial regions. He had heavy brow ridges, a sloping forehead, an out-thrust jaw, and heavier bones and muscles than we do. But his brain was about the same size as ours, he had roughly the same stature, and he was generally more like us than not.

Shelter from the cold *could not always be found in caves, so* Homo sapiens *became an increasingly adept engineer. This reconstruction of an ice age dwelling is made of intricately assembled mammoth bones and amply lined with animal skins.*

Then a new actor appeared on the human stage. It is generally agreed that man's ancestors evolved first in Africa, one branch then migrating to Asia more than a million years ago. Which branch spawned the modern form of *Homo sapiens*—ourselves—is open to question, but by about 50,000 years ago the Neanderthals had clearly been supplanted.

What happened to the Neanderthals is yet another mystery of the last ice age.

There is no evidence at all that modern man wiped them out. It is possible that the two types interbred and that the purely Neanderthal characteristics were absorbed by the new population. Or it may simply be that the Neanderthals were unable to compete with their more ingenious relatives.

To be sure, it was ingenuity that set modern man apart. Neanderthal hunters, for example, engaged their quarry at close quarters with knives, clubs, and spears. The newcomers had a better idea: the spear thrower, with which they could whip a killing shot from 50 feet away. Another innovation was a small sliver of bone, sharpened at one end and drilled with a flint punch at the other—in other words, the sewing needle. All in all, the appearance of modern man was marked by a dramatic leap forward in technology. And one result may have been to give some of the weakened species of mammals a last push into oblivion.

The ice age itself was destined to be forgotten over the course of time. Even as Asiatic seal hunters moved east across Beringia 15,000 years ago, the world's weather was growing warmer. Within 10,000 years the great ice sheets would be gone, except in Antarctica and Greenland and a handful of high mountain ranges. Only in relatively recent times did a few pioneering geologists realize that the same distinctive marks left by retreating glaciers in the Alps could be found in places such as Scotland, where the presence of ice sheets had never been suspected. And it was not until the 1830's that scientists began to accept the notion that ice might in fact be responsible for much of the variety in the planet's terrain.

At first it appeared that a single ice age had occurred. Bit by bit, the evidence came to suggest two, three, even four glaciations. But only with the aid of new technologies has it become possible to collect and analyze traces of past climates, deposited layer by layer in ocean sediment and deep in the ice that still caps Antarctica and Greenland. And these climate records have disclosed a much longer history of ice ages than anyone had suspected.

Each glacial cycle lasted some 90,000 to 100,000 years, and the cold spell that ended about 10,000 years ago was just the latest in a succession of ice ages

THE MYSTERIOUS MAMMOTH

In life, they resembled elephants but often sported thick shaggy fur. In death, the frozen carcasses and fossil bones of mammoths and mastodons were transformed by human imagination into the remains of fantastic and impossible creatures. It was long believed in China that mammoths were subterranean animals, described in one book as "the underground rat of the north." Fully preserved mammoths can still be found in Siberia today, entombed for at least 10,000 years in frozen earth yet remarkably, even eerily, well preserved.

Elsewhere in the world, mammoth remains usually take the form of fossilized bones and teeth, fossils more than large enough to bring legends to life. One scholar noted that an elephant's skull has a roughly circular area in the center—the nasal cavity—that could easily be mistaken for a single, large eye socket. Discoveries of such things by early Greek seafarers might well have fueled stories of one-eyed ogres that became the basis for Polyphemus, the monstrous Cyclops in Homer's epic poem *The Odyssey*.

In Renaissance Europe, mammoth tusks were prized as unicorn horns, renowned for their medicinal power. Other traditions concerned giants that lived in ancient times. Saint Christopher, for one, was long held to be a giant, and across Western Europe

Impressively life-size, this replica of a woolly mammoth stands 14 feet tall.

mammoth bones were venerated as his remains. Even when nearly complete mammoth specimens were uncovered in the 17th century, the implications were generally ignored: people would not easily give up their beliefs in such cherished creatures as unicorns and giants. As late as 1706, a mastodon tooth found in upstate New York was attributed to a giant killed in the biblical Deluge. "Without a doubt," wrote an observer, "he waded as long as he could keep his head above water, but must at length be confounded with all other creatures."

Poignant in death, this baby mammoth was unearthed in Siberia.

dating back at least 3 million years. The relatively warm intervals between them, called interglacials, have lasted only 10,000 to 12,000 years each. This 3-million-year string of ice ages is, in turn, but an episode in a much longer span of time that began some 30 to 40 million years ago when the landmass of Antarctica drifted to the South Pole and began to freeze over. Indeed, we seem to be living in a warm moment in a very cold era.

The climate records are especially provocative because when they are combined with what we know about the mechanics of our solar system, they appear to solve the mystery of what causes the ice to come and go. Regular variations in the earth's orbit around the sun and the orientation of its axis coincide very closely with the new sedimentary evidence of past climates. Evidently the slight reduction in sunlight

that occurs when the earth is farthest from the sun and tilted at its greatest angle is enough to tip the climate into an ice age. When enough ice covers the planet's surface, solar radiation is reflected away rather than being stored as warmth.

Perhaps the most intriguing question about the ice ages is when the next glacial epoch will begin. Are we living at the very end of an interglacial period—and on the brink of another plunge into the cold—or is the earth due for a few more millennia of relative warmth? Only our distant descendants will know. One thing is certain: another ice age would be a tremendous challenge for mankind, although there seems no doubt that his scientific and organizational ability would rise to that challenge. If the past record teaches nothing else, it affirms that the human race has always thrived on physical adversity.

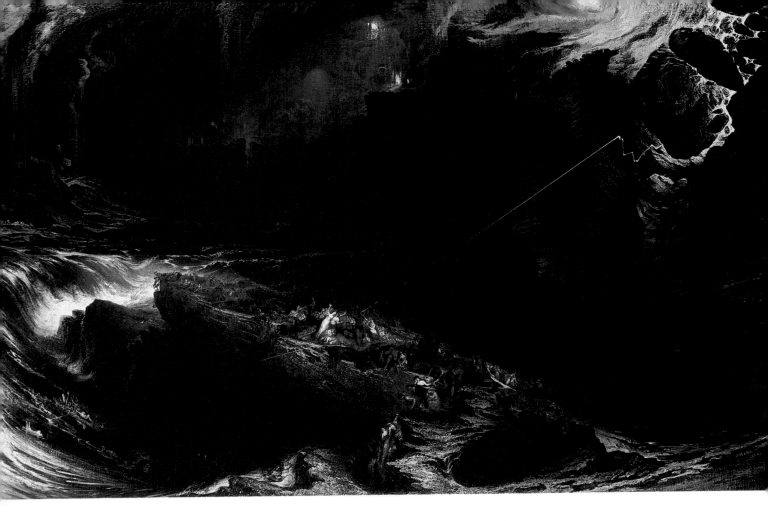

Noah's Flood

Global destruction ends with a promise of new life

I T WAS THE ULTIMATE disaster: a cataclysm so overwhelming that it brought the world to an end and heralded a second Creation. The story of Noah and the Flood, so powerfully told in the Book of Genesis, is one of human wickedness and divine wrath, of one man's righteousness and God's infinite justice and mercy. For the biblical narrator the Deluge was by no means a natural disaster but rather a divinely directed event that set human history on a new course.

From the beginning of the Genesis flood account, it is clear that events are unfolding in an age of marvels, when giants with superhuman powers walk the earth and men live prodigiously long lives. The fifth chapter of Genesis chronicles the 10 generations in the male line from Adam to Noah. These antediluvian patriarchs were between 65 and 190 years old when they sired their first children. Most lived past the age of 900, although none reached a full millennium. The longest-lived was Methuselah, Noah's grandfather,

who died in the Flood when he was 969 years old.

Unlike his predecessors, Noah waited until the age of 500 to father his three sons, Shem, Ham, and Japheth. And it was a century after their birth—1,656 years after the creation of Adam, according to the biblical genealogy—that the Flood came.

The world before the Flood was corrupted by the evil of mankind.

The earth that God had created and pronounced "good" at the beginning of the biblical account was now a corrupt place, filled with human violence and lawlessness. "The Lord saw that the wickedness of man was great in the earth, and that every imagination of the thoughts of his heart was only evil continually." Regretting His creation, God decided to send a

24

"And the waters prevailed so mightily upon the earth that all the high mountains under the whole heaven were covered." Genesis 7:19. "The Deluge" was painted by English artist John Martin in 1834.

great flood that would blot out "man and beast and creeping things and birds of the air, for I am sorry that I have made them."

Alone among men, Noah found favor with God. Because he was a righteous man, "blameless in his generation," Noah and his immediate family, and through them all future generations of mankind, would be spared the impending destruction. To save this tiny remnant of humanity, God told Noah to make "an ark of gopher wood." The Hebrew word *tevah*, usually translated as "ark," evidently means "chest" or "box," thereby implying that the vessel may not have been shaped like a ship. In fact, the Bible story never suggests that Noah could navigate the ark or even see outside it. *Gopher* is simply a transliteration of a Hebrew word that some scholars believe means "cypress." God further instructed Noah to build rooms within the ark and to cover the massive houseboat with pitch to make it waterproof.

Noah, his wife, their three sons, and their wives were the ark's only human passengers. But because all nonaquatic animals had been doomed along with mankind, a remnant of the animal world also had to be assembled. At least one male and female "of every living thing of all flesh" were brought into the ark to be kept alive by Noah and his family.

If we could match our calendar to the biblical chronology, we could say that the Flood began on February 17, in the 600th year of Noah's life. On that day "all the fountains of the great deep burst forth, and the windows of the heavens were opened." The wording of this description is significant, for it is a very specific reference to the creation story in the first chapter of Genesis. In the beginning, God had brought order out of chaos by creating a "firmament," a solid dome called Heaven, separating the celestial from the earthly waters. But now, as the waters trapped beneath the earth gushed upward and the heavenly waters burst through the opened windows of the firmament, God plunged the earth back into chaos.

It rained for 40 days and 40 nights, until the highest mountains on earth were under some 20 feet of water. Except for the ark's passengers, every air-breathing land creature on earth drowned—"birds, cattle, beasts, all swarming creatures that swarm upon the earth, and every man; everything on the dry land in whose nostrils was the breath of life died."

After 40 days the rains stopped, and a wind blew over the earth. The waters gradually subsided, and 150 days after the Flood began (July 17 on our calen-

dar) the ark rested upon "the mountains of Ararat."

Noah remained in the ark for several months after it landed. On November 10 he sent out a raven and then a dove "to see if the waters had subsided from the face of the ground." The raven "went to and fro until the waters were dried up from the earth," but the dove, finding "no place to set her foot," returned to the ark. A week later Noah released the dove once more, and this time it returned with a fresh olive leaf in its beak, a sure sign that life was starting over. When it was sent out again the following week, the dove did not come back.

Only on the first day of the new year did Noah remove the covering of the ark and look outside, and what he saw was dry ground. On February 27, one year and 10 days after the Deluge began, God sent Noah and his family and all the animals out of the ark. The first thing Noah did was to build an altar and offer animal sacrifices to God. When God "smelled the pleasing odor," He made a new covenant with Noah, his descendants, and all living creatures, promising never again to punish the entire earth for the evil of mankind but to maintain the regularity of the cycles of the seasons without fail. God blessed Noah and renewed the command given to Adam to "be fruitful and multiply." And the rainbow, God said, would be the sign of the new covenant, a reminder "that never again shall all flesh be cut off by the waters of a flood."

Noah directs the building of the ark in this 9th-century A.D. Italian ivory relief. According to Genesis, the ark was made of gopher wood and sealed with pitch. The three-decked vessel measured about 450 feet long, 75 feet wide, and 45 feet high.

ANCIENT GREAT FLOODS

Many scholars believe that the biblical flood narrative weaves together two separate Hebrew traditions—as is evident in the text's many repetitions and inconsistencies. Though the two traditions were probably not combined until about the fifth century B.C., the older version was first recorded some five centuries earlier.

The Gilgamesh flood story on a 7th-century B.C. tablet.

Related to the biblical account, but far older, are Mesopotamian flood stories, such as the one contained in the *Epic of Gilgamesh*. Composed no later than 2000 B.C., the poem tells the story of the hero-king Gilgamesh and his quest for immortality. To learn the secret of eternal life, Gilgamesh seeks out Utnapishtim, the Babylonian Noah, who after surviving a universal flood was immortalized by the gods. But as he tells his story, Utnapishtim makes it clear that he has no secret to impart.

Led by the warlike Enlil, the council of the gods decided—for unstated reasons—to destroy mankind by a flood. But the god Ea warned Utnapishtim and told him to build a cube-shaped vessel and to bring into it "the seed of all living things." After Utnapishtim, his family, craftsmen, a boatman, and assorted animals were safely on board, the tempest began. It raged on for six days, and when it was over, "all of mankind had returned to clay." Seven days after the ship landed on Mount Nisir, Utnapishtim first sent out a dove, which came back to him, then a swallow, which also returned, and finally a raven, which stayed away. After emptying the ship, Utnapishtim offered sacrifices to the gods, who "smelled the sweet savor" and came crowding around. They debated the wisdom of destroying mankind for its sins, until even Enlil relented and made Utnapishtim and his wife immortal.

The similarities between the Utnapishtim and Noah stories have convinced many scholars that the biblical narrative was derived from Mesopotamian sources. Yet the Hebrew version differs significantly from any possible antecedents. Its account of specific human evil, divine retribution, and God's solemn, life-affirming covenant with creation is far removed from the arbitrary world of Utnapishtim and his quarrelsome gods.

The story of Noah and the Flood is one of the best-known passages in the Bible and a special favorite of children the world over. But its fascination is by no means limited to the young. The biblical account of the Deluge has given rise to much religious debate and archeological research. Was there really a universal flood, and if so, can evidence of it be found?

At one time, the appearance of shell fossils on mountaintops seemed incontrovertible proof that the entire earth had once been submerged. Today, however, we know that continental drift and other geologic forces explain the fossil records better than the theory of a universal flood does.

But is there other evidence? If a relatively minor inundation can leave behind thousands of tons of mud and silt, the biblical Deluge should have deposited a massive flood layer throughout the globe. Yet the search for such a universal flood layer has proved fruitless. Even in Israel, the home of the Scriptures, where excavations of sites such as Jericho have revealed settlements dating as far back as 8000 B.C., no evidence of the interruption of life by massive flooding has ever been unearthed.

The situation is different, however, in Mesopotamia. In the valley of the Tigris and Euphrates rivers, signs of destructive floods have been found at several sites.

Archeologist Woolley *and his crew stand over a Mesopotamian burial pit in 1929. Excavations here revealed a flood layer dating from about 3500 B.C.*

Christian tradition *designated this peak in northeast Turkey as Mount Ararat, where the ark is said to have landed.*

The most famous is the ancient Sumerian city of Ur. There, in 1929, excavations led by the British archeologist Sir Charles Leonard Woolley revealed that the levels of occupation at the site were interrupted by an eight-foot-thick layer of mud containing no traces of human habitation and dating from about 3500 B.C.

Was the evidence of an ancient flood in Mesopotamia linked to the Deluge?

It was Mrs. Woolley who, upon seeing the mud layer at Ur, first ventured the opinion that "of course, it's the Flood." And to an extent she was right. The break in the life of Ur was the result of a great flood, but not of *the* flood. Leonard Woolley's own excavations at a nearby site uncovered no flood layer at all, proving that the inundation at Ur was a local phenomenon.

Similar flood deposits were discovered by other archeologists in the sites of ancient Mesopotamian cities such as Nineveh and Kish, but these floods probably occurred at different times than the one at Ur and were also purely local. Such inundations may have been the basis of the various Mesopotamian flood legends from which the more recent biblical account seems to be derived, but none can lay claim to being the universal flood described in the Bible.

Despite the lack of archeological evidence of Noah's Flood, the hope of finding traces of his ark has long attracted people to the mountain in northeast Turkey traditionally held to be Mount Ararat. Since the mountain was first scaled in 1829, several explorers have mounted expeditions in search of the vessel. The most promising piece of evidence was discovered by a French industrialist named Fernand Navarra. According to Navarra's account of his 1955 Ararat expedition, he found hand-worked timber and other wood fragments in a glacial crevasse about 14,000 feet up the mountain. The forestry experts who first examined Navarra's find dated it at about 3000 B.C. But tests using the carbon-14 dating method indicated that the timber was cut sometime between the sixth and the ninth centuries A.D. Navarra's wooden structure, scientists believe, was more likely a shrine built by local monks to commemorate the ark than the ark itself.

Whether the Genesis flood story is based on an actual universal deluge, on a devastating local inundation that worked its way into mythology, or on the collective memory of the countless floods that have plagued man wherever he has dwelt may never be known and ultimately matters little. Rather, it is the religious and moral impact of Noah's story that has made it live so powerfully in the traditions of Judaism, Christianity, and Islam. Unlike the Mesopotamian legends, in which a flood is unleashed by capricious gods for uncertain reasons, the biblical account is a specific indictment of man's potential for evil and a clear revelation of God's character. The story vividly portrays God's deadly wrath against human wickedness as well as His concern for the continuity and prosperity of life on earth. For this, the greatest of all disaster stories, ends with a ringing affirmation of life and a renewal of hope.

The Making of the Sahara

Luxuriant haven for man and beast turns into a desert wasteland

THE GREATEST DESERT on earth—a vast, forbidding world of barren mountains and parched plateaus, gravel plains and endless seas of sand—stretches more than 3,000 miles across the whole of northern Africa, from the Atlantic Ocean to the Red Sea. It is a land of violent contrasts and extreme conditions, where life is difficult at best. Yet some 10,000 years ago, the region we now call the Sahara—a name derived from the Arabic word for desert—was in a green and fertile phase in which rain-swollen rivers flowed from tree-covered mountains, and hippopotamuses wallowed in lakes and lagoons. On the vast North African grasslands, leopards stalked ostriches and gazelles; elephants, rhinoceroses, and giraffes found plentiful vegetation to eat. People also thrived there, at first hunting game, later raising enormous herds of cattle. And for thousands of years, these hunters and herdsmen of the Sahara recorded their lives on cliff walls and cave roofs. Prehistoric rock engravings and paintings have been preserved throughout the region, but they are most abundant— and most beautiful—in the remote and rugged heart of the desert, among the fantastic rock formations of the Tassili n'Ajjer plateaus of southern Algeria.

How did this verdant land teeming with wildlife turn into one of the driest and most inhospitable places on the planet? The Tassili n'Ajjer picture galleries illustrate a part of the story, but only the most recent part, for the drying out of the Sahara was a disaster that took eons to unfold.

During the age of the dinosaurs, lush Saharan rain forests provided abundant food for the giant reptiles.

Today's Sahara is, in fact, the result of hundreds of millions of years of geologic and climatic change. Traces of ancient glaciers have been found in rocks throughout the Tassili n'Ajjer plateaus—evidence of a remote past when parts of the Sahara were buried under an ice cap. The enormous sea that covered most of the area during the Carboniferous period, about 300 million years ago, eventually gave way to luxuriant tropical landscapes inhabited by dinosaurs. Early in the Cretaceous period, some 130 million years ago, the dinosaurs disappeared from the Saharan region, and large parts of what is now desert lay underwater once more. In time, the Cretaceous seas were themselves

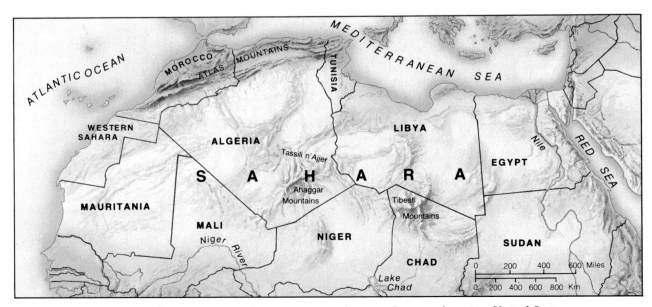

The Sahara includes parts of 11 countries and covers an area almost as large as the entire United States.

Two prehistoric hunters stalk their prey, once abundant in the heart of the Sahara, on the wall of a shallow cave in the Tassili n'Ajjer region.

Created some 5,500 years ago, this Tassili n'Ajjer rock painting shows what life was like then. Long-horned cattle return from pasture (right); tethered calves stand in front of oval huts (left) while people converse or watch over children.

replaced by a moist environment of marshes and lakes—and never again would so much of North Africa be submerged.

Over the last 2.5 million years, climatic changes comparable to those that caused alternating ice ages and periods of interglacial warming in Europe also influenced rainfall and weather patterns in North Africa. Dry phases, when desert conditions prevailed and spread, alternated with humid periods, when great networks of rivers and lakes supported large animal and human populations.

Radar images taken by the space shuttle *Columbia* in 1981 over the hot sands of southern Egypt and northern Sudan revealed the buried remains of Old Stone Age campsites. The radar also revealed underground traces of rivers and streams that more than 200,000 years ago carved out valleys as wide as that of the Nile River.

Fossil finds in the Libyan Desert, now one of the hottest and most barren stretches of the Sahara, show that during one of its wet phases the region was home to *Stegotetrabeledon syrticus*, a giant mastodon much bigger than a modern elephant and equipped with four massive eight-foot-long tusks. The vegetation in this now searing wasteland must have been abundant indeed to satisfy the needs of such a huge and voracious plant eater.

In the course of its evolution, the Sahara has been both larger and considerably smaller than it is today. Fifteen thousand years ago an expanding desert created sand dunes some 300 miles south of its present boundary. On the other hand, perhaps as recently as 7,000 years ago, Lake Chad covered more than 10 times the area it now does and reached 400 miles north of its present shores into what is now desert terrain. Farther to the west, the Niger River once flowed into Lake Arawan, a body of water that today is little more than a sea of sand in central Mali.

But despite the recurrences of moist periods, the

Sahara ultimately could not escape the consequences of its geography and climate. Continental drift has placed North Africa in the earth's equatorial arid belt, where—except under extraordinary circumstances, such as the ebb and flow of an ice age—constant high atmospheric pressure produces air that is simply too dry for clouds and rain to form. The peculiar nature of the ancient Sahara's drainage system also played a crucial role in creating the desert. Instead of flowing into the sea, Saharan waterways ran from the mountains into closed basins in the lowlands. During wet periods these powerful rivers and streams shaped and eroded the mountains and deposited the resulting debris in the basins, gradually filling them. The result

of this process was the formation of the Saharan gravel plains, known as regs. During dry phases the wind took over the work of erosion, sifting out grains of sand and heaping them up in undulating sand seas, called ergs, at the outer edges of the desert, beyond the gravel plains.

The most recent of the Sahara's wet phases began 12,000 to 10,000 years ago, toward the end of the last glacial period. The oldest of the Tassili n'Ajjer rock engravings and paintings, dating from the sixth millennium B.C. or earlier, depict hunters of a Negroid race, who wore animal skins and masks and stalked their prey with clubs, lances, and boomerangs. Though crude, the art of these early Saharan hunter-gatherers

Worlds of Harsh Beauty: The Deserts

THINK OF A DESERT, and the image of vast, undulating dune fields is likely to come to mind. Yet such "seas of sand" account for only a small fraction of the world's deserts. From rugged mountains and steep-sided plateaus to salt flats and Arctic tundra, deserts comprise a wide range of landforms and climatic conditions. All deserts, however, share one common feature: a lack of moisture. By definition, a desert is a nearly barren area in which rainfall is so scarce or irregular that the land cannot adequately support vegetation. Semi-arid, arid, and extreme desert zones cover about one-third of the earth's total landmass. And every year an estimated 27,000 square miles of land turn into desert.

What makes a desert so dry? The world's great tropical deserts—the Sahara and the Kalahari Desert in Africa and the Great Australian Desert—are all located near the Tropic of Cancer or of Capricorn in zones of almost permanent high atmospheric pressure. Such conditions produce air so dry that very little moisture can ever condense in it. Deserts located in the middle latitudes, such as the Gobi in central Asia and the Mojave in the western United States, are dry because they are either very far away from an ocean or are separated from it by a major mountain range. A third type of desert is the cold desert of the Arctic and Antarctic regions, in which the air is simply too frigid to hold much moisture.

Temperatures in cold deserts usually do not rise much above 50° F, and then only during the short summer season. In hot deserts, however, temperatures can plunge from searing to frigid

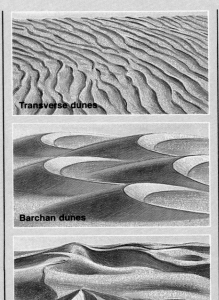

Transverse dunes

Barchan dunes

Star-shaped dunes

Shaped by the wind, dunes take on a variety of different forms, as shown above.

overnight, as the intense heat absorbed during the day is quickly radiated back into space after sundown.

Some rain falls even in the driest deserts, and a cloudburst over barren ground can create flash floods and temporary streams of great erosive power. It is the combined action of water and wind that has sculpted the characteristic landforms of the desert:

- **Alluvial Fan.** A fan-shaped deposit of rock debris laid down most often by a swiftly flowing mountain stream as it enters a level plain or open valley.

- **Arroyo, or Wadi.** A normally dry streambed that turns into a temporary watercourse after heavy rain.

- **Bolson.** A broad desert basin with no outlet. Streams from nearby mountains often create *alluvial fans* along the edge of bolsons.

- **Desert Pavement.** A mosaic-like surface of closely packed pebbles.

- **Dune.** An ever-changing mound or ridge of windblown sand.

- **Erg.** A Saharan term for a desert area covered with sand dunes.

- **Hammada.** A Saharan term for a desert surface of wind-eroded bedrock.

- **Pediment.** A gently sloping, boulder-strewn area of bedrock that borders mountain bases.

- **Playa.** A shallow basin in which temporary lakes form and quickly evaporate, leaving behind salt deposits.

- **Reg.** A Saharan term for a desert surface of smooth stones and gravel.

Despite the formidable challenges they present, few desert regions are completely devoid of life. Approximately 4 percent of the world's people live in deserts. And even as unpromising a place as the Tassili n'Ajjer supports a hardy population of trees, wildflowers, lizards, scorpions, and butterflies, while in scattered water holes, called *gueltas,* fish, frogs, shrimp, and mollusks manage to survive.

reveals a rich, game-filled landscape, very similar to the savannas of sub-Saharan East Africa today. But the art also chronicles the gradual drying out of the area. By about 4000 B.C. the Sahara could no longer provide enough food for herds of elephants and other large game, which either died out or drifted south in search of better grazing lands. The hunter-gatherers were replaced by nomads from the east—possibly from the Upper Nile Valley—who kept huge herds of cattle and flocks of sheep and goats. These pastoral people were also the skilled artists who created some of the most spectacular of the Tassili n'Ajjer rock paintings.

The art of the Saharan golden age, between 4000 and 2000 B.C., shows herds of cattle being led to pasture and men armed with bows and arrows hunting wild sheep, antelopes, gazelles, and other, smaller game. In many campsite scenes, women prepare food while their children play. Other paintings recreate ceremonies meant to ward off illness or remove spells from animals. That these were peaceful, prosperous times for the Sahara is evident from the size of the herds shown in the rock paintings and the numerous depictions of people dancing, playing, wearing elaborate costumes, or simply engaged in friendly conversation.

It is also from this period that we have living proof of the Sahara's former bounty. For in remote valleys of the Tassili n'Ajjer, a few ancient cypress and olive trees, some possibly 3,000 to 4,000 years old, still cling to life. Twisted and gnarled and unable to reproduce themselves, the Tassili's prehistoric trees survive, however precariously, on the meager rains that fall from time to time. Along with the giant sequoias of California, these relics of a green Sahara are among the oldest living things on earth.

By about 2500 B.C. the culture of the herdsmen went into sharp decline as the drying of the Sahara accelerated. Less rain fell; streams, marshes, and watering holes disappeared at a faster and faster pace, and vegetation withered. The pastoral tribes were forced to hunt out of necessity rather than for sport, as had been their custom. Eventually they vanished altogether, probably driven south by their need for water and new grazing lands for their herds. Cattle, on which the golden-age culture of the Sahara had been

The sandstone plateaus of the Tassili n'Ajjer were carved by the erosive power of running water when the Sahara was a wetter, greener place.

based and whose intense grazing in all likelihood contributed to the region's decline, disappeared from Saharan art sometime about 1000 B.C.

Into the ever-evolving desert rode a new and warlike tribe of horsemen.

Invading warriors from the north, riding horses and chariots, replaced the herdsmen as the dominant people of an increasingly arid Sahara. Instead of quiet pastoral scenes, fierce battles become the subject of the last of the Tassili n'Ajjer rock paintings, which are stiff and colorless in comparison with the art of the previous period.

By the beginning of the Christian Era, horses could no longer negotiate the Sahara and were soon replaced by camels, a clear sign that by then the desert was an accomplished fact. For all but a hardy few—mostly bands of nomads—human life in the Sahara outside the oases had become virtually impossible.

31

Thera: Great Destroyer

A colossal eruption shakes the Mediterranean world

THE IMMENSE BAY is flanked on three sides by towering cliffs, whose jagged striations of black, gray, pink, and rust bear witness to one of nature's greatest upheavals, sometime in the distant past. Villages, dazzling white in the morning sun, perch precariously atop the crescent-shaped cliffs of the largest island. Nearby, plumes of smoke rise from a pair of smaller islands, mounds of brown and black rubble that appear all the more ominous against their setting in the violet-blue waters.

There is no mistaking this place: the huge circular basin, the monstrous, blasted cliffs, the smoking islands in the center—these are the ruins of a mighty volcano, the aftermath of an eruption of unimaginable force at a time almost beyond remembering.

Today the cluster of five islands is often called Santorini, a name bestowed by its medieval Venetian rulers in homage to Saint Irene. It belongs to the Cyclades, the chain of islands strung out to the southeast of the Greek mainland in that part of the Mediterranean known since antiquity as the Aegean Sea. A

scene of peace and beauty, of warm sun and fragrant breezes, it is also a place of death, of violence and destruction on the mightiest of scales.

Three thousand five hundred years ago Santorini was a single verdant island of surpassing beauty, some 10 miles in diameter and rising nearly a mile to a handsomely symmetrical mountain peak. It was not Santorini then: there is no record of what it was called—though later it came to be known as Thera, after the ancient Spartan hero Theras, descendant of one of Jason's legendary Argonauts, who settled there. With the island of Crete, it formed part of the ancient world's greatest maritime civilization, dominating the eastern Mediterranean for some 1,500 years during the Bronze Age.

Crete was the home of the Minoan kingdom, a vigorous society built on trade that reached out to all corners of the known world. Frescoes in the Minoan style excavated on Santorini show small keeled vessels, a noteworthy fact at a time when the best that such great powers as Egypt and Mesopotamia could

The breathtaking beauty *of Santorini—or Thera, to use its Greek name—belies the cataclysmic violence that produced it. Across the bay from the town of Phira are, left to right, the smaller islands of Nea Kameni, Aspronisi, Palea Kameni, and Therasia.*

sons, carpenters, and other craftsmen, as well as artists of great skill and originality.

Then, by a stroke of nature, Thera was gone, destroyed in a volcanic convulsion so violent as to erase all direct memory of its existence. Historical records contain no account of the cataclysm, no mention whatever—at least no direct mention. Instead, historians have had to play detective, drawing on a variety of disciplines to reconstruct what actually happened. Archeology, geology, oceanography, meteorology, and volcanology have all told their tales. Scattered clues drawn from ancient literature, Greek mythology, and other sources help to fill out this elusive story.

The first sign that something momentous was going to happen probably came as a volley of light earth tremors.

It was summer. A strong wind was blowing from the north and kept most of the great Minoan fleet in port. Harvest time was still weeks off, and on Thera the great stone jars used to store wheat, barley, dried fruit, and other staples were nearly empty. Every day merchants scanned the horizon for signs of the vessels that were their lifeline to trading partners across the Mediterranean. Then began the earth tremors that signaled a far more profound threat.

There must have been meetings, perhaps heated debates between those who urged evacuation and others who saw no cause for alarm. At the very least, precautions were taken. Houses recently uncovered at Akrotiri contained no items of gold, silver, or other precious belongings, suggesting that such things were gathered up for quick departure. In many instances, utensils and supplies have been found in basement storerooms, presumably to protect them from shock.

There followed an earthquake of exceptional violence. Houses collapsed; stone walls cracked and crumbled. At one place the shaking first split and then compacted a staircase as if by a blow from a giant fist. Though there were no signs of volcanic activity yet, the aftershocks were enough to convince even the most stubborn holdouts that it was time to leave. Evacuation began, and from all indications it was carried out in the typically ordered fashion of things Minoan. Some of the people may have made for the Greek mainland, 125 miles away, but a more likely course was toward the familiar haven of Crete.

manage was large, flat-bottomed river craft. Boats of this kind were able to traverse more than 200 miles—the average distance between landfalls on the Mediterranean—in a day and a half. This meant that the Minoans' ships could range quite far from home, trading grain, pottery, and marble for the copper and tin they needed to make bronze. Indeed, Cycladic pottery dating from the 18th century B.C. has been found in such distant locations as Marseilles, in France, and on the Spanish island of Minorca.

This golden culture left behind a language known as Linear A, which has not yet been completely deciphered. But Minoan art and architecture found at Akrotiri, the main excavation site on Thera, bespeak a high standard of living, enjoyed by a comfortable, cultivated upper class. The houses of the well-to-do were adorned by expertly rendered murals and other striking artworks. Depictions of animals, for example, reveal an understanding of line and movement remarkable in any age. Even women's fashions, as displayed in numerous contemporary paintings, show a captivating sense of style.

The town itself likewise reflected a high degree of technical development and social organization. Its houses of two, three, and four stories were skillfully designed and solidly built, and a well-maintained system of drains ran beneath Akrotiri's streets. Clearly, though a small island separated from Crete by 70 miles of open water, Thera was prosperous and sophisticated enough to support a sizable class of ma-

What happened next? For a while, nothing—though archeologists disagree as to whether the lull was measurable in days, weeks, or longer. Residents trickled back to begin the weary task of cleaning up and rebuilding, leaving evidence visible today in the excavations at Akrotiri: a path cleared, the rubble piled at intervals along it; a window frame enlarged into a doorway; an improvised cooking hearth set up outside a ruined wall. In one spot a bathtub was hauled to a rooftop, perhaps to catch rainwater.

But rebuilding came abruptly to a halt as the gleaming island destroyed itself from within. The final cataclysm may have taken as long as two years, reducing Thera gradually to an ash-coated wasteland, or just two unimaginably violent days. The time span is unclear, but the sequence of events can be read in the layers of ash in the immense quarry south of the clifftop town of Phira. The eruption first produced a shower of pumice, blanketing the island with what could have been mistaken for a light snowfall, then with larger lumps of the same rock, and then with the distinctive rose-colored pumice for which Thera is famous.

How long this shower continued is open to speculation, but when the end came, it was on a tremendous scale. Judging from what is now known about volcanic eruptions, it is safe to say that the top of the mountain burst open, releasing a blast of compressed material and superheated gases outward at speeds exceeding 1,200 miles per hour.

A pillar of smoke and ash rose more than 20 miles above the Mediterranean.

An immense volcanic cloud reached high into the stratosphere, accompanied by a salvo of colossal booms that could be heard from central Africa to Scandinavia and from the Persian Gulf to the Rock of Gibraltar. Airborne dust turned day into night hun-

Under the Volcano: Thera's Mighty Engine

THERE ARE MORE than 500 active volcanoes in the world today, most of them found along the great fault lines—convergences of giant plates that make up the earth's crust beneath the continents and sea floors. One of the major fault lines, the meeting of the great African plate and the various crust pieces forming the Eurasian plate, runs roughly west-to-east across the Mediterranean. Since prehistoric times the two plates have been pushing slowly in contrary directions, and one of the ar-eas where the stress is greatest lies near Crete and Thera.

A grinding process called subduction forces one plate under the other, and the resulting friction and heat cause basaltic rock to melt along the leading edge. Volcanic magma—a kind of liquid fire made of partially molten rock, chemicals, and minerals—works its way inexorably toward the surface. Over thousands of years it accumulates in a magma chamber, an opening in the rock layer anywhere from 3 to 100 miles below the earth's surface. As convection stirs it, melted sedimentary rock from the overriding plate adds to its mass, while silica and water pump in extra steam pressure.

In many cases, that pressure is released through tremors, steam, lava flows, and minor eruptions. But if a volcano's main vents become plugged up by hardened magma, the result is, in effect, a mighty time bomb—as the people of the Mediterranean world discovered 35 centuries ago.

The first stage of Thera's destruction was an explosion that blew off the mountaintop and sent a column of gas, lava, pumice, and ash upward at more than 1,200 miles an hour.

A later eruption of gas and magma formed a cloud so dense that it collapsed under its own weight, sending a superheated avalanche down Thera's flanks and into the crater.

Once enough of the mountain was gone, water poured into the gaping crater and exploded on contact with the red-hot magma, carving an ever-larger bay out of the remains.

dreds of miles distant, fell to earth in large quantities across a vast area, and probably affected sunsets and weather conditions around the world.

The expulsion of ash and volcanic matter fractured Thera's symmetrical cone in several places, opening the giant magma chamber beneath it to the sea. Billions of gallons of seawater poured into the white-hot abyss, triggering a series of titanic explosions. They blew away 32 cubic miles of the island—far more than in the largest eruption for which records exist—and sent giant sea waves smashing onto the coast of Crete and beyond. Some believe that the force of the eruption and the shape and depth of the sea bed in that part of the Aegean could have produced waves that reached a height of 200 to 300 feet as they crashed ashore.

Such a combination of earthquake, water, ash, and fire may have fatally weakened the Minoan civilization of Crete, leaving traces only in the confused folk memory handed down as legend—and in another,

quite unexpected place: the writings of the great philosopher Plato.

In about 350 B.C., Plato related the story of a lost kingdom called Atlantis, first described to the Athenian poet-statesman Solon during a visit to Egypt around 600 B.C. In Plato's account, an Egyptian priest tells of a "great and marvelous power, which held sway over all the island and over many other islands," and also describes it as belonging to great antiquity, warlike in nature, and in any case located outside the Strait of Gibraltar, in the Atlantic. According to the story, "there occurred portentous earthquakes and floods, and one grievous day and night befell them, when the whole body of your warriors was swallowed up by the earth, and the island of Atlantis was swallowed up by the sea and vanished."

For centuries, scholars have been discussing the disappearance of Atlantis and trying to link it to a historical event. Some think that a mistranslation of figures resulted in greatly exaggerated time periods, and that the Atlantis destruction belongs not to very early antiquity but to the second millennium B.C.—the time of Thera's eruption and the subsequent demise of Minoan civilization. They note that numerous geographical and topographical features of Solon's description of Atlantis fit locations on Crete and Thera exactly.

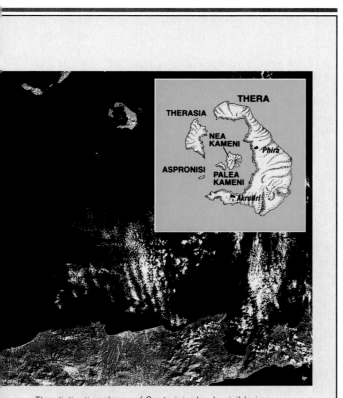

The distinctive shape of Santorini, clearly visible in a satellite photograph that also shows Crete, 70 miles to the south, leaves no doubt that the circular cluster of five islands (detailed in inset) is but a remnant of the much larger island destroyed by the same volcanic forces that created it.

The Atlantis legend and others may have been attempts to understand a cataclysm that could not be rationally explained.

Viewed from the perspective of modern science, it is unlikely that a vast landmass such as Plato describes could have sunk anywhere in the Atlantic. Yet the notion of Atlantis is a strangely persistent one. It has been suggested that Atlantis was a kind of amalgam of many lost-world legends, from the biblical Garden of Eden to Homer's Elysian Fields to the mystical realms of Celtic and Teutonic myth. Such a theory mirrors a basic truth: all peoples seem to need an Atlantis, some land of great accomplishment and high purpose in a yesterday beyond remembering.

The few other early references to this most momentous of big bangs are oblique, tantalizing, and open to freewheeling interpretation. A rich source is the mythology of ancient Greece. Indeed, it is almost inevitable that such a prodigious eruption would have found its way into legend—precisely because it was too vast, its destructiveness too great, to be explained in rational terms by anyone living in the Bronze Age.

In one famous myth, Jason and the Argonauts, returning home with the Golden Fleece, sailed northward from the Libyan coast toward Crete but were prevented from landing by Talos, "the bronze sentinel, who pelted the *Argo* with rocks, as was his custom."

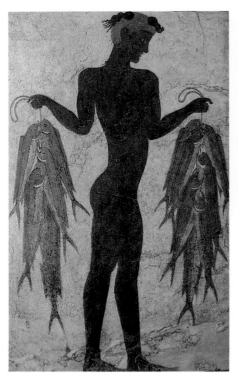

The vivid frescoes of Akrotiri reveal a society of wealth and sophistication whose

The riches of the bountiful sea are displayed by a young fisherman, possibly as a ritual offering to one of Thera's ancient deities.

Medea then bewitched the monster, and as he staggered about he grazed his heel against a rock, his life-giving divine ichor ran out "like molten lead," and he died. Read the "heel" as a small secondary vent and the "ichor" as molten lava, and it is not difficult to see Talos as a mighty volcano in eruption, raining volcanic "bombs" on the weary and hapless mariners.

Another legend concerns the birth of the god Apollo on the island of Delos, which lies about 65 miles north of Thera in the Aegean Sea. According to one tradition, the island—originally called Asterie, or "star island"—had fallen from the sky like a star and floated freely around the Aegean. Only after Apollo's birth did it become anchored in a fixed position and acquire the name Delos. This and other legends of movable islands may well have had their origins in sightings by ancient sailors of huge masses of floating pumice expelled by Thera. In recent centuries, in the Pacific, less powerful eruptions than Thera's have produced floating mounds of pumice more than 25 miles long—far larger than the small island of Delos.

And what of the Phaeacians, those bright and enterprising souls in Homer's *Odyssey,* noted for seamanship, for their speed in conveying goods and passengers to distant points, for their dancing and love of hot baths and comfortable beds? They incurred the wrath of Poseidon, god of the sea, by helping Odysseus on his way home to Ithaca. As punishment, the god threatened to turn their ship to stone and "cover up their city with a great mountain."

Might this story contain an echo of real events—from a time when huge walls of water smashed into the northeastern coast of Crete, crippling a mighty trading fleet and dealing a mortal blow to the proud Minoan civilization? One of the earliest Greek poets, Hesiod, writing in the 8th century B.C., used distinctly volcanic imagery to describe a battle at sea between Zeus and the giant monster Typhon: "And the heat of them both gripped the purple sea, the heat of thunder and lightning and of fire from such a monster, the heat of fiery storm-winds and flaming thunderbolts. And the whole earth and firmament and sea boiled. And long waves spreading out in circles went seething over the headlands." The poet was drawing on centuries-old folklore that obviously included knowledge of the effects of a massive eruption.

Despite such parallels, historians have yet to reach a consensus about the Minoans' fate. Some believe that the final destruction of the Minoan kingdom happened not through a natural upheaval but some time later, through invasion and conquest. Most likely, in this view, Crete survived the ordeal of fire, water, and ash but was left weakened and vulnerable to attack from the Greek mainland over a period of months or even years.

In any event, the Minoans may not have been the only people affected by the cataclysm on Thera. Geological evidence makes it clear that Mediterranean winds blew Thera's immense cloud of burning ash in a southeasterly direction. A provocative theory put forward by some scholars proposed that the traditional dating of events in the ancient world contained crucial flaws, and that if they were corrected, a vivid account of the eruption and its far-reaching consequences could be found in the Old Testament.

"The Lord went before them by day in a pillar of cloud to lead them along the way," says the Book of Exodus, recounting the flight of Moses and his Hebrew followers from bondage in Egypt, "and by night

formidable navy safeguarded Thera's seaports and kept the vital shipping lanes open to commerce.

in a pillar of fire to give them light." What was this great pillar, and what was the "thick darkness in all the land of Egypt three days"? The curvature of the earth's surface is such that a column of ash blown high into the stratosphere above Thera, though almost 500 miles away, would have been dramatically visible from the Nile Delta by night or day. Likewise, the southeasterly moving ash cloud could easily have caused three days of profound darkness.

Were the miraculous events described in the Book of Exodus really connected to the eruption of Thera?

The idea of a connection between Thera and the Exodus narrative gained adherents and stirred the imagination, but it also generated intense controversy. The long-accepted date of the eruption, based on archeological evidence, was about 1470 B.C. This put it within two centuries of the period in which many scholars place the Exodus—a gap proponents of the theory blamed on erroneous dating of Egypt's early dynasties. Now, however, new techniques are enabling geologists to date prehistoric events with great accuracy, and studies published in the mid-1980's established almost beyond question that Thera erupted not in the 15th century B.C. but in the 17th—probably in the year 1628 B.C. With a single stroke these findings profoundly altered our view of the ancient Mediterranean world, deepening the mystery surrounding the Minoans and making a link between Thera and the Exodus, however intriguing to contemplate, all but impossible to support.

Today, the twin outcroppings of bare brown and black rocks in the center of the bay serve as reminders that Thera is by no means dead. The islands are called Palea Kameni and Nea Kameni ("Old Burnt" and

"New Burnt"). An eruption there in 197 B.C. was described by the Greek geographer Strabo: "Midway between Thera and Therasia, flames came bursting up from the sea for four days, causing the water to seethe and flare up. Gradually an island emerged and was built up, as though it had been forged by implements out of a red-hot mass." This was the birth of Palea Kameni. In 1707 a similar upheaval created Nea Kameni, which was tripled in size by yet another eruption in 1866.

"As visitors to the Kameni islands can testify," one commentator wrote not long ago, "it is necessary only to scratch the surface to feel temperatures that owe nothing to the heat of the sun." The geologist A. G. Galanopoulos described "cone-shaped depressions of fine ash, among scatters of pumice and heaps of rock, black, reddish and dusted with the bright efflorescence of sulfur. It is an oppressive scene, every harsh effect is repeated again and again with the cumulative insistence of nightmare. At the summit, the latest crater still faintly bubbles and emits puffs of mephitic vapor. It is as though all the world's slag heaps and spoil tips had been combined in a senseless but menacing composition."

"This savage island," he goes on, ". . . is merely the consequence of a few relatively minor eruptions, spread over the last 200 years; the calm circle of waters, which seemed so reassuring, is nothing more than the gigantic hole blown in the earth's surface 3,500 years ago when the ancient island . . . was swallowed up by the sea and vanished; the sunny cliffs being the torn sides of the crater."

What lies in store? Will the great "bronze sentinel" be heard from once more, to rain ruin on these historic lands? Will the stresses set in motion by the collisions of great pieces of the earth's crust ever again find catastrophic release in this setting of benevolent sunshine and wine-dark sea? There is no way to know. For the moment, at least, Thera keeps its secrets well.

The Plague of Athens

War and pestilence herald the end of Greek golden age

THE GLORY OF GREECE was Athens in the days of Pericles. Under this brilliant soldier-statesman, fifth-century B.C. Athens was the setting for an unparalleled explosion of creativity in politics, art, and philosophy. Nearly 2,500 years later, the achievements of Periclean Athens—democratic government, the architectural masterpieces on the Acropolis, the sculptures of Phidias, the dramas of Sophocles and Euripides, the philosophy of Socrates, a general striving for excellence in all things—still shape our notions of a civilized society.

Yet in 431 B.C., at the height of its power and prestige, Athens, and most of the Greek world with it, embarked on a fratricidal war that would drag on for more than a quarter century and bring down the curtain on the Athenian Empire. The Peloponnesian War pitted democratic Athens and its sea-based confederacy against the land-based power of autocratic Sparta and its Peloponnesian allies. Athens entered the war with every expectation of quick success; but it could not anticipate the devastating plague that would wipe out between a quarter and a third of its population and tear apart the fabric of Athenian society.

From the beginning, the Athenians knew that on land they were no match for the Peloponnesian armies, but at sea they were practically invincible. Pericles therefore proposed that Athens avoid land battles and relinquish the surrounding countryside of Attica to the enemy. Since war in those days was fought mainly during the spring and summer months, the rural population would be sheltered for the season within the city and its Long Walls, the 4-mile-long, 550-foot-wide defensive corridor that linked Athens and the harbor town of Piraeus. According to the plan, the Peloponnesians would be free to pillage a depopulated Attica while the Athenian fleet laid waste the coasts of the Peloponnesus. If the Athenians bided their time and tended their navy, victory would be assured.

During the first year of the war, all went as planned. There were few engagements and few casualties. For those Athenians who fell in battle that year, Pericles delivered his famous funeral oration, a landmark speech that, as recorded by the historian Thucydides in his *History of the Peloponnesian War*, brilliantly captured the values and ideals of Athenian civilization at its zenith.

As the fighting season of 430 B.C. approached, the farmers and villagers of Attica once again sought refuge in Athens. Those with relatives in the city moved in with them so that soon nearly every house was crowded; those who could find no such accommodations built shacks under the open sky and prepared to endure the six or more weeks that the invasion could be expected to last.

The Peloponnesian armies, led by the Spartan king Archidamus, invaded on schedule and immediately began devastating the countryside around Athens. Anything that the people of Attica had managed to rebuild since the last invasion was put to the torch, and the smoke of burning fields and buildings was plainly visible from the beleaguered city. While Sparta and its allies continued their depredations far from their home, base, Pericles seized the opportunity to lead an expedition against the city of Epidaurus, a formidable Spartan ally on the Peloponnesian coast.

But even before Pericles set sail—in fact, within only a few days of the Peloponnesians' arrival in Atti-

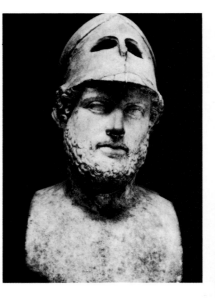

War with Sparta *and plague in Athens clouded the final years of Pericles' rule. The great Athenian leader is shown above in his characteristic battle helmet. At right, enemy ships attack the Athenian harbor of Piraeus. Because the plague started in Piraeus, the Athenians at first suspected the Spartans of poisoning the harbor town's reservoirs.*

ca—a plague that probably originated in Ethiopia and moved from there into Egypt, Libya, and Persia, invaded Greece with a terrifying swiftness. The first cases were reported in Piraeus, but the disease spread like wildfire into desperately overcrowded Athens. In an account that would remain for centuries a model of medical reporting, Thucydides described in harrowing detail the course of a disease that he himself suffered and survived:

"People in perfect health suddenly began to have burning feelings in the head; their eyes became red and inflamed; inside their mouths there was bleeding from the throat and tongue, and the breath became unnatural and unpleasant. The next symptoms were sneezing and hoarseness of voice, and before long the pain settled on the chest and was accompanied by coughing. Next the stomach was affected with aches and with vomitings of every kind of bile that has been given a name by the medical profession, all this being accompanied by great pain and difficulty. In most cases there were attacks of ineffectual retching, producing violent spasms. . . . Externally the body was not very hot to the touch, nor was there any pallor: the skin was rather reddish and livid, breaking out into small pustules and ulcers. But inside there was a feeling of burning, so that people could not bear the touch even of the lightest linen clothing, but wanted to be completely naked, and indeed most of all would have liked to plunge into cold water." No amount of water, however, could slake the plague victims' thirst.

Many of the sick hurled themselves into water tanks in an effort to relieve a thirst that could not be quenched.

Sleeplessness and "the desperate feeling of not being able to keep still" completed the list of initial plague symptoms, all of which occurred within the first week of illness. Remarkably, reported Thucydides, "there was still some strength left on the seventh or eighth day, which was the time when, in most cases, death came from the internal fever." Patients who lived beyond eight days could expect to die eventually from weakness caused by "violent ulceration and uncontrollable diarrhea."

Those who survived the disease usually became

A 5th-century B.C. Greek vase shows a doctor bleeding a patient.

THE ART OF GREEK MEDICINE

The foremost physician of golden age Greece was Hippocrates, the Father of Medicine. Rejecting the notion of disease as divine punishment, Hippocrates and his followers regarded illness as a naturally occurring malfunction of the body. Health was believed to be a state of balance among the basic bodily fluids, or humors: blood, phlegm, yellow bile, and black bile. Sickness was an imbalance among the humors. The doctor's task was to identify the disease and predict its outcome by carefully observing his patient. Treatment, which involved diet, exercise or rest, and drugs, was aimed at relieving symptoms and reinforcing the body's healing powers.

Ancient Greek medicine was more craft than profession. Itinerant doctors would vie for patients in village marketplaces. Large towns might have resident physicians, whose offices would be equipped with bronze surgical instruments, clean towels and bandages, and potable water. Still popular in Periclean Greece was the ancient cult of temple cures. A patient would spend one or more nights in a temple of Aesculapius, the god of healing, in the hope that the deity would visit him in a dream and effect a cure.

Greek doctors could diagnose and treat many diseases and perform a wide range of surgical procedures, but they knew little about the body's inner workings and even less about disease transmission. They attributed plagues to miasmas, or poisonous air, and had no weapons with which to fight epidemics like the plague of Athens.

immune to further attacks, but many were left permanently scarred. The plague "affected the genitals, the fingers, and the toes, and many of those who recovered lost the use of these members." Some survivors went blind; others suffered temporary amnesia, "not knowing who they were themselves and being unable to recognize their friends."

Effective medical treatment for the plague simply did not exist. "What did good in some cases did harm in others. Those with naturally strong constitutions were no better able than the weak to resist the disease, which carried away all alike, even those who were treated and dieted with the greatest care." Doctors and others who tried to care for the sick died in such great numbers ("like sheep," says Thucydides) that people grew afraid to visit plague victims, and entire households perished "through lack of any attention."

With enemy armies outside the walls and plague within, the Athenians were caught in a terrible trap. Especially hard hit were the peasants and villagers who had crowded into the city. "There were no houses for them, and, living as they did during the hot season in badly ventilated huts, they died like flies. The bodies of the dying were heaped one on top of the other, and half-dead creatures could be seen staggering about in the streets or flocking around the fountains in their desire for water." Even scavenging birds and dogs became infected and soon learned to avoid the corpses of plague victims.

After raiding the Peloponnesus but failing to take his main objective, Epidaurus, Pericles returned home to find Athens in the tight grip of the plague. The Peloponnesian forces had already withdrawn from Attica—driven off by the plague, some said, although as Thucydides points out, the invasion that year lasted longer than any other.

From the summer of 430 B.C. through the spring of 428, the plague worked its deadly way through Athens.

Fear of contagion caused the Peloponnesians to cancel their summer offensive in 429, but they returned to Attica the following summer, after the plague seemed to have abated somewhat. This respite did not last long, however. The disease struck Athens again with full force in the winter of 427 and remained in the city for one more year before finally dying out.

The exact number of people who succumbed to the plague will never be known. According to Thucydides, the disease killed 4,400 hoplites (fully armed infantrymen) out of an estimated 15,500 in the Athenian army. Three hundred cavalrymen, out of 1,000, also perished. If the army's 28 to 30 percent mortality rate is applied to Attica's estimated population of 315,000, then the plague may have taken as many as 90,000 lives in Athens and the surrounding countryside.

As for the nature and cause of the disease, "I must leave that," wrote Thucydides, "to be considered by other writers. . . . I myself shall merely describe what it was like, and set down the symptoms, knowledge of which will enable it to be recognized, if it should ever break out again." Yet despite Thucydides' clear and detailed description, modern science has been unable to recognize what the plague of Athens actually was.

Over the years the disease has been identified as smallpox, bubonic plague, scarlet fever, measles, typhus, typhoid fever, and Rift Valley fever, but objections can be raised against each of these candidates. It has been suggested that two or more still extant diseases—influenza followed by toxic shock syndrome, for example—may have struck almost simultaneously and reinforced each other to produce a virulent plague. It is also quite possible that the plague described by Thucydides no longer exists or has evolved into a much less virulent disease such as measles.

Whatever the plague may have been, Thucydides left no doubt about its wrenching effect on Athenian society. The people's initial reaction was to attribute the plague to human causes that could be understood and combated. It was rumored at first that the Peloponnesians had poisoned the reservoirs of Piraeus, but as the death toll mounted in Athens—a city whose wells were out of the enemy's reach—that hypothesis was discredited. If no human agents were involved, then the gods were surely to blame. People remembered an old oracular prophecy that a war with the Peloponnesians would coincide with an outbreak of plague. It was also known that before the war began, the Spartans had consulted the oracle of Apollo at Delphi and that the god had promised to aid them. To the Athenians, divine intervention helped to explain why the Peloponnesus had largely escaped the pestilence, while Attica was being devastated.

As the epidemic spread, however, it became clear that attributing the disease to the gods did not help get rid of it. With bodies quickly piling up and death literally in the air, despair took hold of the city, and men, reported Thucydides, "became indifferent to the very rule of religion or of law." Funeral ceremonies were ignored or haphazardly carried out. One corpse would be thrown on top of another on a funeral pyre, and bodies were left lying in temples, a sacrilege that would have been unthinkable only a few weeks before. In this "state of unprecedented lawlessness," pleasure seeking and self-indulgence became the standards of the moment.

Angry and demoralized, Athens turned against Pericles and even attempted to sue for peace without his consent. In an extraordinary speech before the Athenian Assembly in the summer of 430 B.C., Pericles succeeded in rallying the people and re-engaging their support for his policies and the cause of Athens. But with bitterness against him still running high, Pericles was relieved of his command and tried for mismanagement of funds. (He was found guilty, but fined only a modest sum.) The old statesman was restored to power in 429—Athens having quickly discovered that it had no leaders worthy of replacing him—but by then he had lost his sister and his two legitimate sons to the plague and may have contracted the disease himself. In the autumn of the same year, Pericles died. With his passing, Athens entered a period of corruption and misrule that would lead to the city's defeat by Sparta in 404 B.C. The death of Pericles marked the end of a golden moment not only for Athens and Greece but for all of Western civilization.

***The biblical plague of David** is the subject of this engraving, which is based on a 17th-century French painting. But such details as the dead dog in the foreground and the thirsty plague victims at the background are drawn from Thucydides' account of the plague of Athens.*

The Burning of Rome

Capital of the Caesars laid waste by mystery fire

IT WAS WELL KNOWN in Nero's Rome that the artistic emperor hated the look of the ancient city—with its narrow streets, teeming slums, and haphazard layout—and that he dreamed of rebuilding it according to his own plans. He got his chance early in the morning of July 19, A.D. 64, when a fire broke out in a row of shops near the Circus Maximus, the site of Rome's spectacular chariot races, south of the Palatine Hill. Fed by the combustible goods in the shops and fanned by the wind, the flames quickly leaped to the arena itself and consumed it. With no solid masonry structures in the vicinity to block its path, the fire spread rapidly to other parts of the crowded city.

"Furiously the destroying flames swept on," wrote the eminent Roman historian Tacitus, "first over the level ground, then up the heights, then again plunging into the hollows, with a rapidity which outstripped all efforts to cope with them." Rome's tortuous streets were a hodgepodge of shops, temples, densely packed tenements, and large, mostly wooden houses, all extremely vulnerable to fire.

As proud imperial Rome became fuel for the raging inferno, fear and panic gripped the city.

Tacitus described the ensuing horror in these words: "Terrified, shrieking women, helpless old and young, people intent on their own safety, people unselfishly supporting invalids and waiting for them, fugitives and lingerers alike—all heightened the confusion. When people looked back, menacing flames sprang

The Great Fire of Rome broke out early in the morning of July 19, A.D. 64, in a row of shops around the Circus Maximus, ancient Rome's great racetrack. This 18th-century French painting (left) depicts the fire's early stages. As the Circus Maximus burns in the background, panic-stricken citizens seek refuge and perhaps a means of escape along the banks of the Tiber River.

Gladiators fight lions and one another in this fanciful reconstruction of the Circus Maximus (below). Rebuilt by Nero after the fire and enlarged by later emperors, the arena eventually could seat an estimated 250,000 fans.

up before them or outflanked them. When they escaped to a neighboring quarter, the fire followed—even districts believed remote proved to be involved."

A horde of suddenly homeless victims took refuge in underground tombs. "Finally, with no idea where or what to flee," Tacitus continued, "they crowded on to the country roads, or lay in the fields. Some who had lost everything—even their food for the day—could have escaped but preferred to die. So did others who had failed to rescue their loved ones."

Menacing gangs of thugs roamed the city, brandishing flaming torches and preventing the already overwhelmed fire fighters from performing their duties. In anticipation of greater plunder—or as rumor had it, on orders of the emperor—the looters tried to spread the fire through the unprotected wealthier districts of the city.

Nero, who was staying at his villa in Antium, 35 miles from Rome, rushed back to the city in time to see his new palace, the Domus Transitoria, engulfed by flames. Immediately he set to work directing fire-fighting and relief efforts. Many public buildings and even the emperor's own private gardens were made available to house homeless refugees; food brought in

from nearby towns was sold at greatly reduced prices.

The fire raged unchecked for six days. It was put out only after a vast number of buildings standing in its path were razed, thus forcing the fire to feed upon itself. But just as the first blaze was subsiding, another one broke out to the north of the Capitoline Hill. Because this part of Rome was less congested, the second fire took fewer lives than the first, but it caused even more widespread damage to temples and other public buildings.

Finally, after nine days of unbridled destruction, the Great Fire of Rome was extinguished. Unknown thousands of citizens had lost their lives, and perhaps hundreds of thousands more were left homeless. Of the city's 14 districts, only 4 escaped unharmed. "Three were levelled to the ground," reported Tacitus. "The other seven were reduced to a few scorched and mangled ruins." Lost forever in the blaze were masterpieces of Greek art as well as Rome's oldest and most venerated landmarks, such as the palace of Numa, the second king of Rome; the Temple of Vesta, where the statues of Rome's guardian deities were kept; and the Temple of Jupiter Stator, said to have been dedicated by Romulus himself, one of the city's twin founders. According to the historian Suetonius, the fire destroyed "every ancient monument of historical interest that had hitherto survived." Not since the sacking of Rome by the Gauls 4½ centuries earlier had the city undergone such an ordeal.

To clear Rome of debris and limit pillaging, Nero closed off the devasted areas and prohibited even homeowners and tenants from visiting the ruins of their former residences. The same ships that had brought grain to the beleaguered city were now ordered to transport rubble out of it.

Rebuilding Rome was a massive and costly undertaking that Nero tackled with vigor. First he instituted a series of building-code reforms intended to prevent such catastrophic fires in the future. The city was to be rebuilt according to a central plan, with wider streets laid out in an orderly, geometric pattern and plenty of open spaces designed to hinder the spread of fire. The limit on building heights, set by the emperor Augustus but long ignored, was rigorously enforced. New buildings had to be freestanding—shared walls were banned—and they had to be constructed of fire-resistant stone up to a specified height. To reduce congestion in the city, new tenements were required to have an inner courtyard as well as a portico projecting out over the street. Nero magnanimously offered to pay for the porticoes, which were also meant to provide refuge from falling debris in case of fire. Finally, running water was made available for public use throughout the city, and officials were appointed to protect and monitor the water supply.

The new, orderly Rome received mixed reviews, with some citizens complaining about the lack of shade and many others lamenting the loss of the old monuments. Still, it was undeniable that a spectacular city was rising from the ashes of old Rome. With his usual flair for the extravagant, Nero filled the city with triumphal arches, rebuilt structures lost to the fire, such as the Temple of Vesta and the Circus Maximus, on an even grander scale, and erected a huge arena near what is now the site of St. Peter's Basilica. And to replace the ruined Domus Transitoria, which had never completely satisfied him anyway, Nero embarked on the most ambitious of all his building projects. Named the Domus Aurea, or Golden House, for the

abundance of gold, ivory, and precious stones that adorned it, the new imperial residence was intended to be the crowning achievement of Nero's Rome.

More than a mere palace, the Golden House was a series of pavilions, linked by porticoes, which together formed a small city in the very heart of Rome. The complex—including temples, baths, gardens, woods, grottoes, fields, fountains, and an enormous artificial lake that later became the site of the Colosseum— covered as many as 200 acres. Towering over the entrance to the Golden House, and visible from nearly all of the city, was a 120-foot-tall gilded bronze statue

FIGHTING FIRES IN ANCIENT ROME

In the days of the Roman Republic, the job of fighting fires was entrusted to bands of slaves known as the Familia Publica. Under the authority of public magistrates, these primitive fire brigades were stationed by the gates and walls of the city and equipped with little more than water buckets. Augmenting the Familia Publica were fire-fighting crews maintained by private citizens either for financial gain or to enhance their political careers.

After a disastrous fire in A.D. 6, the emperor Augustus replaced this highly inefficient system with the corps of Vigiles, the world's first truly professional fire department. The Vigiles were divided into seven units, or cohorts, each responsible for 2 of Rome's 14 administrative districts. The roughly 1,000 men in each cohort were named according to the tasks they carried out during a fire. Using buckets of woven and tarred esparto grass, the Aquarii, or water carriers, formed bucket brigades between a water source and the site of the fire. The Siphonarii squirted water at the fire by means of a *siphos*, a brass hand pump resembling a four-foot-long hypodermic needle. The Uncinarii were hook men, who grappled burning roofs and walls with hooked lances. Other equipment used by Roman fire fighters included axes, ladders, blankets, sponges, brooms, wickerwork mats, and possibly, even an early type of chemical fire extinguisher. The Siphonarii may also have used a doublecylinder force pump—a rudimentary version of the modern fire engine.

The Vigiles were also responsible for policing the city at night, capturing runaway slaves, preventing thievery at the public baths, and enforcing fire prevention codes. The corps of Vigiles lasted some 500 years despite its dismal—and still unexplained—failure to respond to the Great Fire of A.D. 64.

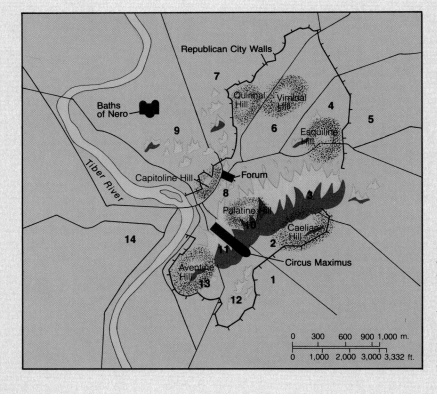

This map of Rome at the time of Nero shows the 14 administrative districts into which the city was divided. The fire of A.D. 64 destroyed 3 districts and damaged 7 others. It began in District 11, which was leveled along with Districts 10 and 3. The second phase of the fire began north of the Capitoline Hill. Only Districts 1, 5, 6, and 14 escaped harm.

Nero surveys his devastated capital. Although rumors circulated in Rome that the emperor himself had ordered the burning of the city, Nero acted quickly and with great energy to provide relief to the fire's victims and to erect a splendid new city on the ruins of the old.

of Nero, a monument to the emperor's megalomania.

Despite Nero's well-documented efforts to assist the victims of the fire and rebuild the city, he could not squelch the persistent rumors that he was somehow responsible for the burning of Rome. The stories of Nero's complicity began circulating the night the fire started—and spread almost as quickly. According to Suetonius, not only did Nero have the fire set but at the height of the conflagration he climbed the Tower of Maecenas, "put on his tragedian's costume and sang *The Fall of Troy* from beginning to end." Tacitus, however, had the performance taking place on a private stage, and later versions of the story gave Nero a lyre and eventually a fiddle. This image of the emperor "fiddling while Rome burned" has come down to us essentially intact—and still unproven.

With the people of Rome reeling from the effects of the fire, Nero at first tried to attribute the disaster to divine anger. To placate the gods, he ordered a round of religious ceremonies, sacred banquets, and nightly vigils. When that failed to distract the populace, Nero turned to Rome's small Christian community for a scapegoat. Although there is no hard evidence that a major persecution of Christians took place under Nero, Tacitus reported that "large numbers [of Christians] were condemned—not so much for incendiarism as for their anti-social tendencies. . . . Dressed in wild animals' skins, they were torn to pieces by dogs, or crucified." The historian even claims that Nero used Christians as living torches to light up his garden at night. According to Christian tradition, one of the victims of the purge was the Apostle Peter, who was crucified in Nero's new arena on the Vatican Hill.

The persecutions, if they did indeed occur, seemed to have backfired, for the Romans reportedly began to feel compassion for the brutally martyred Christians and continued to hold Nero responsible for the blaze.

The Great Fire marked the beginning of the end of Nero's reign.

The enormous costs of rebuilding Rome, and especially of constructing the Golden House, bled the city and the empire and fueled resentment against Nero. His depravity and growing list of murder victims—among them his mother, his pregnant wife, and his former tutor, the philosopher Seneca—were becoming intolerable. In June A.D. 68 the Senate declared Nero a public enemy and condemned him to a slave's ignominious death by flogging. Abandoned by his palace guard, courtiers, and friends, Nero chose instead to commit suicide by slitting his own throat.

After Nero's death, his successors converted large parts of the Golden House to public use and used the rest as foundations for new structures. Today all that remains of Nero's palace are subterranean rooms buried beneath the ruins of later buildings. As for Nero's giant statue, no one really knows what happened to it. Some sources say that it was dragged by a team of 24 elephants to a site in front of the Colosseum—in fact, the proximity of the colossal statue may have given the new arena its name. Eventually the sculpture vanished without a trace, thus becoming the last of the unsolved mysteries surrounding the Great Fire of Rome.

The Wrath of Vesuvius

Pompeii and Herculaneum perish in a colossal eruption

GAIUS PLINIUS SECUNDUS, better known to us as Pliny the Elder, began the last full day of his life with a regimen comfortable in its familiarity: at least an hour stretched out in the sun, then a quick plunge into cold water, followed by a hearty lunch. He had just settled down to an afternoon's reading and writing when his sister burst in on his reverie. It was unusual, she said, for so sunny a summer day, but an enormous, strange-looking cloud had appeared in the sky to the northeast. It seemed to be expanding, growing darker. Hadn't he best take a look?

The day was August 24, A.D. 79. Pliny had arrived just a few weeks before, commissioned by the emperor Titus to take command of the Roman fleet stationed at Misenum, at the mouth of the Bay of Naples in the region of southern Italy known as Campania. The emperor's kindness had been well-timed: Pliny was 56 and overweight and in recent years had suffered increasingly from asthma and a series of related respiratory complaints. He was ready to slow down.

The Roman world of the first century A.D. esteemed him as a natural historian and scholar of the highest standing. As a naval officer he had traveled widely, helping secure Rome's hegemony throughout the far-flung empire. Misenum, though strategically important, was a relatively peaceful place. Nearly 20 miles across the deep blue of the bay, sharp eyes could make out Herculaneum, a summer resort for affluent Romans, and 9 miles to its southeast the thriving commercial and agricultural center of Pompeii.

Pliny laid aside his books and climbed to the top of a nearby hill to observe the strange cloud. What he saw

comes down to us in a vivid account transcribed by his nephew, Pliny the Younger.

"The cloud was rising; watchers from our distance could not tell from which mountain, though later it was known to be Vesuvius. In appearance and shape it was like a tree—the umbrella pine would give the best idea of it. Like an immense tree trunk, it was projected into the air, and opened out with branches."

For most Romans, the suggestion that Vesuvius might be even a dormant volcano seemed absurd. Since time before memory it had been there, towering benevolently above a landscape of shining beauty and rare fertility. Olive groves and fruit orchards prospered on its slopes, yielding apples, figs, pears, cherries, and other delights. There was grain in plenty. Grapes from Vesuvian vineyards were famed for their size and the richness of their wine.

The area's blend of brilliant sunshine and cooling sea breezes attracted both summer visitors and well-to-do year-round residents, whose opulent villas were

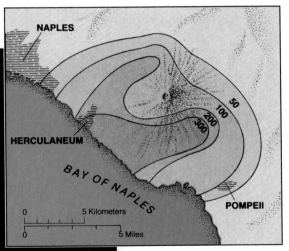

The awesome power
of Vesuvius captivated Europe's imagination after the dramatic discoveries of Pompeii and Herculaneum in the early 1700's. A sense of the mountain's raw, elemental fury is conveyed in this painting by the 18th-century French artist Pierre-Jacques Volaire. The map above shows the Bay of Naples and the depth (in meters) of volcanic deposits that buried the two sites.

the talk of all Rome. Pompeii and Herculaneum offered something for everyone—whether the spectacular games in the 16,000-seat amphitheater, the magnificent Forum Baths on the Via del Foro, or the lavishly appointed brothels and the dozens of drinking houses lining "Sin Street," the Vicolo del Lupanare.

The nearest thing to an eruption most locals had heard of was the revolt led by the Thracian slave and gladiator Spartacus, who in 73 B.C. escaped with 70 companions and took refuge high on the slopes of Vesuvius. When Roman troops thought they had the fugitives trapped, Spartacus led his followers to freedom by having them lower themselves on wild grapevines down the steep far side of the mountain; he went on to organize a mass rebellion that for nearly two years held much of southern Italy at bay.

Vesuvius had in fact been giving warnings—but only to those willing to recognize them.

Not 20 miles distant lay the smoking caverns and volcanic steam geysers of the Phlegraean Fields, regarded since ancient times as a doorway to Hades. At nearby Baiae, mineral springs gushed hot from untold depths. Various early chroniclers, including the Greek geographer Strabo, had noted the mountain's remarkably volcanic shape and speculated about its origins.

But little, it seemed, could disturb the honeyed tranquillity of Campania and its verdant 6,000-foot mountain. Even when a violent earthquake heavily damaged Herculaneum and Pompeii on February 5, A.D. 62 (or 63, according to some accounts), all thoughts were soon turned toward rebuilding—and improving—both cities. Work started slowly, probably because much of the labor available in Rome was pressed into rebuilding the capital after the devastating fire of A.D. 64. Gradually, though, Pompeii and Herculaneum emerged glistening and renewed from their own rubble.

The sciences of seismology and volcanology lay nearly two millennia in the future. There was no way anyone could have known that this entire region lay along one of the great fault lines of the earth's crust, the meeting point of the giant African and Eurasian continental plates. And there was certainly no way of knowing that the grinding of one granite and basalt plate beneath the other created stupendous pressures that even then were working their way upward, forcing tons of magma, or molten rock, inexorably toward the surface.

Around midday on August 24 they burst forth with a great bellowing noise and a roar like a thunderclap, cracking the mountain open like a walnut and shooting a billowing cloud of fire, ash, and pumice 12 miles

Still buried at Herculaneum, the Villa of the Papyri was duplicated to house the J. Paul Getty Museum in California.

into the Mediterranean sky. Watching from his vantage point at Misenum, Pliny the Elder realized he was witnessing a major natural event, one that demanded closer scientific investigation. He ordered a small galley made ready, then sought out his 17-year-old nephew. Would the lad like to accompany him to examine this rare occurrence?

"I answered that I preferred to study," Pliny the Younger wrote later, "as he himself had assigned me some work to do." Moments before he was due to depart, the elder Pliny received an urgent note from a woman named Rectina, wife of his colleague Caesius Bassus, pleading for rescue from her villa on a slope of the mountain accessible only from the sea.

"He now saw his expedition in a new light," his nephew wrote. "What he had begun in the spirit of a scientist, he carried on as a hero." He ordered out a good part of the fleet, and set his course directly across the bay, where the towering cloud had begun visibly raining ash and fire.

A brisk southeasterly wind had directed the eruption's initial fury against Pompeii. First came a smoldering blizzard of ash, pumice, and dense, jagged

rocks, some as much as eight inches in diameter. Many Pompeiians were no doubt killed or injured by these heavy projectiles, plummeting to earth from thousands of feet in the air. Additionally, as the afternoon wore on, the steady buildup of pumice must have caused roofs to collapse all over the city, triggering a mass evacuation.

Back at Misenum with his mother, Pliny the Younger spent the rest of the day in study, dined, and tried vainly to sleep. "For several days we had experienced earth shocks, which hardly alarmed us as they are frequent in Campania. But that night they became so violent that it seemed the world was not only being shaken, but turned upside down." After several hours of acting as though nothing were the matter, mother and son acknowledged their danger and took to the road, joining crowds of others moving north along the coast. The earth shook even more fiercely, and the roaring and booming increased as the sea suddenly appeared to recede, as if presaging a giant tidal wave.

"In the other direction loomed a horrible black cloud ripped by sudden bursts of fire, writhing snakelike, and parting to reveal great tongues of fire larger than lightning," the young man wrote. "Soon after, the cloud began to descend upon the earth and cover the sea. It had already surrounded and obscured Capreae, and blotted out Cape Misenum." Then, abruptly, darkness was upon them—"the darkness of a sealed room without lights."

"To be heard were only the shrill cries of women, the wailing of children, the shouting of men."

Pliny the Elder, meanwhile, had run into trouble during the afternoon as he neared the shore close to Pompeii. "The ashes were falling on the ships," his nephew learned from the accounts of survivors, "thicker and hotter the closer they approached, and also pumice stones and cinders, blackened, scorched, and scattered by the fires. Shallows suddenly were encountered, and landing was made difficult because the shore was blocked by rubble from the mountain. The pilot urged that they turn back, and my uncle hesitated." Then, with the exclamation "Fortune favors the brave!"—ever the scholar, Pliny was quoting Vergil—he changed course southward toward the seaside village of Stabiae, where he found his old friend Pomponianus.

Panic was running rampant by then. In an effort to calm his crew, his friend, and a steady stream of arrivals, Pliny seems to have made a great show of taking a leisurely bath, then dining with high spirits and great appetite. The night, meanwhile, was even more terrifying than the day. Great sheets of fire flashed from and around the mountaintop. The booming and roaring continued unabated, and ash was still falling as Pliny retired to bed.

Before he knew it, it was morning and Pomponianus was shaking him, imploring him to wake up. "The walls of the house were swaying with repeated violent shocks, and seemed to move in one direction and then another, as if shifted from their foundations." What was worse—to endure the terrible trembling and swaying indoors, or to go outside and be choked, pelted, and burned by the unceasing rain of pumice and ash? At length, as Pliny the Younger rather wryly observed, they chose the latter course, "my uncle moved by the stronger reasons and his companions by the stronger fears."

They found a scene that could have been an artist's vision of hell. Though by now well into daytime, the world remained

From a seaside villa *much like this one, Pliny the Elder first glimpsed the eruption that would claim his life.*

The fertile slopes *of Vesuvius, famed for their vineyards, are watched over by Dionysus, the god of wine, and a snake, which Romans considered a sign of good luck, in this 1st-century* A.D. *mural from Pompeii.*

49

black. A wild sea tossed the ships anchored in the harbor like toys. Lightning split the sky, fire flashed from the mountain, and an overpowering stench of sulfur filled the air.

What happened next is subject to interpretation. According to his nephew, Pliny twice called for water, then collapsed, unable to breathe. "I assume," Pliny the Younger wrote, "that his breathing was impeded by the dense vapors, and his windpipe blocked—for constitutionally it was narrow and weak, and often inflamed." But some historians have speculated that this heavy, aging man had simply overtaxed himself and suffered a fatal heart attack. In any event, when his friends returned later to look for him, "his body was found intact, without injury, and clad as in life. He looked more like a sleeper than a dead man."

It was on that same morning that the people of Pompeii were suddenly and horribly annihilated.

Bearing down on Pompeii the morning of the 25th was what geologists call a ground surge—a deadly mass of pumice and ash mixed with condensed, superheated steam, racing along at 60 miles an hour. In its path were many of the inhabitants who had fled the previous afternoon and returned later, thinking the worst was over. It overtook them wherever they were—in their homes packing up valuables, or in public buildings and marketplaces looking for loved ones, or on the roads trying desperately to flee again. There was neither refuge nor escape. It found them, suffocated them, and buried them.

The combination of ash rain, pumice, and moisture that killed so wantonly also had another effect, one ultimately beneficial to history. As the mixture dried, it formed a perfect mold of each corpse it surrounded; centuries later, when time and decay had done their work, the mold was all that was left. During the 1860's the first of the great Pompeii excavators, Giuseppi Fiorelli, pumped plaster of Paris into the molds and produced casts of each victim at the moment of death, accurate down to the folds of their clothing and, in some instances, even the looks on their faces.

Amedeo Maiuri, director of antiquities for Campania from 1927 to 1961, reconstructed in heartbreaking detail the last moments of a group of 13 Pompeiians overtaken by the lethal ash cloud as they attempted to flee. From their dress, possessions, location, and other evidence yielded by the plaster casts, he deduced that they were members of two farming families and one merchant's family, all living on the city's south side near the Nucian Gate, farthest from Vesuvius. It is easy to imagine them running blindly through impenetrable darkness, calling out desperately to one another. One of the farming families led the way.

"First came a servant," Maiuri concluded, "carrying over his shoulder a bag hastily filled with provisions.

The victims of Pompeii *were preserved with meticulous fidelity by the same volcanic material that killed them. The ash that buried the residents at left hardened quickly around their bodies. The resulting molds, left hollow after the soft tissues decayed, were filled with plaster to form the eerily detailed figures visible today. The watchdog below, held by a chain fixed to his collar, likewise remains frozen in an agonizing portrait of death.*

The morning sun *brightens one of the streets of Pompeii as Vesuvius looms serenely on the horizon, less than six miles to the northwest. About 7:30 A.M. on August 25, A.D. 79, the first deadly wave of hot gas and ash roared across that stretch of countryside at speeds between 60 and 120 miles an hour.*

arm pressed against a mound of earth and his back bent in a supreme effort to rise, to fight off the black demon that had him by the throat, and to come to the aid of his family. Bent thus, he appeared to us not as the frozen nakedness of a plaster cast, but as a living man of flesh and blood." Pompeii, in Maiuri's words, "was not burned to death; it was smothered. The very pall of rock and ash that took the city's life preserved it more beautifully than the most skilled museum curator could have done. . . . In effect, we are excavating not a ruin but a marvelously intact museum."

But Vesuvius had more—and worse—in store. Though scarcely five miles below the volcano's peak, Herculaneum had escaped that first day's horrors. As stupefying as the explosion, shocks, and sheer noise must have been, the winds blowing destruction on Pompeii had kept the worst of the ash rain away from the resort. Whereas Pompeii had been buried beneath as much as 12 feet of pumice and smoking debris on August 24, only 8 inches had fallen on Herculaneum. Many residents, assuming fate had been kinder to them than to their neighbors a few miles away, decided to return to their homes.

We found him where he fell, near the wall of a vegetable garden—a cabbage patch, by the look of the furrows. The man was still in a crouched position, suggesting not so much the weight of the sack as the dense darkness and the violent, eruption-born winds through which he struggled.

"Next, hand in hand, came the farmer's two little boys, about four and five. . . . Finally came the children's parents, the farmer supporting his trembling wife. They had fallen with faces to the ground, as if to hide the agony of suffocation. The two boys, on the contrary, had died facing the sky, their expressions peaceful, as if, after a few tears, they had resigned themselves to sleep."

One after another the cast figures emerged, complete even to clothes, hairstyles, and agonized expressions. But for Maiuri, the final figure, that of the merchant, was the most poignant of all. "He was not lying down but still sitting upright, with his right

Shortly after midnight, as Pliny the Younger was groping his way out of Misenum with his mother in tow, and his uncle, at Stabiae, was making a great show of turning in for the night, Vesuvius spoke again. The volcano had been blowing flame, gas, and debris into the air for nearly 12 hours, forming the immense cloud that had first attracted his uncle's attention. Now saturated with superheated debris, the towering fountain collapsed on itself and sent destruction cascading down on Herculaneum and the immediate surroundings of Vesuvius. In all likelihood it was this that Pliny the Younger was watching when he described how the "cloud sank down to earth and covered the sea."

The first impact sent a ground surge, a great blast of enormously hot air and debris, through the city in seconds, searing everything in its path. Hard behind it came the noxious, boiling avalanche itself—a deadly brew of volcanic matter, ash, steam, and rocks. There was no warning, no time to agonize over whether to go outside or stay indoors, no time to pack belongings or scoop up more than a handful of valuables. It struck within five minutes after the explosion, ripping giant columns from their bases and tossing them about like matchsticks, pulverizing stone walls, and baking everything in its path in temperatures as high as 752° F. Those left alive could only run, screaming, for any available shelter.

Scholars long assumed that most of the resort's 4,500 inhabitants had escaped the previous day. However, recent discoveries of perfectly preserved skeletal remains suggest a different, and appalling, sequence of events. Scores, perhaps hundreds, sought refuge at Herculaneum's marina, under the huge vaulted arches of the Suburban Baths, a majestic, sturdy building that opened out onto the water and was used for storing small boats during the winter months. But the tumultuous sea offered no escape. It is difficult to imagine the depth of their horror as they cowered under the arches and watched the sea roll back as if tipped away in a basin, then turn and rush toward them again in colossal waves—all while the roiling, steaming avalanche crushed its way in through every door and window.

A second surge must have hit the helpless town like a giant fist.

An hour later another scalding cloud sped down the mountainside. It blew a woman off a terrace 60 feet above the marina, slammed a soldier face down on his scabbard, flipped a boat and boatman into the air like dolls. Excavations since the early 1980's have yielded skeletal remains of the doomed, frozen in their last seconds of fear. A woman of obvious means, fingers

HERCULANEUM TELLS ITS STORY

It was the purest of accidents, a chance discovery in February 1980 by municipal workers digging trenches at an excavation site. And it changed forever the world's perception of what happened to Herculaneum that long-ago August when death coursed down the slopes of Vesuvius.

Excavation of Herculaneum and its more famous neighbor, Pompeii, had gone on intermittently since an earlier moment of good fortune, when a well digger's spade broke through to an underground amphitheater in Herculaneum in 1709. In contrast to Pompeii's cover of pumice and ash, which could be shoveled away, Herculaneum lay hidden under 65 feet of cementlike volcanic matter, which had to be laboriously drilled and chiseled away. Most of the early digging there, as in Pompeii, had been done chiefly by treasure hunters who tunneled into the ruins and carried off furniture, statuary, jewels—anything of potential value.

After more than 200 years of digging, in fact, Herculaneum had yielded only 10 skeletons, and they told no discernible story. The assumption was that while Pompeii was being deluged with 12 feet of wind-borne ash and pumice, most residents of Herculaneum had sufficient time to pack what they needed and flee.

So it rested until 1980, when the workmen struck something unexpected: the ancient skeleton of a Roman woman, heavily jeweled gold rings still in place on her fingers. Further probing yielded another skeleton, then another, and another. At that point, archeologists took over, and before they were finished they had unearthed hundreds of skeletons, many clustered in and around five large chambers of a building that had once been a beachfront marina. Clearly, the old assumptions were wrong. Not only had the people of Herculaneum not made an easy escape—something terrible had stopped them in their tracks.

But what? Intensive study of the skeletons by anthropologists and others soon began to disclose secrets 19 centuries old. Amid the evidence were valuable clues about the health, occupations, and social standing of the doomed inhabitants of Herculaneum —and about what had taken place in those last unimaginable moments.

One young woman whose remains were found among a group huddled in the first chamber, for example, had died cradling an infant in her arms. A mother and child, it appeared—but on closer scrutiny the picture changed. From notches and other features in the woman's bones, one scientist was able to deduce that she had

Rings still shining brightly on her hand, an affluent resident of Herculaneum lies where a fast-moving volcanic surge struck her down in the early-morning darkness of August 25, A.D. 79.

bejeweled with still-bright rings, lies beneath one of the great arches. In a nearby corner, huddled together in a final, despairing attempt at protection, is what one excavator has called "a masterpiece of pathos"—seven adults, four children, and a baby, preserved for all time by the thick, scalding muck that killed them.

If Pompeii could rightly be described as "a marvelously intact museum," Herculaneum has proved even more amazing, a perfectly frozen moment in history. There, still in place, are all the traces of day-to-day life interrupted by cataclysm. Loaves of bread sit intact in bakers' ovens and on family tables, alongside fruit, eggs, a bowl of seemingly fresh walnuts, and vegetables ready to be eaten. A box of expensive glassware sits half unpacked and wood cabinets half built, with the carpenter's tools lying nearby. A sick boy lies in his bed, his lunch of chicken untouched on a plate beside him. In short, every evidence of the clock stopped at a moment of supreme catastrophe.

In all, six surges and six seething waves struck the town, each leaving a demarcation line as it hardened. Finally, 18 hours after it had begun, the long ordeal ended. Daylight penetrated the gloom and revealed a scene of barely imaginable destruction. Herculaneum lay entombed beneath 60 feet of solidifying volcanic slag. Like Pompeii it was gone, struck down and buried with a terrible abruptness, its very existence destined to be forgotten as the centuries passed.

Vesuvius has erupted no fewer than 70 times since that fearful day, most recently in 1944. Today the bottom of the crater is sealed shut. Not even a small plume of smoke rises into the clear sky above it. But that placid appearance is deceptive. As those who know its history can affirm, the same immense pressures that triggered the great catastrophe of A.D. 79 could even now be building up in the magma chamber far below, and the mighty voice of Vesuvius may one day be heard again above the Bay of Naples.

been unmarried, raised in a poor family, and was probably employed as a governess for the well-fed, expensively dressed child whom she tried to protect when the avalanche of searing gas and lava swept in. Her decay-free teeth (like those of the wealthier residents) further indicated a diet low in sugar; apparently the opulent lifestyle of Herculaneum did not include overindulgence in sweets.

It may be that the Herculaneum excavations will never rival those at Pompeii for size or accessibility. Many buildings cannot be reached because they lie directly under those of the modern city of Ercolano. Meanwhile, unsolved mysteries still tantalize the imagination. The sprawling Villa of the Papyri, first explored in the mid-18th century, is thought to hold an unparalleled library of ancient manuscripts. Some 1,800 scrolled books were found at that time, but experts believe that further chambers may yet be unearthed, perhaps containing lost treasures of classical Greek literature.

How many people really died at Herculaneum? Where are they? What other revelations await excavators here? The discoveries of the early 1980's raised many questions, but they also left no doubt that the answers will be well worth seeking.

Like a monstrous apparition, this hardened flow of volcanic ash fills the doorway of a public bathhouse in Herculaneum, still seemingly trying to force its way inside. So powerful was the surge that it not only hurled a massive marble basin across the room but embedded it with shattered window glass.

Earthquake at Alexandria

Mediterranean lands hit by giant sea waves

A GREAT PART of the Roman Empire was jolted awake by a violent earthquake early in the morning of July 21, A.D. 365. As often happens when an earthquake originates under the ocean floor, the greatest damage to life and property was caused not by the quake itself but by the tsunami, or giant sea wave, that the quake set in motion. In the words of Saint Jerome, the contemporary scholar and doctor of the church, the floods that followed were so immense that it "seemed as though God was threatening a second deluge, or all things were returning to original chaos." Most severely affected were the coasts of Sicily, Dalmatia (now part of Yugoslavia), Greece, and Egypt. According to one story, the citizens of the Greek seaside town of Epidaurus, terrified by the oncoming wave, ran for help to Saint Hilarion, the revered monk and mystic, who was living among them at the time. Led to the shore by the townspeople, the old man made the sign of the cross three times in the sand and stretched out his hands to the sea. Miraculously, the wave hesitated, then bowed, and finally retreated. Across the Mediterranean the citizens of the Egyptian port of Alexandria were not so lucky. For it was their glittering city on the western edge of the Nile Delta that was to bear the brunt of the cataclysm.

With its wide harbor, world-famous library, and even more renowned lighthouse—the last was one of the Seven Wonders of Antiquity—Alexandria had long been a major commercial and cultural hub of the Greco-Roman world. Founded by Alexander the Great in 332 B.C., the city quickly attracted the leading scholars of the day. Here Euclid wrote his famous treatise on geometry about 300 B.C. and Eratosthenes first calculated the earth's circumference. The city was also the scene of Cleopatra's seductions and intrigues, which would end in her suicide and Rome's conquest of Egypt in 30 B.C. Although Alexandria's political importance declined under Roman rule, the city retained much of its intellectual pre-eminence throughout the first centuries of the Christian Era. By the middle of the fourth century A.D., Alexandria had become a leading center of Christian thought and a battleground for the forces of heresy and orthodoxy.

On that fateful morning in July, the people of Alexandria were struck by "horrible phenomena," wrote the contemporary historian Ammianus Marcellinus, "such as are related to us neither in fable nor in truthful history. For a little after daybreak, preceded by heavy and repeated thunder and lightning, the whole of the firm and solid earth was shaken and

Royal palaces lined the Great Port of ancient Alexandria. The two obelisks are probably the same ones later known as Cleopatra's Needles, which today stand in London and New York.

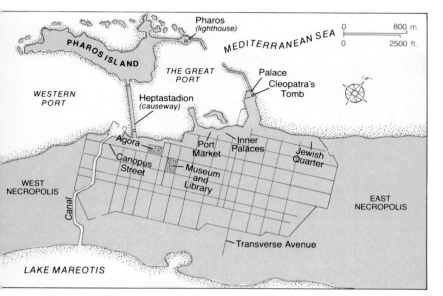

Alexandria's lighthouse, shown (right) in a fanciful reconstruction, commanded the approach to the Great Port (above) and, despite its exposed position, survived the earthquake and tsunami of A.D. 365.

trembled." As the quake itself subsided, the waters of the Mediterranean began pulling away ominously from the coasts, "so that in the abyss of the deep thus revealed men saw many kinds of sea-creatures stuck fast in the slime; and vast mountains and deep valleys, which Nature, the creator, had hidden in the unplumbed depths . . . first saw the beams of the sun." Many people, thinking that the worst might be over, ventured into the suddenly shallow waters to gather stranded fish with their bare hands.

But the worst was by no means over. The rapid drop in water level was soon followed by a tremendous wave that came crashing down on the city with all its terrifying power and fury. Ammianus described the scene in these words: "The roaring sea, resenting, as it were, this forced retreat, rose in its turn . . . dashed mightily upon islands and broad stretches of the mainland, and levelled innumerable buildings. . . . The great mass of waters, returning when it was least expected, killed many thousands of men by drowning." The unwise fishermen were no doubt among the drowned. So great was the force of the water that it lifted large ships and deposited them on the tops of buildings or carried them as far as two miles inland. Later, when the waters had receded, many ships "were found to have been destroyed, and the lifeless bodies of shipwrecked persons lay floating on their backs or on their faces." In all, some 50,000 Alexandrians are thought to have perished in the earthquake and ensuing inundation.

In an age when extraordinary events were routinely attributed to God's will and disasters were viewed as divine punishment for man's sin, the earthquake caused astonishment and fear throughout the decaying Roman Empire. People apprehensively recalled previous calamities and spoke of this one as only a preview of worse things to come. But Alexandria itself—and its remarkably sturdy lighthouse—endured, and for generations afterward its citizens commemorated the earthquake and flood of 365 with a yearly festival. On each anniversary of the disaster, according to the fifth-century lawyer and historian Sozomen, Alexandrians would make "a general illumination throughout the city," offer "thankful prayers to God," and celebrate "very brilliantly and piously" their city's survival.

55

Killer Quake at Antioch

A stroke of nature's fury destroys a brilliant metropolis

ON MAY 29 in the year 526, the great city of Antioch bustled with even more energy than usual. The next day was the feast of the Ascension, and the city was filled to overflowing with thousands of visitors come to share in the observances. At such a time, indeed at any time, Antioch was an exciting place to visit. Situated on the Orontes River about 20 miles upstream from the Mediterranean coast in present-day Syria, it controlled key trade routes linking Europe with the entire Near East. For more than half a millennium Antioch had flourished as a center of cosmopolitan life, first as a royal capital under the Seleucid dynasty, then as the provincial capital of Syria in the Roman Empire, and finally, after the imperial capital was moved to Constantinople, as a vitally important commercial center of the Byzantine Empire. Sixth-century Antioch boasted all the trappings of prestige and power. There were impressive marble colonnades, wide paved streets in the Roman style, ornate public baths, theaters and amphitheaters, marketplaces, churches, and monuments—even a regular system of oil-burning street lamps—all enclosed by a massive stone wall.

Antioch had also been a true cradle of Christianity, supporting one of the most important early church communities and providing a secure base from which the Apostle Paul carried out his mission to the Gentiles. (It was there, in fact, that the term *Christian* was first applied to the followers of Jesus Christ.) Little wonder, then, that the Fair Crown of the Orient, as Antioch was called, served as a magnet for worshipers from miles around on so joyous an occasion as Ascension Day.

By dusk most of the people had gone indoors to dine, their spirits no doubt stirring with anticipation of the day to come. It was then, just a bit after 6 o'clock, that the earthquake struck, so suddenly that its victims had no chance to react. Whole buildings caved in almost instantaneously, their walls and ceilings crashing down with a roar that mixed with the cries of terror and pain. The timing of the quake was as bad as it could possibly have been. Not only because countless thousands of visitors were on hand for Ascension Day, but because so many were indoors for the evening meal, the collapsing buildings took an especially heavy toll. Perhaps even more awful than the convulsions of those first few minutes was the eerie silence that followed as survivors cowered in confusion and numbing fear.

The good life of ancient Antioch is captured in this 3rd-century mosaic of a celestial drinking contest between Heracles and Dionysus, entertained by a graceful dancer.

56

A sweeping vista greeted revelers departing from "The House of the Drinking Contest," as it was named by excavators.

But the stillness did not last. Waves of aftershocks compounded the torment and destruction. Then, as if to make the agony complete, the crippled city was engulfed by fire. So intense and fast-moving was the blaze that survivors described how "fire fell down from heaven instead of rain." Many were burned to death as the surging flames blocked their escape; many more were asphyxiated or consumed as they lay trapped beneath the piles of smoking debris.

"Sparks of fire filled the air and burned like lightning," wrote John Malalas, a resident who may have been the only eyewitness to leave an account of the disaster. "Except for the soil of the fields, the fire surrounded everything in the city, as if it had received a command from God that every living thing should be burned." In addition, nearly every building that had withstood the earthquake was destroyed or badly damaged by the conflagration. "Not a single dwelling, nor any sort of house" escaped the flames, Malalas reported. "No holy church, nor monastery, nor any other holy place was left unruined."

Particularly shocking was the fate of Antioch's crowning glory, the golden-domed Great Church, built two centuries earlier by the Roman emperor Constantine himself and renowned for its beauty. "After everything else had fallen by the wrath of God," wrote Malalas, the Great Church "remained standing for five days after the punishment. But suddenly even it caught on fire and collapsed to the ground."

All the suffering wrought by nature was compounded by human wickedness.

The toll was horrendous. Perhaps 250,000 to 300,000 people lost their lives, either killed instantly or left to starve, bleed, or burn to death beneath the tons of rubble. Meanwhile, as dazed survivors scrambled away from the ruins, they were set upon by packs of bandits, who took their valuables and murdered anyone who tried to resist. The more brazen criminals streamed into the city in search of treasure, looting the ruins and stripping pearls, gold, and precious stones from the corpses.

The most infamous thief was an official named Thomas, who gathered his slaves at one of the city's gates and over the course of four days amassed a fortune from the hapless escapees. He suddenly collapsed and died, however, and his ill-gotten gains—along with the rest of his property—were triumphantly dispersed among the people.

The story of Thomas's death and other accounts of brigands who met a similar fate were widely circulated as examples of divine retribution. And the people, in the midst of their sorrow, found further indications of supernatural favor. "Pregnant women, who had been buried in the ruins, after 21 days came out whole," reported Malalas. "Many also gave birth to children under the debris which covered the ground, and came out after some days with newborn infants unscathed, alive with the children borne by them. . . . And many other even more wonderful and incredible things happened, which no human tongue can express, and of which only the immortal God knows the secret."

Most miraculous and inspiring of all, it was said that three days after the earthquake, weary survivors looked up to see a vision of the Holy Cross in the sky. They fell to their knees and prayed as the manifestation hovered overhead for more than an hour.

While the people of Antioch bravely tried to reestablish their lives, the outside world was dumbfounded. "The splendor of the city, its good climate, and the beauty of its churches," reflected Malalas, "were such that those strangers who had seen them before, and came there afterwards, exclaimed: 'So utterly has this great refuge, this peaceful harbor of the world, been desolated!'"

To stunned contemporaries, who saw in every act of nature a reflection of God's purpose, the destruction of such a city was almost incomprehensible. An earthquake was not a reflection of natural activity, but an

THE MARTYR OF ANTIOCH

Although the great earthquake of 526 was a profound shock to the people of Antioch, other such convulsions had marked the city's long history—and one in particular had caused more than physical destruction. In December of A.D. 115, a massive quake struck Antioch during a visit by the Roman emperor Trajan, whose host was the provincial governor and future emperor, Hadrian. The two

barely escaped with their lives as the city suffered widespread damage and a heavy toll of dead and injured.

As was often the case, this disaster was viewed as punishment for some offense against the gods—and in an era of rising persecution, it was all too easy to blame the city's Christian minority. Many were killed by mobs, and the bishop of Antioch, Ignatius, was taken in chains to Rome for trial. On

the way, he wrote letters and spoke to church members in cities across Asia Minor, counseling courage and steadfastness. His own courage was soon put to the ultimate test. Condemned by an imperial tribunal, Ignatius implored church leaders to make no efforts on his behalf, and about A.D. 117 became perhaps the first Christian martyr to be killed by wild animals in the Roman Colosseum.

Saint Ignatius of Antioch became one of the early church's most inspiring figures. His cruel death in the arena, a fate shared by countless others during the next 200 years, is vividly recalled in this 10th-century illustration.

ominous message. What else could explain the cracking and trembling of the earth that God had created solid? To be sure, people of the region were accustomed to passing geologic disturbances, from sonorous rumblings beneath the surface of the earth to occasional rockslides and minor shocks. Indeed, in the years after the installation of Justin I on the Byzantine throne in Constantinople in 518, such events had become even more frequent. But the most violent episodes had occurred elsewhere.

What could it mean that this of all places had been singled out to be so brutally laid waste?

If the famed Greek city of Corinth collapsed in ruins, and if the same fate befell other sites in Asia and Europe—even so, they could scarcely be compared to Antioch. Rich, powerful, renowned as a center of religious thought, Antioch not only rivaled Constantinople and Alexandria in the empire's temporal affairs but ranked with Rome and Jerusalem in the spiritual life of Christendom.

"As soon as he heard of it," John Malalas wrote of the emperor Justin, "he took off his crown and the purple robe, mourned for a long time and wept." A crash program was launched to bring Antioch back to life. The imperial family urgently wanted a restoration of the city's commercial and religious vitality: it was too important to lose. Troops were dispatched to seek out survivors and to begin the formidable task of rebuilding. When Justin named his nephew Justinian coemperor a year after the earthquake, Justinian and his wife, Theodora, sent great sums to fund the construction of new churches, baths, and a hospice. The message from the throne was loud and clear: Antioch must rise again.

But as events would prove, even the most determined efforts of Byzantine officials were futile. In a word, Antioch was doomed. Aftershocks continued to reverberate through the sundered ground for the next year and a half, and for the first time in centuries the people of Antioch began to move away from their beloved city. Decline in one area spawned further decline in another. Trade fell because of the loss of life and property, and the commercial stagnation in turn drove more people away.

Then in November 528 another massive earthquake ripped through Antioch and claimed about 5,000 lives—a number that would undoubtedly have been higher but for the exodus that had already taken place. This time the destruction was immediate. The new structures, built with such purposeful optimism in the preceding months, fell in ruins, just as the buildings they were meant to replace had crumbled.

In two and a half years Antioch had suffered two devastating earthquakes. No surprise, then, that people continued to move away from this blighted spot. Some survivors, inspired by the dream of a pious Christian, inscribed above their doors the words "Christ is with us—stand." But for others, faith was overwhelmed by fear.

Once again Justinian (now sole emperor after the death of his uncle) warmly encouraged reconstruction with a generous allocation of funds; he even relieved the city of paying taxes for three years. Attention was paid to the spiritual dimension as well. After someone reportedly found a written injunction that warned, "And thou, wretched city, shalt not be called by the name of Antiochus," the name was promptly changed to Theopolis, meaning "City of God."

The Antioch Chalice, *made of silver and gilt with intricate carvings on the outer shell, was unearthed around 1910. Reputed at first to be the legendary Holy Grail, the wine cup used by Jesus and the Apostles at the Last Supper, it is now known to date from the 6th century* A.D. *Even so, it remains one of the most prized relics of the early Christian world.*

During Justinian's reign there were no more earthquakes approaching the magnitude of those in 526 and 528, but the damage had already been done. It was more than a great city that trembled to its foundations. When "Antioch the Great collapsed by the wrath of God," as Malalas put it, the spirit and self-confidence of a much larger community were sorely tested. The consequences would be felt for generations, as the Byzantine Empire began to lose its way and succumb to invaders.

For Antioch itself the deathblow was finally dealt by a man-made disaster, the onslaught of war. In 540 the city was captured and sacked by the Persians, and just two years later those who remained were ravaged by the plague that was overwhelming Justinian's domain. With this the battered metropolis limped off the pages of history, never to regain even a trace of the brilliance it had taken for granted until the 29th of May in 526.

Great Pestilence in Constantinople

Epidemic deals deathblow to the Byzantine Empire

IN THE 15TH YEAR of the emperor Justinian's reign, A.D. 542, the Great Plague struck Constantinople, the nerve center of the Byzantine Empire. For four terrifying months it held the metropolis in its grip. As spring turned to summer, so many of the citizenry fell victim that Constantinople came to a virtual standstill; at the height of the contagion the daily death toll may have reached 10,000 or more. Even the 59-year-old emperor was taken ill, though news of his confinement was kept from the already frightened populace.

How did disease race so easily from peasant to potentate? No one at the time understood how the plague was transmitted, which made it all the more terrifying. In 541 it was first recognized in the Egyptian harbor town of Pelusium. Next it tore through Alexandria and the rest of the country before moving northward to attack Palestine and Syria. "From there it spread over the whole world," observed the historian Procopius. The catastrophe was so overwhelming that "the whole human race came near to being annihilated." Most probably this was the earliest pandemic on record.

Much of what we know about the plague in Justinian's time comes from the writings of Procopius, who was a native of Caesarea in Palestine. As legal adviser to the general Belisarius, he accompanied his patron on missions throughout the Mediterranean world and was in Constantinople when the plague erupted. His eyewitness account details the course of the disease and the hideous suffering it brought to the populace.

At the outset of the affliction, all victims seemed to experience similar symptoms. "They had a sudden fever, some when just roused from sleep, others while walking about, and others while otherwise engaged, without any regard to what they were doing." It was a curious, "languid sort" of fever, so much so that "not one of those who had contracted the disease expected to die from it." However, very soon a swelling developed, usually below the abdomen, but also in the armpit, on the thighs, and in some cases near the ears. At this point the disease usually took a turn for the worse, although no one could predict the outcome. Some died suddenly and without warning; others were not so fortunate. "For there ensued with some a deep coma, with others a violent delirium. . . . Those who were under the spell of the coma forgot all those who were familiar to them and seemed to be sleeping constantly. . . . But those who were seized with delirium suffered from insomnia and were victims of a distorted imagination; for they suspected that men

Justinian's capital, Constantinople, is shown in this painting from a 15th-century manuscript. The emperor's beloved church, the domed Hagia Sophia, dominates the walled city. An equestrian statue of Justinian can be seen at left.

were coming upon them to destroy them, and they would become excited and rush off in flight, crying out at the top of their voices." Exorcists were sometimes summoned, but to no avail.

The most wretched death, however, was reserved for the sufferer who remained conscious and mentally competent as the swellings grew, causing excruciating pain until the end. In some cases, a discharge of pus seemed to lead to recovery; in others, the swelling disappeared, but the victim died as if poisoned from within. Some survivors apparently regained complete health; others lisped or experienced other speech difficulties for the rest of their lives.

Those who were well enough to care for the sick were soon exhausted by the ordeal. "For when the patients fell from their beds and lay rolling upon the floor, they kept putting them back in place, and when they were struggling to rush headlong out of their houses, they would force them back by shoving and

60

pulling against them." As the plague intensified and carried off more and more victims, there were not enough people to dispose of the bodies—or places in which to put them. Procopius described the ensuing chaos: "When it came about that all the tombs which had existed previously were filled with the dead, then they dug up all the places about the city one after the other, laid the dead there, each one as he could, and departed; but later on, those who were making these trenches, no longer able to keep up with the number of the dying, mounted the towers of the fortification in Sycae [across the waters of the Golden Horn], and tearing off the roofs threw the bodies in there in complete disorder; and they piled them up just as each one happened to fall, and filled practically all the towers with corpses, and then covered them again with their roofs."

Despite the chaos, the people of Constantinople tried to maintain their composure. Showing an astonishing strength of community, volunteer groups formed to dispose of the thousands of rotting corpses. Grants of food and money in the emperor's name were distributed to supplicants. The churches of the city continued to hold services; not surprisingly, perhaps, the survivors were said to worship more fervently than in less stressful times. Public entertainments were continued, and dignitaries of rival nations were received with pomp. Justinian's wife, Theodora, engaged in social activities even as her husband lay on his sickbed.

As August drew to a close, the Great Plague seemed to relinquish its hold on the city, having done its worst in one fell swoop. Although Justinian may not have realized it during that summer of death, the plague had probably dealt the final and most telling blow to his hopes of reviving the declining Roman Empire. Winter would halt the disease altogether, aided by the dispersion of the population in the outlying rural areas. Yet the deadly organism would hold on to life. Though the bacillus retreated, it was by no means conquered. When it attacked again, in the 14th century, it did so with a fury that would earn it a new and sinister name: the Black Death.

JUSTINIAN AND HIS CONSORT, THEODORA

When Justinian inherited the throne of the eastern Roman Empire from his uncle Justin in 527, he determined to restore to Constantinople (originally known as Byzantium) the political and military glory of ancient Rome.

Born of peasant stock, Justinian had attained this loftiest of ranks through a combination of talent and sheer will—with an added dash of luck. His greatest ally in his ambition to renew the empire was his wife, Theodora, a onetime actress and prostitute. An explicit account of her supposed sexual activities, written by Procopius, was kept secret by its author for fear of reprisals, and it did not come to the

The emperor Justinian

public's attention for at least two centuries after his death.

The truth about Theodora, however, was at best complex and never fully known. After all, it was the court of Byzantium that would give rise to that byword for devious and labyrinthine intrigue, *Byzantine*.

Anyone sharing the emperor's enormous power would be subject to envy and slander, particularly a woman who was born, as Theodora was, the daughter of the animal keeper of the Constantinople circus. When he died, she was forced as a very young girl to go on the stage, which was not a respectable profession.

Whatever her past, Theodora was forceful, intelligent, and an undeniable beauty. Even a malicious enemy would concede that she was "fair of face and of a very graceful, though small, person; her complexion was moderately colorful, if somewhat pale; and her eyes were dazzling and vivacious." Justinian was soundly smitten. Over the determined objections of his royal aunt, he took her as his mistress. When opportunity presented itself, he had his uncle, the emperor Justin, change the law of the land so that he could marry this commoner.

The strange union, derided by many at the time, was to become one of history's strongest marriages. Theodora was officially named empress, and her name appears on documents of state. She was the originator of laws designed to protect the rights of women, and she founded charitable institutions for the care of reformed prostitutes. When Theodora died in 548, Justinian seemed to lose both ambition and ability. The years until his death in 565 saw a steady deterioration of his capacity to govern and increased weakening of his influence throughout the empire.

The empress Theodora

Famine in Egypt

Failure of Nile floods brings hunger to an ancient land

EGYPT, AS THE GREEKS long ago observed, is the gift of the Nile. Without the silt-laden river the country would be a searing desert all the way to its Mediterranean shores. But a land that depends for its very life on the rise and fall of one river is also disastrously subject to that river's unpredictable mercies.

From before the days of the pharaohs to well into the 20th century, Egyptians awaited the annual flooding of the Nile with excitement and a degree of apprehension. In a typical year the river would begin to rise in late June and continue to swell throughout the summer. After cresting in mid-September, the floodwaters would recede, leaving behind a thick layer of rich silt for the fellahin, or peasants, to cultivate.

In medieval Egypt the minimum amount the Nile had to rise to produce a good crop was reckoned at 16 cubits, or about 28 feet. (A cubit, defined as the distance from the elbow to the tip of the middle finger, equals about 21 inches.) This level was called the sultan's water, because once the river reached it, farmers had to pay a tax on their land. A rise of 18 cubits might produce enough food to last the country two years. If the river rose above 20 cubits, however, large stretches of land would be flooded too long to be planted. At the other extreme, a rise of less than 16 cubits could mean a dramatic shortfall in the year's crop; two such failures in a row usually spelled disaster.

Writing in the year 1204, the Baghdad-born scholar, scientist, and historian Abd al-Latif observed that only 20 times since the beginning of the Islamic era (A.D. 622) had the Nile not exceeded "14 cubits and some fingers," and only about 6 times had it "stopped at 13 cubits and some fingers." In 1200, however, the Nile failed to reach even 13 cubits, "a thing extremely rare." As Latif recounts in his chilling chronicles of the famine years 1200–02, this failure of the Nile marked the beginning of what may have been one of the worst natural catastrophes in Egyptian history; certainly by Latif's account it was one of the saddest and most gruesome.

The summer began as usual that year, with the Nile showing its normal signs of rising toward the end of June. Yet two months earlier something quite out of the ordinary had occurred. "They had observed in the waters of the river a green tint," wrote Latif. "This tint acquired progressively more intensity, and the smell of the water took on a fetid and corrupt character." Boiling the water did not improve its taste or smell, and people began drinking well water instead.

Latif, who had come to Cairo several years earlier to teach at the renowned al-Azhar Mosque, conducted a series of experiments on the water and found it to be choked with vegetable matter. He correctly attributed the condition to a shortage of rain at the river's source.

As the summer wore on, the Nile's strange color disappeared, but so too did the promise of a good rise. By the ninth of September the river had reached its maximum level for the year: a disastrous 12 cubits and 21 fingers. Then it began to drop.

With the threat of a famine looming ever closer, the new year, reported Latif, "announced itself like a monster." Food prices rose, and people began to abandon the parched countryside in favor of the main provincial towns. Those who could, fled the country altogether, seeking refuge throughout North Africa

Since the time of the pharaohs, nilometers, such as the one at Aswan shown above in a 19th-century print, were used to measure the Nile's annual rise. For millennia Egypt depended on the yearly Nile flood (right) to soak its fields with silt-laden, life-giving water.

and the Middle East. An "infinite multitude," however, wound up in the cities of Misr and Cairo, where all they found was "an appalling famine and a frightful mortality." By March 1201 "the air was corrupted, the plague and contagion began to make itself felt, and the poor, pressed by the famine which struck them always, ate carrion, corpses, dogs . . . and the filth of animals. This went on a long time, until they began to eat little children."

From this point on, Abd al-Latif's account becomes a record of unrelieved deprivation and extraordinary barbarism, culminating in a prolonged siege of cannibalism that affected every level of society. "It was not rare to surprise people with little children roasted or boiled. . . . I myself saw a small roasted child in a basket. They carried it to the Governor and led in at the same time a man and a woman who, they said, were the father and mother of the child. The Governor condemned them to be burned alive."

Despite such punishments, the practice of cannibalism spread throughout the country during the first year of the famine. In the beginning, observed Latif, "horror and astonishment caused by these extraordinary

meals were such that the crimes became the subject of all conversation. . . . But subsequently, they accustomed themselves to such things, and conceived quite a taste for these detestable foods."

Adults and infants alike were abducted for human consumption, and graves were ransacked for food.

There were reports of storerooms full of human bones picked clean and of cauldrons bobbing with the heads of small children. Young girls were routinely sold into slavery for a pittance by their own parents in the hope that the buyers would at least keep the children alive.

For those who escaped being eaten by their neighbors or the bands of marauders that roamed city and countryside, death by starvation was often the only alternative. "As for the number of the poor who perished from exhaustion and hunger, God alone knows," wrote Latif. "In the streets where I trod, there was no single one where the feet or the eyes did not meet with

a corpse or a man in the throes of mortal agony. . . . They carried away, particularly from Cairo, each day between 100 and 500 dead bodies. . . . At Misr the number of the dead was incalculable: they could not inter them, but contented themselves with throwing them outside the town."

As their poorest citizens died and those able to move beyond the famine zone did so, towns around Cairo and in the provinces fell silent. A traveler could pass through a large town without finding a single living soul. Through the open doors of the houses one could see piles of corpses, "some reduced to rottenness, others still fresh." The road to Damascus, the main thoroughfare leading in and out of Cairo, "had become like a banqueting room for birds and wild beasts, who gorged themselves on the flesh of the corpses."

About April 1201 the Nile again turned green and noxious—a terrifying omen for a desperate land. Two months later the river cleared and began its feeble increase. After several fits and starts, the Nile reached its maximum level for the year in early September: 15 cubits and 16 fingers. Although short of the sultan's water, such a rise might still have ended the famine had the river not immediately begun to decline. As a result, in some areas the floods were felt "like the ghost of an inundation." Even fields that had been sufficiently flooded were left fallow because their owners lacked the money to cultivate them.

With a second Nile failure now a certainty, the prices of Egypt's staples—beans, barley, and wheat— rose to new heights, and the country headed into another year of famine, depopulated, exhausted, and with few resources. "Everything was in the same state" as in the first year, wrote Latif, and there was little hope of improvement. "Fewer of the poor perished," but only because they had already been "uniquely reduced to a small number." The practice of cannibalism waned, more as a result of exhaustion

ABD AL-LATIF: PHYSICIAN AND CHRONICLER OF EGYPT'S TRAGEDY

Our knowledge of the Egyptian famine of 1200–02 is derived primarily from an eyewitness account written by one of the most versatile scholars of the medieval Arab world. Abd al-Latif was born in Baghdad in 1162. In the course of his education, Latif committed to memory the entire Koran, as well as books on history, philosophy, theology, law, languages, and the sciences, especially medicine.

At age 28, Latif embarked on a trip that took him to Turkey, Greece, Syria, and Egypt. During his travels, he studied and taught at some of the leading centers of Islamic learning. He was befriended by Saladin, the great sultan of Egypt and foe of the Crusaders, and among the scholars he met in Cairo was the revered Jewish thinker and physician Maimonides.

It was during a second, extended stay in Cairo beginning in 1197 that Latif witnessed the great famine. Throughout the ordeal, Latif recorded what he saw and heard with scrupulous precision. His tone is that of the compassionate scientist—moved by human suffering but always ready to learn from it. Hearing that the bodies of an estimated 20,000 famine victims had been piled up in a place called Al Maks, Latif went there, and ignoring the Islamic ban on anatomical studies, began to examine skeletons. He discovered, among other things, that the lower jawbone was a single bone rather than a jointed one—an extraordinary finding in that it contradicted Galen, the second-century A.D. Greek physician whose writings were the medical bible of Latif's day.

In the years following the famine, Latif continued to travel extensively, teaching and writing some 165 books in all. His treatise on the human body remained a standard Arabic textbook for centuries. His *History of Egypt* was lost, but an extract containing only events that Latif himself witnessed, such as the great famine, survived and was translated into English in 1965. Abd al-Latif died at the age of 69 in Baghdad, where he had stopped briefly while on a pilgrimage to Mecca.

A physician instructs his assistant in the preparation of a poultice in this page from a 13th-century Arabic copy of a 1st-century A.D. Greco-Roman work on the medicinal use of drugs and herbs.

As it still does today in parts of Africa, hunger forced masses of people to migrate in search of food during Egypt's great famine of 1200–02. "Often it happened," wrote chronicler Abd al-Latif, "that among the crowd of emigrants, a woman became separated from her children, and . . . the unhappy little ones wandered, tired and hungry until death ended their sufferings."

and a shortage of victims, perhaps, than of revulsion.

As an example of Egypt's depopulation, Latif cites the rush-mat makers of Misr, whose numbers plummeted from 900 to 15 in two years, and "one could not but apply the same proportion to the other professions." A lack of tenants caused rents in Egyptian cities to drop by as much as 85 percent. Even the price of wheat declined. Although it was still a scarce commodity, the greatly reduced number of potential buyers lowered the grain's market value.

Within two years, hunger, disease, or cannibalistic murder claimed the lives of unknown thousands of Egyptians.

Between July 1200 and April 1202, the number of deaths officially registered in Egypt rose to nearly 111,000. But even this great number was "less than nothing," wrote Latif, "if one compares it to the infinite multitude of those whom death carried off, or who had been eaten, in all the cities, the country districts, and on the roads."

As often happened in Egypt in the wake of a famine, plague broke out in several parts of the country early in 1202, just as the year's meager crops were about to be sown. So rapidly did the disease spread that peasants dropped dead at their plows. "People worthy of trust" told Latif that in a single day at Alexandria the imam, or prayer leader, said funeral prayers for 700 people. And in just one month, an inheritance passed to 40 heirs in quick succession.

The final blow came early in the morning of May 20, 1202, when a series of violent earthquakes struck Egypt. Felt throughout Syria and perhaps as far north as Armenia, the quakes "loosened buildings, made the doors shake and cracked the roofs and the rafters." Port cities were inundated, ships were hurled up onto the shore, and people disappeared without a trace.

Although the quakes added considerably to the famine's death toll, they at least heralded the end of this particular time of trial for Egypt. Through the second winter of the famine, the Nile had run so low that it could be forded on foot in some places, and in February it had turned green again, causing great alarm. After reaching its low point about the time of the quake, the Nile began to rise slowly. From mid-June to mid-July it rose only four fingers, which led the people to form "a very bad opinion of the rise for that year; despair was general. They imagined that something extraordinary had happened to the sources of the Nile."

But after the middle of July the river began to swell once more. It quickly reached an encouraging height of three cubits before stalling for a brief but terrifying two days. And then the "waters came again in great abundance," wrote Latif. "They increased by very strong progression and it was said that mountains of water precipitated themselves one on the others." On September 4, 1202, the Nile rose to a height of just under 16 cubits and remained there for two days before falling away slowly. After two years of starvation and death, the specter of famine left Egypt—at least for the moment. For not until the building of the Aswan High Dam in our own century would Egypt's dependence on the annual flooding of the Nile finally end.

Drought in the American Southwest

Ancient pueblo builders abandon parched homeland

SOME DISASTERS STRIKE with the explosive abruptness of a lightning bolt. Others unfold slowly, gnawing away at the foundations of people's lives. So it was for the Anasazi people, pre-Columbian ancestors of the modern Pueblo Indians of the southwestern United States. Toward the end of the 13th century, a prolonged drought devastated the already arid lands of the Anasazi. Springs evaporated, the water table dropped, and crops withered in the summer heat. Impelled by lack of rain, soil erosion, and social pressures that we can only surmise, the Anasazi began abandoning their spectacular stone settlements, or pueblos, in search of less hostile conditions.

The Anasazi heartland was never an easy or hospitable place. The Colorado Plateau, which extends from northern Utah through southwestern Colorado into central Arizona and New Mexico, includes vast undulating tablelands cut by narrow gorges and bleak sandstone ridges. Steep-sided mesas rise from alkali barrens in some parts of the region. Elsewhere the thin soil sprouts a meager covering of sagebrush, greasewood, and desert grasses. But there are also wooded areas, covered with juniper and piñon trees, and in the canyon bottoms, sporadic streams feed oases of cottonwood and willow. Icy winds gust across the plateau in winter. Summers are dry, dusty, and hot. Scattered showers may bring occasional relief, and thunderstorms, though infrequent, can turn desert streams into raging, flood-producing torrents. Some years, parts of the plateau get no rain at all.

Unpromising as the Anasazi's land might seem, their ancestors had been living on it for millennia.

As far back as 12,000 years ago, this region was home to Stone Age bands of hunter-gatherers, who roamed the plateau in search of food. About 1500 B.C. the cultivation of corn was introduced into the area. By the early centuries of the Christian Era, the peoples of the Southwest were living a more sedentary life, and three distinct cultural groups began to emerge. The Hohokam lived in the lowland deserts of what is now Arizona and became expert irrigation farmers. The Mogollon, avid hunters and accomplished potters, inhabited the mountains and valleys south of the Colorado Plateau. The Anasazi settled on the plateau itself.

Known as the Basket Makers for their skill in weaving baskets, the early Anasazi dwelled in makeshift shelters or in caves at the base of cliffs and canyon walls. They lived on game and wild plants, supplemented by a few cultivated crops. But from roughly A.D. 500, the lives of the Anasazi began to change dramatically. They had learned the craft of pottery making and were becoming increasingly proficient at it. The more efficient bow and arrow replaced the stone-tipped spear and the atlatl, or wooden spear thrower. Cultivated corn, squash, and beans now formed a more substantial part of the Anasazi's diet.

As the Anasazi gained agricultural skills and gave

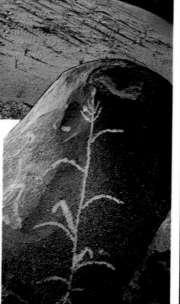

The staff of life *for the Anasazi, corn, was coaxed from the desert much as it is today by their Hopi descendants. Above, corn plants ripen in a Hopi field in Arizona. Centuries ago, an Anasazi carver paid tribute to the corn on a rock face (right) in New Mexico.*

Members of the Snake Society dance around the village plaza in this reconstruction of the dramatic Hopi snake ceremony.

FESTIVE RITES TO SUMMON THE RAIN

Ceremonial dances to invoke rain and ensure good harvests were as much a part of Anasazi agriculture as planting the seed and gathering the crop. If the practices of the Anasazi's descendants, the modern Pueblo Indians of the American Southwest, can be taken as a guide, preparations for the most sacred of these dances would begin months in advance, as the men of the pueblo entered their clan kivas to fashion the dancers' elaborate costumes and eerie wooden masks.

Each dancer would impersonate a kachina—one of the spirits that in ancient times had lived among the people and taught them to farm. Though long since departed, the ka-chinas returned at festival time to enter the bodies of the dancers. Since one of the kachinas' functions was to make rain, the dancers' regalia glittered with watery symbols: kilts and cloaks patterned with clouds and lightning bolts, masks splattered with raindrops, stone and turquoise pendants fashioned in the shape of frogs and other water creatures. Some dancers carried lightning-shaped wands; others wore eagle feathers, which were associated with the sun, or spruce boughs, suggestive of mountains, rain, and long life. Although only men wore kachina costumes, the entire community gathered in the village plaza to watch the lines of swaying, foot-stomping dancers move to the rhythm of drums, flutes, and rattles.

Kachina dances play a central role in the spiritual life of the Hopi and Zuni tribes of Pueblo Indians. But perhaps the most spectacular of the ancient rituals still performed today is the Hopi snake ceremony, a nine-day event held in late August, when timely rains will ensure a good harvest in the fall. At the climax of the ceremony, dancers circle the village plaza, carrying live snakes—symbols of lightning and rain—in their mouths. When the dance is finished, the snakes are released in the desert to convey the Hopi's prayers for rain to the spirits of the underworld.

up their nomadic ways, their housing became more permanent. By A.D. 300, some Anasazi families had started living in small shelters of mud-daubed timber, which they erected over saucerlike depressions dug into the soil. Later generations modified the plan, excavating the floor to greater depths, smoothing it with clay, and erecting timber roofs held up by wooden posts. Cool in summer and well protected from the chill winter gales, these pit houses provided natural year-round insulation. Aboveground storehouses—built first of branches and mud and later of stone—held the winter's supply of food. Sometime after A.D. 850, the Anasazi made the transition to living above ground. The storerooms evolved into houses, side chambers were added to accommodate relatives, and the first multifamily pueblos began to take shape.

Perhaps the most important innovation in Anasazi life involved control of the water supply. At first this effort may have been entrusted mostly to tribal elders and medicine men, who would puff ceremonial pipes

Pueblo Bonito, *the Anasazi's greatest architectural achievement, today lies abandoned and in ruins under the New Mexico sun. Built of sandstone and timber, Pueblo Bonito in its heyday covered more than three acres. At the heart of the community were the great kivas, huge circular chambers used for religious and social functions.*

los of Chaco Canyon in New Mexico are today silent witnesses to the extraordinary skills of the Anasazi builders. Along a nine-mile stretch of Chaco Canyon stood at least eight "great houses"—massive housing projects with thick masonry walls and accommodations for scores of families. As in the old pit houses, pueblo rooms were entered through openings in the roofs. The pit houses themselves were retained in the form of kivas, underground ceremonial chambers that served as clubhouses and religious centers for the men of the community.

The largest of the Chaco Canyon great houses was Pueblo Bonito—Spanish for "Beautiful Village." This magnificent D-shaped structure rose in five or more terraced stories, its windows and roof entryways fronting on a grand central plaza. At the height of its development, Pueblo Bonito contained more than 800 rooms and may have housed a population of more than 1,000. The complex included some 30 kivas, 2 of which measured 60 feet in diameter. A system of well-engineered roads led out from Chaco Canyon to smaller communities in the countryside. Archeologists have uncovered a hundred or more of these outlying villages, spread across an area of 30,000 square miles—so vast was the extent of Chaco influence.

Only a large, highly organized society could have mobilized the manpower necessary to build the great community houses and to maintain the croplands and irrigation systems that supported them. Yet the Anasazi seem to have been a people without defined social classes. There were no kings or aristocrats and no downtrodden peasants. Tribal elders, sitting in conference in the kivas, undoubtedly conducted the community's affairs, but they seem to have lived no differently than their neighbors. Everyone, in fact, shared in the bounty of Anasazi life, which followed a well-ordered rhythm of labor and ceremony, dance and harvest.

But the very growth of Anasazi prosperity carried the seeds of its own decline. One factor in the increasing affluence may have been a long period of unusually wet, stable weather that set in about A.D. 900. Steady rainfall levels meant that crop yields could be

and stage ritual dances to ensure favorable weather. But about A.D. 1000, in the northern reaches of the San Juan River valley in Colorado, Anasazi farmers developed a more practical approach. They began building diversion dams on canyon slopes to slow the runoff from whatever rain happened to fall. In some cases, a network of channels along canyon bottoms spread the water to neatly squared-off garden plots. Crop yields increased and populations burgeoned.

So began the golden age of the Anasazi. The small pueblos of earlier days gave way to thriving developments of astonishing size and complexity. The cliff dwellings of Mesa Verde, Colorado, and of Canyon de Chelly, Arizona, and especially the multitiered pueb-

predicted and surplus harvests set aside to feed an expanding population. The security of these reserves was deceptive, however. Poor farmland was brought into cultivation, and soon the Anasazi came to depend on the added crops. To supply their ever-growing need for firewood and building materials, the Anasazi engaged in intensive log cutting in the surrounding mountains. This inevitably led to the deterioration of the region's watershed; stripped of tree cover, the soil began to lose its capacity to store moisture. The delicate relationship between nature and man's needs was losing its balance.

Sometime after 1150 the climate underwent a subtle but far-reaching change. Fluctuations in rainfall became more frequent and severe, so that years of abundance would alternate with unforeseen periods of drought. When crops failed in the marginal fields, supplies of grain would run dangerously low. Then in 1276 the rains stopped altogether.

Year after year, for the next two decades, precipitation remained well below normal in the lands of the Anasazi. Although less snow fell in the high country, the spring meltwater would cascade down the now denuded slopes in devastating flash floods. Little moisture would seep into the ground or trickle down to the springs at the canyon heads. Wood for heating and building, already hard to come by, grew even scarcer. With the land's resources strained to capacity, famine threatening, and relief nowhere in sight, Anasazi society began to unravel.

As the sun beat down on Anasazi fields, no ritual pipe or ceremonial dance could save the withering corn.

The process was as slow and inexorable as the drought itself. At first, families who farmed the drier fields, where nothing would now grow, began leaving the pueblos to fend for themselves. Disputes may have broken out over ownership of land or the division of the increasingly scant harvests. Some pueblos may have had to take up arms to defend their dwindling grain reserves. Hunting parties would scour the countryside for game and come back empty-handed, for the animals too were abandoning the region.

But the Anasazi had withstood drought and scarcity in the past. What made them abandon their ancestral homeland now? The exact answer may never be known, but it seems that a complex combination of environmental and social factors—uncertain rainfall, depletion of wood supplies, soil erosion, population pressures, factionalism, and the breakdown of community ties—fueled a tendency, common throughout the pre-Columbian Americas, to abandon settlements once they were no longer viable. In fact, with the

exception of the Chaco sites, Anasazi pueblos were rarely inhabited for more than 80 years.

Whatever may have been the reasons for their migration, the Anasazi now scattered in many directions throughout Arizona and New Mexico. Eventually, they resettled, primarily along the Little Colorado River and the northern Rio Grande. By 1300, the pueblos of the Colorado Plateau, from Mesa Verde to Chaco Canyon, had fallen silent, abandoned forever to the locust and the rattlesnake. The Navajos and Utes who later occupied the region avoided the ancient pueblos for fear of the Anasazi ghosts that were said to haunt them.

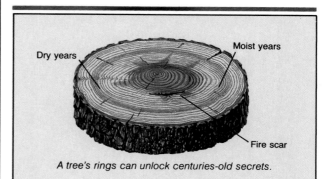

A tree's rings can unlock centuries-old secrets.

Trees Help Date Anasazi Past

DENDROCHRONOLOGY, or tree-ring dating, has provided many clues about the prehistory of the American Southwest. The technique is based on the fact that temperate-zone trees add a new layer of wood every year. When such a tree is felled, the rings in its trunk reveal the tree's age and much else about its history and growth patterns. Drought, for example, which inhibits a tree's growth, is reflected in narrow rings.

Since similar trees growing in the same region at the same time exhibit nearly identical rings, scientists have been able to create centuries-long timelines for a region based on its tree-ring data. This is done by matching the inner rings of a newly felled tree with the outer rings of a tree cut down when the first specimen was a sapling and then continuing the process as far back as possible. A wooden beam from an ancient house, for example, can be compared with the regional "master chart" and accurately dated. In the Southwest, where the technique was developed and has proved most successful, the tree-ring-based timeline extends back to about 300 B.C.. It has revealed that the oldest wood used at Pueblo Bonito was from a tree felled in about A.D. 850; the newest, in A.D. 1130. A succession of narrow tree rings, corresponding to the years 1276 to 1299, indicates a severe drought during the years the Anasazi were abandoning their homeland.

TRAGEDY ON A GLOBAL SCALE

The Black Death

Europe is ravaged by history's most ferocious epidemic

IN OCTOBER 1347 a dozen trading galleys of the Genoese merchant fleet put into Messina on Sicily across the Strait of Messina from the toe of Italy. They had sailed from the East, probably from the Black Sea, where they had loaded spices and silk as part of their regular trade with the caravans of Asia. But they also brought something terrible. The sailors, according to one chronicler, were racked with "sickness clinging to their very bones." Within days the people of Messina began to sicken and die. Horrified, they drove the plague ships back out to sea.

But the fatal seed had been planted. The sickness burned through Messina: a sudden, terrible fever, a few days of great pain, then death. Many fled to the countryside, carrying the pestilence with them. The citizens of Messina begged that the relics of Saint Agatha be brought from nearby Catania, but the Catanians forcibly prevented their archbishop from complying. Instead, he dipped the relics in holy water and took that to Messina, where he encountered "demons transfigured into the shape of dogs, who wrought grievous harm upon the bodies of the citizens." A few

days later, after returning to Catania, the churchman died of the plague. The disease meanwhile stalked south and west across Sicily.

Genoa and Venice—two of Europe's largest cities, along with Florence and Paris—were infected in much the same manner in January 1348. One account says that three plague-stricken galleys arrived in Genoa from Kaffa, a fortified trading outpost on the Black Sea that had come under siege by a Tartar army. A virulent outbreak of plague had decimated the Tartar troops, forcing them to abandon the siege—but not before catapulting some of the diseased corpses over the fortress walls. The infection spread quickly among the defenders, and those who did not succumb at once scrambled aboard their ships and set out for the Mediterranean.

When they reached Genoa, however, the ill-fated vessels were driven off with flaming arrows because no one would touch them—though again, as in Messina, the damage had already been done. These and other galleys struggled west along the Mediterranean coast, spreading the plague to the seaports of France and Spain. In Italy, meantime, Pisa was soon contaminated, and from there the disease spread through northern Italy and into central Europe. Florence, with its population of nearly 100,000, was suffering the first cases within a few weeks of the plague's landing at Genoa.

Giovanni Boccaccio was one of the surviving eyewitnesses of the plague in Florence. He later described it in his famed *Decameron*, a collection of tales supposedly told by a group of young aristocrats secluded in a villa for 10 days during the outbreak. "It began both in men and women with certain swellings in the groin or under the armpit. They grew to the size of a small apple or an egg, more or less, and were vulgarly called tumors. In a short space of time these tumors spread from the two parts named all over the body. Soon after this the symptoms changed and black or purple spots appeared on the arms or thighs or any other part of the body. Sometimes a few large ones, sometimes many little ones. These spots were a certain sign of death, just as the original tumor had been and still remained." The whole course of the disease, he reported, lasted three days.

Of the city's panic Boccaccio wrote, "such terror was struck into the hearts of men and women by this

Death triumphant gallops through a helpless population in this painting by an anonymous Dutch artist. The plague's psychological impact on Europe, echoing for generations to come, was reflected most vividly in countless images of a leering, exultant skeleton. "No thought is born in me," wrote Michelangelo two centuries later, "that has not 'Death' engraved upon it."

calamity that brother abandoned brother, and the uncle his nephew, and sister her brother, and very often the wife her husband. What is even worse and nearly incredible is that fathers and mothers refused to see and tend their children, as if they had not been theirs." And of the mortality: "Dead bodies filled every corner. Most of them were treated in the same manner by the survivors, who were more concerned to get rid of their rotting bodies than moved by charity towards the dead. With the aid of porters, if they could get them, they carried the bodies out of the houses and laid them at the doors, where every morning quantities of the dead might be seen."

The churchyards were soon overwhelmed by the flood of death. A citizen of Siena recorded the nightmarish consequences: "None could be found to bury the dead for money or for friendship. . . . And in many places in Siena great pits were dug and piled deep with the multitude of dead. . . . And I, Agnolo di Tura, called the Fat, buried my five children with my own hands. And there were also those who were so sparsely covered with earth that the dogs dragged them forth and devoured many bodies."

The plague raged for four months in Florence and may have left as many as 65,000 dead. During the next three years the same nightmare would be repeated again and again throughout Europe. So fast were people dying that in many towns and cities the corpses (and often, no doubt, near-corpses) were simply piled up daily in the street and carted off by whoever was willing, for a high enough fee, to dispose of them.

This fearsome thing was not content to kill. It tortured its victims and made them loathsome in their last hours.

A French chronicler recorded in grim detail that "all the matter which exuded from their bodies let off an unbearable stench; sweat, excrement, spittle, breath, so fetid as to be overpowering; urine turbid, thick, black or red."

The symptoms described by Boccaccio and his contemporaries were the hallmarks of bubonic plague, named for the buboes—swellings of the lymph glands, usually in the groin and armpit—that form on human victims. The disease is caused by the bacillus *Yersinia pestis*, which is carried by some wild rodents and spread from them by fleas. In some cases the swellings break on their own and the sufferer recovers. But for most victims in the 14th century—upwards of 80 percent—they meant a death sentence.

An even more virulent form, pneumonic plague, occurs when bubonic plague develops into pneumonia. Fatal to almost every person it infected, pneumonic plague spread directly from one person to another in droplets of moisture on exhaled air, doing its deadly work in anywhere from two days to two weeks. So efficient was the transmission of this invisible menace that a mere glance from a dying person was widely believed to be lethal.

A third variety that compounded the outbreaks was septicemic plague, an infection of the blood so potent that its victim might go to bed well and die in his sleep, or drop dead in the street, having started the morning healthy.

The epidemic we know as the Black Death—a name first applied two centuries later—originated in a harsh and remote region of Central Asia. There, in the vicinity of Lake Issyk-Kul in what is now the Soviet Union, *Yersinia pestis* is found in the Mongolian marmot, a squirrel-like rodent also called a tarbagan. No one knows whether floods, overpopulation, or some other cause prompted the carriers of this disease to spill out of their isolated neighborhood. In any case, disease-bearing fleas spread to the black rat, and the rats carried them into the main arteries of civilization. Evidence shows human infection in Asia by the late 1330's; it progressed west to the Crimea, and from there began its lethal journey to Europe.

Once unleashed, the plague traveled wherever man provided suitable transportation. It entered southern Europe by ship, alighting on a population that was probably free of the disease, and then was carried across the whole continent by the routes of commerce. Rats and their fleas, ensconced in shipments of grain, took *Yersinia pestis* from one town or village to infect rats in the next. Infected fleas can survive in cargoes of wool or cloth for weeks without their hosts, finding new rats in the shops and storerooms where they are unloaded. Moscow caught the plague not directly from the Crimea, but late in the epidemic through trade with northern European countries. It descended on the Middle East from Constantinople and other major ports, and on North Africa from Sicily. A ship adrift in the North Sea, its crewmen all dead, reportedly carried the contagion to Norway.

All the while, the possibility that rats and fleas were the bearers of destruction was never suspected.

The black rat, *Rattus rattus*, lives in close proximity to man and did so especially in medieval Europe. Black rats infested houses in cities and towns, finding ideal living conditions in the wood and clay structures. In villages they joined the farm animals sharing the peasants' quarters. Before the onset of the Black Death they must have died in large numbers and been especially evident in cities, but their presence and death went unremarked in accounts of the time.

An eerie procession *of Flagellants, whose bizarre and bloody rituals became familiar throughout plague-stricken Europe, is depicted in this 15th-century illumination from a French manuscript.*

The plague, consuming Europe from south to north, inexplicably spared a few small areas—one in present-day Belgium, another in the southwest of France, a larger one in Bohemia. In Milan, when the first cases were reported, the infected houses were ordered bricked up, with sick and well alike left inside to die. This draconian measure scarcely seems adequate to have saved the city, but Milan was indeed spared a devastating outbreak, the only major European city to be so fortunate.

By March the disease had settled on Avignon, seat of the papacy for most of the previous half century, where it raged for seven months, killing perhaps half the city's 50,000 residents. So heavy was the death toll at its peak, in fact, that the pope consecrated the waters of the Rhone in order that bodies could be thrown into the river. By June the plague reached Paris, reducing that vibrant capital to a shuttered, looted charnel house, populated by the dead and by those who could not or would not escape.

In villages, where most of Europe's people lived, tilling the land of the nobility and the church, the plague likely came first as a tale told by a traveler of disaster in foreign lands (which might be anywhere beyond the next province). Perhaps the priest spoke of it from the pulpit. Then the sickness appeared in the next village, then at home: first one person, then another—then what seemed like continuous dying. When it passed, many houses stood empty. Livestock wandered untended; crops rotted in the fields.

The pestilence brought dread to every hearth. "The contagious nature of the disease is indeed the most terrible of all the terrors," wrote a Flemish priest, "for when anyone who is infected by it dies, all who see him in his sickness, or visit him, or do any business with him, or even carry him to the grave, quickly follow him thither, and there is no known means of protection."

Wherever plague struck, people could plainly see—if not comprehend—what was happening around them. Many of those with the means to do so fled, like the storytellers of Boccaccio's *Decameron,* from towns and cities to isolation in the country. The medical profession could contribute precious little. While doctors had useful treatments for some common ailments, their basic understanding of disease still owed a great deal more to astrology than it did to science.

Gui de Chauliac, physician to the papal court, wrote that this disease in particular was "shameful for the physicians, who could give no help at all, especially as, out of fear of infection, they hesitated to visit the sick." In fairness, their fear was well founded: doctors who ministered to plague-stricken patients usually died. Some physicians recommended seclusion, preferably sheltered from wind—especially the south wind—and well away from the coasts and swampy regions that gave rise to corrupted mists.

For those who had to stay in cities, strong scents—aromatic woods and powders to burn on the hearth or pieces of amber or waxy concoctions called smelling apples to carry—were thought to counteract poisoned air. There was a notion that foul odors were especially effective in warding off the pestilence, and some people visited public latrines daily to imbibe the stench. Inactivity was favored because exercise increased the consumption of tainted air.

The papal physician, whatever his estimate of other doctors, brought a scientific spirit to his own duties. He made accurate observations of the disease, discerning two distinct forms at work and recognizing that pneumonic plague was the deadlier. And he prescribed a successful regimen for his principal patient, Pope Clement VI, confining him alone in his palace to sit and sleep

between two roaring fires until the dying passed. (All the other rulers of Europe escaped death, too, except King Alfonso of Spain, who died when plague decimated his army near Gibraltar.) Out of 450 members of the papal Curia, 94 died during the plague at Avignon—an enviably low death rate compared to that of the population at large.

The causes of the plague were open to debate, but its ultimate explanation was never doubted in Christendom: punishment by God for the innumerable sins of the age. In October 1348, a year after the plague first touched Europe, William Edendon, bishop of Winchester, began a letter to his clergy: "A voice in Rama has been heard; much weeping and crying has sounded throughout the various countries of the globe. . . . this cruel plague, as we have heard, has already begun singularly to afflict the various coasts of the realm of England." Drawing what seemed an inescapable conclusion, he remarked that "it is much to be feared that man's sensuality . . . has now fallen into deeper malice and justly provoked the Divine

Scapegoats doomed by bigotry and fear, Jews are burned alive as the plague approaches Cologne (left). Less barbaric but no more effective in resisting the pestilence was the prayerful, frenzied Dance of Death.

wrath by a multitude of sins to this chastisement."

But the plague did not respect piety. The parish priest who tended the sick was likely to be one of its early victims. Church records in England chart the march of disease with a surge of clerical vacancies, and when the pestilence appeared in a monastic community it might well leave no survivors at all.

Nor was it death alone that emptied Europe's pulpits: many priests obeyed the powerful instinct for survival and fled their dying congregations. In January 1349 the bishop of Bath and Wells, in a letter to the priests of his diocese, told them to advise their parishioners, "in particular those who are now sick or should fall sick in the future, that, if they are on the point of death and cannot secure the services of a priest, then they should make confession to each other."

In Germany the pervasive terror swelled the ranks of a movement called the Brethren of the Cross, or the Flagellants, who sought to placate God's anger by acts of extreme penitence, most especially self-flagellation. The practice of mortifying the flesh may have first appeared in Europe in some Italian monasteries in the early 11th century. Two centuries later, again in Italy, devout men gathered to scourge themselves after a series of disasters beset their province. Then, in the 14th century, the Black Death brought the movement to a crescendo.

The Flagellants, at the beginning of their rapid upsurge in Germany, were a tightly disciplined community. Anyone wishing to join had to confess all sins, promise to scourge himself three times a day for 33 days (one day for each year Christ spent on earth), and provide sufficient funds to pay for food during the period. Every new communicant agreed to be obedient to the master of a pilgrimage and not to change clothes, bathe, shave, sleep in a bed, or have any contact with the opposite sex during the allotted 33 days.

The Brethren went from town to town, usually in groups of a few hundred but sometimes more than a thousand strong. They wore simple robes marked by red crosses and cowls that hid their faces, marching two by two behind the master and two lieutenants who bore banners of gold and purple. When they entered a town or village, they held a service, stripped to the waist, formed a circle, and lay down so that the master could move among them and whip those who chose postures symbolic of certain sins. Then the pilgrims would rise and flail themselves with scourges of leather thongs studded with metal at the ends. The Brethren chanted throughout their painful

show of penance, eventually reaching a frenzy, as the watching crowd wailed and groaned.

By the middle of 1349, the Brethren were active in Germany, Hungary, Poland, and the Low Countries. As if in keeping with the terrible times, what had begun in devotion soon careened out of control. Masters claimed the right to hear confession and the power to exorcise evil spirits, even to raise the dead. At length, in October 1349 Clement VI issued a papal bull ordering the Brethren suppressed.

The Flagellants also contributed to another horror of the 14th century —this one man-made.

Clement listed among other charges "shedding the blood of Jews, whom Christian piety accepts and sustains." The Flagellants had indeed done so, with unmistakable zeal, but they were not alone. As plague swept across Europe, people looked in every direction for others to blame. Some settled on lepers, others on foreigners; but almost everywhere Jews found themselves branded as secret agents of destruction.

In the spring of 1348 there was a massacre of Jews in southern France. Then a celebrated trial in Switzerland dramatically raised the level of hatred and hysteria. Jews were accused at Chillon of poisoning wells, and 11 confessions were extracted by torture, implicating every member of the Jewish community in the plot. The confessions were circulated to nearby cities, and persecution spread with them.

The violence flared across Europe in a sad imitation of the plague itself. At Basel, in Switzerland, the Jews were locked in wooden buildings and burned; at Speyer, in Germany, their murdered bodies were loaded in giant wine casks and pushed into the Rhine; at Strasbourg, in France, 2,000 were killed on a single day in February 1349. By March the wave of murder seemed to have stopped. Then in July, the Brethren appeared in Frankfurt and marched directly to the Jewish quarter, where they initiated a slaughter. In Brussels the mere news that a column of Flagellants would arrive shortly was enough to trigger a massacre. When the plague subsided in Europe, so did the killings, though by then there were few Jewish communities left intact anywhere in western Europe.

"Wretched, terrible, destructive year" begins a note scratched in 1350 on the wall of St. Mary's

The beaked mask of a doctor held spices to repel tainted air.

THE PAINFUL SCIENCE OF MEDIEVAL MEDICINE

To physicians of the 14th century, bubonic plague was an absolute, sinister mystery, no more comprehensible than an atomic bomb would have been. While some branches of science could claim modest advances, medical knowledge had remained at a virtual standstill for a thousand years. An individual's health was still thought to be governed by the four bodily fluids known as humors, and influenced by astrological and other obscure forces. The idea that a disease might be caused by tiny organisms such as bacteria—and that they might be spread by rats and fleas—was a breakthrough reserved for later centuries.

As with the theory of medicine, its practice was an accumulation of remedies and rituals that had been handed down unquestioningly from one generation to another. In some areas, to be sure, medieval doctors were quite competent: they knew how to set broken bones, dress wounds, extract decayed teeth, prepare herbal medications, and perform various surgical procedures. But when confronted with a disease like the plague, they turned to an ancient repertoire of useless, often gruesome treatments. The most familiar was bloodletting, rou-tinely prescribed for everything from headaches to cancer. The theory was that bleeding drained off excess humors and restored a healthy balance; in fact, it only diminished a patient's chances of recovery. Potions containing pulverized gold and precious gems were prescribed for wealthy sufferers, and the buboes of plague victims were often lanced or cauterized with hot irons, methods as ineffective as they were excruciating. There was, however, at least one important public-health policy that emerged from the plague years: before being allowed into a city, possible carriers were isolated for a period eventually fixed at 40 days—or, in Italian, a *quarantina*.

An impressively robed physician lances a bubo on the neck of a plague victim.

Church in Ashwell, England. The inscription stands as a bitter summary of the plague years, which ended by 1351, having claimed perhaps a third of Europe's population—20 million souls or more. The stunned people of Europe went about trying to restore a semblance of normality to their lives, though little could seem normal after the Great Dying. In the words of the Italian poet Petrarch, "a vast and dreadful solitude" lay like a shroud on survivors everywhere. "Oh happy posterity," he wrote, addressing readers of the future, "who will not experience such abysmal woe and will look upon our testimony as a fable." But his vision of posterity proved too optimistic. The sickness struck Europe again 10 years later and would reappear often in centuries to come, alternately subsiding and flourishing until its last cataclysmic outbreak in Marseilles in 1720.

Such a calamity was bound to have far-reaching consequences. The feudal system, already on the decline, was further weakened by the disappearance of millions of peasants whose labor had been its foundation. Survivors found that their labor commanded wages far higher than any they had known before.

Indeed, there was a modest economic boom in many areas, fueled by people who had lost their entire families—and suddenly had inherited wealth to spend.

Unquestioning acceptance of church authority was eroded not only by the spectacle of priests deserting their flocks, but by the church's utter powerlessness to slow the juggernaut of death. A new skepticism arose, compounded by the lack of able young churchmen to replace those who had died, that would culminate finally in the Protestant Reformation.

"And I, Brother John Clyn, of the Order of Friars Minor and of the convent of Kilkenny, wrote in this book those notable things which happened in my time, which I saw with my own eyes, or which I learned from people worthy of belief." So says the account of a dying monk in Ireland who had watched his fellows die around him. "And, lest the writing perish with the writer and the work fail with the laborer, I leave parchment to continue this work, if perchance any man survive and any of the race of Adam escape this pestilence and carry on the work which I have begun." And finally, two last words that speak all too eloquently for his time: "Great dearth."

Mysterious Sweating Sickness

A lethal fever hits England repeatedly, then vanishes

"IN THE YEAR of our Lord God 1485, shortly after the seventh day of August . . . there chanced a disease among the people, lasting the rest of that month & all September, which for sudden sharpness and unwont cruelness passed the pestilence. . . . It immediately killed some in opening their windows, some in playing with children in their street doors, some in one hour, many in two it destroyed, & at the longest, to them that merrily dined, it gave a sorrowful Supper."

Thus began Dr. John Caius's 1552 book *Counsel Against the Disease Called the Sweat.* In April of the previous year, Caius, one of England's most eminent physicians, had witnessed another outbreak of the same terrifying disease in Shrewsbury in west-central England. From there it had spread southeast to the Channel coast and north all the way to the Scottish border before petering out in September.

Caius could find no precedent for the English sweating sickness, or *sudor anglicus,* in medical histories. It seems to have erupted in August 1485 among the victorious troops of Henry Tudor just after the Battle of Bosworth Field ended the historic Wars of the Roses. Infected soldiers afterward drifted toward London, carrying the disease with them. Within three weeks the sickness had killed two lord mayors, four aldermen, many noblemen, and countless ordinary Britons. Henry Tudor's coronation as King Henry VII had to be postponed, and Oxford University was shut down for six weeks while the faculty and students either took to their beds to die or fled the city in hopes of avoiding the dread disease.

Sometime in late autumn, the sweating sickness vanished as mysteriously as it had come. Some said that a violent storm had swept over the south of

The Battle of Bosworth Field *marked the fall of Richard III—and the rise of England's mysterious sweating sickness.*

England and carried it out to sea. At any rate it seemed to be gone for good, with no recurrences the next year or the year after—none, in fact, for a generation.

But it did return, directed by a timetable as inscrutable as its origins. In the summer of 1508 it reappeared suddenly, counting several high-ranking officials among its victims and prompting King Henry to move from place to place, always, so he hoped, one step ahead of the fast-spreading contagion. Then, following what was to become a pattern, its potency decreased rather quickly, and by mid-autumn the disease had faded away once again.

Eight more summers came and went. Then in 1517 the sickness struck with even greater impact than before. Sweating fever nearly claimed the life of Henry VIII's powerful chancellor, Cardinal Wolsey, reportedly killed more than 400 students at Oxford, and took so high a toll in London that the famed statesman Sir Thomas More remarked in a letter, "I assure you there is less danger in the ranks of war than in this city."

A hallmark of the disease was that it struck without warning, usually during the night or toward early morning, with the onset of a profound chill and tremors. Soon the victim was beset with headache, backache, thirst, loss of appetite, shortness of breath, and extremely high fever. The attack was likely to climax in a few hours, followed by either a quick recovery or a fatal coma.

Prominent among the many odd features of this sickness was its predilection for the English. Though other diseases routinely crossed and recrossed the Channel, the sweat was almost exclusively an English disease. Only during the terrible epidemic of 1528 did it gain significant ground on the Continent, reaching Germany the following year and spreading from there through northern and central Europe.

After a decade-long respite, the disease made its fourth appearance in June 1528, this time afflicting King Henry's newest lover and future wife, Anne Boleyn. She recovered, but many others were not so lucky as the disease spread with such terrifying virulence that it was dubbed "the great dying."

The specific cause of the sweat was a subject of speculation more than real knowledge. Caius suggested that "evil mists & exhalations drawn out of the ground by the sun" were a probable cause, triggered perhaps by astrological influences. He went on to propose that the sweat favored the English because they consumed too much meat, an excess of infected fruits, and an overabundance of spirits, noting that it was prosperous, middle-aged males—who lived high off the hog—who seemed most vulnerable.

In truth, the poor did seem to be more resistant to the disease than their better-off countrymen, perhaps because those who lived—and survived—in squalid conditions built up a degree of immunity. But the poor also seldom used physicians, whose cures could be

Two who recovered *from bouts of the fever were Cardinal Wolsey (right), and young Anne Boleyn, who survived the 1528 outbreak only to be executed later by her husband, Henry VIII.*

more deadly than the disease. One popular treatment was to have a team of keepers prevent a patient from sleeping, on the theory that victims often died in a state of deep sleep or coma. "Put strong wind or sharp vinegar into his nose," suggested one treatise, "talking to him all the while."

The fever made its last appearance in London in 1551, prompting Caius to write his book, and since then many others have attempted to apply scientific explanations to the questions surrounding it. What exactly was the disease, and where did it come from? Why did it recur at such irregular intervals? Where did it hibernate in the meantime? What really made it choose English victims almost exclusively, and men much more often than women? And why, after the 1551 flare-up, did it vanish from medical history?

Some symptoms suggest other illnesses such as influenza, scarlet fever, typhus, and meningitis. A more likely connection, however, can be made with relapsing fever, an infectious disease transmitted by a virus that can be harbored in the ticks or lice of small mammals or birds for many years with no apparent effect on humans. Then, through a complex set of circumstances—weather conditions, lowered immunity owing to poor diet, population shifts, or a mutation of the virus itself—the infection erupts.

In the end, though, such theories remain in the realm of speculation—intriguing, even ingenious, but never conclusive. After more than 400 years, the questions still have no answers. And in all likelihood, this perplexing disease will remain as mystifying to the 21st century as it was to the 16th.

Smallpox in Mexico

Old World scourge helps topple mighty Aztec empire

OF ALL THE WEAPONS the Spaniards brought with them to conquer Mexico—steel swords, muskets, cannon, armor, and horses—none would prove so deadly as smallpox. Hernán Cortés and his band of some 550 soldier-adventurers landed near the site of modern Vera Cruz on Holy Thursday, 1519. Within three years, 2 to 3.5 million Mexican Indians, according to conservative estimates, had died of the newly imported disease, and Spanish Mexico City was rising on the ruins of the fabled Aztec capital of Tenochtitlán.

For more than a decade before Cortés sailed from Cuba to conquer Mexico, portents of disaster had plagued the Aztec nation: a mysterious tongue of fire lit up the heavens; a holy shrine burst into flames; a comet raced across a clear afternoon sky; the waters of Lake Texcoco, which surrounded the island city of Tenochtitlán, suddenly boiled up on a calm day.

The apprehensions of the Aztecs and of their superstitious emperor Montezuma were heightened in 1517 by disturbing reports from the land of the Mayas in the far-off Yucatan. A race of white men, it seems, had

arrived from across the ocean and engaged in skirmishes with the local people. The following year a tax collector returning from the Gulf Coast informed Montezuma that he had seen and traded with bearded, white-faced men who sailed the sea on "winged towers" and whose weapons spewed out deadly flames. The "winged towers" were the ships of Juan de Grijalva, whom the Spanish governor of Cuba, Diego Velásquez, had sent to explore the Yucatan coast. Montezuma, however, became convinced that these strange encounters signaled the imminent return of the plumed serpent god, Quetzalcoatl.

Long ago, the Aztecs believed, Quetzalcoatl had appeared on earth in the guise of a prophet-king, bearded and pale-skinned. Driven off to the east by the god of the night sky, Quetzalcoatl vowed to return one day to reclaim his throne. The idea that Cortés might be Quetzalcoatl haunted Montezuma and eventually enabled the Spaniard to enter Tenochtitlán as the emperor's guest—without having to fire a shot.

From the start Cortés was lucky, but he was also

Montezuma greets Cortés in this artist's impression of one of history's great encounters. Within two years of this fateful day, Montezuma's empire would lie in ruins, a victim, in part, of a deadly Spanish import—smallpox.

one of those men who, to a great extent, make their own luck. His bold decision to colonize Mexico and found the settlement of Vera Cruz, for example, far exceeded his mandate from Diego Velásquez. And in a stunning act of self-assurance, Cortés burned his own ships in order to discourage potential deserters before setting off on his historic march from Vera Cruz to Tenochtitlán on August 16, 1519.

Cortés took with him some 350 soldiers and one invaluable ally—his Indian interpreter, adviser, and mistress, Malinche, or Doña Marina, as the Spaniards called her. In another stroke of good luck, Cortés had acquired this brilliant, high-born woman as a peace offering after an early skirmish with the Indians along the Tabascan coast. On the way to Tenochtitlán, Doña Marina helped Cortés forge alliances with disgruntled subjects and enemies of the tyrannical Aztecs. The most important of these alliances was with the Tlaxcalans, a fiercely independent people who had long resisted Aztec dominion. Defeated by Cortés in September 1519, the Tlaxcalans offered to join him as allies and went on to play a crucial role in the Spanish conquest.

From Tenochtitlán, Montezuma anxiously kept abreast of Cortés's movements and sent a succession of ambassadors bearing gold and jewels and promises of much more to come if Cortés would stay away from the city. But the gold only whetted the Spaniards' appetite, and as they drew ever closer to his capital, a vacillating Montezuma prepared to receive them.

The meeting of Montezuma and Cortés took place on November 8, 1519, on one of the causeways that connected Tenochtitlán to the mainland. Under the gaze of thousands of his subjects, Montezuma welcomed the Spanish commander as the long-awaited divinity come to rule once again in Mexico. In the city, the Spaniards were lodged in the treasure-filled palace of Montezuma's father. The emperor exchanged visits with Cortés and arranged for the Spaniards a tour of Tenochtitlán, by all accounts one of the most spectacular cities of the 16th-century world. The visitors were especially impressed by Tenochtitlán's teeming markets but were horrified by its temples, whose walls dripped with the blood of human sacrifices.

Despite Montezuma's show of cooperation, Cortés mistrusted him and sensed the increasing hatred of a populace that vastly outnumbered his combined Spanish and Tlaxcalan forces. The Spaniards' lust for gold and their obvious revulsion at the Aztecs' blood rituals fueled the Indians' hostility and eventually convinced even Montezuma that he was not dealing with Quetzalcoatl. Feeling exposed and vulnerable, Cortés took Montezuma hostage. But instead of securing the submission of the Aztecs, Cortés's action undermined what little confidence they had left in their weak emperor. In a desperate attempt to placate and perhaps rid himself of his captors, Montezuma handed over the treasure in his father's palace to the Spaniards, thereby alienating his people even more without satisfying the Spaniards' greed.

With Montezuma under his control, Cortés now had to turn his attention to Vera Cruz, where a Spanish army of more than 1,500 men under the command of Pánfilo de Narváez had landed on April 23, 1520. Narváez arrived in Mexico with orders from Cuba's governor to curb Cortés's growing power. But Narváez was no match for the wily and experienced conquistador. Leaving Pedro de Alvarado in charge at Tenochtitlán, Cortés rushed to the coast, where he quickly outmaneuvered Narváez and took over his army.

Narváez brought with him the final weapon that would help Cortés seal the fate of the Aztecs.

In addition to supplying Cortés with badly needed reinforcements, the Narváez expedition introduced the deadly disease smallpox to the American mainland. Characterized by aching pains, high fever, and a distinctive, often disfiguring skin rash, smallpox was highly contagious and frequently fatal, especially when introduced into populations that had had no previous contact with the virus that causes the disease. Smallpox had made its way from Spain to the Americas in 1507, when a terrible epidemic broke out among the vulnerable Indians of the Caribbean island of Hispaniola. A second epidemic, this one probably introduced by African slaves, began in Hispaniola in 1518. By May 1519, the disease had killed up to one-third of the island's Indians and had spread to Puerto Rico and Cuba, where it was raging at the time of Narváez's departure. At least one of Narváez's men—according to some accounts, an African slave named Francisco de Baguia—had smallpox when he arrived in Mexico and, as part of Cortés's newly reinforced army, carried it with him to Tenochtitlán.

During Cortés's absence from the Mexican capital, Alvarado had ordered a senseless massacre of hundreds of unarmed Aztec noblemen engaged in a religious festival. As word of the outrage spread through

Tenochtitlán, *island capital of the Aztecs, was a city of floating gardens, lavish palaces—and bloodied temples. This 16th-century plan, probably based on a sketch by Cortés, shows the city before it was conquered by Spanish arms and a killer disease.*

the city, the people rose up to attack the Spaniards and besiege them in their palace stronghold. Montezuma attempted to calm the situation and to a degree succeeded. By the time Cortés returned to relieve the trapped garrison, a deadly quiet prevailed in Tenochtitlán. The next day, under the leadership of Montezuma's more forceful brother Cuitlahuac, the Aztecs renewed their assault on the Spaniards and in a series of violent clashes came close to overwhelming them. When Montezuma climbed the roof of his father's palace to argue once more for peace, the people responded with stones and arrows. Montezuma was injured in the attack and three days later died—whether of his wounds, at the hands of the Spaniards, or perhaps of despair remains unclear. What is clear, however, is that without the measure of protection afforded by his royal hostage, Cortés was on his own.

The Spaniards' only hope now lay in escape, but that would be far from easy. The new emperor, Cuitlahuac, had the bridges in the city's causeways removed in order to prevent a retreat to the mainland. With an ingenuity born of desperation, the Spaniards devised a portable wooden bridge capable of spanning the gaps in the causeways. On the night of June 30, 1520, a night remembered in Mexican history as the Spaniards' *Noche Triste* ("Sad Night"), Cortés and his men, accompanied by their Tlaxcalan allies, began their escape. The fleeing soldiers made it across the first gap in the Tacuba causeway, but then their portable

bridge got stuck. At the second gap, the massacre began in earnest. Burdened by their armor and by the treasure they could not bring themselves to leave behind, the Spaniards toppled into Lake Texcoco and either sank or provided easy targets for the Aztecs, who came surging out of the night in their canoes. Eventually the pile of bodies, weapons, wagons, and treasure chests grew tall enough to serve as a platform for the surviving soldiers to scramble over. The same horrible scene was repeated at the next gap in the causeway, but this time with far fewer participants.

Cortés, Doña Marina, and remnants of the Spanish forces managed to escape from Tenochtitlán and fought their way to the safety of Tlaxcala. But the toll of *La Noche Triste* was devastating. It is estimated that as many as two-thirds of Cortés's men were killed or dragged off to sacrificial altars. The Spaniards also lost all of their artillery, most of their horses, and most of the treasure they valued so highly.

The Aztecs had defeated the Spanish, but a new foe was waiting in the wings.

To the Aztecs, it must have seemed as if they had routed the enemy, but once again Cortés's luck held. For among the dead at Tenochtitlán was at least one smallpox victim. As the Aztecs looted the corpses of the enemy, they came in contact for the first time with the lethal virus. Within two weeks, the Indians began to fall to the disease they called "the great leprosy." Coursing through the nonimmune population like a prairie fire, the virus covered its fevered victims with raw pustules and reduced the strongest to helpless-

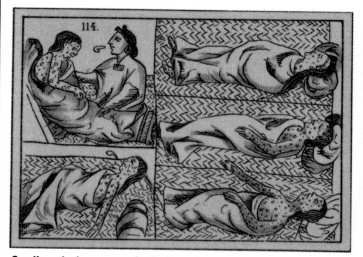

Smallpox lesions *cover the bodies of Aztec victims in this drawing from a postconquest history of the Aztecs known as the Florentine Codex.*

82

THE ERADICATION OF SMALLPOX: A TRIUMPH OF MODERN MEDICINE

Attempts to inoculate against smallpox may be almost as ancient as the millennia-old disease itself. In medieval China, dried, powdered smallpox scabs were inhaled through ivory straws. In the Middle East, variolation, as the practice was called, involved introducing smallpox pus into the bloodstream through a small wound. When all went well, the patient would develop a mild case of smallpox, recover quickly, and become immune for life. Occasionally, however, the induced disease proved fatal, or the inoculated person would transmit a full-blown case to someone else and perhaps trigger an epidemic.

Variolation had long been practiced in Europe, but only as folk medicine. In the early 18th century, the wife of the British ambassador to Turkey, Lady Mary Montagu, saw many people being successfully variolated in Constantinople. Upon her return to London in 1718, she became an enthusiastic promoter of the technique and conferred a measure of respectability on it.

During a smallpox epidemic in 1757, an eight-year-old orphan named Edward Jenner was taken to the local apothecary to be variolated. In preparation, the boy had undergone the usual six weeks of bleedings and starvation. Jenner never forgot the ordeal. During another epidemic in 1778, Jenner, by then an eminent physician, noticed that dairymaids who had caught cowpox—a mild disease of cows and humans—seemed immune to smallpox. After years of research, Jenner set out to test his theory. On May 14, 1796, he inoculated a young boy with cowpox pus. When the boy was inoculated with smallpox pus on July 1, he did not contract the disease.

Jenner's vaccine (from *vacca*, Latin for "cow") soon became widely known and used. In 1978, some 200 years after Jenner first began seriously to consider cowpox as a smallpox preventive, the World Health Organization (WHO) reported the last known death from smallpox. A vaccination campaign launched by WHO in 1967 had succeeded in finally wiping out one of the world's ancient scourges.

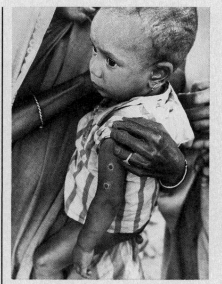

A child in Bangladesh displays the scars of smallpox vaccination—his guarantee against the disease that before it was wiped out in the late 1970's might have killed him or left him blind.

---

ness. "They could no longer walk," wrote Fray Toribio Motolinía some 20 years later in his *History of the Indians of New Spain*. "They could do no more than lie down. . . . They couldn't bestir their bodies, neither to lie face down, nor on their backs, nor to turn from one side to the other. And when they did move, they cried out. In death, many [bodies] were like sticky, compacted, hard grain." Of those who survived the disease, many were left scarred, some were blinded.

Nor was the disease confined to Tenochtitlán. According to Fray Motolinía, "When the smallpox began to attack the Indians it became so great a pestilence among them throughout the land that in most provinces more than half the population died. . . . they died in heaps, like bedbugs. Many others died of starvation, because, as they were all taken sick at once, they could not care for each other, nor was there anyone to give them bread or anything else."

Everywhere in Mexico, people were dying of smallpox—everywhere, that is, except in the camps of the invaders. Like most European adults at the time, Cortés and his men had probably survived a childhood exposure and were thus immune. While the Aztecs grew weaker, Cortés spent 5½ months recouping his losses and preparing for the final campaign against Tenochtitlán. He had supplies and reinforcements brought in from Vera Cruz and built a fleet of portable brigantines to counter the Aztec canoes. On December 28, 1520, Cortés set out from Tlaxcala at the head of an army of 600 Spaniards and 10,000 Tlaxcalans; other Indian recruits would eventually increase the Spanish forces to more than 100,000 men. After assembling his portable navy on Lake Texcoco and subduing the lakeside areas, Cortés began his siege of Tenochtitlán in late April 1521. By then Cuitlahuac had died of the pox and his army had been decimated. Even so, the new emperor, Cuauhtémoc, mounted a heroic defense that lasted more than three months. On August 13, 1521, starving, disease-racked Tenochtitlán fell. No sooner had the city been captured than the Spaniards began to raze it; with its capital destroyed, the great Aztec empire fell apart.

Estimates of the number of Mexicans killed by smallpox in this first great mainland epidemic range from 2 million to as many as 15 million, or perhaps half Mexico's population in the early 16th century. Within months of Tenochtitlán's fall, smallpox moved south with the Spaniards into Maya country. Between 1525 and 1527 the disease reached the Inca empire in Peru, where, as it had done for Cortés, smallpox would open the way for Francisco Pizarro to claim his own glittering New World prize.

London's Great Plague

"Dreadful visitation" kills thousands in English capital

THE EPIDEMIC ANNOUNCED itself slowly. In December 1664 a death by plague was officially recorded in St. Giles-in-the-Fields, an out-parish, or suburb, of London. A second plague death, also in St. Giles, was registered the following February. Other cases probably went unreported in and around London that winter. Such isolated instances of bubonic plague were not uncommon in London. Ever since the arrival of the Black Death in the 14th century, hardly a year had gone by without at least a few people dying of the disease; in bad years, the toll reached several thousands. The year 1665 ranked among the worst.

With its horrendous overcrowding and unhygienic conditions, 17th-century London was especially susceptible to epidemics. Economic prosperity had greatly increased the capital's population, which by 1665 was about 500,000. In both the old City of London and its outlying communities, rat-infested slums lacked running water and basic sanitation facilities. Under such conditions, plague outbreaks were frequent throughout the first half of the century.

In the early months of 1665, a cold wave so severe that the Thames froze twice may have delayed the Great Plague for a while, but with the arrival of warm weather in April, the death toll began to rise. Bills of Mortality—official weekly listings of new deaths and their causes—were compiled systematically beginning in the plague year of 1603, and though notoriously unreliable, they give an approximate idea of the epidemic's progress in 1665. In the week of April 18, the bills listed two plague deaths, both in St. Giles. Nine deaths were recorded in the first week of May: three in St. Giles, five in other out-parishes, and one within the walls of the City itself. On May 12 King Charles II recognized the existence of an epidemic and appointed a committee "to consider of the best means of preventing the spreading of the infection." In the last week of May, as the disease spread through the out-parishes, 17 new deaths were recorded.

A heat wave in early June heralded the start of a long, hot summer of death. The number of recorded plague fatalities more than doubled in the first week of the month and trebled the next. Samuel Pepys, the naval administrator whose famous diary contains a

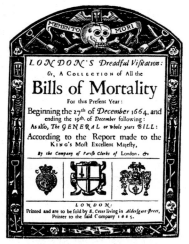

The plague's lethal toll in 1665 was recorded in official Bills of Mortality, published weekly.

vivid account of the plague years, wrote that on June 7, "much against my will, I did in Drury Lane see two or three houses marked with a red cross upon the doors, and 'Lord have mercy upon us!' writ there; which was a sad sight to me, being the first of the kind that, to my remembrance, I ever saw."

The red cross and pious entreaty that so rattled Pepys were plague quarantine signs. On May 4, the King's Bench had instructed the City and its dependencies to begin shutting up infected houses. On June 19 the Lord Mayor reinstated the Plague Orders of 1646. This meant that a household suspected of infection would be visited by an official "searcher," usually a destitute old woman who received a small fee for confirming deaths, ascertaining their cause, and ferreting out plague cases. If a suspect showed the hard swellings or purplish spots symptomatic of the plague, his house would be marked and his entire household locked up inside until the victim or victims recovered or died (usually the latter). Even more dreadful was the fate of those sent to the pest houses, the five hospitals on the outskirts of London in which plague victims were isolated. Walled in with dozens of sick and dying strangers, an inmate had little hope of survival. Not surprisingly, plague cases were seriously underreported as victims and their families tried to conceal the true nature of their misfortune.

The role of the flea and the rat in transmitting the plague bacillus to man was not fully understood until the 20th century. Without that basic knowledge, Londoners in the 17th century could do little to combat the plague, and often what they did was counterproductive. Dogs and cats were slaughtered at public expense because they were suspected of being plague carriers—a move that allowed rats, the real culprits, to proliferate. Because the plague was also thought to be carried in the air, ineffective fires and stink pots were used to cleanse it of its poisons. Tobacco was widely regarded as a plague preventative, since tobacconists, rumor had it, never caught the plague. Medical care, such as it was, became increasingly hard to find as doctors either died of the disease or fled the city.

Regardless of what was done or not done, the depopulation of London continued at a staggering pace.

Those who could afford to, sought refuge in the countryside, leaving the poor to die in London. On June 21 Pepys reported finding "all the town, almost going out of town, the coaches and waggons being all full of people going into the country." On July 7 despairing Londoners learned that the king and his court had joined the exodus of well-to-do citizens. Courageous civil servants such as Pepys stayed in London and risked their lives to help keep the government functioning.

By late July, 2,000 people a week were dying. Carts roamed the streets all night, their drivers ringing bells and shouting "Bring out your dead." Corpses were dumped into communal pits outside the walls and hastily covered with a thin layer of soil. From graveyards and plague pits, a nauseating stench filled the air.

The epidemic peaked in the week of September 12, when 7,165 plague deaths were recorded. By then London's desolation was beyond imagining. Government and commerce were virtually suspended. Entire streets were boarded up, their houses marked with red crosses. There was hardly any traffic, and grass grew in once busy squares. But as summer turned to fall, the plague began to wane. Mortality rates declined throughout October, and toward the end of November Pepys rejoiced to learn that the disease had taken *only* "600 and odd" lives in a week. On New Year's Eve he reported that "the plague is abated almost to nothing." Although cases continued to crop up in 1666, especially in the provinces, the epidemic in London was effectively over. Officially, the Great Plague killed 68,596 Londoners. But if underreporting is taken into account, the toll may have exceeded 100,000.

For generations afterward, the pest houses were kept in readiness for the plague's return. But that never happened. Popular wisdom wrongly credited the Great Fire of 1666 with cleansing London of infection. Scientists point to a gradual improvement in hygiene as well as to the eventual replacement in England of the black rat by the brown rat, a creature that prefers to live at a greater distance from man than its black cousin. Whatever the reason, London's worst plague since the Black Death was also its last.

Death rules the countryside outside London in this contemporary woodcut of the 1665 plague. At left, a doomed mother displays purplish plague spots. Fleeing Londoners, right, are stopped by armed villagers fearing contagion. The prayer "Lord, have mercy" was part of the quarantine notice written on plague victims' houses.

The Great Fire of London

*Blaze in Pudding Lane kindles one of the worst
urban conflagrations on record*

KING CHARLES II HIMSELF had warned London of its peril. In April 1665 the king wrote a letter to the lord mayor of London, complaining of fire hazards in the City, the ancient heart of the English capital. Still a largely medieval town, London in the mid-17th century was dirty and overcrowded, its narrow streets and alleys densely packed with overhanging, timber-framed houses. Building codes, which since the 12th century had called for party walls to be built of brick or stone, were routinely ignored. The king urged the City's governors to enforce the building codes more rigorously and gave them the authority to imprison violators. Nearly a year and a half later, however, nothing had come of the king's warnings, and by Sunday, September 2, 1666, after a dry, hot summer, London was a tinderbox ready to explode.

The disaster began in one of the City's meanest, narrowest streets, Pudding Lane, which led down to the Thames River near London Bridge. Among the tumbledown, pitch-coated wooden houses on Pudding Lane stood the home of the king's baker, Thomas Farynor, and it was there, in Farynor's downstairs bakery, that fire broke out about 1 or 2 o'clock in the morning of September 2. Farynor later testified that he had banked the fire in his oven around 10 o'clock on Saturday night, and that there was no way embers from the oven could have ignited a pile of kindling lying nearby. Whether the fire had been deliberately set (as Farynor claimed), or was due to carelessness (as is more likely), Farynor's assistant woke up at 2 in the morning to find the house full of smoke. Flames already engulfed the bakery, but Farynor and most of his household managed to escape by climbing out a window of the upstairs living quarters onto a gutter and from there to the roof of a neighboring building. Farynor's maid, however, refused to budge. Paralyzed

As London burns, throngs of people seek safety along the Thames in this contemporary Dutch school painting of the Great Fire. On London Bridge, houses blaze, while flames begin to consume Old St. Paul's Cathedral (center). At right, the Tower of London stands unscathed.

Diarist Samuel Pepys
helped keep the government functioning in London during the plague of 1665 and worked tirelessly to save his city during the fire of 1666. His writings are a vivid source of information about both disasters.

by fear, she stayed behind to die in the flames.

The fire advanced slowly at first. Farynor's house is said to have burned for an hour before the flames spread next door. Even when a sharp northeast wind blew sparks that ignited the nearby Star Inn, the fire seemed little different from countless other City slum fires that had been more or less quickly put out. The lord mayor, Sir Thomas Bludworth, arrived on the scene at about 3 A.M., greatly annoyed at being aroused at such an ungodly hour. After surveying what to him looked like a local fire that could be easily extinguished, the lord mayor went back home to bed.

At about the same time, Samuel Pepys, the diarist and a hero of the previous year's plague, was awakened by his maid Jane with a report of a fire in the City. He looked out a window and thinking the fire was "far enough off," went back to bed. The confidence of both the lord mayor and Pepys might have

been justified had Farynor's house not been so close to Thames Street, whose cellars and warehouses were filled with highly flammable goods. Once it hit Thames Street, the fire began to go out of control. Local fire fighters, armed only with leather buckets and hand-held pumps, could do little to stop the growing inferno. By 8 A.M., the Church of St. Magnus the Martyr, at the foot of London Bridge, was burning fiercely, and once the church was gone, there was nothing to prevent the fire from attacking the bridge.

Pepys had awakened about 7 A.M. and heard from Jane that "above 300 houses have been burned down tonight by the fire we saw, and that it is now burning down all Fish Street, by London Bridge." Alarmed, Pepys walked to the Tower of London and from its heights saw "the houses at that end of the bridge all on fire." Not only was London Bridge one of the City's oldest landmarks and most important thoroughfares, the double row of houses it supported made it a populous residential and shopping quarter as well. Along with many of the bridge houses, the fire destroyed the wooden water wheels set in the bridge's northern arches. Since these wheels pumped most of the City's water supply, fire fighters lost an important resource almost at the outset of the conflagration.

An energetic man not given to sitting out a crisis, Pepys made his way to the Thames and hired a boat to ferry him upstream past the fire. From his vantage point on the river, Pepys witnessed a scene of terrible chaos as the London riverfront went up in flames. "Everybody endeavouring to remove their goods," he reported, "and flinging into the river or bringing them into lighters [barges] that lay off."

In London's burning waterside, the poor clung to their homes "till the very fire touched them," wrote Pepys.

Like many of the City's riverfront residents, even the pigeons, Pepys noticed, "were loth to leave their houses, but hovered about the windows and balconies, till they, some of them, burned their wings, and fell down." When the flames finally compelled people to flee, they ran into boats or clambered "from one pair of stairs by the waterside to another."

With the blaze continuing to spread under the influence of a "mighty high" wind—and his fellow Londoners apparently more concerned with saving their goods than with putting out the fire—Pepys decided to continue on to the royal palace at Whitehall and alert the king. Upon hearing Pepys's report, and his warning that "unless His Majesty did command houses to be pulled down, nothing could stop the fire," King Charles sent Pepys back to the City with an order for the lord mayor "to spare no houses."

As it happened, the lord mayor had already ordered the City's militia to begin clearing firebreaks. But the work was hampered by landlords reluctant to have their property pulled down. Only when their houses were on the brink of destruction would many owners allow the militia, armed with axes and fire hooks, to demolish them. And by then it was often too late to check the flames. When Pepys, who had returned to the City by coach, caught up with the lord mayor and delivered the king's message, Sir Thomas replied, "Lord! what can I do? I am spent: people will not obey me. I have been pulling down houses, but the fire overtakes us faster than we can do it."

By afternoon, Pepys found the streets "full of nothing but people; and horses and carts loaden with goods, ready to run over one another, and removing goods from one burned house to another." The Thames, he wrote, was "full of lighters and boats taking in goods and good goods swimming in the water." Carters and boatmen raised their fares outrageously, profiting by their neighbors' misfortunes. The king, accompanied by his brother, the duke of York, sailed downstream by barge from Whitehall to see the fire for himself and was shocked by its extent and intensity. That afternoon, continued Pepys,

"all over the Thames, with one's face in the wind, you were almost burned with a shower of fire-drops," and by nightfall, "we saw the fire as only one entire arch of fire from this to the other side the bridge, and in a bow up the hill for an arch of above a mile long; it made me weep to see it."

Monday morning, with one-sixteenth of the City already ablaze, the flames turned inland to invade the wealthier residential neighborhoods. Perhaps for the first time, Londoners began fully to realize how serious the fire had become. With the post office destroyed and the official *London Gazette* ceasing publication after its Monday edition, rumors of foreign conspiracy and arson ran rampant in the City. As soon as he became aware of London's deteriorating situation, King Charles set aside the authority of the lord mayor and placed the duke of York in charge of the fire-fighting forces. Seven fire posts were established at the perimeter of the fire, with 30 foot soldiers and 100 civilians assigned to each post. All day Monday the duke worked side by side with his men, while the king himself visited the City several times. But it was all to no avail. By midnight the fire, spreading north and west, covered four times the area it had consumed only 24 hours earlier. Among the day's casualties was

The new London that arose from the ashes of the Great Fire was painted in the 18th century by the Italian artist Canaletto. The spires of churches designed by England's great architect Sir Christopher Wren punctuate the skyline. Dominating the scene by its size and splendor is Wren's masterpiece, the new St. Paul's Cathedral.

The monument to the Great Fire, depicted at right in a 17th-century print, was completed in 1677. It stands not far from where the fire began. In the relief at the tower's base (above), King Charles II, dressed in Roman garb, is shown offering aid to the ruined City.

the century-old Royal Exchange, in whose arcades City merchants met to conduct the nation's foreign trade.

Even worse was in store on Tuesday. The king and his brother spent the entire day in the City, riding from post to post and even joining the bucket brigades. Despite these royal efforts, more of London burned on Tuesday than on the previous two days combined. Ludgate Hill, the Old Bailey, and Fleet Street were all ablaze. The Guildhall, where the City held its court and kept its records, caught fire too, yet its massive stone walls and the crypt that housed the records survived the Great Fire, as they would survive German bombs during the blitz of 1940.

In a desperate effort to contain the raging fire, houses in its path were blown up with gunpowder.

The use of explosives to create firebreaks had been suggested as early as Sunday, but the plan was deemed too hazardous. Finally, on Tuesday night, wrote Pepys, began "the practice of blowing up of houses in Tower Street, those next the Tower." This tactic eventually kept the fire from spreading east and saved the Tower of London and the Admiralty office.

Elsewhere, however, the blaze continued to spread until at about 8 P.M. Old St. Paul's Cathedral, the largest church in England, caught fire. With its great stone walls, lead-sheathed roof, and spacious churchyard to protect it, the church, though dilapidated, had been considered immune from the blaze. No one, however, had counted on the wind, which wafted a cinder onto some boards used to patch a leak on the roof. The burning boards kindled the beams below, and soon flames from the church leapt so high that a schoolboy was able to read by their light a mile away. So intense was the heat that stones burst like grenades and the six acres of lead roof dripped to the floor in a fiery rain. The cathedral took with it the little Church of St. Faith, located in the greater building's vaulted basement. St. Faith's was the church of the booksellers' guild, and here its members had stowed wares valued at up to £200,000, among which may have been almost the entire Third Folio edition of Shakespeare's plays. In one of the greatest losses resulting from the fire, none of the contents of St. Faith's survived.

The winds abated late Tuesday night, and despite a few sporadic outbursts, the fire began to burn itself out on Wednesday. When it was over, 80 percent of the City was in ashes. Lost in the fire were 87 parish churches and the halls of 44 City livery companies, or guilds. In addition to the post office, Guildhall, and Royal Exchange, the fire leveled the Customhouse, Newgate Prison, and many libraries and hospitals. Ninety percent of the City's houses were destroyed, and between 100,000 and 200,000 people were left homeless. Only 6 people were reported to have died in the fire, but many more may have succumbed to starvation, disease, and other hardships afterwards.

The fire struck at a particularly unfortunate time for London: the City was still recovering from the plague and England was at war with France and Holland. Not surprisingly, rumors that the fire had been set by French or Dutch agents precipitated savage assaults on foreigners. A crazed Frenchman, for example, confessed to starting the fire, and although his story was full of contradictions, public feeling ran so high that he was convicted and hanged anyway.

But good also came of the disaster. Although the ruins smoldered through March 1667, the City was rebuilt, this time in brick and stone and according to strictly enforced building codes. London emerged from its ordeal a neater, cleaner, safer, and more modern city than it had ever been.

The most far-reaching of the fire's legacies, however, may have been the Fire Company founded by Dr. Nicholas Barbon in 1667. The world's first fire insurance firm not only guaranteed householders against loss by fire, it also maintained fire engines and a force of uniformed fire fighters to safeguard the houses it insured. And to each protected house, the company affixed its symbol—a phoenix rising from the flames.

Twin cones of Mount Etna eject ash and lava on Catania below; only part of the castle (left) survived the holocaust.

Mount Etna Erupts—Again

*Fiery lava from "the mouth of hell" devours
village after village*

RISING MORE THAN 1,700 FEET above the sea, with a mantle of snow clinging to its summit many months of the year, Mount Etna is the presiding deity of the island of Sicily. But she can be a goddess of wrath as well as of beauty. The fertile fields and orchards on the broad lower slopes, the majestic views from the towns high on the flanks, the white plume drifting airily from the peak—these tell only half the story of the mountain whose name derives from the Greek word meaning "I burn."

Etna, in fact, "burns" 10 to 20 times every century, making it one of the most active volcanoes in the world. Typically, its sides split open in glowing fissures; molten lava heated to 1800° F pours down its slopes; the earth shakes; the surf recedes from the shore, to return sometimes in tidal waves to engulf the coastal villages in sea water.

Set in a wilderness or on some remote barren island in the North Atlantic, Etna would probably be a mere geological curiosity. But this is not the case; it stands on an island adjacent to one of the most crowded nations of Europe. Because the island is endowed with a long growing season and fertile soils, which have been enriched by centuries of volcanic renewal, a teeming population has gathered around the base of the mountain. As a result, this highly active volcano can also be one of the world's deadliest.

From the beginning of recorded history, Etna has erupted some 200 times, not counting innumerable minor ventings. Ancient writers who took notice of Etna's fiery activity include Hesiod, Aeschylus, Pindar, Cicero, Vergil, Lucretius, and Ovid, among others. One of the most lethal explosions, followed by a devastating earthquake, occurred in 1169. It killed

15,000 people in the port city of Catania alone, some 18 miles from the mountain's base. Many of Catania's citizens had crowded into the cathedral to pray for divine intercession when the earth heaved and the building collapsed on the worshipers.

The most violent eruption, however, occurred 500 years later, in 1669. Early that year Etna had vented rock and gases 22 times without threatening life or property. But on the evening of Friday, March 8, wrote the bishop of Catania: "The sun was observed before its setting to appear of a pale and dead colour. . . . The same night happened in this city, as well as the whole country hereabouts, a terrible and unusual earthquake, whose strong and unequal motions, joined with horrible roarings from Mongibello [a local name for Etna], exceedingly frightened the inhabitants."

That night of terror was only the beginning. "This dreadful convulsion of the earth," the bishop continued, "was immediately followed on Monday, March 11, about 10 at night, by three terrible eruptions."

In the fury and violence that followed, huge boulders, some weighing as much as 300 pounds, were shot several miles through the air, "whilst the whole air was filled with smoke, burning cinders, and ashes, which fell like a fiery rain. . . . This fiery and burning deluge immediately spread itself to about six miles in breadth, seeming to be somewhat of the colour of melted and burning glass."

A section of the town of Nicolosi and several smaller hamlets were destroyed in the quakes. The mountain split open along a line 6 feet wide and nearly 10 miles long, six massive holes later opening in the fissure and emitting flame, smoke, sulfurous gas, and lava. The thundering could be heard 50 miles away.

The eruption, as is usually the case with Etna, was primarily a venting from craters on the sides rather than at the summit. The mountain had probably already blown off its central cone and was in the process of creating several new subsidiary craters.

The frightened people turned to their saints. "As the fire approached," the bishop reported, "the religious everywhere appeared with much devotion, carrying in procession their relics, especially those of St. Agatha, the famous martyr of Catania." Some lashed themselves with whips. Some shouted out "with great complaints and cries, expressing their dreadful expectation of the events of those prodigious fiery inundations."

In the meantime, one Diego Pappalardo led 50 men out to meet the approaching river of lava. These intrepid fighters covered themselves with wet cowhides for protection from the intense heat. They carried iron bars, shovels, and other implements to attack the congealed and relatively cool crust that covered the lava tongue. Their intention was to open a diversionary channel, thereby relieving the pressure in the main tongue and perhaps changing the course of the flow, which was headed straight for their city.

This first recorded attempt in history to divert a lava flow appeared successful enough to alarm the citizens of the nearby town of Paterno, toward which a new channel now directed itself. Five hundred men of Paterno set upon Pappalardo and his 50, drove them off, and saved their town.

The lava was once more bearing down on Catania. Slowly, inexorably the fiery torrent reached the city walls, hastily built for protection, climbed their 60-foot height like a satanic growth, and curled over the top. Soon Catania was flooded with the superheated ooze. Much of Catania, the island's biggest city, was wiped out; only the keep of its castle remained intact.

Lord Winchilsea, a British ambassador who had sailed from Malta to Catania to see the eruption, reported to his sovereign, Charles II: "I assure your majesty no pen can express how terrible it is, nor can all the art and industry of the world quench, or divert that which is burning in the country."

Undeniably, many lost their lives. According to the official count, 20,000 died in the disaster, but the unofficial tally reached 100,000.

A tortuous river of boiling lava races down Etna's scarred slopes at a frightening speed of 15 feet per second. This photograph was taken during the 1971 eruption, one of the many such events in Etna's long history as Europe's most active volcano. Ancient observers blamed the volcanic activity on the Roman fire god Vulcan, from whose name the word volcano is derived.

Windstorm in Britain

Tempest leaves trail of destruction on land and at sea

F OR TWO SOLID WEEKS in November 1703 unusually strong Atlantic gales and rainsqualls battered England and Wales. After what must have seemed an eternity of exceptionally foul weather—even for England—Thursday, November 25, dawned calm and clear. On land, people began to look forward to a peaceful night's sleep, uninterrupted by howling winds and rattling roofs. In the anchorages and roadsteads outside English harbors, where an unprecedented number of ships of all descriptions had gathered to ride out the storm, seamen prepared to weigh anchor and set sail within a day or two.

Among those anxious to be underway was Henry Winstanley, architect of the famous Eddystone lighthouse. Located in the English Channel, 14 miles southwest of Plymouth, the four-year-old structure was considered by some, including its architect, to be

indestructible. Winstanley had assembled a work party to carry out routine repairs on the lighthouse but had been unable to depart because of the weather. Early on Friday morning, November 26, Winstanley and his crew sailed out from Plymouth and landed on the Eddystone Rocks that afternoon.

The favorable conditions that permitted Winstanley to reach his lighthouse continued through Friday evening. But the day's fair weather turned out to be the calm before the most destructive storm ever recorded in Britain. Shortly before midnight, the tempest that would go down in British history as the Great Storm began its rampage across southern England and Wales.

Some meteorologists believe that the Great Storm was a freak West Indian hurricane that instead of dying out over the Atlantic gained new strength as it crossed the ocean. Whatever its origins, the storm

Unrivaled in the history of England, *the Great Storm of 1703 destroyed hundreds of vessels lying at anchor in the English Channel (left) and claimed the lives of some 8,000 sailors. The Eddystone lighthouse (above), built to resist the severest storms, disappeared without a trace.*

brought with it little rain, no thunder, and only scattered reports of lightning. It was a windstorm, pure and simple, of an intensity no one in England had ever experienced, accompanied by a deafening noise that no one who heard it would ever forget. Relentless and strange, the roar of the wind was probably the most alarming aspect of a night full of terrors.

By 2 A.M. on Saturday, the winds had reached a velocity of more than 100 miles per hour; they remained at peak strength for three hours and did not die down until about 8 o'clock that morning. Blowing from the southwest, the storm swept over Cornwall in the west of England and created a tidal wave in the Severn River eight feet higher than any ever recorded there. The wind-driven wall of water flooded the countryside for miles around. In the warehouses of Bristol harbor, flooding caused the loss of £150,000 worth of goods. Throughout southern England, the wind reduced more than 800 houses to rubble and damaged thousands more. Windmills collapsed by the hundreds, chimneys by the thousands. Tens, perhaps hundreds, of thousands of trees were uprooted. (Southern England suffered a similar loss much more recently. On October 15, 1987, a freak storm toppled

up to 100,000 trees in and around London, including rare, centuries-old chestnuts, beeches, willows, and oaks in the capital's great public parks and gardens.)

So strong was the wind that birds were knocked out of the air and hurled against buildings to their deaths. Many church spires suffered heavy damage; seven were knocked down completely. At least 100 churches lost the lead lining of their roofs—heavy sheets of metal that in some cases were rolled up "like so much paper" and blown away. Tiles ripped off the roofs of houses hit the ground with such force that they penetrated up to eight inches into it. Even with their houses about to fall on their heads, people did not dare go outside for fear of being struck down by flying debris. In his account of the Great Storm, Daniel Defoe, author of *Robinson Crusoe,* reports that the loss of tiles was so great that their price jumped from 21 shillings to £6 per thousand.

With damages estimated at £1 million, London after the storm looked as though a bomb had hit it—its roofless houses open to the elements and rubble piled high in the streets. "I question very much," wrote Defoe of the devastation, "if anybody believed the hundredth part of what they saw."

The Great Storm claimed at least 123 lives on land, probably a low estimate considering the number of bodies that may have been lost in the rubble. Offshore and in the river mouths, the storm's toll, both in lost lives and lost ships, was much graver—especially for a maritime nation like England, then at war with France.

Hurricane-force winds ripped ships from their anchorages and smashed them against one another or onto the shore. Many vessels had their masts snapped off and either sank or were driven helplessly out to sea. Those ships that could do so ran before the storm—some were carried clear across to Norway—and a week afterward, British Navy and merchant shipping in various states of distress dotted the North Sea. Of the crowded and flooded Thames, Defoe wrote, "It was a strange sight to see all the ships in the river blown away. . . . No anchors or landfast, no cables or mooring would hold them, the chains which lay cross the river for the moorings of ships, all gave way."

In the chaos of that one night, some 8,000 British sailors may have died. The Royal Navy lost 15 warships, 1,500 seamen, and 1 admiral. The merchant service fared even worse, with several hundred of its vessels thought to have been destroyed.

Among the night's casualties were Henry Winstanley, his work crew, and his "indestructible" lighthouse. On Friday night, the Eddystone light had sent out its yellow beam as usual until just before midnight, when the hurricane struck. The next morning, only the Eddystone Rocks remained. Winstanley, who had once expressed a desire to be inside his creation during "the greatest storm that ever was," had tragically been granted his wish.

The Lisbon Earthquake

Portugal's metropolis leveled by quakes, floods, and fire

ALL SAINTS' DAY, November 1, 1755, dawned clear and bright over the ancient city of Lisbon. Built, like Rome, on seven hills and ideally situated for trade near the mouth of the Tagus River, Lisbon in the mid-18th century was a bustling city of some 275,000 people, the proud and wealthy hub of a far-flung empire, and one of Europe's major commercial ports. But in this Age of Enlightenment, Lisbon was in many ways a backward city, better known for its piety than for progressive thinking. On that sunny autumn morning in 1755, church bells throughout the city summoned the faithful to mass. As thousands of Lisbon's citizens made their way to church or knelt in prayer, a violent upheaval of the sea floor somewhere out in the Atlantic sent a massive convulsion racing toward the Portuguese mainland. Lisbon's ordeal by earthquake had begun.

Around 9:40 A.M., a strange, ominous noise, "resembling the hollow distant rumbling of thunder," according to one eyewitness account, heralded the first of the shocks that would devastate Lisbon that day. Church bells began ringing out on their own, the enormous chandeliers in the city's ancient cathedral swung wildly, and buildings were shaken to their foundations. Panic-stricken worshipers from the cathedral and the nearby Church of St. Anthony crowded into the cathedral square and prayed for deliverance. After a brief lull, a louder, more destructive tremor rocked the city, bringing down buildings already weakened by the first shock. Large portions of the cathedral and of St. Anthony's collapsed and in the words of a survivor, "buried every soul as they were standing there crowded together." Similar catastrophes occurred throughout Lisbon—especially in the lower part of the city near the riverfront—as churches and convents, shops and warehouses, palaces and simple homes crumbled in a horrifying wave of destruction.

A visiting British merchant named Braddock was writing a letter in his apartment when the disaster struck. In his detailed account of the earthquake, Braddock wrote that the second tremor shook his house "with such violence, that the upper stories immediately fell, and though my apartment (which

was the first floor) did not share the same fate . . . it was with no small difficulty I kept my feet, and expected nothing less than to be soon crushed to death, as the walls continued rocking to and fro in the frightfullest manner, opening in several large places; large stones falling down on every side from the cracks; and the ends of most of the rafters starting out from the roof. To add to this terrifying scene, the sky in a moment became so gloomy, that I could now distinguish no particular object."

So many buildings had collapsed in Lisbon—when it was all over, some 17,000 out of an estimated 20,000 houses were destroyed—that a blinding cloud of dust blotted out the morning sunlight. To make matters

Giant waves from the Tagus River threaten Lisbon's collapsing waterfront in this contemporary engraving of the city's great earthquake of 1755. Thousands of Lisbon residents who survived the initial quakes perished in the ensuing fires and floods.

worse, a third shock hit the city about 15 minutes after the first. According to a Portuguese eyewitness named António Pereira, "The whole tract of country about Lisbon was seen to heave like the swelling of the billows in a storm." Although the city would suffer aftershocks throughout the day and for many days to come, the major earthquake damage was caused by the first three tremors, all within about 15 minutes.

No sooner had the dust begun to settle than fires ignited by toppled church candles and unattended kitchen hearths started spreading from several points in the ruined city. Fanned by northeast winds, the blaze raged on for five or six days, destroying in its wake much of what the earthquake had left standing. Small shopkeepers tried to save their inventories by setting up salvage dumps in the Terreiro do Paço, but fire soon destroyed Lisbon's great riverside square and all the goods piled up in it. Elsewhere, priceless archives and warehouses full of silks and spices went up in flames. Among the city landmarks that more or less survived the earthquake only to be gutted by fire were the newly built opera house, the lavish Patriarchal Church, and the royal palace itself with its magnificent furnishings and its libraries containing more than 70,000 volumes. It did not go unnoticed, especially among Lisbon's English Protestant community, that one of the first buildings to burn was the headquarters of the Inquisition. And anyone who could still manage a chuckle must have done so upon learning that the brothels on Suja Street had survived intact.

The dead, the dying, and the injured choked the streets of Lisbon.

Nearly everyone in the city was affected by the disaster. "Here, mothers with infants in their arms; there, ladies richly dressed," wrote the Englishman Braddock, "priests, friars, gentlemen, mechanics . . . some had their backs or thighs broken, others vast stones on their breasts; some lay almost buried in the rubbish."

The rescue of a little Lisbon girl from the rubble of the earthquake is depicted in this painting commissioned by the child's father in thanksgiving for her miraculous survival.

Like many other survivors, Braddock struggled over rubble and corpses to reach the banks of the Tagus, where he would be relatively safe from falling buildings. Standing amid the frantic mobs near the waterfront about an hour after the first quake hit, Braddock heard a chilling cry: "The sea is coming in; we shall be all lost."

After appearing to ebb out to sea, the waters of the Tagus suddenly reared up to an unimaginable height and then came crashing down on the city. "In an instant there appeared, at some small distance, a large body of water, rising as it were like a mountain," wrote Braddock. "We all immediately ran for our lives, as fast as possible; many were actually swept away, and the rest above their waist in water at a good distance from the banks. For my own part, I had the narrowest escape, and should certainly have been lost, had I not grasped a large beam that lay on the ground, till the water returned to its channel, which it did almost at the same instant, with equal rapidity."

The phenomenon described by Braddock was a tsunami, or seismic sea wave—a common sequel to earthquakes that originate underwater. Within a few minutes, three waves—one of which may have been up to 50 feet high—swept through the lower city and then receded, dragging unknown numbers of screaming victims to their deaths in the Tagus. Not surprisingly, many of those still alive in Lisbon began to think that the world was coming to an end.

Some 30,000 Lisbon residents may have died in the earthquake and its aftermath, although estimates range from 15,000 to more than 75,000 dead. The whole of southwestern Portugal suffered extensive damage, as did cities in Morocco and other places in North Africa. Tremors were felt throughout the rest of Portugal, in Spain and southern France, and possibly farther north; chandeliers were observed swaying in churches as far away as Holland and Germany. The sea waves triggered by the earthquake were recorded in England at about 2 P.M. and reached the West Indies some four hours later. Throughout Europe, the levels of lakes, rivers, ponds, springs, and canals underwent unusual fluctuations that day.

Back in the still trembling and burning city of Lisbon, looters began to scavenge among the ruins, and escaped convicts and galley slaves robbed the living and the dead. Lisbon's streets and squares were mobbed with people not knowing where to turn or screaming for absolution before they died. Terrified by the continuing fires and aftershocks and by wild rumors of worse things to come, hordes of hysterical refugees clogged the roads leading to open country.

The moment was right for a leader to step forward and restore order and hope to the ruined city.

With death and destruction everywhere, Portugal's government essentially collapsed—until one man dared to take charge. He was the 56-year-old minister for foreign affairs and war, Sebastião José de Carvalho e Mello, the future marquis de Pombal. After the quake, Pombal made his way to the suburban palace at Belém, where the young king, José Manuel, was staying. The distraught monarch welcomed Pombal and gave him command of Lisbon. For the next few days Pombal lived in his coach, gulping down broth brought by his wife, while he worked to revive Lisbon.

To keep plunder as well as skilled laborers from streaming out of the city, Pombal posted army units at Lisbon's gates. He organized fire-fighting and demolition brigades and secured church approval to bury the dead at sea, thereby removing the threat of disease as well as the awful stench of rotting corpses. Temporary housing was arranged for the homeless, and public kitchens and food distribution centers were set up. Both Portuguese and foreign ships were ordered to unload their provisions and sell them at pre-earthquake prices. Rents, too, were kept from skyrocketing, and landlords were forbidden to throw tenants out on the street. To discourage thievery and profiteering, Pombal had several gallows erected in Lisbon, and the bodies of 34 looters soon dangled in full public view.

Under Pombal's leadership, Lisbon began to revive. Timber supplies were brought into the city. Limekilns for mortar and ovens for bricks and tiles were built at top speed. To dispell public apathy, Pombal asked the clergy to stop dwelling on Portugal's sins and God's wrath. The astute minister also realized the value of accurate news over rumor in keeping up morale: the *Gazeta de Lisboa*, the city's influential weekly, never skipped an issue. Because commerce was the city's lifeline, Portuguese ships set sail to reassure the kingdom's colonies and trading partners that Lisbon was open for business. And within months of the quake, Pombal had drawn up a master plan for rebuilding the city. Today, Lisbon's *Baixa*, or lower town, built according to Pombal's vision, remains one of the finest examples of 18th-century European town planning.

Although Lisbon's recovery was relatively rapid for the time, the All Saints' Day disaster had a long-lasting effect on European thought and beliefs. Why did devout Lisbon become the object of God's anger? (Portuguese clergy railed against the city's wealth and tolerance of heretics; Protestant northerners tended to blame the Inquisition and "Popish idolatry.") How could a just God indiscriminately kill thousands of the good and the bad alike, or even more puzzling, allow the Suja Street brothels to survive while so many churches came crashing down? What purpose could the slaughter of innocent children possibly serve? Such questions haunted people throughout Europe.

The Lisbon earthquake undermined many of the prevailing philosophical assumptions of the Enlightenment. Most severely confounded, perhaps, were those who believed in a harmonious and divinely ordered universe in which everything that happens is for the best. The struggles of these optimists to reconcile "the best of all possible worlds" with the reality of Lisbon was wickedly satirized in Voltaire's novel *Candide*. Having survived the quake, Candide, "terrified almost out of his wits, covered with blood, and trembling violently, said to himself: 'If this is the best of all possible worlds, whatever must the others be like?'"

To the real survivors of the earthquake, however, the philosophical debates occasioned by their suffering must have been of secondary concern. For the people of Lisbon the task at hand was to pick up the pieces of their lives—and to pray that the terrible rumble of an earthquake never again be heard in their land.

THE DAWN OF MODERN SEISMOLOGY

The Lisbon earthquake of 1755 was the first to be subjected to rigorous scientific investigation. The marquis de Pombal, the energetic minister in charge of restoring Lisbon, had a questionnaire sent to every parish in Portugal requesting such information as the time and duration of the shocks and aftershocks, the height of sea waves, and the number of people killed. Preserved in Portugal's National Archives, the replies to Pombal's questionnaire proved to be a mine of information on the earthquake and its effects.

One of Pombal's concerns was to dispel the popular notion that the disaster was the result of God's ire rather than a natural phenomenon—a concern shared by Enlightenment scientists who sought to discover the true nature of earthquakes. Speculation, however, sometimes took odd turns. The Dutch theoretician J. F. Dryfhout, for example, believed that veins of explosives riddled the earth and that a subterranean blast had set the ground beneath Lisbon moving.

The greatest contribution to seismology in the wake of the Lisbon disaster came from an Englishman named John Michell. In a treatise published in 1760, Michell described earthquakes as waves set in motion by "shifting masses of rock miles below the surface"—a definition that in essence holds up today.

This seismometer, made in Italy in 1751, employs a pendulum bob to detect and measure tremors.

Eruption in the Land of Ice and Fire

Deadly volcanic gases poison Iceland

A record volume of lava erupted from Iceland's Lakagígar fissure in 1783. Above, craters in the fissure's northeast branch lead up to Mount Laki in the background. The map at left tracks the lava flow from June through September 1, 1783.

THE WORST DISASTER ever to hit Iceland was announced by a series of earthquakes that began on June 1, 1783, lasted for a week, and probably caused little alarm at first. Iceland is an earthquake-prone land, born of volcanoes and riddled with fissures, and its people had long since grown accustomed to the earth's tremblings. Some 200 volcanoes, and thousands of lesser craters, dot this stark North Atlantic island, and one of them rumbles to life every five years or so. But no matter how used to quakes and eruptions Icelanders may have been, nothing in their experience could have prepared them for the catastrophe that was brewing underground in early June 1783.

At about 9 o'clock in the morning of June 8, the Lakagígar fissure in southeastern Iceland burst open with extreme violence. Giant fountains of lava shot into the air, and billowing clouds of debris darkened the skies and deposited ash over a wide area. The initial explosive phase of the eruption lasted only a few days; by June 11 a lava flood, typical of Icelandic fissure eruptions but of a size unprecedented in historical times, was pouring out of the Lakagígar fissure.

Low-rising Mount Laki divides the fissure—actually a 15-mile-long row of about 115 craters—into two nearly equal sections. Between June 8 and July 29, the eruption was confined to the section southwest of the mountain. During the 50 days it was active, this part of Lakagígar spewed out lava at a rate of some 6,540 cubic yards a second, or about twice the discharge of the Rhine River near its mouth. Flowing in a southwesterly direction, a river of molten rock replaced the River Skaftá in its bed, which in some places was more than 600 feet deep, and soon overflowed its banks onto surrounding pasturelands and farms. Fed by an uninterrupted supply of lava, the seething torrent continued its progress down the Skaftá Valley throughout June and much of July. It swept over the brink of what had been the Stapafoss waterfall on July 17 and formed a 10-to-15-mile-wide fan-shaped delta in the coastal lowlands before coming to a halt on July 20. Nine days later, the section of Lakagígar northeast of Mount Laki came to life, sending a second stream of lava coursing down the bed of the Hverfisfljót River, which like the Skaftá before it, disappeared under the assault of molten rock.

The Lakagígar eruption continued in force into September and did not fully die out until early February 1784. When it was all over, about 3 cubic miles of new lava covered an area of more than 200 square miles. (Imagine an area the size of Chicago buried in 75 feet

Fountains of molten rock shoot up from the earth during a modern-day fissure eruption at Krafla in northeastern Ice-

land. As continental drift tears Iceland apart, new fissures continue to erupt within the island's volcanic zones.

of lava.) Fourteen farmsteads and two churches were completely engulfed by molten rock; another 30 farms were severely damaged. But the lava, which moved slowly, killed no one directly; rather, Iceland's tragedy came from the ashes and especially the toxic gases that accompanied the lava out of the earth's depths.

Lakagígar's ash production was limited mostly to the first explosive stage of the eruption. For the next eight months, however, the fissure emitted enormous quantities of foul-smelling sulfur dioxide and two other deadly gases, carbon dioxide and fluorine. A noxious blue haze formed over Iceland and lingered there all summer and fall. By late June, the haze had spread throughout continental Europe and was drifting over western Asia and North Africa. Iceland's volcanic pollution spoiled crops in Scotland, ruined the finish on copper pots in England, and deposited dust on northern Italy. Benjamin Franklin, who at the time was the United States plenipotentiary in France, correctly linked the unusually cold winter of 1783–84 with the sun-obscuring haze of the previous summer; he also speculated that the haze might have been caused by volcanic activity in Iceland.

If the blue haze caused foul odors and stinging eyes in the European mainland, its effects on Iceland itself were catastrophic. Trees withered and died, crops yellowed, and grass all but ceased to grow. With toxic chemicals poisoning the pasturelands, Iceland's livestock, the mainstay of a poor economy, began to sicken and die. Jón Steingrímsson, a local pastor who witnessed the eruption, recorded in harrowing detail

the disease and mortality that swept through the island. "The horses lost all flesh, on some the hide rotted all along the back; manes and tails decayed and came off at a sharp pull." A similar disease afflicted sheep and cattle, and many of the people, too, developed deformities throughout their bodies.

Boils and growths appeared on the bodies of sick Icelanders; their gums swelled, and their hair fell out.

About three-quarters of Iceland's sheep and horses and one-half of its cattle died of gas poisoning or starvation. Fish, which along with mutton was an important part of the Icelandic diet, disappeared from the island's polluted coastal waters and did not return for almost a year. The ensuing famine, still known in Iceland as the Haze Famine, claimed more than 10,000 lives, roughly one-fifth of the country's population, within three years.

Other volcanoes may have erupted with a louder bang or caused greater immediate damage, but none in human memory has produced such a massive outpouring of lava as the Lakagígar eruption of 1783. In the annals of vulcanology, Lakagígar is a landmark event. But in Iceland, the lava flood and the famine it caused remain the darkest page in that nation's history. Decades of hardship went by before the land, herds, and people of Iceland recovered.

Yellow Fever in Saint-Domingue

Caribbean isle becomes a death trap for European armies

HAITI TODAY IS one of the poorest nations on earth. Yet two centuries ago this tiny country occupying the western third of the Caribbean island of Hispaniola was the jewel among France's colonial possessions. The slave-based plantations of Saint-Domingue, as Haiti was then known, produced lucrative crops of sugar, coffee, cacao, indigo, and cotton. In 1789, near the height of its prosperity, a phenomenal $140 million worth of goods flowed in and out of Saint-Domingue. Just 15 years later, however, the fabled colony lay in ruins. From the ashes of colonial Saint-Domingue rose the independent black republic of Haiti, a nation that to a great extent owes its birth to a mosquito and the terrible virus it carries.

Named for the jaundice that often afflicts its victims, yellow fever was no stranger to the Caribbean. Although questions remain as to when and how the disease reached the New World, it seems to have crossed the Atlantic in the 1640's aboard slave ships sailing from West Africa—where yellow fever probably originated—to the West Indies. From then on, the disease would sweep periodically through the Caribbean, showing a particular affinity for seamen and newly arrived colonists from northern Europe.

No one knew at the time what caused yellow fever or how the dreadful disease was spread.

Before the method of its transmission was discovered in the late 19th century, yellow fever was thought to be communicated directly from person to person, even though the usual anticontagion measures—isolating the victims, disinfecting their clothes and quarters, cremating their corpses—did not seem to work. We now know that the yellow fever virus is spread by mosquitoes, most often by one species, *Aedes aegypti*. An urban mosquito, *Aedes* lays its eggs primarily in man-made water containers such as barrels and cisterns. It also breeds in ships' water stores, which explains how it reached the Americas in the first place.

Yellow fever either kills its victims within days or confers lifelong immunity on those who recover. West African blacks brought as slaves to the New World had probably been exposed to a mild infection as children and were thus immune. As yellow fever took hold in South America and the West Indies, native-born inhabitants, whether of African, European, or mixed blood, also acquired immunity. By 1790, yellow fever was a relatively rare occurrence among the largely immune native population of Saint-Domingue. But *Aedes aegypti*, and the yellow fever virus with it, was still very much a presence on the island. All that was needed for a major epidemic to break out was the arrival on the scene of a large nonimmune population. In September 1793 just such a group—in the form of 600 British troops—landed in Saint-Domingue.

The troubles that brought the British to Saint-Domingue date from 1789, when word of the French Revolution began reaching the island, and they had their origins in the colony's complex racial and class structure. At the top were the rich whites, who ran Saint-Domingue's affairs. A second class of whites, comprised of artisans, shopkeepers, and small-time planters, envied the white elite while bitterly resenting the success of Saint-Domingue's third class, the so-called free persons of color. Descendants, for the most part, of white masters and their slave mistresses, the freedmen of color were French citizens, and many of them had achieved wealth and position in the colony. Throughout the second half of the 18th century, however, discriminatory laws had deprived the freedmen of many of their rights and privileges.

The majority of Saint-Domingue's people, however, existed outside the social hierarchy and were often horribly mistreated. These were the black slaves, on whose labor the whole system rested. By 1791, there were about half a million blacks in Saint-Domingue, and if any group had cause to rebel, it was this one.

In this steamy cauldron of race and class hatreds France's revolutionary message of liberty, equality, and brotherhood found a receptive audience. Especially enthusiastic were the freedmen of color, who saw in the revolution a chance to regain their full rights as French citizens. Against a background of mounting tensions between whites and coloreds, the black slaves unexpectedly took matters into their own hands. In August 1791 they began a revolt that would make the mother country's Reign of Terror seem tame by comparison. Atrocities occurred on both sides, but in the end, Saint-Domingue's vastly outnumbered whites had either been killed or fled the country.

The French government sent commissioners to Saint-Domingue to restore order and to negotiate with the black and colored guerrilla forces vying for control of the colony. Among the leaders of the black guerrillas was a remarkable former slave named François Dominique Toussaint L'Ouverture. After the slave

revolt, in the spring of 1793, Toussaint went over to the Spanish side of Hispaniola, where he made a name for himself fighting with the Spanish against remnants of the French colonial forces. Within a year, however, the French commissioners had formally abolished slavery in Saint-Domingue, the British had invaded the island, and Toussaint had changed sides. In May 1794 Toussaint and 4,000 black troops joined the French in their fight against the British.

Why the British chose to meddle in Saint-Domingue is not entirely clear. Perhaps they feared for the stability of their own Caribbean colonies. Or possibly Britain, then at war with France, hoped to harass its enemy and in the process take over the profitable French sugar trade. Whatever the reasons may have been, the British troops proved more than a match for Saint-Domingue's French and native-born defenders. The redcoats, whose numbers rose to nearly 4,000 within nine months, seized key positions along the coast and from there drove inland. In June 1794 the capital of Port-au-Prince fell to the British, and Toussaint was forced to retreat into the mountains of the interior.

But just as a final British victory seemed at hand, yellow fever intervened with a vengeance. An unusually hot and rainy season had created the ideal conditions for mosquito breeding. And the British themselves provided easy targets for the yellow fever virus. Most of them had come directly from Europe and were thus dangerously vulnerable to infection. No sooner had Port-au-Prince been conquered than huge num-

bers of British soldiers began dying of yellow fever.

The first signs of the disease were usually fatigue, headache, dizziness, and a raging fever. Bouts of nausea and vomiting often followed. As the virus attacked the liver, the victim's skin and eyeballs might turn yellow. Continued high fever, the vomiting of partly digested blood, delirium, a falling pulse rate, and in the later stages, generalized hemorrhage more often than not led to death within a week or so.

Adding to the British mortality rates in Saint-Domingue was the presence of other diseases, particular-

A CONQUEROR OF ARMIES IS VANQUISHED AT LAST

It was commonly called yellow jack, after the yellow flags displayed by quarantined ships, and in 1900 it was killing American soldiers stationed in Cuba after the Spanish-American War. Yellow fever had plagued the New World for at least 2½ centuries, yet its mode of transmission remained unknown. In 1881 a Cuban physician, Dr. Carlos Juan Finlay, had proposed that the *Aedes aegypti* mosquito was responsible for spreading yellow fever, but his theory was largely ignored. Nearly 20 years later, the United States Army appointed a commission to investigate the disease that was threatening its forces in Cuba.

On June 25, 1900, the Yellow Fever Commission, headed by Dr. Walter Reed, convened near Havana and soon began testing Dr. Finlay's theory. Volunteers, including members of the commission, were exposed to *Aedes aegypti*. Two commission members, Drs. James Carroll and Jesse Lazear, contracted yellow fever; Carroll recovered, but Lazear died of the disease. Thanks largely to the heroism

The mosquito Aedes aegypti.

A volunteer is exposed to infected mosquitoes in this portrait of the Yellow Fever Commission in Cuba. The commission head, Dr. Walter Reed, stands at center.

of the volunteers, Reed's team was able to prove by the end of 1900 that *Aedes aegypti* was indeed the yellow fever carrier. To control the disease, therefore, the mosquito and its watery breeding grounds had to be wiped out. Within a year, an eradication cam-

paign led by sanitation expert Major William Gorgas rid Havana of yellow fever. A similar campaign launched by Gorgas in 1904 in fever-plagued Panama eliminated the disease from that country and opened the way to the completion of the Panama Canal.

---

ly malaria. In late June 1796 Lieutenant Thomas Howard of the York Hussars described in his diary the terrible disease that was decimating his regiment: "Men were taken ill at dinner, who had been in the most apparent Health during the Morn:, & were carried to their [graves] at Night. . . . hundreds, almost were absolutely drowned in their own Blood, bursting from them at every Pore." While the symptoms described by Lieutenant Howard could be those of yellow fever, the disease's rapid progression also indicates a type of malaria known as pernicious malaria.

There is no specific treatment for yellow fever, and those that were tried in Saint-Domingue—dousings with cold water, bleedings, blisterings, and heavy doses of mercury, arsenic, calomel, and other drugs—were at best ineffective. Not surprisingly, of the soldiers who entered Saint-Domingue's understaffed and overcrowded hospitals "very few ever came out," observed Lieutenant Howard, "except to their Graves."

Between June and December 1794, 2,000 British soldiers died of yellow fever in Saint-Domingue. After declining in the early months of 1795, the fever toll began to soar again in May. The 96th regiment, which arrived from Ireland in April 1795, lost 41 percent of its ranks by July 1. Fresh troops arriving in August and October seemed to step off their ships directly to

their deaths. The grim pattern was repeated the following year as 600 soldiers died every month during the terrible summer of 1796.

Although yellow fever continued to spread rapidly in 1797, it took fewer lives that year, as the British forces finally became acclimatized to conditions on the island.

Despite a decline in mortality, the Saint-Domingue war was proving too costly for the British to sustain.

Harried by Toussaint's guerrilla forces and decimated by disease, the British had had enough. In October 1798 Britain negotiated a peace with Toussaint and withdrew its remaining men from the island. In the five years of the occupation, Britain had committed 20,200 troops to Saint-Domingue. Of these, an estimated 12,700 soldiers died, 95 percent of them from fever, and another 1,500 were discharged and sent home as invalids; some 2,500 seamen may also have perished in the course of the campaign.

With the British gone, Toussaint endeavored to revive Saint-Domingue's economy. He sent his followers back to the plantations, guaranteeing the former slaves their freedom and a share of the profits. He encouraged exiled planters to return to Saint-Domingue and extended his protection to them. In an amazingly short time, a measure of prosperity did return to the country, despite the ongoing struggle between black and colored factions. By the early months of 1801, Toussaint had defeated his rivals in Saint-Domingue, conquered the Spanish part of the island, and emerged as Hispaniola's sole master. Resisting a formal break with France, however, Toussaint repeatedly protested his loyalty to the government in Paris.

While Toussaint was consolidating his power over Saint-Domingue, France's new first consul, Napoleon Bonaparte, was plotting his downfall. Angered by Toussaint's seizure of power, Napoleon determined to crush "the Gilded African" and reassert personal control over the colony as the first step in the creation of a New World empire that would stretch from the Caribbean to Canada by way of the Louisiana Territory.

An army of 23,000 veteran troops under the command of Napoleon's brother-in-law Charles Leclerc landed in Saint-Domingue in late January 1802. Toussaint's forces offered stiff resistance at first, but by April his chief officers had surrendered, and in early June Toussaint himself was seized and sent to France, where he died in jail of cold and starvation less than a year later. Even before Toussaint's capture, however, the French soldiers, like the British before them, had begun to die of yellow fever in terrifying numbers. On June 11 Leclerc wrote home that "If the First Consul wishes to have an army at San Domingo in October, he must send it from France, for the ravages of this disease are simply indescribable." Leclerc himself succumbed to yellow fever in November, by which time war and disease had claimed about half his army.

Although 10,000 French reinforcements reached Saint-Domingue in the autumn of 1802, Leclerc's death marked the turning point in Napoleon's New World schemes. In April 1803 Louisiana was sold to the United States, and seven months later the French withdrew from Saint-Domingue. At war's end, 24,000 French soldiers, out of a force of 33,000, had died; another 7,000 lay dying, most of them of yellow fever.

On January 1, 1804, Toussaint's successor, General Jean Jacques Dessalines, proclaimed the independence of Saint-Domingue, which from then on would be called by the island's Indian name, Haiti. A deadly mosquito and a determined guerrilla force had thus helped create the first fully independent black republic. Yet 13 years of civil strife, invasions, and disease bequeathed to the infant nation a legacy of poverty and misrule that Haiti still struggles to overcome.

Fighting for freedom, *rebel slaves battle French troops in Saint-Domingue in this 19th-century print. With yellow fever as their ally, an army of former slaves went on to defeat the forces of Great Britain and France.*

Forgotten Quake at New Madrid

For nearly two months, violent convulsions wrack America's heartland

"**V**ISIT NEW MADRID (While It's Still There)," proclaims the legend on a T-shirt designed by James Cravens, merchant and dabbler in the local politics of New Madrid (pronounced *mad*-rid), Missouri. When queried about the significance of the neatly stenciled words, Cravens, a man of boundless good humor, is likely to chuckle warmly. The message, it seems, is a bit of whimsy, an ironic reflection of the bravado of the 3,000 and more citizens who make their homes atop the most active earthquake zone in the eastern half of North America.

For New Madrid, standing beside a broad loop on the Mississippi River near the point where the borders of Kentucky, Tennessee, and Missouri meet, has, in fact, been wiped out once before. And as James Cravens's T-shirt wryly predicts, it will almost certainly be gone again one day.

New Madrid's first disappearance was caused by what has been called the greatest sequence of earthquakes ever to have occurred in the recorded history of eastern North America. The final devastating blow was delivered on February 7, 1812, by an earthquake more powerful in terms of magnitude than either the one that helped destroy San Francisco in 1906 or the

Reelfoot Lake in Tennessee was formed by a sinking of the earth's surface during the New Madrid earthquakes.

one that claimed some 10,000 lives in Mexico City in 1985. And—almost unbelievably—this truly great earthquake had been preceded by two monstrous quakes on December 16, 1811, and January 23, 1812. Throughout that fateful winter, witnesses reported that the ground seemed never to be at rest. Between December 16, 1811, and March 15 the following year, one observer counted a total of 1,874 shocks.

The shivering of the land was felt as far away as Quebec in Canada to the north and New Orleans to the south.

The people of New Madrid were not alone in their alarm. The vibrations rattled windows and chandeliers in Washington, D.C., 750 miles east of New Madrid, and aroused the sleeping residents of Pittsburgh, Pennsylvania. And in Charleston, South Carolina, they set church bells ringing, causing people to rush out into the streets in search of the fire they thought the bells were heralding. In fact, scientists later determined that the quakes were felt over an area of at least 1.5 million square miles—nearly half the area of the present-day continental United States. Moreover, the quake of February 7 would be counted among the most violent ever to have occurred in North America.

What brought on the shattering destruction in that winter of 1811–12? The answer lies some 3 to 12 miles beneath the surface of the earth. For that is where scientists have discovered a weakness in the rock, a fault that runs diagonally for about 150 miles from a point in northeastern Arkansas to a spot just north of Cairo, Illinois.

This fault is under tremendous and ever-increasing stress brought about by very slow but ceaseless movement of the vast geological plate on which North America rests. The western edge of the North American plate, moving southeast, grinds relentlessly against the Pacific plate, a situation that causes stress to build up along the fault. Most of the time the rock gives ground reluctantly and in small concessions, each of which sets off a quiver on the surface above.

Some 200 to 300 of these micro-quakes occur each year, but most of them go undetected by all but the most sensitive instruments. The windows of the town do not rattle, and the people don't feel a thing. As Cravens says, "You don't sit around and even think about it." The people of New Madrid echo his sentiments. If anything, they seem amused by all the fuss that is periodically focused on their town—amusement that is aptly expressed by the words on yet another popular local T-shirt: "It's Our Fault—The New Madrid Earthquake."

The farmers and merchants who lived in the area in the winter of 1811–12, on the other hand, were anything but amused by the events that befell them. Late

THE GREAT EARTHQUAKE AT NEW MADRID

"Then the houses crumbled, the trees waved together, the ground sunk; while ever and anon vivid flashes of lightning, gleaming through the troubled clouds of night, rendered the darkness doubly horrible"

The terrifying fury of the quakes that rattled New Madrid is recaptured in this engraving from an 1851 work.

on the night of Sunday, December 15, 1811, none knew of the disaster that was about to engulf them. Except for a group of French settlers who were dancing away the evening at a boisterous party, most of the residents of New Madrid and the nearby communities of Big and Little Prairie were asleep in their beds.

Up and down the Mississippi, too, flat-bottomed barges bound for New Orleans had been moored securely, tied up for the night to trees on islands or along the river's banks. John Bradbury, a Scottish naturalist, was on one such boat, tied up to a small island about 100 miles south of New Madrid as the sky began to darken on the chill evening of December 15. Returning from a plant-collecting trip along the far reaches of the Missouri River, Bradbury left us a vivid eyewitness account of the earthquake.

As far as is known, he slept soundly until about 2 A.M., when, suddenly, something at once both frightening and incomprehensible shattered his repose. He woke up in a daze to hear "a most tremendous noise . . . equal to the loudest thunder, but more hollow and vibrating." To this terrifying din was added an eerie "screaming of the geese," leading the still-disoriented Bradbury to conclude that "all nature was in a state of dissolution." The geese and other birds seemed to be in the grip of some uncontrollable panic, for they descended in huge numbers on boats all along the river, while on land, smaller birds alighted on the heads and shoulders of equally panicked humans.

Flashes of light electrified the night sky, and a foul, sulfurous odor stung the nostrils of all who rushed from their homes in terror. Fissures opened in the land, sometimes splitting huge trees vertically, leaving each riven tree trunk straddling the crevasse as if some subterranean woodsman had swung an ax upward from within the earth. With an angry roar, massive chunks of the Mississippi's banks plunged into the boiling water, setting in motion surging waves that swept boats helplessly in all directions. Water, mud, and sand shot upward from rents in the ground, and rocks and clods of soil weighing up to 20 pounds were hurled scores of yards through the air.

Worst of all was the rocking and trembling of the solid ground itself. One young boy later recalled seeing the earth rolling in waves several feet in height. Great slabs of land were thrown upward while others dropped as if giant trapdoors had suddenly opened beneath them. As the terrain tilted, water spilled from some lakes as if from a tipped dishpan. In other places swampy land dropped suddenly and without warning, and water poured in from outlets that had in an instant become inlets.

One such event took place in the northwest corner of Tennessee, where a new body of water, Reelfoot Lake, was born overnight from a swamp. When the earthquake struck, the entire bottom of the swamp dropped down, permitting water from nearby Reelfoot Creek to rush backward into the depression. Now 18 miles long by 5 miles wide, the lake today is a watery playground for local residents. But grim reminders of its violent origin remain—the protruding stumps of dead cypresses that were killed when the lake was formed.

Although New Madrid itself this time was spared, the towns of Big Prairie and Little Prairie just to the south were completely destroyed by the paroxysm. The fact that the earthquake's epicenter lay not directly under the towns that it so mightily rocked, but rather in northeastern Arkansas some 65 miles away, is striking testimony to the power of the December convulsion.

As the sky began to brighten on the morning of December 16, the inhabitants of the region around New Madrid might well have heaved sighs of relief, believing that their time of horror had ended. Little did they know that the worst was still to come. The earth continued to jiggle relentlessly, with movements that one witness likened to the tremors of "the flesh of a beef just killed." On January 23, 1812, the jiggling turned to thunder once more, and an earthquake nearly as powerful in magnitude as that of December 16 rocked the land. Then came the final, most destructive blow on February 7.

The land this time heaved its own rumbling sigh, releasing a torrent of pent-up stress that totally leveled New Madrid. The bed of the Mississippi, moreover, was moved so violently as to build two roaring waterfalls where none had been before—one above and the other below New Madrid. And the river, as if affronted, appeared to recoil and reverse its flow. It is believed that part of the riverbed was lifted up and formed an obstruction, causing the Mississippi to run northward for a time. After a few hours, the obstacle was worn down and the waters resumed their normal course toward the Gulf of Mexico. The falls, made of sand and mud, were also soon worn away and no longer exist.

What does remain is the memory of the greatest series of earthquakes ever to strike eastern North America. Casualties from the quake, fortunately, were few. New Madrid's total population at the time was only about 1,000, while a mere 30 or so families lived in the tiny settlements at Big Prairie and Little Prairie. Most people, moreover, lived in log cabins, resilient structures that took a lot of shaking before

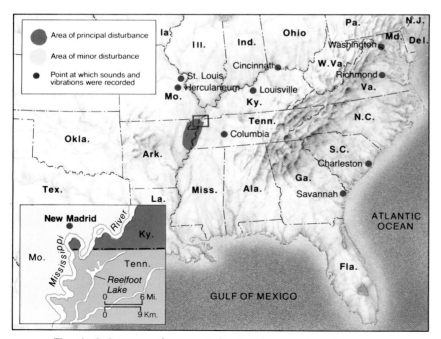

The shaded area on the map indicates the extent of visible surface damage caused by the New Madrid earthquakes.

HUNTING BEARS IN EARTHQUAKE COUNTRY

The winter of 1825–26 was a banner season for frontiersman Davy Crockett; in just seven months, he claimed, he killed a grand total of 105 bears. But one of them must have stood out as something special, even for that legendary hunter.

The time was early January 1826, and Crockett was hunting the territory between the Obion River and Reelfoot Lake—a creation of the New Madrid earthquake—in northwestern Tennessee. Travel was difficult and "mighty slow," he noted, "on account of the cracks in the earth occasioned by the earthquakes." Even so, after nightfall his dogs managed to tree a bear and Crockett shot it down. Wounded, it fought fiercely with the dogs until at last it "got down into one of the cracks that the earthquakes had made in the ground, about four feet deep, and I could tell the biting end of him by the hollering of my dogs." In the scuffle that followed, Crockett misplaced his gun, and so he finished off the bear as only Davy Crockett could: he crawled into the crack and, barehanded, stabbed the beast to

death with his butchering knife. It was an exploit, an awestruck companion exclaimed, that he wouldn't have attempted "for all the bears in the woods."

Nor were Crockett's earthquake adventures quite over with that episode. The next night, he goes on to tell us, "We had laid down by our fire, and about ten o'clock there came a most

terrible earthquake, which shook the earth so that we were rocked about like we had been in a cradle. We were very much alarmed; for though we were accustomed to feel earthquakes, we were now right in the region which had been torn to pieces by them in 1812, and we thought it might take a notion and swallow us up, like the big fish did Jonah."

An illustration from Buffalo Bill Cody's 1888 biography of Davy Crockett depicts the legendary frontiersman and his trusty dogs in the throes of their famous nighttime fight with an angry black bear.

---

they tumbled down. By that time, most of the inhabitants had fled their homes, with the result that only a handful of people were killed on land. A greater but unknown number may, however, have been lost to the angry waters of the Mississippi.

Today, in contrast, the region is far from sparsely populated. Where once only a few thousand people lived and worked—mostly farmers and trappers in rude frontier settlements—there now are millions. Large cities such as Memphis, Tennessee, and Evansville, Indiana, have sprung up within the zone potentially threatened by any future New Madrid earthquake.

And, in the words of one expert, "We're due for an earthquake of 6.5 [on the Richter scale] by the turn of the century," which could occur anywhere in the central U.S. seismic zone. The seven states that would suffer most from such a quake are Kentucky, Indiana, Illinois, Missouri, Tennessee, Arkansas, and Mississippi. Although the ground motion of a 6.5 quake would be 20 times weaker than either of the quakes that struck the region in December 1811 or February 1812, it would be much more severe than a magnitude 6 quake in California, for example, because of the geology of the area.

Will such a calamity come again to the New Madrid

region? And, if so, when? Scientists have uncovered clues to the answers by studying rock formations and the behavior of the earth in the area. These suggest that a big earthquake like the ones that struck in the winter of 1811–12 comes only every 500 to 1,800 years. But what about less destructive quakes? Speaking of these, one scientist has concluded that "the New Madrid fault has stored up enough strain energy since 1812 to be capable of producing, right now, a very large earthquake of 7.6." And, he adds, "It's not a matter of 'if.' It's 'when.'"

As to how destructive the next New Madrid earthquake might be, that's anyone's guess. Lesser but still damaging earthquakes occur in the region about once every 75 to 100 years. Since the last such quake to strike the region occurred nearly a century ago, it might be prudent, the experts suggest, to expect one in the very near future.

How do the people of New Madrid respond to these dire predictions? "It's farthest from our minds, really," declares the publisher of the local newspaper. "Nobody takes it seriously here."

Maybe so. But that T-shirt with its ominous legend, "Visit New Madrid (While It's Still There)," surely makes one wonder.

*A **grim reaper*** *in the form of hail, snow, and frost killed off young summer crops across the Northeast.*

The Year Without a Summer

Mysterious cold waves trigger devastating crop failures

HIRAM HARWOOD must have sensed something was wrong the moment he opened his eyes early on Thursday morning. The calendar said June, but he could have sworn it was a day in February; there was a chill in the air that usually meant snow on the way. In the rich, rolling land around Bennington, Vermont, where Hiram worked a small family farm with his father, days like this were known as late as April and, this year, even in May. But June?

Harwood was a meticulous diarist, and in his entry for that day, June 6, 1816, he wrote that "about 8 A.M. [it] began to snow—continued more or less till past 2 P.M. The heads of all the mountains on every side were crowned with snow. The most gloomy and extraordinary weather ever seen."

Friday, he noted, was no better: "In ploughfields and other parts the surface of the ground was stiff with frost—the leaves of the trees were blackened—past 6 in the morning a wash-tub full of rain water was scum'd with ice."

The unwelcome snowfall had blanketed most of the Northeast and parts of northern Pennsylvania. The Bangor *Register* in Maine reported snow falling "in beautiful large flakes, some of which as they struck the ground covered spots two inches [in] diameter." Under the headline "Melancholy Weather," the Danville, Vermont, *North Star* recorded snowdrifts of up to 20 inches and conditions on Saturday that were "more severe than it generally is during the . . . winter. It was indeed a gloomy and tedious period."

The numbing cold continued for five days. Freezing temperatures, frost, and intermittent snow killed off much of the corn, staple crop of New England agriculture. By Tuesday, though, the worst seemed to be over, and farmers throughout the region set about replowing, replanting, and replacing corn, beans, cucumbers, squash, and other less hardy crops.

Over the next four weeks, life returned to normal, and the new plantings began to take hold. Wheat and rye, especially, seemed to prosper. Some farmers, looking back on the anxious days of June, poked fun at one another for their panic over "famine fever." But in early July the cold and killing frost came again.

One ominous fact was now clear: in many communities in the northern half of the nation, there would be a very thin harvest that year. Any lingering hopes for a recovery were crushed by a recurrence of frost and snow in August and then another in September. Grain prices during the winter of 1816–17 went through the ceiling: corn, usually 75 cents a bushel, more than doubled in price; oats leaped from 12 cents to 92, wheat from 50 cents to $2.75.

"There was great destitution among the people the next winter and spring," wrote one chronicler. "The farmers in some instances were reduced to the last extremity, and many cattle died. The poorer men could not buy corn at the exorbitant prices for which it was sold. In the autumn, stock was sold at extremely low prices on account of the lack of hay and corn."

With no alternative, some turned to killing raccoons and groundhogs and foraging for wild onions and other edible plants. Pigeons became game birds. Farmers fed mackerel to their livestock and would remember 1816, accordingly, as "mackerel year."

However severe the effects in the United States, they could not begin to compare with the distress across much of Europe. France, especially, was still reeling from the shocks of revolution followed by nearly two decades of the Napoleonic Wars.

Spring came late, and with it heavy rains and chilly temperatures (aptly named "Napoleonic weather") that made for meager harvests across France. Food prices skyrocketed beyond the reach of all but the very rich. A government tax on wheat triggered riots in Poitiers, Toulouse, and other agricultural centers. In the Loire Valley, hunger and indignation exploded into violence as hundreds of angry citizens attacked grain carts en route to market. What little was harvested was of unusually poor quality.

Conditions elsewhere were hardly better. A letter from London, published in a New York newspaper in June, reported that "from the Baltic to Breslau—the greater part of the land sown with winter grain has been obliged to be ploughed up. . . . of the [wheat] that remains standing scarcely one-third part of a crop is to be expected."

Throughout the farmlands of East Anglia in England, tension had been high since an abnormally cold spring pushed up the price of wheat while at the same time holding down agricultural employment and wages. In May, rioters armed with sticks and iron spikes, and carrying banners proclaiming "Bread or Blood," stampeded through several towns, looting and vandalizing. After the summer frosts, such discontent

One local hero whose green thumb helped others survive is remembered on this New Hampshire tombstone.

spread quickly throughout Great Britain. At Dundee, in Scotland, a mob of 2,000 plundered nearly 100 food shops, then looted and burned the home of a local grain dealer.

Correspondents in Ireland reported that "a famine in this unfortunate country is inevitable for the harvests entirely failed from the badness of the weather." There was indeed a famine—and along with it a typhus epidemic that killed an estimated 50,000 people over the next two years.

Things were perhaps at their worst in landlocked Switzerland, especially in Zurich, center of the European grain market since medieval times. By the spring of 1817, famine had become a Swiss national emergency. Efforts to replant had been thwarted when seed supplies ran out. Unemployment soared, and bands of youths prowled back streets of towns and cities looking for stray cats to cut up and eat. Sections of the country that had grain refused to sell it even to neighboring regions. Great grain-trading firms bought Russian wheat at Italian ports—only to lose it to bands of hungry raiders in the high mountain passes en route home.

Inevitably, masses of people on both sides of the Atlantic found themselves asking the same question: why?

If the consequences of the freakish cold were all too clear, explanations were harder to find. What caprice of nature had caused this plague of winter weather in what should have been high summer?

Many Americans saw the calamity as a warning from God. From Maine to Georgia they flocked to churches, swelling Sunday morning attendance and feeding a sharp upswing in evangelism. Of those who looked to science for explanations, some claimed it was a result of sunspots, which were increasingly visible to the naked eye early and late in the day. One German scientist cited ship's logs to prove that there had been an eruption of Arctic icebergs. Other theorists wound up blaming Benjamin Franklin, whose experiments decades earlier with electricity and lightning rods remained a topic of controversy. According to one school of thought, much of the heat that warmed the continents was electrical and flowed below the crust of the earth. Franklin's lightning rods had disrupted that

Halfway around the world from Mount Tambora, a pervasive yellowish haze caused by volcanic dust probably inspired *the dramatic sky in "Decline of the Carthaginian Empire," painted in 1817 by the British artist J. M. W. Turner.*

flow, the reasoning went, and so brought on this plague of unseasonably cold weather.

Ironically, a theory developed years earlier by the same Benjamin Franklin turned out to be closer to the truth than anyone could have guessed. In 1784 Franklin had blamed the unusually cold summer of 1783, and the bitter winter that followed, on volcanic eruptions in Iceland. He conjectured that dust and "smoke" issuing from these explosions might have formed the mysterious "dry fog" that seemed to veil the sun during much of that time, resulting in dramatically cooler temperatures.

A century would pass, however, before the world would know how right he had been. In 1816 a sea voyage of many weeks separated Europe and America from such faraway locales as Sumatra and other islands of the Dutch East Indies. A volcanic eruption on a remote island, reported only sketchily, would not have attracted much attention—even if, as was the case, the eruption turned out to be one of the most powerful on record. In April 1815, 13,000-foot Mount Tambora on an island east of Java erupted with stupendous force, shooting an estimated 1.7 million tons of ash and debris into the air, killing more than 10,000 islanders immediately and some 82,000 more from disease and starvation in the following months. It cast a blanket of ash over a million square miles, could be heard 1,600 miles away, and turned day into night within a radius of 370 miles.

A large quantity of the volcanic ash did not fall to earth but floated high in the stratosphere as a fine dust, light as talcum, circling the globe at an altitude of some 25 miles. At this height it functioned as a vast filter, reflecting sunlight back into space while allowing heat to escape from the lower atmosphere.

None of this was known to scientists of the day. The Tambora disaster went all but unreported, save for scattered accounts assembed by Sir Thomas Stamford Raffles, British lieutenant governor of Java. Not until 1920 did William J. Humphreys, of the U.S. Weather Bureau, publish a landmark study linking Tambora to the worldwide weather disturbances of 1816. Humphreys also noted that two other major eruptions had preceded the Tambora cataclysm—Soufrière, on St. Vincent Island in the West Indies, in 1812, and Mount Mayon, on Luzon in the Philippines, in 1814.

Once that connection was established, it became possible to explain a number of distinctive side effects: the smoky yellow skies and other somber tints used by the British painter J. M. W. Turner in his 1817 "Decline of the Carthaginian Empire" and other works from this period; dazzling sunsets throughout the northern latitudes, blending shades of orange, purple, and pink; newspaper stories in Baltimore and Annapolis, Maryland, reporting snowfalls in April and May tinted by red, blue, and brown dust; a newspaper item in Washington, D.C., noting that "the whole atmosphere is filled with a thick haze, the inconvenience of which is not diminished by the clouds of impalpable dust which floats in the air." Another side effect was a widely viewed aura around the sun, which seemed to dim its intensity—allowing sunspots to be seen more clearly and spurring newspaper comment that "the Sun's rays, it has been frequently remarked, have not their usual power. . . . there appears to be less intensity of light as well as heat." Finally, Benjamin Franklin's mysterious "dry fog" of 1783 makes perfect sense as a description of volcanic dust.

In view of the year's privations, it is not surprising to note that the elections of November 1816 turned more incumbent congressmen out of office than any on record. When the House of Representatives reconvened early in 1817, fully 70 percent of the members were new. Also not surprising was a sharp increase in the number of people abandoning northeastern farms for greener pastures in Ohio and Indiana. "On some days," noted the Zanesville, Ohio, *Messenger* in October 1816, "from forty to fifty wagons have passed the Muskingum at this place. The emigrants are from almost every state north and east of the Potomack . . . travelling in various modes—some on foot, some on horses, and others in different kinds of vehicles, from the ponderous Pennsylvania wagon, to the light New England pleasure carriage."

Not all the effects of the weather of 1816 were to prove unwelcome. The poet Lord Byron had left England for good and joined his friends Mary and Percy Bysshe Shelley at a villa near Lake Geneva. The cold, wet weather of that summer kept them housebound, and they amused themselves by writing ghost stories—one of which was Mary Shelley's *Frankenstein*.

While New England experienced one year of hardship, the impact on Europe proved deeper and longer-lasting.

Recovery was relatively fast in the United States. The 1817 New England harvest was bountiful, helping to compensate for the damage of the previous year. Europe was another matter: the disastrous weather of 1816 was but one chapter in a continuing story of crisis and upheaval. It was a pivotal one, however, helping to precipitate the great bank panic and depression that gripped the Continent in 1818–19.

If nothing else, the aftermath of Tambora's eruption provided a stark example of how unpredictable and far-reaching the effects of a single, violent convulsion of nature can be. It remains to be pondered what the impact might be if several such convulsions coincided—hardly a rare phenomenon in the planet's history. William J. Humphreys, for one, came to the sobering conclusion that volcanic ash blown into the stratosphere even once every two years would result in temperatures low enough to "cover the earth with a mantle of snow so extensive as to be self-perpetuating . . . and thereby initiate at least a cool period or, under the most favorable conditions, even an ice age."

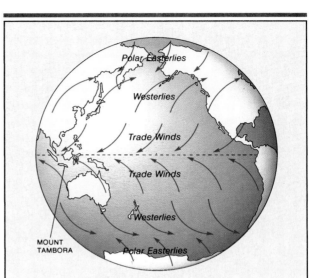

A schematic diagram of the wind patterns that influence weather and climate worldwide outlines the Northern Hemisphere's three dominant systems and their mirror-image counterparts to the south.

Earth's Restless Ocean of Air

TO MOST PEOPLE of the early 19th century, it would have sounded fantastic to suggest that a force as basic as the weather could be governed by events on a small island halfway around the globe. Yet the earth has revealed itself to be an intricate mechanism in which any natural occurrence may have wide-ranging consequences — and few events have made that point more dramatically than the April 1815 eruption of Mount Tambora.

The atmosphere up to a height of about 10 miles contains three broad zones of wind currents in each hemisphere — westward near the equator and poles, eastward in the middle latitudes — that help orchestrate the world's basic weather patterns. The volcanic debris produced by most eruptions rises only a few miles into the air and is soon washed back to earth by rain and snow. But Tambora's colossal explosion propelled a huge volume of ash as high as 25 miles into the stratosphere, far above any rain clouds, where it could remain aloft for several years. The stratosphere's powerful east-west winds picked up the powdery debris and began to carry it around the globe, gradually broadening its range from the equator to higher latitudes. Within a year, large amounts of ash veiled the skies above North America and Europe, and since sunlight striking the earth at a more acute angle had to pass through a thicker veil of dust, the climatic effect there was magnified. Indeed, average temperatures in those latitudes may have dropped more than 4°F worldwide in 1816, and that summer remains the coldest on the records of cities as far apart as New Haven, Connecticut, and Geneva, Switzerland.

Fighting fear with fire, *citizens of Marseilles and countless other cities sought to disinfect the air with roaring bonfires.*

Cholera Sweeps the World

Millions succumb to a mysterious and terrible disease

IT WAS EARLY AUTUMN of 1831, and rumors had been circulating since April through the busy harbor of Sunderland, near Newcastle on England's northeast coast. They were about the quarantine, a government order slapping a 15-day hold on all shipping coming in first from Russia, then in June from the Baltic and from Germany. It was the deadly cholera, people said, a new and mysterious disease, brought to Europe from India. A horrible thing: the diarrhea was merciless, then the cramps, agonizing pain, unbearable thirst; the blood congealed like tar, the body shrank, turned blue, then cold—and then you died. And it happened fast. A man could wake healthy at sunrise, they said, and be dead of the thing by dusk.

According to some tavern talk, it had already reached Sunderland—but no one seemed to know anything more. William Sproat must have heard the talk and most likely shrugged it off. A typical York-

shireman, Sproat belied his 60 years by the vigor with which he pitched into every workday at the harbor, where he made a good living as a keelman on a coal barge. He had always been the picture of health; he lived well and never went hungry. But for nearly a week he had been troubled by queasiness in the stomach and bouts of diarrhea. On Wednesday, October 19, Sproat felt so sick that he missed a day's work. Thursday was worse. But on Friday he seemed to take a turn for the better.

Then on Saturday afternoon the cramps hit him again, along with more of the shivering and diarrhea. A local doctor was summoned and arrived to find Sproat "evidently sinking; pulse almost imperceptible and extremities cold, skin dry, eyes sunk, lips blue, features shrunk, he spoke in whispers, violent vomiting and purging, cramps of the calves of the legs and complete prostration of strength."

Two other doctors were called in, and they agreed on what they found. For months, Sunderland had been trying to deny to itself that the dreaded Asiatic cholera had at last made a beachhead in England. Even when several unmistakable cases had been reported, news had been suppressed. Now there was no doubt. William Sproat died in a coma the following Wednesday. Within 24 hours, his son and granddaughter were desperately ill with the same symptoms. Cholera had officially landed on British shores and now walked among the people of Sunderland.

Records from Asia more than 2,000 years old described a disease whose terrible symptoms were becoming all too familiar.

Though unknown in Europe, cholera was hardly a new disease. Some accounts establish its presence in Tibet and the Indian subcontinent as early as the fourth century B.C. A temple of that period discovered at Gujarat in western India reportedly bore an inscription eerily reminiscent of William Sproat's agony: "The lips blue, the face haggard, the eyes hollow, the stomach sunk in, the limbs contracted and crumpled as if by fire, those are the signs of the great illness which, invoked by a malediction of the priests, comes down to slay the brave."

But the "great illness" remained an Asian phenomenon until the fateful year 1817, when a major outbreak of cholera burst on the scene. This time no borders seemed able to contain it: in less than a decade it had spread to China, Japan, and Arabia, moved into Persia and Syria, and north toward the Caspian Sea, on the very doorstep of Europe, where it halted during the memorably cold winter of 1823–24.

By mid-1829, cholera was active again. Moving east, west, and north along the great routes of trade and religious pilgrimage, it advanced steadily toward the great population centers of Europe. The international medical community buzzed with speculation: How did it travel? Was it contagious? Probably in some fashion—yet it often seemed to defy the usual contagion patterns. People apparently unconnected with a cholera victim would suddenly, mysteriously, fall ill with the telltale symptoms—while those actually handling the sick and the dead just as often escaped. Was it in the atmosphere, climate, humidity?

By the autumn of 1830, the disease was in Moscow, the following spring in St. Petersburg on the shores of the Baltic. From there it jumped easily to Finland and Poland, south into Hungary, and finally to Austria. By summer, outbreaks had been reported in Berlin and shortly afterward in Hamburg and the Netherlands.

British politicians, doctors, scientists, and the general public watched in fearful fascination. "It is with deep concern," King William IV told the opening session of Parliament on June 21, 1831, "that I have to announce to you the continued progress of a formidable disease . . . in the eastern parts of Europe. . . . Precautions should be taken . . . against the introduction of so dangerous a malady into this country." Then came Sunderland, and William Sproat's moment in history. The wait was over.

Yet apart from its symptoms and its awesome power to kill, little was understood about cholera. "We know of absolutely no other disease in which the utter powerlessness of the healing art is manifested as [in] cholera," was one physician's despairing cry. Some recommended large doses of calomel, a mercury compound normally used as a purgative, or even castor oil and other agents, presumably to flush out the system. Others suggested ammonia, arsenic, phosphorus, rhubarb, opium, and even mutton broth. Still others favored electric shock treatments or the application of red-hot irons to various parts of the body.

Cholera, meanwhile, marched on. By March 1832, it began to spread across England and jumped to Ireland, then across the Atlantic to Canada and the United States. It took hold in France, Belgium, Norway, and Holland. The German poet Heinrich Heine, who was in Paris that spring, wrote a riveting account. On March 29, the day cholera's arrival in Paris was announced, the people "mocked the fear of cholera and the disease itself. That night the balls were more crowded than usual: hysterical laughter almost drowned out the loud music. Suddenly, the most light-

Head-to-toe protection *suggested to Vienna's residents included herb-laden pouches, a potion-filled basket, bulky overshoes, and other ingenious but useless paraphernalia.*

"Death's Dispensary," the title of this 1866 cartoon, scarcely overstated the hazard posed by public water pumps, which were still common in London and elsewhere despite the discoveries made years earlier by Dr. John Snow.

hearted of the harlequins felt his legs growing cold, and took off his mask; to the astonishment of everyone present, he revealed a face turned violet-blue.

"It was clear that this was no practical joke: laughter died away, and carriages filled with revelers took them from the ball straight to the Hotel Dieu, the Central Hospital, where, still arrayed in their carnival attire, they soon died."

Across the Atlantic, Americans had been well warned of the danger. Committees were formed and doctors exchanged views as to the best course of action when cholera arrived on American shores. The disease made first landfall in Quebec and Montreal. Then on June 26 an Irish immigrant worker in New York City fell ill with all the classic symptoms. He was followed by his two children and his wife, all of whom died within the week. There was no mistaking the nature and identity of his affliction.

Nor was there any mistaking the consequences around the crowded city. Strict quarantines were imposed. Shops closed down—with an immediate upsurge in the number of reported burglaries. Hearses came and went, barely able to keep up with the rampant death rate. Dead bodies lay abandoned in gutters.

New Yorkers who could fled the city for what they saw as sanctuary in the country. Not all found it an easy journey, however. Those crossing Long Island Sound ran into volleys of gunfire from Rhode Islanders determined not to let the deadly pestilence in. From New York State, cholera radiated outward, traveling the Erie Canal to the Midwest, riding the inland roads and coastal waterways to New Orleans, where it claimed more than 5,000 lives. Local militia at Ypsilanti, Michigan, opened fire on a mail stage arriving

from Detroit, where cholera had been reported. Waxing and waning through the seasons, it remained a curse of American life for most of the next two years.

After the first cholera wave broke over Europe and North America, movements for social reform were fueled by the obvious link between incidence of the disease and the primitive conditions under which the working classes were forced to live. The rise of industry and the building of factories had transformed many small towns into major cities almost overnight; rows of cramped, dreary terraced houses sprouted like weeds along town perimeters as overcrowded larger buildings decayed into tenements. Streets were awash with a mixture of stagnant rainwater, putrefying food leavings, filth, human and animal excrement. Sewage, industrial waste, carcasses of slaughtered animals, and all other imaginable forms of refuse matter were dumped untreated into the Thames.

Cholera returned to England in 1848 and ravaged the population throughout 1849, leaving behind a death toll of some 130,000. In that year, Dr. John Snow published his own opinions on the vexing question of how the disease was transmitted. Snow was already noted as an expert in the use of ether and chloroform, newly introduced as safe and effective anesthetics. Cholera was not breathed in through the lungs at all, he contended; instead it was swallowed, then spread through the excretions of infected people into sources of drinking water used by others—not an uncommon occurrence in a time of widespread squalor and primitive sanitary conditions.

There was little Snow could do to test his opinions, however, until the disease struck again. He hadn't long to wait. In August 1854 it surfaced in London, and he was ready to find evidence to corroborate what was now widely known as "Doctor Snow's theory."

At the corner of Broad and Cambridge streets stood a water pump that served the hundreds living at close

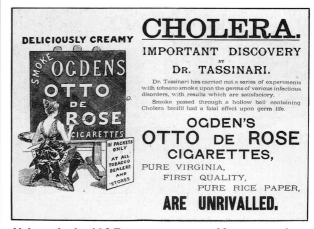

Light up for health? Even cigarettes could masquerade as cholera fighters, so desperate were people for a cure.

quarters in the surrounding honeycomb of back streets. Snow took samples of the water and found the small white ricelike particles that are telltale signs of the diarrhea excretions of cholera victims. He obtained an inventory of cholera deaths in the neighborhood for a recent week and found that nearly all of them had lived within a short distance of the Broad Street pump.

Every new clue pointed to the same grim conclusion: somehow, the Broad Street water pump was killing people.

Evidence accumulated, from the brewery in Broad Street, where not a single man died of cholera—and where the workers drank either free beer or water from the company's own well—to the factory down the street that always kept two tubs full of water from the Broad Street pump for its workers, and reported 18 employees dead of cholera. Finally, Snow had seen enough. He persuaded city officials to remove the handle from the Broad Street pump—and cholera deaths in the area tapered off almost to nothing.

The pattern continued, cholera rolling across land and sea to break, wave upon wave, on distant shores. The intermittent epidemics of 1846–62 gave way to another in 1864, then again in 1881 and 1899, the last persisting until 1923 throughout Europe, Asia, Africa, and the Americas.

In 1883, working first in Egypt, then in India, the German bacteriologist Robert Koch at last isolated and identified the short, thick, curved microorganism responsible for cholera. It was a great personal triumph for Koch, who had come to early prominence for his work in isolating the anthrax and tuberculosis bacilli.

"Cholera," Koch wrote, "does not come into being spontaneously—out of nothing. It is a disease that attacks only those who have swallowed the comma bacillus." That bacillus, he added, could not be inhaled—vindicating England's John Snow, as well as solving the riddle of why people treating cholera victims often remained healthy themselves. Increased understanding of the disease also made it clear that the widespread use of purgatives and laxatives had been the worst treatments possible. The classic symptoms of bluish lips, dry skin, and violent muscle cramps turned out to be caused by the rapid dehydration that accompanies the onset of cholera.

The disease persists today, probably afflicting more victims than ever before, but only where overcrowding, inadequate diet, and poor housing and sanitation are still predominant. These conditions prevail in southern Asia, cholera's ancient incubator, and Africa south of the Sahara. Cholera is no longer the killer it once was, however, as medicine has developed effective treatments using antibiotics and blood transfusions. Though vaccination is widespread in such regions, the vaccine is effective in only about 50 percent of cases, and then for no more than 18 months.

In short, there is really no way of eradicating cholera, save care and attention to the way great numbers of people live. It remains hovering in the wings like a sinister shadow, ever patient, awaiting its chance once again to carry death abroad in the world.

Florence Nightingale answered her country's call and won worldwide recognition for her profession when she left England in 1854 with a team of nurses to care for British troops during the Crimean War. Rifles and artillery proved to be less deadly weapons than cholera, which killed tens of thousands of soldiers on both sides.

Famine in Ireland

Blighted potato crop triggers national tragedy

IT'S THE WARM WIND of the ocean that makes Ireland the Emerald Isle. Parts of County Donegal lie nearly as far north on the globe as Moscow; even the southernmost counties touch a parallel that runs hundreds of miles north of Quebec. Yet the land is clothed in velvet green—a gift of the Gulf Stream, which brings a touch of tropical warmth from the distant Caribbean. Snow, ice, severe cold, all are rare. A little fire of peat, an inefficient but plentiful fuel, has usually sufficed to warm a country cottage.

It was this same gentle wind, however, that in the summer of 1845 helped bring on a calamity that decimated the Irish people—a succession of famine, disease, and death whose like had never been seen even in a land accustomed to bitter hardship. This was not a sudden, violent upheaval, but a silent process that stole upon the island and found conditions tailor-made for disaster. By the time it was over, some 1.5 million people had died—in a country of perhaps 8 million—and a million more had fled overseas. Some emigrated to Canada or Australia, but most chose the United States; and by the impact of their sheer num-

bers, they set American history on a new course.

Ironically, it was from America that the fungus responsible for the potato blight had come, most likely crossing the Atlantic in the damp hold of a ship. The first sign of trouble was a report in August 1845 that potatoes on the Isle of Wight in the English Channel were spoiling in the fields, evidently stricken by the same fungus that had appeared in North America three years earlier. Yet neither this report nor later news of potato crops rotting in Holland, France, and other parts of Great Britain alerted the government to the full extent of the danger. The potato crop had been attacked by a variety of pests over the years, but the people always managed to get through the bad times.

Never before, however, had the Irish leaned so heavily on this one crop. By the 1840's potatoes were the mainstay of the average diet—indeed, often the only solid food available. The countryside had been divided and subdivided so many times that a typical tenant farmer's holding might comprise less than an acre. Nearly half the rural populace lived in window-less mud cabins—the poorer the family, the more

The dreaded sight of a landlord's agent meant eviction — and likely death from starvation, disease, or exposure—for thousands of peasant families across Ireland's blighted countryside. The agent often encouraged hungry neighbors to glean whatever food they could from the tenant's field while the cottage was being "tumbled," torn down to clear the site for a more profitable planting of wheat or barley.

children there seemed to be—and all that stood between them and starvation was the ubiquitous potato. Nutritious and fast-growing, potatoes were planted in every nook and cranny, on the side of a hill or the edge of a bog. The larger fields, meanwhile, were reserved for the cash crops, mainly wheat and oats, which the peasants sold to pay the rent.

And the rent had to be paid. Under English law the landlord was a lord in the strictest sense: he could evict at will. Even in the years before 1845, to be evicted for any reason meant hunger and severe privation. After the famine had set in, the House of Commons was told, eviction was "tantamount to a sentence of death by slow torture."

Everything depended, then, on the cash crop to pay the rent and the potato crop to feed the family. This "lumper" or "spud" on which the Irish staked their fate was a hardy plant, growing in such abundance that tons were thrown away in the best years. But that was exactly the problem—unlike grains, surplus potatoes couldn't be stored from one year to the next.

This was the land over which the wet sea breezes of 1845 blew, carrying the deadly spore of the fungus *Phytophthora infestans*. Throughout August reports accumulated of a "fearful malady" in the potato fields of Europe, yet so far Ireland had been spared. Then in September 1845 the editor of England's *Gardeners' Chronicle and Horticultural Gazette* dramatically announced: "We stop the Press with very great regret to announce that the potato Murrain has unequivocally

declared itself in Ireland. The crops about Dublin are suddenly perishing."

A fringe of white on the leaves provided the first sign that a potato plant had been infected. Under a microscope, that whitish substance showed up as a dense network of filaments and countless pear-shaped spore capsules. With moist air and mild temperatures, the spores multiplied rapidly and then, agitated by wind, rain, or the spade, showered themselves on nearby plants and earth. When conditions were right, whole fields could be afflicted in a very short time.

A sickly odor rose from these fields, and a worse one pervaded the potatoes themselves when harvested.

People would enter fields in the morning that had been green with promise the day before, and find a spreading blackness, softness, and slime on leaf and stalk. As the Irish learned a year after the first outbreak, even some tubers that appeared healthy might be contaminated. If these were used as seed for the next crop, that too would be subject to the blight.

And so it happened. The harvest of 1845 was a toll of misery and a fearful omen. Some areas were spared, but the next year disaster was universal. In August 1846 a priest named Father Mathew wrote: "On the 27th of last month I passed from Cork to Dublin, and this doomed plant bloomed in all luxuriance of an abundant harvest. Returning on the third [of August] I beheld with sorrow one wide waste of putrefying vegetation. In many places the wretched people were seated on the fences of their decaying gardens, wringing their hands and wailing bitterly the destruction that had left them foodless."

The winter of 1846–47 was unusually severe. A

A telltale patch of white on the leaves of a potato plant was the all-too-familiar calling card of Phytophthora infestans, *the fungus responsible for the killing blight that swept across Ireland like a firestorm. Favored by cool, damp weather, the fungus could destroy healthy plants in a matter of days, leaving the potatoes inedible and filling the air with a nauseous stench.*

117

justice of the peace wrote from Cork in December: "The alarming prospect cannot be exaggerated. . . . I assure you that unless something is immediately done the people must die." Later that ghastly winter he appealed directly to the duke of Wellington, hero of Waterloo, describing an effort he had just made to distribute bread in the nearby hamlet of Skibbereen. Inside one hovel he found heaps of rags from which issued "a low moaning." He saw feverish children, a woman, and "what had once been a man."

Outside, a crowd of the starving surrounded him: "My clothes were nearly torn off in my endeavour to escape from the throng of pestilence around, when my neckcloth was seized from behind. . . . I found myself grasped by a woman with an infant just born in her arms and the remains of a filthy sack across her loins—the sole covering of herself and baby. . . . A mother, herself in a fever, was seen the same day to drag out the corpse of her child, a girl about twelve, perfectly naked, and leave it half covered with stones. In another house, within 500 yards of the cavalry station at Skibbereen, the dispensary doctor found seven wretches lying unable to move, under the same cloak. One had been dead many hours, but the others were unable to move either themselves or the corpse."

No sense of urgency about mass starvation disrupts the gentlemanly conversation between Prime Minister Robert Peel and opposition leader Lord John Russell in an 1846 cartoon. Even less alarmed is the lion, which bears a curious resemblance to Queen Victoria.

The wretchedness of these people appalled relief officials and other eyewitnesses, who did what little they could. A local relief official reported in December 1846 to his superiors: "Although a man not easily moved, I confess myself unmanned by the extent and intensity of suffering I witnessed, more especially among the women and little children, crowds of whom were to be seen scattered over the turnip fields, like a flock of famishing crows, devouring the raw turnips, and mostly half-naked, shivering in the snow and sleet, uttering exclamations of despair, whilst their children were screaming with hunger."

"Pray do something for them," wrote one inspector. "Let me beg of you to attend to this. I cannot express their condition."

The British government responded with a number of relief programs, but their efforts were disorganized, intermittent, and hampered by political obstacles. The most glaring barrier was that imposed by England's long-standing Corn Laws, which blocked the importation of grain that could have alleviated Ireland's hunger. The laws' original purpose had been simple—to assure high profits for English landowners by keeping out foreign produce—but their effect now was to deepen the famine.

To his credit, Prime Minister Robert Peel fought for and won repeal of the Corn Laws in 1846, a battle that cost him his office soon afterward. As a practical matter, though, repeal made little difference. Many landlords and food brokers continued throughout the crisis to ship grain and livestock from Ireland to England; in effect, the starving were compelled to feed the relatively well-off. One Irish writer described the pain of watching "immense herds of cattle, sheep, and hogs . . . floating off on every tide, out of every one of our thirteen seaports, bound for England; and the landlords were receiving their rents, and going to England to spend them." To the exporters, though, it made sense to sell the food abroad, since the Irish had no money to buy it with anyway.

Another obstacle was the notion that too much help would spoil the Irish, making them lazy and dependent. Peel's government established several makework projects—building roads, harbors, and the like—but paid the laborers less than was necessary to feed a family. And the 1847 Poor Relief Act denied aid to any man who rented a plot of more than a quarter-acre, even when his miserable piece of ground produced nothing but blight.

Finally, there was a feeling among many British leaders, often bluntly expressed, that the famine might not be such a bad thing. "They live in a horrible island and have no history of their own worth the least

THE IRISH IN AMERICA

America midway through the 19th century was feeling the first great wave of what became a torrent of European immigration—1.6 million people pouring in during the 1840's alone. Of that number, nearly half were Irish peasants fleeing their ravaged homeland, with another 900,000 to follow during the 1850's. Reluctant to put their trust in farming again, most settled in northeastern cities, chiefly Boston, Philadelphia, and New York (which by 1860 was being called "the largest Irish city in the world").

Despite the glowing accounts many had heard, however, life in America proved to be anything but easy. Home was likely to be in a teeming tenement or shantytown, and steady work was hard to find. Most of the Irish were unskilled and semiliterate, and they faced the added barrier of anti-Catholic bigotry, which for years made "No Irish need apply" a familiar footnote on help-wanted signs.

But centuries of British rule had honed an ability to survive under adverse conditions. The men provided the cheap labor needed to build the nation's burgeoning system of canals and railroads; the women worked as housemaids or seamstresses; their children took whatever odd jobs they could find. Together they managed to make ends meet, and sometimes even to send back enough money to pay for relatives' passage and help

Irish pride—and political clout—were never more conspicuous than on Saint Patrick's Day, as indicated by this view of New York's gala 1874 parade.

support others who stayed behind.

The Irish also brought with them a talent for social and political organization, and they found in the neighborhood-based politics of the big cities an arena in which they could compete with growing success. In the early 1870's, Irish-born "Honest John" Kelly became head of New York's infamous Tammany Hall. By the 1880's both New York and Boston had Irish-born mayors, launching a succession of Irish-Americans who wielded big-city political power, including the power of patronage. As if by magic, the number of Irish in civil service jobs swelled—policemen, firemen, teachers, municipal clerks, and the like—and with this new access to the mainstream of American life came an end to the quest begun years before in the blighted potato fields of Ireland.

---

notice," the poet Alfred Lord Tennyson wrote of the Irish. "Could not anyone blow up that horrible island with dynamite and carry it off in pieces—a long way off?" Ireland was a conquered country, its populace kept in check by an army of occupation. To most absentee landlords, who might not see their estates from one year to the next, the tenants scarcely existed as human beings. When hundreds of thousands were evicted and their cottages "tumbled" to make space for cash crops or pasturage, no great outcry ensued.

In 1847 there was a good harvest, and the suffering abated somewhat. But the blight hit hard again in 1848 and renewed Ireland's miseries, bringing on not only more starvation but also devastating outbreaks of typhus, cholera, and scurvy. Lord John Russell, Peel's successor as prime minister, reacted by blaming the Irish themselves for remaining so dependent on the potato crop—"How can such a people be assist-

ed?" he complained—as though they had a choice.

At length, in 1849, the blight ended and Ireland returned to being merely a poor country, not a starving one. But among the survivors there remained a profound bitterness over British policies that had allowed a million and a half people to die, a bitterness that would not soon dissipate. As Ireland suffered through its long ordeal, a way of life was extinguished too. Before the Great Hunger, recalled a survivor, "there was no trade in the world then but some man of Beltany could try it—the best weavers in the country were there; there were masons, carpenters, coopers, thatchers and every kind of tradesman you could name in this townland; and after the famine years neither tale nor tidings of them was to be found."

Said another: "Sports and pastimes disappeared. Poetry, music, and dancing stopped. They lost and forgot them all."

Fires in Wisconsin

On the day Chicago burns, northern woodlands become a vast inferno

ONE OF AMERICA'S great disasters might just as well have happened in a void so far as public knowledge of it is concerned. This was the tragedy of the Peshtigo forest fire in Wisconsin, on the evening of October 8, 1871, during which some 1,200 people lost their lives. By an incomparable irony of fate, this happened also to be the night when, in the barn of a Mrs. O'Leary, a cow supposedly kicked over a lantern that set Chicago on fire and burned it down to the edge of the lake.

Peshtigo was a typical lumber town of the pineries. It stood along both sides of the small, swift Peshtigo River, which flowed six miles southeast to enter Lake Michigan's Green Bay. A narrow-gauge railroad connected the town with its port of Peshtigo Harbor. The town was new and booming. A fragrant blanket of sawdust already lay in its houses. It had been built quickly around the sawmill and factory of the Peshtigo Company, a well-heeled concern headed by William Butler Ogden, Chicago's first mayor.

If anything more was needed to guarantee the town's future, it was, of course, a railroad. The boon of rail connection was already assured by the fact that the Peshtigo Company's president, Ogden, was also an official of the Chicago and North Western Railroad, which even then, in the summer of 1871, was extending its line from Fort Howard, on Green Bay, northward through Peshtigo to the twin sawmill cities of Marinette, Wisconsin, and Menominee, Michigan.

Then, to cap the pride of the new industrial town, came Luther B. Noyes to found the *Marinette and Peshtigo Eagle*. The weekly, true enough, was printed in nearby Marinette, but it carried the news of both towns. Editor Noyes started his newspaper in June, with three months to spare before the biggest story he was ever to print blew into town.

The town was lively with newly arrived settlers, with loggers and mill hands and drummers. The immense forest, dominated by pine and spruce, began at the town's edge and ran west and north, beyond the knowing of men save for a few timber cruisers. It was broken by several openings near Peshtigo where homesteaders had settled. Because of their fine old maples, these openings were known as the Upper, the Middle, and the Lower Sugar Bush.

Though Luther Noyes was alert to chronicle every step made by the railroad construction crews, he kept one eye of his *Eagle* on the weather, noting more than once that "the woods are terribly dry," and he hailed with joy "a smart shower" on July 8, which he said was the first rain in more than two months. The rest of July and all of August and September were rainless.

On September 9 the *Eagle* reported that "Mulligan's brigade of choppers, axes in hand, armed and equipped as the railroad authorities direct, 32 strong, rank and file, passed this place on Saturday enroute for the north side of the river, to clear the track for the railroad between Peshtigo and Marinette." A week later the paper noted "heavy fires northeast of the village [Peshtigo] in the woods." Mulligan's brigade was doing its work. On September 30 the *Eagle* said: "Last Sunday all hands turned out to fight fire in the woods near the Peshtigo factory."

A feeling of unease became apparent in the local paper as heat and scattered fires continued to build.

October came in, bringing a new sharpness of the early morning air but becoming hot enough at midday. Here, as elsewhere, the coming of fall gave notice of plans for the social season. Yet the *Eagle's* weather eye remained clear. Editor Noyes did not like the look of things. On October 7 he remarked that "fires are still lurking in the woods around Marinette, ready to pounce upon any portion of the village in the event of a favorable wind." There was further foreboding in an observation by the Peshtigo correspondent who wrote: "Unless we have rain soon, God only knows how soon a conflagration may sweep this town." All was ready.

Peshtigo awoke on the eighth of October to find a copper sun in the sky and a village that lay baked and sultry in an autumn heat such as no man could recall. The air was deathly still. So were the large flocks of crows, pigeons, and smaller birds that were seen to form and fly away, making no sound. By noon the copper sun disappeared. A strange yellow half-light, which came from no visible source, reflected eerily from the sawdust streets and plank sidewalks.

The villagers attended church services, then sat down to heavy Sabbath dinners. At the Peshtigo Company's big boardinghouse the unmarried employees got an extra-good meal. The afternoon wore on, hot and still, and smoky enough to make eyes run. By

Numerous small conflagrations *culminated in a mass fire that ravaged 2,400 square miles of Wisconsin woodlands.*

suppertime black and white ashes, borne into town on a still-leisurely wind, were drifting through screenless windows and getting into the food.

John Cameron, a timber cruiser, had just returned to town from a trip up the river. He sat now on the steps of the company's boardinghouse while night closed down on this village in the forest. He could see a sullen red over the treetops to the southwest. The smoke gradually thickened. At about 9 o'clock he thought he could hear a new noise in the night, a low moaning, soft, deep, far off, as of a distant waterfall. He knew it wasn't water. Presently it grew into a roar. John Cameron had heard big winds in his time but

nothing quite like the sound that was now welling up back in the timber.

In the village the wind freshened to rustle the few trees that stood along the river. Then it fell, and a moody silence covered everything—everything, that is, save for that deep roar far off to the southwest. Or was it far off? Cameron was trying to make up his mind about it when a whirling slab of fire came down out of nowhere to fall fair in the sawdust street near the boardinghouse. It was followed by another slab of fire, then another. Cameron got to his feet to shout a warning. "Fire!" he yelled. As if in answer to his cry, fire poured down on the village like rain.

The sole refuge from the deadly flames for panic-stricken residents was the Peshtigo River, which ran through the middle of town.

In a flash—it seemed to Cameron—the splintered pine sidewalks were blazing. Startled men and women crowded onto doorsteps and into yards. The top of a house leaped with sudden flame, then tore away on the wind. Down the street trotted a legion of house and barn cats, stopping to look back, then trotting on again. A deer, wide-eyed and trembling, flitted out of the woods and stood stock-still in the midst of town dogs, who whimpered and sniffed but made no move to attack the wild creature.

Cameron and many other people started to flee down the east side of the river. Far too many others ran to the bridge, and there they were met by panic-stricken people from the west side. Humans, horses, cows, wagons—they met head-on. The bridge started to burn. Some were trampled underfoot; others fell into the water, where they might swim or drown. The sawmill by the east end of the bridge seemed to explode in flames. The logs in the millpond began to smoke, then to light up. Cameron and others saw things they never forgot. Forty years afterward, Cameron's voice choked as he told of watching pretty Helga Rockstad as she ran down a blazing sidewalk, her blonde hair streaming, and of seeing that long hair leap into flame that stopped Helga in her tracks. Searching the scene next morning, Cameron "found two nickel garter buckles and some gray-white ashes."

Though the river was being swept by sheets of fire, it was probably the safest place that night.

On the west side of town, Father Pernin, the Catholic priest, had been sensing danger. At nightfall he started to dig a trench in his yard. Into it he put his trunks, books, and church ornaments, covering them with earth. Then he paused to look around. Out of the southwest was rolling a firestorm that lighted the whole horizon. The priest turned his horse loose. Then he went into his house to notice that his pet jay was fluttering wildly in its cage, "uttering noises of alarm." Picking up the tabernacle with its revered objects, he ran into the yard, put them into the buggy,

got between the shafts, and started for the river. The fiery hurricane struck with full force. The priest was knocked down and got up to find the buggy had been blown over on its side. He ran for the river.

Standing in water to his neck, Father Pernin watched the bright tongues reach out over the stream to set the hair on the heads of men and women to burning. The heads quickly disappeared beneath the water. Some came up again, some didn't. But down the banks tumbled more humans seeking damp harbor from the storm. With them came cows, pigs, and dogs.

Down past the refugees in the river a burning log floated swiftly. More logs came after it, all afire and hissing from steam, forming a steady procession of danger because they knocked people off their legs, then moved on, still hissing. Then, among these long, floating torches came a sight that survivors were to remember—a cow swimming with the current, with a woman hanging onto one horn.

Clinging to logs were little Amelia Slaughter, age nine, and her mother and sister, dousing their heads when the ribbons of fire reached out, then bobbing up to breathe and watch the drama that surrounded them. They were fairly close to the factory when a mighty gust of wind hit the structure. The building seemed to explode and to vomit a torrent of fire in the form of thousands of blazing tubs and buckets and handles and clothespins, which tore through the night like small meteors. Refugees in the water now had to duck these missiles, which exploded in clouds of steam. The water was beginning to get warm, but it was still wet. It saved hundreds that night and drowned no more than 20. Between 9 and 10 o'clock the entire town was burned clean.

On its way to the village the fire had taken its toll in the Sugar Bush neighborhood southwest of town. Next day, "within thirty rods of L. H. Hill's barn," were found the bodies of 13 people, 23 horses, 15 sheep, 2 cows, 2 calves, and 1 dog. In the Middle Bush the Joseph Diedrick family of five was wiped out; Mrs. Diedrick was found standing upright and dead, leaning against a tree. In the Lower Bush Mr. and Mrs. Charles Towsley and three children died, but not from fire: their throats had been cut. William Curtis, a lone homesteader, was another who did not want to be burned alive. He was found in his well, the bucket chain wrapped tightly around his neck.

When the fire had swept the Sugar Bush and Peshtigo, it raced northeast, straight for the sawmill cities of Marinette and Menominee. The citizens there were digging trenches, hauling water, and wetting down roofs. Most of the women and children went to the docks to board steamers, which then put out into the lake to remain until next day. The two towns had seemed doomed, but the long range of sand hills south of Marinette deflected the fire to the west of the city, though it lashed out to destroy a planing mill, a sawmill, and the Catholic church. Menominee suffered little damage. The fire leaped the broad Menominee River, however, and went raging on to strike with deadly fury the settlement of Birch Creek, Michigan.

Dawn on the ninth was little more than twilight. The surface of Green Bay was so obscured that two men were stationed on the dock at Menominee, lifting and dropping heavy planks to serve as a signal of port to smoke-bound steamers bringing relief supplies from Escanaba. The sun could not be seen, yet the deep gloom lifted enough to show survivors that both sides of Green Bay were a desolation of charred trees, burning peat bogs, and communities where "the sandy streets glisten with a frightful smoothness, and calcined fragments are all that remain of hundreds of peaceful homes."

Late on October 9 rain began to fall, just about 26 hours too late. On the fourteenth the *Eagle* came out with a Fire Extra. It was a single sheet, one quarter the size of the paper's usual horse-blanket format. It carried the turned rule, the mourning mark of printers. Editor Noyes apologized for the dwarfed *Eagle* when there was so much news, and explained that his regular shipment of paper had not arrived from Chicago; and Chicago, so he heard, had suffered quite a fire of its own. So it had, and because of it, weeks were to pass before *Harper's Weekly*, the news magazine of the day, got around to the horror in the Wisconsin backwoods.

The Fury of a Firestorm

The swirling pillar of smoke and flame pulls in strong winds at treetop level and throws off burning firebrands higher up.

FIRE FIGHTERS CALL IT a blowup, that crucial moment when a forest fire suddenly, and often unexpectedly, explodes in its scope and intensity and is transformed into a seething mass of flames, known as a moving firestorm. Not even experts can predict when such a fire will develop, but recognizable danger signals are the presence of dry and plentiful fuel—wood or grass, for instance—and strong, low-level winds.

Once a firestorm has begun, it fuels itself. Rising convective heat forms a towering column—it can grow to a height of more than five miles—which usually leans forward a little, ahead of the fire itself. Oxygen-rich replacement air is sucked into the base of the column, where it mixes with the burning fuels and in turn rises. Great bubbles of unburned gases sometimes rise within a column before they explode into a fierce pyrotechnical display. In 1967, at the height of a severe drought, one fire in northern Idaho blackened 50,000 acres in nine hours.

Within the great fire itself, whirlwinds that can range up to 500 feet in diameter pick up whole trees and toss them around like straws. It is these large and small firebrands that perpetuate the fire as the whirlwinds hurl them far in advance—at times for a distance of several miles—of the moving wall of flame. Wherever firebrands land, they ignite their own small fires, called spot fires, which grow and eventually merge with the main firestorm and help to sustain its advance.

Fire fighters are helpless in the face of a firestorm. The intensity of the heat, the rapid advance, and a virtual rain of embers make a frontal attack impossible. There is nothing they can do but stand back at a safe distance and watch. A blowup will end when nature takes a hand, rains begin, the lethal winds at last die down, or the fire has consumed all the available fuel. Then, and only then, can the fire fighters move in and finish the job.

As downtown Chicago burns, *frantic throngs seek safety across a Chicago River bridge in this Currier and Ives print.*

The Great Chicago Fire

Thousands flee as Windy City is gutted by flames

WHERE IT STARTED has never been in doubt. The conflagration that would destroy some 18,000 buildings and leave an estimated 100,000 people homeless began early Sunday evening, October 8, 1871, in the barn behind Mr. and Mrs. Patrick O'Leary's frame house at 137 DeKoven Street on Chicago's West Side. Just how the fire started is quite another matter. Legend has it that Mrs. O'Leary's cow—probably the most famous animal in the city's history—grew restive while being milked and kicked over a lighted kerosene lamp, instantly setting the barn on fire. In her sworn testimony after the fire, however, Mrs. O'Leary insisted that she, Mr. O'Leary, and their five children were all in bed when the fire broke out.

Overlooked in this version of the fire's origins is the possible role of Dennis "Peg Leg" Sullivan, a one-legged drayman who was a boarder in the O'Learys'

house. Some historians of the disaster believe that Sullivan, of whose drinking Mrs. O'Leary supposedly disapproved, slipped into the barn for a few nips and accidentally set off the blaze while lighting his pipe. But in a sworn statement—an affidavit signed with an "X"—Sullivan maintained that he was not in the barn when the fire started. Rather, having seen the flames from across the street, he rushed over to the barn, yelled out "Fire! Fire!" and then went inside, where he tried to free Mrs. O'Leary's horse and cows. In the commotion, Sullivan lost his wooden leg when it stuck in a crack in the barn floor, but he managed to hobble out by clinging to the neck of a singed calf.

What really happened on that warm October night in Mrs. O'Leary's barn will probably never be known. But no matter what Mrs. O'Leary, her cow, or Peg Leg Sullivan may or may not have done to start the fire, the real culprits of the story were the flimsy wooden

Fire ended here

The charred heart *of the city— shaded on this map —included the business district and posh North Side neighborhoods.*

Chicago River North Branch

Chicago River

Chicago River South Branch

Fire started here

structures prevalent throughout Chicago as well as the drought that was turning the city, in the words of historian Robert Cromie, into "a huge potential bonfire waiting to be lit."

Before the fire, Chicago had 55 miles of pine-block streets and 651 miles of wooden sidewalks. Even the thoroughfares in the newly opened Union Stockyards were paved with wooden blocks to protect the hooves of cattle, sheep, and hogs on their way to the killing pens. The ships in the Chicago River were made of wood, and so were the bridges that spanned it. In Chicago, wrote Cromie, "there were wooden fences, wooden barns and outbuildings, wooden stables behind the wealthier homes—often containing a wooden carriage, hay, firewood and oil." An estimated 65 percent of the city's 60,000 buildings were constructed entirely of lumber. In the poorer residential areas, cheaply built wooden houses stood next to lumber and coal yards, paint sheds, furniture factories, and other industrial-use buildings filled with flammable goods. Kindling and wood shavings for starting fires were stored beneath houses or in ubiquitous backyard sheds. Fire and building codes, deficient to begin with, were routinely disregarded.

Chicago's fire hazards were not confined to the cottages of the poor. Although the city boasted some fine brick and masonry structures, many of its solid-looking buildings were actually jerry-built affairs hiding behind false fronts. On September 1, 1871, the

Chicago Tribune deplored the city's "miles of fire traps, pleasing to the eye, looking substantial, but all sham and shingles." (Ironically, the *Tribune*'s supposedly fireproof headquarters at Madison and Dearborn streets was itself destroyed in the Great Fire.)

Compounding the city's vulnerability was the drought—one of the worst in recent memory—that had plagued the Great Plains during the summer and into the fall of 1871. Between July 3 and the night of the fire, only 2½ inches of rain had fallen on Chicago, and even that fell in brief showers that did little to moisten the parched city.

Not surprisingly, under such conditions fires had been breaking out in Chicago all summer long. By the first week of October, the five-ton bell in the tower of Cook County Courthouse was sounding the fire alarm as many as seven times a day. Sometime between 10 P.M. and 11 P.M. on Saturday, October 7, the night before the main event, one of the worst fires in Chicago's history broke out in a lumber mill on Canal Street, also in the West Side, causing some $750,000 worth of damage over a four-block area. The 16-hour battle against the fire, in which all 29 of the city's fire-fighting companies participated, knocked out 4 companies, injured many firemen, and, coming at the end of a week of intense activity, left all of them exhausted. Engine Company No. 6, in fact, returned to its station from the Canal Street fire less than an hour before it was summoned to DeKoven Street to fight the fire in the O'Learys' barn. It is just possible that had the firemen not been so tired this latest blaze might not have flared out of control.

In the critical first hour of the fire, human error and confusion laid the groundwork for disaster.

Neighbors of the O'Learys first noticed the flames in the barn about 8:45 P.M. on Sunday evening. A DeKoven Street resident named Dennis Kogan (who may have been Peg Leg Sullivan's drinking companion in the barn) is said to have roused the O'Learys. Another neighbor, William Lee, rushed to the nearest fire alarm box, located at Goll's drug store three blocks away. Lee got there at about 9 P.M., but for reasons that are not clear, the alarm either was not sent out immediately or failed to register at the courthouse, headquarters of the city's telegraph fire alarm system. It was not until 9:20 P.M., when the watchman in the tower of Engine Company No. 6 noticed the fire, that an alarm was first sounded.

A fire watchman was also stationed in the cupola of the courthouse, but there too confusion reigned. William Brown, the telegraph operator on duty at the courthouse that night, noticed a light in the direction of DeKoven Street shortly after 9 P.M., but thinking that it was only a minor rekindling of the previous night's fire, he did nothing about it. Meanwhile, up in the cupola, watchman Mathias Schaffer not only waited until 9:30 P.M. to sound an alarm, he also misjudged the location of the fire and ordered Brown to ring the wrong alarm box. The result was that precious minutes were lost and vital equipment failed to reach the fire at a time when it still might have been contained.

Engine Company No. 6 thundered up DeKoven Street at 9:24 P.M., some 40 minutes after the blaze was first noticed. By then the fire was burning briskly and, fanned by a mild wind, had spread north from the O'Leary barn to nearby barns and sheds. Within 10 minutes, Engine Company No. 5 was also at the scene of the fire, but equipment failure promptly knocked it out of operation. Although other companies were on their way, the loss of Engine Company No. 5, was a serious setback for the firemen and for the city.

Any hopes that the blaze would be quickly contained were dashed at about 10 P.M., when the wind blew flaming brands and sparks five blocks north onto the steeple of St. Paul's Church, which ignited almost at once. St. Paul's next-door neighbor was a furniture-finishing factory packed with flammable goods. In short order, the blaze from the burning factory eclipsed the one that was roaring at the doomed church. From that point on, despite the valiant efforts of the fire fighters, there was little anyone could do to stop the northward advance of the flames.

Feeding on itself and on the heat of the flames, the wind blowing from the southwest gained so much strength that by 11 P.M. it was hurling burning debris two miles out into Lake Michigan. At 11:30 P.M., fanned by 60-miles-per-hour winds, the fire jumped the south branch of the Chicago River—which had been expected to check the blaze—and established a foothold in the city's South Side in the new stable of the Parmelee Omnibus and Stage Co. A half hour later the fire was sweeping through the saloons, bordellos, and shanties of a slum called Conley's Patch. With Conley's Patch gone, Chicago's downtown business district was next. One by one, some of the proudest buildings in the Midwest's fastest-growing city went up in flames, or were turned into stone shells that remained too hot to enter for days afterward. The

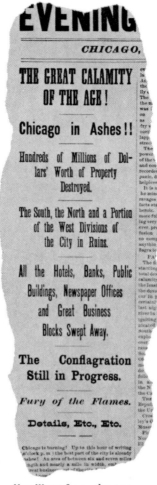

Headlines *from the one-page edition of the Chicago* Evening Journal, *issued while the fire still raged, dramatically outlined the city's plight.*

unfinished Grand Pacific Hotel, the post office, the customs house, the newly renovated Crosby's Opera House (scheduled to reopen with a gala concert on October 9), the giant Field & Lieter dry goods store, and the "fireproof" *Chicago Tribune* building were all razed.

Flaming debris had set small fires on the courthouse cupola as early as 10 P.M., but the watchman had been able to put them out at first. Eventually, the heat in the courthouse grew so intense that the windows melted and the masonry began to crumble. At 1:30 A.M. the men in the tower were forced to evacuate the building, and 35 minutes later the giant courthouse bell came crashing down into the basement.

As the *Chicago Post* reported on October 17, the downtown district at the height of the blaze was a scene of utter chaos: "Everywhere, dust, smoke, flame, heat, thunder of falling walls, crackle of fire, hissing of water, panting of engines, shouts, braying of trumpets, wind, tumult, and uproar." Thomas Byrne, a member of Hose Elevator Company No. 2, later recalled that "you couldn't see anything over you but fire. No clouds, no stars, nothing but fire."

Victories for the fire fighters were few and far between that night. A huge steam pump at the Oriental Flouring Mills was used to keep the mills and adjacent lumberyards under a steady stream of water for hours, a tactic that saved the mills and kept the fire from moving west. Blowing up wooden buildings in the path of the fire also prevented it from advancing south. And many Chicagoans were hoping that the main portion of the Chicago River would keep the blaze from spreading to the elegant residential quarters of the North Side, but that was not to be. In the early hours of Monday morning, buildings on the north bank of the river were catching fire, and soon the air over the North Side was as thick with flying sparks and debris as it was on the South Side. Judge Lambert Tree, a respected Chicago jurist and North Side resident, later recalled that "the size of some of this burning material hurled through the air [seemed] almost incredible." From the roof of his house, Tree watched as a flaming object "fully as large as an ordinary bed pillow" flew by.

As the fire worked its way through the North Side, a piece of burning debris ignited the roof of the city waterworks, whose pumps, protected behind thick stone walls, had been working flawlessly throughout

Scene on the prairie monday night.

The homeless taking refuge in a church

The on-the-scene sketches of Alfred R. Waud, published in the magazine Every Saturday, *provide vivid glimpses of Chicago in the midst of its worst disaster. With his writer-colleague Ralph Keeler, Waud rushed to Chicago from St. Louis on Monday, October 9, and got there in time to see parts of the city still in flames.*

On the night he arrived, Waud sketched refugees huddled on the prairie outside Chicago (above, left). The following Sunday, Waud and Keeler were stopped and questioned by a soldier on patrol (above, right). Earlier that day, the artist drew homeless people (right) taking refuge in a church spared by the fire. Chicago churches, noted Keeler, "were thronged on this Sabbath morning."

the night. Despite the solid wall, the building's interior flooring and woodwork were soon ablaze, and by 3 A.M. Monday, the pumps went out of action for good. Water would continue to flow for a while from the city's reservoirs, but Chicago had essentially lost its water supply. Although fire companies came to help from as far away as Milwaukee and Cincinnati, without water there was nothing they could do. Chicago's fire fighters had to put down their equipment and concede their city to the flames.

North Side residents, many of whom had awakened to watch the burning of the South Side, now watched in horror as the flames licked at their own doorsteps. Refugees from the South Side who had raced over the Chicago River bridges to the North Side were forced to run for their lives once more. All told, about 75,000 of Chicago's approximately 335,000 residents took to the streets during the course of the fire. Some attempted to flee west over bridges jammed with panicky horses,

overloaded vehicles, and refugees struggling with their personal belongings. Others headed north to Lincoln Park or east to the beaches along Lake Michigan. When the heat and smoke became too intense, many of those assembled on the beaches waded out as far as possible into the lake, keeping all but their heads submerged and ducking under the water when flaming timbers fell among them.

In the panic and confusion of the moment, people chose to save the strangest things: feather dusters, a fireplace mantel, a stovepipe, empty bird cages, even a wooden Indian. One resident was seen fleeing with a rooster perched on his shoulder. Servants of the wealthy were kept busy burying silverware and other valuables, including—amazingly enough—a number of grand pianos. Taking advantage of the pandemonium in the city, looters, both amateur and professional, set to work pillaging stores and private homes. To maintain law and order, Chicago mayor Roswell B. Mason

127

quickly called in United States Army troops under the command of Gen. Philip Sheridan, of Civil War fame. A special force of Pinkerton's Preventive Police was also brought in to patrol the burned districts and discourage looters in no uncertain terms. Any person caught stealing would be killed, stated Allan Pinkerton's directive to his men; "no Mercy Shall be shown them, but Death shall be their fate." Despite this stern approach, Chicago's crime rate soared for several weeks after the fire.

All day Monday the flames continued their relentless spread north. By noon they were lapping at the southern edges of Lincoln Park. By 5 P.M. the Chicago Avenue bridge, an important escape route to the west, had caught fire and was soon reduced to a twisted heap of glowing metal. Finally, about 11 P.M., as the winds died down and scattered showers began to fall, the Great Chicago Fire burned itself out, after raging for nearly 24 hours. The last building to go up in flames was a doctor's house on Fullerton Street, which at the time was the northern boundary of Lincoln Park. The heart of the once proud metropolis was reduced to little more than a heap of rubble and ashes.

For days after the fire, coal piles smoldered throughout the ruined city.

The fire is thought to have killed some 300 people, although many more bodies may have been lost in the debris and gone uncounted. Flames consumed an area of 2,124 acres and destroyed an estimated $196 million worth of property. But these figures do not even begin to convey the extent of Chicago's ruin, for those burned acres represented the very center of the

city's commercial, cultural, and civic life. In a one-page, one-story edition, Monday's *Evening Journal* tallied the city's losses: "All the principal hotels, all the public buildings, all the banks, all the newspaper offices, all the places of amusement, nearly all the great business edifices, nearly all the railroad depots, the water works, the gas works, several churches, and thousands of private residences and stores have been consumed. The proud, noble magnificent Chicago of yesterday is to-day a mere shadow of what it was." On the same page, however, an upbeat Board of Trade announced that its directors would be meeting the next day on Canal Street to help put the stricken city back on its feet.

Indeed, Chicago began recovering from its immolation with remarkable speed. Western Union resumed its telegraph service Tuesday morning. By Thursday, all the city's major newspapers were back in operation. Within eight days, the main water supply was reactivated, and emergency gas was being piped in from the West Side through temporary connections to the burned districts. Banks and businesses set up headquarters in tents and sheds and quickly went back into operation. Typical of the spirit of the city in its time of crisis was the sign put up by William Kerfoot on his makeshift real estate office: "All gone but wife, children, and energy."

Although some merchants took advantage of the situation to send prices skyrocketing, tales of the generosity and resilience displayed by Chicagoans abound. One West Side butcher gave meat away to people who could not afford to pay for it. The owner of a new South Side building cut rents by 10 percent, even for tenants who had already signed leases. Solomon A. Smith, president of the Merchants Savings, Loan & Trust Co., managed to save his bank's cash and secu-

rities from the fire but not its records. Smith nevertheless repaid his depositors in full on their word alone. The Chicago fire even spawned a new type of credit scheme. Because his furniture store had come through the disaster unscathed, a grateful John Smyth devised the installment plan to help his hard-pressed customers refurnish their homes. Smyth's version of the plan, however, was a model of philanthropy: he never took a penny in interest from anybody.

In no time at all, Chicago mobilized to feed, shelter, and care for an army of homeless people.

Four days after the fire, Mayor Mason charged the Chicago Relief and Aid Society—an organization founded in 1850 for the purpose of feeding and sheltering the poor—with the monumental task of providing for Chicago's homeless. By the time the society closed its books on the disaster on April 30, 1874, it had overseen the distribution of nearly $5 million in cash, goods, and services to victims of the fire. It found jobs for more than 20,000 workers, provided medical care to some 90,000 patients, and vaccinated 64,000 people against smallpox. In one of its most astonishing achievements, the society built 5,000 homes, providing shelter for 25,000 people—all within just over a month of the fire. The houses cost $125 each to build and furnish but were given free of charge to the needy.

The Great Chicago Fire triggered a national and international outpouring of charitable contributions. Help seemed to be coming in from everywhere: President Ulysses S. Grant sent $1,000 from his personal funds; the newsboys of Cincinnati donated two days' pay; the United States Army quartermaster stores contributed 10,000 blankets; even the inmates and guards of the Charlestown State Prison in Boston raised exactly $617.32 for the Chicago relief effort. Food shipments came in by rail from the rest of Illinois as well as from Iowa and Missouri. Chicago's great commercial rivals put competitiveness aside and made large contributions to the city's restoration: New York City sent nearly $1 million; Boston, more than $400,000; and Philadelphia, more than $300,000. Money also poured in from countries around the world. The most generous contributor was England, which, in addition to a cash gift of $435,000, sent 12,000 books to replenish Chicago's libraries. (Some of the volumes were autographed by their donors, who included such luminaries as Alfred Lord Tennyson, John Ruskin, Thomas Carlyle, and Queen Victoria herself.)

Six weeks after the fire, 212 brick and stone buildings were going up in Chicago's South Side. Within a year, the burned districts of the city had acquired some $40 million worth of new buildings, most of them bigger, finer, and more solidly constructed than those they replaced. By 1880 Chicagoans had wiped out all traces of the fire, except for the memory. From the ashes of its greatest catastrophe arose a stronger, safer, and prouder Chicago than ever before—and an architectural showcase for the entire nation.

After the fire, *downtown Chicago was little more than a rubble-strewn wasteland. In this panoramic view of the ruins, the walls of St. Paul's Universalist Church stand at left. Behind and to the right of the church are the shells of the post office, courthouse, and Board of Trade buildings.*

The Year of the Locusts

Billions of ravenous insects infest prairie homesteads

"AUGUST 1, 1874, is a day that will always be remembered by the then inhabitants of Kansas. . . . For several days there had been quite a few hoppers around, but this day there was a haze in the air and the sun was veiled almost like Indian summer. They began, toward night, dropping to earth, and it seemed as if we were in a big snowstorm where the air was filled with enormous-size flakes."

These are the words of Mary Lyon, a Kansas pioneer woman who witnessed and wrote about the worst invasion of locusts—grasshoppers, or "hoppers," as the locals called them—in United States history. During the summer of 1874, and during each of the following three summers, hordes of Rocky Mountain locusts embarked on a feeding frenzy of unprecedented proportions from the Dakota Territory to Texas and from the Rockies to the Mississippi River.

After several years of drought and poor harvests, the farmers of the Great Plains had been anticipating a change of fortune in 1874. But their hopes were shattered by the sudden arrival of the locusts—more than 120 billion of them in a swarm that measured 100 miles wide, 300 miles long, and up to a mile deep. Carried on the winds from their breeding grounds just east of the Rockies, the insects brought destruction and ruin wherever they alighted.

From afar, the dark cloud of locusts could be mistaken for an oncoming dust storm or perhaps an unseasonable squall. But up close, there was no mistaking them. "When they came down," remembered one eyewitness, "they struck the ground so hard it sounded almost like hail." On the ground, they formed a living, breathing carpet, inches deep and stretching as far as the eye could see. As they ate, the unsettling noise of millions of tiny insect jaws hard at work could be heard far and wide.

The corn crop was usually the first to go, quickly followed by other grains, fruits, and vegetables. The locusts would even eat bulbs and root vegetables out of the ground—onions seemed to be a special favorite.

Once the cultivated crops had been consumed, the omnivorous insects turned to weeds and the leaves and bark of trees. When these, too, were gone, they attacked wooden tool handles and fence slats, leather harnesses, window curtains, mosquito netting, and even the clothes on people's backs.

Locusts crawled through hair and down shirts and dresses. Men had to tie strings around their trouser cuffs to keep the insects from crawling up their legs. The pests invaded the farmhouses and ate everything inside. "And on retiring to bed," recalled Mary Lyon, "we had to shake them out of the bedding."

Chickens and turkeys ate locusts until they got sick; hogs and poultry that fed on the insects took on their flavor and became completely inedible. Locust excrement colored rivers and streams a dark brown; locust carcasses polluted the wells. The locust plague even hampered railroad service. Heaps of insects crushed by a train made the rails slimy

Hungry locusts threaten fields in Wright County, Iowa, during the summer of 1874. In a vain effort to drive off the pests with smoke, farmers ignite stacks of straw covered with damp grass.

AN ANCIENT NEMESIS STILL HAUNTS MANKIND

Locust swarms have plagued human settlements since prehistoric times. One of the earliest depictions of the pest—an Egyptian tomb painting dating from the 15th century B.C.—shows a locust perched on top of a papyrus blossom. Beginning with the Egyptian plague described in the Book of Exodus, the Bible mentions grasshoppers and locusts more than 30 times. The insects also appear in the art of the Aztecs and of other American Indian tribes, evidence that locusts infested the New World long before the arrival of Europeans.

During their nonmigratory phase, plague locusts live as solitary individuals and do not stray far from their breeding areas. But given the right conditions—enough rain over the breeding grounds to allow many eggs to hatch at the same time and enough food to allow many insects to mature together—the young locusts undergo a transformation. Their color changes, they become more active, and they begin to seek one another out—the first steps in the development of a wide-ranging and destructive swarm.

The Rocky Mountain locusts that blighted the Great Plains more than a century ago may well be extinct today—no living specimen has been reported since the early 1900's. But other locust species still swarm periodically—and to devastating effect—in Africa, Asia, the western United States, and elsewhere in the world. Fortunately, the severity of modern invasions has been reduced by the use of pesticides. Scientists are also experimenting with other, safer methods, including genetic engineering, to control these age-old pests.

Oblivious to the threat the insects pose, an Ethiopian child scampers through a swarm of locusts during a 1968 invasion.

and caused the wheels to lose traction. Railroad crews had to cover the tracks with sand in order to get the train moving again.

Typically, hoppers remained in one place until there was no food left. This usually took only two or three days, but sometimes the swarm stayed on for as long as a week waiting for the winds to carry them to new pastures and orchards. Behind them, the locusts left ravaged farmhouses, barren fields, and buried in the soil, the eggs that would produce the plague's next generation. The following spring, armies of young, wingless locusts would emerge from the ground and after a period of rest, begin to eat everything in sight. When they had stripped their birthplace, the whole colony of still wingless hoppers would embark on a destructive trek in search of food. Eventually the young insects would sprout wings and continue their depredations from the air.

Prairie farmers tried everything they could think of to rid themselves of the locusts. They waved sticks at them, covered garden crops with blankets, poured salt solution on grain, burned smudge fires, let loose their cows and pigs to trample the invaders—all to no avail. Somewhat more successful were the various specially designed machines—hopperdozers some of them were called—that crushed, burned, or trapped the insects on the ground.

Nothing the settlers came up with, however, did much to reduce the swarm or to minimize the damage it caused. In the great locust invasion of 1874 and in the invasions of the next three summers, more than $200 million worth of crops were destroyed, and the lives and livelihoods of thousands of homesteaders were threatened. Some of the homesteaders saw the plague as divine punishment; others viewed it as a sign from God to return to the East, and did so. But the vast majority, unwilling or too poor to go anywhere else, clung to their homesteads and waited for help.

Fearing that the locust plague might discourage potential immigrants, some public officials and local promoters in the West attempted at first to downplay the disaster. Despite their efforts, the news got out, and food, clothing, and cash for the beleaguered farmers came pouring in from the East. When it became clear that relief work was being hampered by corruption as well as by the isolation of many of those most in need, the army stepped in to distribute emergency supplies, and in the process saved many lives.

By 1877 the locust crisis was waning. Farmers noted that the hoppers seemed "used up." The next year, there were few of them to be found. For reasons that remain unclear, the decline of the Rocky Mountain locust continued for the rest of the century. A small swarm was recorded in 1892, but since the early 1900's no living Rocky Mountain locust has been reported. Locusts still plague many parts of the world, including the western United States, but *Melanoplus spretus,* the species that darkened skies and caused so much havoc more than a century ago, might well be extinct—or, say entomologists, the ravenous hoppers might just be lurking out of sight in some remote part of the country, waiting to swarm again someday.

Man and beast toil to cultivate the dry soil of Shensi, one of five Chinese provinces ravaged by the famine of 1876–79.

Famine in China

Hunger and privation lead to violence, cannibalism, and the death of millions

STARVATION HAS BEEN no stranger to the people of China. Throughout most of the nation's recorded history, famines, often triggered by drought, have exacted a terrible toll. But no drought-related famine in recent times has caused more suffering and death than the one that ravaged northern China for three long years beginning in the autumn of 1876.

At best, rainfall in northern China is scant and irregular. Droughts are common, and until recent decades, the region's farmers produced barely enough food, even in good years, to feed a burgeoning population. A year without summer rains—a single failed wheat crop—could spell ruin.

To see them through bad years, the Chinese long relied on a network of surplus grain storage warehouses, but by the late 19th century the ancient granary system had virtually ceased functioning, a victim of neglect, hard times, and corrupt management. At the same time, China's primitive transportation system was in such a state of disrepair that moving relief grain into the interior of the country was a slow and difficult process. With a population of more than 100 million straining an already fragile agricultural system and with an inadequate relief system to fall back on, northern China in the 1870's teetered on the brink of disaster.

The event that finally pushed the region over the brink was a drought that began in 1873. For three years little or no rain fell in the five northern Chinese provinces of Shantung, Chihli, Honan, Shansi, and Shensi. In the winter of 1875, the imperial court in Peking, concerned at the lack of rain in the capital and in other parts of Chihli Province, ordered that special prayers be recited in the state temples. The eight-year-old emperor Kuang-hsü himself implored the gods for rain on behalf of his people.

The next spring, when the rains still had not come, the city magistrate of Ch'ing-chou in Shantung Province resorted to ancient Chinese methods of ending droughts. He issued a decree forbidding the people to eat meat. Then he had his attendants bind his neck, wrists, and feet in chains as a sign of contrition, and thus hobbled, he made his way through the city to the main temple to pray for rain. Forming a procession behind the magistrate was a throng of worshipers decked in wreaths of willow leaves and twigs, the traditional antidrought regalia.

But no matter how fervently the people prayed, it did not rain, and the earth grew more parched and barren. For months, dry winds blew over the plain of Chihli and northern Shantung, burying in dust the scant stalks of wheat that had managed to break through the hardened soil. After three years of drought, crop failures, and soaring food prices, people were starving to death in Shantung by the autumn of 1876.

Among the crowds of peasants praying for rain in Ch'ing-chou the previous spring was a Baptist missionary from Wales named Timothy Richard, who had arrived in northern China six years earlier. Deeply moved by the plight of the people, but also seeing in the drought an opportunity to further his missionary work, Richard traveled throughout Ch'ing-chou prefecture posting yellow placards on town gates with the message that "if the people wanted rain, the best way was to turn from dead idols to the living God."

Richard's mission met with some success, but the situation he encountered in his travels was growing more desperate by the day. In his autobiography Richard reports that in one village he met a group of small boys whose only food was thistles and leaves. As the situation worsened, reports of children sold and women forced into prostitution or slavery proliferated. Hungry villagers turned to robbery, pillaging, and even murder. The government, always fearful of civil disorders and mass uprisings, responded with violent measures of its own—either summary beheadings or the dreaded "sorrow cage," in which criminals were left to die of starvation.

Hunger *was a part of life in China for millennia. This image of a famine victim dates from the 16th century.*

When the last of the grain was gone in 1876, people began to eat "elm bark, buckwheat stalks, turnip leaves, and grass seeds," according to a report Richard wrote to the Baptist Missionary Society in London. "When these are exhausted, they pull down their houses, sell their timber, and it is reported everywhere that many eat the rotten kaoling reeds (sorghum stalks) from the roof. . . . Thousands eat them, and thousands die because they cannot get even that. They sell their clothes and children." With their houses gone, famine victims in some villages sought shelter against the winter cold in enormous underground pits capable of holding as many as 240 persons. Under such crowded conditions, many died, often in a matter of weeks, but vacancies were quickly filled.

Thousands of starving peasants took to the roads in search of something— anything—to eat.

Those who could, fled to Manchuria in the north or Kiangsu in the south, where food was still available. Those who lacked the means or the strength to leave their homes faced a grim future. In some of the smaller villages of Ch'ing-chou prefecture, Richard reported a mortality rate as high as 90 percent. In larger villages, as many as 300 out of 500 families were wiped out. So many corpses piled up in Shantung that eventually they had to be buried in communal pits called "ten thousand men holes." Before it was all over, some 500,000 people died of famine in Shantung Province alone.

In *Famine in China and the Missionary*—an important source for the events of the Great Famine and Timothy Richard's role in it—author P. Richard Bohr reports that as early as June 1876, the court in Peking had begun to provide emergency financial aid to the provinces of Chihli, Shantung, and Honan. In Chihli, grain from government granaries was distributed to the needy, and overdue land taxes went uncollected. As the famine wore on, the collection of land taxes was suspended or deferred in all the stricken provinces, and famine relief taxes were levied on areas not affected by the disaster. The government also encouraged the well-to-do to contribute to the relief effort, and people of means throughout China responded with great generosity.

In addition to money, the Chinese government requisitioned grain from provinces that could supply it, but given the terrible condition of China's roads and its lack of rail transportation at the time, moving the grain to where it was most needed often proved impossible. There was plenty of wheat in the Shantung port of Chefoo, "but that doesn't help a population 200 miles away," reported the *North-China Herald* on July 22, 1876. Not only were the roads bad, but the centuries-old Grand Canal, on which Shantung depended for access to the rice paddies of the lower Yangtze Valley, had become almost unnavigable as a result of the drought and decades of uncontrolled silting and neglect.

From his base at the famine's epicenter in Ch'ingchou, Timothy Richard soon realized that much more had to be done to relieve the people's suffering than the Chinese government was willing or able to do. "I felt that I could not desert the place to save myself," he wrote, "nor could I keep any money while the poor, to whom God had sent me, were starving." Thus began Richard's landmark campaign to raise funds and distribute them among China's famine victims.

Since Richard had no way of obtaining or shipping grain, he limited his operation to the distribution of cash—starting with his own meager savings—to help the needy buy what little food was available. His goal throughout the campaign was to help the neediest cases in the worst-off districts and to distribute what money he had as efficiently as possible. Richard also sought to work with the government in order to avoid offending Chinese sensibilities or giving the appearance of fomenting rebellion among the people.

People around the world heard of the tragedy unfolding in northern China and were moved to help.

To raise funds among China's foreign community, Richard arranged to have his accounts of the Shantung famine published in Shanghai's foreign press. As a direct result of his dispatches, the Shantung Famine Relief Fund Committee was founded in Shanghai in early March 1877 and immediately began soliciting money from the city's foreign residents. Similar organizations were eventually set up throughout China. Less than a year later, the China Famine Relief Fund, an offshoot of the Shanghai committee, issued an

FAMINE NIGHTMARE IN BRITISH INDIA

While millions were dying in China during the famine of 1876–79, a similar tragedy was unfolding in India. As in China, India's great famine was the direct result of drought.

India has always depended for its subsistence on yearly rains called monsoons. Today the threat of famine has abated in India, but in the not-too-distant past, when the rains failed, disaster often followed.

In 1875 and again in 1876, the monsoons did not come to southern India. As millions of acres of parched farmland went unplanted, food prices skyrocketed and the poor began to starve. To make matters worse, the British government was slow to abandon a free trade policy that prevented local officials from lowering food prices or otherwise interfering with the private trade of food. Although

some relief programs were started, this basic government policy doomed millions to starvation and death.

In an article dated August 1, 1877, and quoted in the August 30 edition of *The New York Times*, the editor of the Madras *Times* described in grim detail southern India's misery: "One gentleman passing down a valley in the Wynaad District counted 29 dead bodies on the road. A coffee planter seeking shelter from the rain in a hut found six decomposing corpses in it. On any day and every day mothers may be seen in the streets of Madras offering their children for sale. . . . Information has reached me from Bangalore of two cases of cannibalism already."

In the autumn of 1877, the famine spread to the north too, and the death toll continued to climb. By the time the crisis ended in late 1878, at least 5 million people had died of starvation and disease. From this disaster, however, grew India's Famine Code, a system for detecting the early stages of a famine emergency and providing relief to those in greatest need.

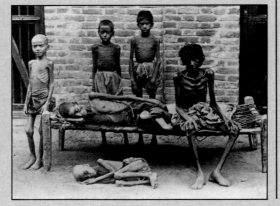

Little more than living skeletons, this Indian family was photographed during the famine that claimed some 1.5 million lives in the states of Bengal and Orissa in 1866–67. The first sign of a famine disaster in India was often the migration of starving families like this one from the countryside to the cities.

urgent appeal for help to Great Britain and the United States. A London committee was founded, and soon money began to pour into China from Britain, the United States, Europe, and the foreign communities of East Asia—the first time a Chinese famine had sparked a coordinated international relief effort.

Richard labored in Shantung through 1876 and most of 1877, but during that time famine had also been raging in Chihli and spreading into Honan, Shensi, and especially Shansi. In late November 1877, confident that the worst was over in Shantung, Richard shifted his charitable and missionary operations to Shansi, now the focus of the disaster.

As in the other afflicted provinces, the famine in Shansi was drought related, but the province's mountainous terrain and poor soil made it even more vulnerable than its neighbors to the effects of drought. In 1877, after years of inadequate rainfall, the spring wheat crop failed, and the few shoots that did grow were eaten by locusts. To make matters worse, landlocked Shansi depended on carts, animals, and human muscle to bring in goods from outside the province. With its pack animals increasingly being killed for food and its tortuous roads often impassable or controlled by brigands, it was more difficult to send relief grain to Shansi than to the other famine provinces. Not surprisingly, the mortality and misery Richard encountered there surpassed even that of Shantung at the height of its agony.

In late January 1878, Richard embarked on a journey through the center of Shansi to assess the extent of the disaster. He traveled with a servant because "it was not safe to travel alone, for many of the starving had become cannibals." The diary Richard kept during his trip provides a graphic picture of Shansi's ordeal. On January 30 he "passed two men apparently just dead. One had good clothes on, but had died of hunger." Further on, "there was a man of about forty walking in front of us, with unsteady steps like a drunken man. A puff of wind blew him over to rise no more." Wolves and foxes, Richard noted, grew fat on human corpses left unburied. Approaching the gate of a city, he saw on one side of it "a pile of naked dead men, heaped on top of each other as though they were pigs in a slaughter-house. On the other side of the

"Suicides in consequence of the famine" is the title of the drawing at left. Starving Chinese "hang themselves from beams, or throw themselves into the rivers."

Imperial government officials (right) distribute aid to the needy, but "the territory is wide and the people are numerous." These poignant scenes of the Great Famine were drawn by a Chinese artist and appeared in a booklet issued in China and, with a translated text, in England to help raise relief funds.

Recalling how Jesus fed the multitudes, Timothy Richard, a missionary hero of the Great Famine, devised a safe way of distributing aid without inciting riots: he had the crowds sit down—as they do at the early 20th-century Chinese soup kitchen shown above.

gate was a similar heap of dead women, their clothing having been taken away to pawn for food." In one village he heard "stories at the inn . . . of parents exchanging their children as they could not eat their own, that men dared not go to the pits for coal as mules, donkeys, and their owners were liable to be killed and eaten."

After two weeks, Richard returned to his base at T'ai-yuan fu, doubting his sanity and thankful for "a respite from the awful sights which we had seen from day to day on our travels." He sent his diary to the Shanghai committee in order to help them elicit sympathy and funds from that city's foreign community.

The winter of 1877 was bitterly cold in Shansi, and as coal prices rose, people tore down their houses and burned the timber in an effort to keep warm. When their last food supplies were gone, they resorted to eating roots, twigs, tree bark, and eventually sawdust, mud, and even cakes made of ground stone mixed with grain or grass seeds—a recipe that in many cases proved fatal. Typhoid fever also broke out that winter, adding thousands to Shansi's death toll. As in Shantung the previous year, those who could tried to flee the province; the rest stayed behind to wage an often futile battle against hunger and death.

Thievery and mob violence became commonplace in the province. Women and children were sold for pennies in the markets, while desperate parents often killed their starving children before committing suicide. Although cannibalism had been reported in other famine provinces, the practice of eating–and selling–human flesh became especially widespread in Shansi.

THE YELLOW RIVER—CHINA'S ANCIENT SORROW—FLOODS AGAIN

Barely a decade after one of the worst famines on record decimated northern China, disaster hit the area once more. On September 28, 1887, the Hwang Ho, or Yellow River, burst from its banks—with fatal results for Honan and Shantung provinces.

Time and again throughout history, the Yellow River—long known as China's Sorrow—has inundated vast areas, leaving millions dead or homeless. It is not an especially powerful river, but owing to a unique set of circumstances, it is a deadly one.

The Yellow River rises in Tibet and follows a circuitous, nearly 3,000-mile-long course to the Gulf of Chihli, an arm of the Yellow Sea. Along the way, it crosses the strange yellow world of the loess plateau. This huge territory straddling Shansi and Shensi provinces is blanketed by the wind-borne, yellowish silt called loess that gives the Yellow River—and seemingly everything else in the region—its distinctive color. By the time the river enters the fertile North China Plain in Honan Province, it carries a yearly average of 1.6 billion tons of silt, making it the world's muddiest river.

As the Yellow River winds its way across the great alluvial plain to the sea, its grade drops, its current slows, and as a result, much of its sediment is deposited in the riverbed itself. So instead of cutting an ever deeper channel, as many aging rivers do, the Yellow is constantly raising its own bed and threatening to overflow its banks.

From time immemorial, the Chinese have tried to contain the river within a system of dikes built of silt and reinforced with enormous bales of sorghum, or kaoling, stalks. (Kaoling roots have a remarkable ability to hold silt and thus create an effective barrier against the river.) The ramparts were positioned as far as eight miles back from either bank, so that if the river overflowed, it would be contained within the wide corridor. But this strategy had two basic flaws: the dikes had to be built ever wider and higher as the floor of the corridor rose with each flooding, and the kaoling bales deteriorated rapidly and required costly repairs year after year. By the 19th century the dikes often stood 30 feet high and 100 feet wide at the base, while the river meandered across the plain as much as 30 feet *above* the surrounding farms and villages.

In the past 3,000 years, the Yellow River has flooded the North China Plain some 1,500 times, but never with more destructiveness than in late September 1887. Exact information about the disaster was hard to come by at first. Communications in China were spotty at best, and few foreigners ventured very far inland. It is known that there had been heavy rains, and that the river had been rising. Even before the break, many had warned that trouble was imminent. But the

Northern China has known more than its share of tragedy. The map at right shows the five provinces affected by the Great Famine of 1876–79, as well as the winding course of the Yellow River. The place names used are those that were current in the late 19th century.

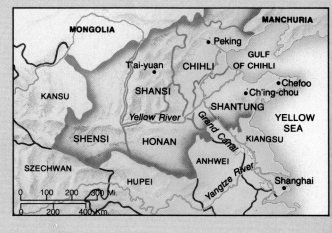

The New York Times of July 6, 1878, quoted a letter from the Roman Catholic bishop of Shansi, Monsignor Louis Monagatta, in which he reported that "until lately the starving people were content to feed on the dead; but now they are slaughtering the living for food. The husband eats his wife; parents are eating their children; and in their turn sons and daughters eat their dead parents."

By late August 1879—after some 5.5 million people had died in Shansi—the crisis abated. In October the drought in northern China finally broke, and the region began to emerge from its long nightmare. Between 1876 and 1879, as many as 13 million people are estimated to have died of starvation or famine-related disease, exhaustion, or violence in northern China. Millions more suffered incalculable hardships.

Richard concluded his relief work in late summer 1879 and resumed his regular missionary activities. During the Great Famine, he and his fellow Protestant relief workers saved as many as 250,000 lives; Roman Catholic workers rescued thousands more. Clearly these figures are nothing in comparison with the total number who died in the catastrophe; they are even "a mere drop in the bucket," as Richard noted, "compared with what the Chinese Government itself did." But they do represent a noble and farsighted effort, and for launching that effort Richard is justly remembered as the founder of famine relief in China. In the years after the famine, Richard devoted much of his time and energy to devising and promoting a modernization plan that he hoped would free China once and for all of the terrible spectre of famine.

official in charge of maintaining the dikes refused to take action; the timing, he claimed, was inauspicious.

The cost of his refusal became known to the outside world only in bits and pieces. On October 27, one month after the flood began, the English-language North-China Herald carried this bulletin: "At the moment of going to press we learn that the Yellow River, which has burst its banks over a very long line, has flooded an immense expanse of country. . . . The loss of life is enormous."

Gradually, the details were filled in. At a sharp bend near the city of Chengchow in Honan, not far from the site of a major break two years earlier, the river had crashed through a decrepit dike wall during the evening of September 28. From a few feet, the gap opened to 100 yards as the walls crumbled, then to more than half a mile when an entire section gave way. Below the breach, the riverbed turned to mud as China's Sorrow surged freely across the flat North China Plain. Towns vanished. Houses were silted over in minutes. An American engineer visiting the scene days later reported seeing "a lake having the superficial area of Lake Ontario"—about 10,000 square miles. At least 1,500 communities were swept away: their inhabitants either drowned or were clinging desperately to anything in sight.

When at last the breach was plugged

After a disastrous Yellow River flood in 1935, workers perform an age-old task: assembling bundles of willow branches (foreground) and bales of kaoling stalks (upper right) for the repair of a breached levee.

and the immense lake began to recede, the damage left behind was almost beyond belief. According to some reports, more than 900,000 people—perhaps as many as 2.5 million—died. Nearly 3 million were missing or homeless.

For the survivors, the next two years were a time of famine, disease, and privation. Nonetheless, in the spring of 1888 an army of workers was rebuilding the dikes; within a year, the task was completed. But restored dikes did not mean that the Yellow River was contained. In the mid-

1930's great floods killed tens of thousands of people and left millions more homeless. In 1938, in an effort to halt the invading Japanese, the Chinese Nationalist army had one of the levees blown up; the ensuing flood killed 500,000 Chinese.

Modern technology has brought hope to those who live at the Yellow River's mercy. But China's Sorrow remains, meandering across the same great plain as it has since memory began. Will it burst free again? Only time, and science, will tell.

Krakatoa Erupts

Earth shaken by the greatest volcanic blast on record

ON SUNDAY AFTERNOON, August 26, 1883, a distant rumbling was heard in the Dutch colonial city of Batavia (now Djakarta, Indonesia). It sounded like salvos of cannon fire—or was it perhaps thunder?—echoing from the west, yet no wars were being fought and the sky was clear. By evening the rumbling had swelled to a thunderous roar. Houses began to shake and windows shattered. People fled their homes in panic. Bright flashes lit the western sky, and foul-smelling smoke choked the city.

At dawn on Monday the sky was still black and the explosions resounded louder than ever. Shortly after noon a giant wave smashed into Batavia's harbor. And all day long the skies rained ash, the obliterating fallout from one of history's mightiest volcanic upheavals.

The eruption of Krakatoa, a triple-cone volcanic island in the Sunda Strait between the Indonesian islands of Java and Sumatra, cast a destructive shadow across 300,000 square miles of southeast Asia. It blew some five cubic miles of searing ash and pumice into the sky and dropped chunks of red-hot debris—some of them eight feet across—over an area larger than France. Great rafts of pumice, a volcanic glass so light it floats, drifted as far away as 7,500 miles across the Indian Ocean, clogging shipping lanes there. The eruption sent atmospheric shock waves circling around the earth more than six times and caused a plume of black vapor to rise as high as 50 miles into the atmosphere. A haze of fine dust caught by the prevailing upper winds temporarily lowered the earth's mean annual temperature and colored sunsets around the world for years.

Krakatoa's detonations set trains of tsunamis, or seismic sea waves, roaring through the Sunda Strait, wiping the shoreline clean of human habitation. Nearly 300 villages were washed away or seriously damaged, and more than 36,000 people lost their lives. Giant waves damaged riverboats in Calcutta, some 2,000 miles away, and raised tides in the English Channel, halfway around the world.

The volcano's final paroxysm, at 10:02 Monday morning, August 27, was per-

The dying Krakatoa *emits a column of ash and vapor thousands of feet high in this 19th-century engraving based on a photograph dated May 27, 1883, three months before the volcano blew itself apart.*

haps the loudest noise ever heard by the human ear. Much of the island had already blown itself away; now the remainder collapsed into its foundations, with an estimated explosive force of 1 million Hiroshima bombs. The report was heard across 7 percent of the earth's surface. People living in central Australia, some 2,250 miles away, mistook Krakatoa's blast for rifle shots. Within four hours the sound had traveled nearly 3,000 miles to the tiny island of Rodriguez in the Indian Ocean, where police chief James Wallis reported hearing "the distant roars of heavy guns."

For all its violence, Krakatoa's upheaval did not come as a total surprise. No region on earth is so prone to volcanic mayhem as Indonesia. At least 76 peaks in the Indonesian archipelago have erupted in historic times and many hundreds more in the dim geologic past. In 1815 a massive convulsion shattered the summit of Tambora, in eastern Indonesia; as many as 90,000 people may have died directly in the blast or as a result of the ensuing tsunamis and famine.

Located in the collision zone between two of the great plates that make up the earth's crust, Krakatoa had already undergone several eruptions, including a prehistoric cataclysm that reshaped the Sunda Strait. In that outburst, the island's original 6,000-foot-high cone vanished into dust, leaving behind several small island fragments around the rim of the caldera, or cavity, that the volcano's collapse had created. Ash and lava continued to bubble up from the caldera's southern rim, until a new, half-mile-high cone, called Rakata, was created. Eventually two smaller cones developed to the north and united with Rakata to form Krakatoa Island.

For centuries the volcano remained quiet. Then in 1680 the smallest of Krakatoa's cones, Perboewatan, came to life. This eruption, which killed off the island's vegetation, was followed by two more centuries of silence. The jungle grew back on Krakatoa, which, as far as anyone knew, had become extinct.

After lying dormant for more than 200 years, mighty Krakatoa began to shudder awake.

In May 1883 minor tremors were felt in the region around Krakatoa, so slight they were barely noticeable. On Sunday, May 20, Perboewatan started thundering and spouting again. At Batavia, 98 miles to the east, the rumblings were heard as "booming sounds, like the firing of artillery."

Ships steaming through the Sunda Strait at the time witnessed a stirring spectacle. To the chaplain of the German warship *Elisabeth*, Krakatoa's vapor plume resembled "a giant cauliflower head." The cauliflower soon blossomed into a huge cloud that covered most of

A tsunami generated by Krakatoa's eruption tore the steamship Berouw from its moorings in Sumatra's Telok Betong harbor and carried it 1½ miles inland.

the sky, and as the *Elisabeth* sailed west out of the strait it received a heavy dousing of volcanic ash.

Most people in the area regarded this early show of force more as entertainment than threat. On May 27 a party of tourists embarked from Batavia on the mail packet *Governor General Loudon* for a close-up view. As the vessel drew near, its passengers marveled at the density of the vapor column, now rising to perhaps 10,000 feet, and at the rosy glow at the column's foot. A few brave souls were ferried ashore to walk on the ash- and pumice-covered beach. Some even climbed the active cinder cone to peer down into the crater itself. Astonishingly, all returned alive.

After a lull in early June, the eruption resumed on June 16 and continued with renewed vigor through the rest of June and July. Government officials in Batavia were becoming alarmed, and on August 11 Captain H. J. G. Ferzenaar of the colonial survey department sailed to Krakatoa to assess the situation. By now the second largest cone, Danan, had opened up, and the entire island was smothered in ash. All vegetation had been destroyed. Smoke, steam, and dust enveloped everything. The captain quickly retreated, declaring further visits inadvisable.

Yet all this time Krakatoa was simply clearing its throat. At 1 o'clock on that fateful August Sunday, the volcano began to go off in earnest. Massive detonations shook the island, one every 10 minutes or so, and by 2 o'clock the vapor plume reached up 17 miles. The blasts increased in frequency and fury during the afternoon, each one releasing huge volumes of lethal, superheated gas and debris, which rolled out into the sea with percussive force. By nightfall the dust cloud hung over an area of 125 square miles. Vivid arcs of static electricity streaked through the murk. And ton upon ton of mud and cinder began to rain down.

A hailstorm of ash and stone battered the decks of

Krakatoa's dust colors the London sky in these views sketched by William Ascroft after sunset on November 26, 1883.

BLUE SUN, RED SKIES: KRAKATOA'S STRANGE INFLUENCE ON THE HEAVENS

In its death throes, Krakatoa sent tiny particles of volcanic dust shooting into the upper stratosphere, where strong winds carried them in a widening band around the earth. This veil of dust particles lingered in the atmosphere for up to three years, refracting the sun's light in ways that startled people from New Zealand to Iceland.

In the weeks immediately following the eruption, the sun appeared "splendidly green" to an observer in Ceylon and "like a blue globe" to a Trinidad resident. In Hawaii, the Reverend S. E. Bishop was the first to describe the whitish corona, or halo, that formed around the sun, a phenomenon known today as Bishop's ring.

The most brilliant of Krakatoa's optical effects, however, were the fiery sunsets—and the even more dramatic afterglows—that lit up the heavens for months after the eruption. From late 1883 through 1886, the British artist William Ascroft regularly sketched the evening sky over Chelsea, London. Ascroft's pastels—two of which are reproduced here—are an invaluable document of Krakatoa's amazing long-distance displays.

the sailing ship *Charles Bal*, bound from Belfast to Hong Kong by way of the Strait of Sunda. "Chains of fire appeared to ascend and descend between [the island] and the sky," Captain W. J. Watson recorded in his log. "The blinding fall of sand and stones, the intense blackness above and around us, broken only by the incessant glare of varied kinds of lightning, and the continued explosive roars of Krakatoa, made our situation a truly awful one."

The *Charles Bal* survived its ordeal more or less unscathed, but many other vessels did not. An estimated 6,500 ships and boats fell victim to Krakatoa's ragings, some swamped by atmospheric gusts or the fall of debris, most capsized by waves that the eruptions generated.

Of all the weapons in Krakatoa's arsenal, the tsunamis took the heaviest toll. They began on the evening of the 26th—long, deep swells at first, rising higher than the highest tide and causing major damage. Ships dragged their anchors at Telok Betong on Sumatra's Lampong Bay, and three feet of water swept over the town pier. At Merak on Java the water rolled in six feet high, flooding a Chinese encampment near the shore and drowning some of its inhabitants.

But during the night, as the volcano's fury mounted, so did the volume and impact of the ocean crests. By 10 P.M. many of the boats at Telok Betong had washed onto the beach. The Javanese coastal town of Anjer was struck by a tsunami, as were most of the other strait towns, including Merak for the second time. Then, starting in the predawn hours of August 27, a sequence of enormous waves rampaged through the strait with such force that they made the earlier undulations seem like ripples in a pond. Generated either by massive flows of gas and molten debris from Krakatoa's inner magma chambers, or else by the collapse of the chambers themselves, the waves dashed against the coast at heights of from 50 to 130 feet.

Trillions of gallons of fast-moving water swept away boats, houses, towns, and people all along the Sunda Strait.

After each surge, the water would recede, and several hours of deceptive calm would ensue. Then another, even greater wave would roll in, killing many of those who had ventured onto the shore during the lull.

The raging waters toppled most of the lighthouses in the Sunda Strait. They surged over the Sumatran town of Kalimbang to a depth of 80 feet and completely swamped Sebesi Island, north of Krakatoa, drowning all 3,000 inhabitants. At Merak, already twice hit, hundreds of people crowded into some stone houses at the top of a 135-foot hill. But a giant wave slammed into these buildings, tearing them apart. Of the town's 3,000 residents, 2 survived.

One of the best eyewitness reports of the disaster came from the mail steamer *Governor General Loudon*, the same ship that had taken tourists to Krakatoa the previous spring. Now transporting a gang of Chinese laborers hired to build a lighthouse off the west coast of Sumatra, the *Loudon* had left Anjer on Sunday afternoon and anchored off Telok Betong that night.

Monday morning brought the first of the major surges. "At about 7 A.M. a tremendous wave came moving in from the sea, which literally blocked the view and moved with tremendous speed," reported a passenger. Meeting the wave head on, the *Loudon* was "lifted up with a dizzying rapidity. The ship made a formidable leap, and immediately afterwards we felt as though we had plunged into the abyss." Unlike most of the ships in the vicinity, the *Loudon* survived the surge. As for the port itself, "all was finished. There, where a few moments ago lived Telok Betong, was nothing but the open sea."

The *Loudon*'s skipper, realizing he could do nothing useful where he was, fired up his engines and headed back toward Anjer to report what he had seen. But as the mail ship tried to get under way, the ash storm gusted in, caking the decks in muck and bringing a cloud of darkness that lasted a full 18 hours. The continuing eruptions stirred up winds that were like a "flying hurricane." No progress was possible.

Early Tuesday morning, conditions improved a bit. The moon shone faintly, and by dawn the sky had cleared enough for the navigator to set a course. Soon the *Loudon* reached Krakatoa, now quiet and diminished to one-third its former size. Of the island's three cones, only a remnant of Rakata still rose above the sea.

At last, late in the afternoon, the *Loudon* dropped anchor at Anjer—more precisely, at the spot where Anjer once stood. Like most communities in the strait, the town lay in utter ruins. After picking up survivors and ferrying them to safety, the *Loudon* went on to complete her ill-starred voyage.

Gradually, the surviving citizens of Java and Sumatra struggled to their feet to count the dead and rebuild their lives. And as soon as the volcanic fires had cooled, life even started moving back to what was left of Krakatoa. Five months after the eruption, a researcher found spiders crawling over the island's ashy remains. Grasses and shrubs began to sprout, and by the 1920's the jungle had returned.

The collapse of Krakatoa created a new undersea caldera four miles across and 900 feet deep—the remains of the volcano's subterranean magma chambers. In late 1927 the sea over the caldera began to churn, and in January 1928 a new volcanic cone emerged. Anak Krakatoa—"Krakatoa's Child," in Malay—has been blasting off at regular intervals ever since. Now some 350 feet tall, this child of Krakatoa will grow as big as its parent in 600 years, say scientists, and may be preparing for a cataclysmic outburst of its own in an even more distant future.

Most of Krakatoa's victims *were killed by the tsunamis that swept over the coastal towns on either side of the Sunda Strait (above). A new volcanic cone, called Anak Krakatoa (left), now rises near the spot where the mighty volcano once raged.*

141

The Blizzard of '88

Paralyzing storm takes Northeast by surprise

OR THE STAFF at the U.S. Signal Service's weather observatory, perched atop the Equitable Life Building on lower Broadway in New York City, Saturday, March 10, 1888, had been a fairly routine day. The only thing at all unusual was the temperature. At 9:30 in the evening, the thermometer outside the window still registered in the 50's. The day had, in fact, been the warmest of the year in the city's mildest winter in 17 years.

With closing time just half an hour away, Sgt. Elias B. Dunn, chief of the observatory, had but one chore left: to issue the forecast for Sunday's weather. With a practiced eye, he sifted through the pile of dispatches on his desk. Arriving by telegraph, telephone, and even carrier pigeon, the reports had come in from points all along the eastern seaboard. They all indicated much the same thing: continued warm and overcast, with perhaps a little rain, then turning fair.

Reassured, Dunn called the night editors at the city's newspapers and read his forecast for Sunday, the 11th: "cloudy, followed by light rain and clearing." And then, bidding his four-man staff goodnight, he locked his desk and left for home.

When Dunn returned to the office on Sunday afternoon, he quickly realized something was afoot. The day had been rainy—much more so than he had forecast. Indeed, the downpour seemed to be increasing, the mercury was falling, and a stiff wind had come up. Anxious for more information, Dunn and his deputy, Francis Long, tried to reach headquarters in Washington, D.C., on their telegraph hookup. Inexplicably, several attempts failed to raise a response.

Unknown to them, a great meteorological drama was unfolding, with two massive weather systems racing toward a collision near Cape Henlopen on the Delaware coast. One, sweeping in from northwestern

142

After a driving rainstorm the night before, astonished New Yorkers awoke on Monday, March 12, 1888, to find a blizzard raging. In all, the city lay buried beneath a total of 20.9 inches of snow.

Canada at an amazing 80 miles an hour, was a giant mass of frigid Arctic air. The other, warm and moisture-laden, was moving up from the Gulf of Mexico.

The two systems met head on, and for a time there was a standoff as warm and cold air masses held each other in check. But eventually the sheer size and momentum of the Arctic system prevailed. The result was, in effect, a winter hurricane, saturated with moisture and powered by violent winds. Eventually the system turned and began to travel northeast, picking up speed as it went.

The effects were terrifying. On Chesapeake Bay the winds first came up late Sunday afternoon, and as the downpour worsened, small craft dashed for any shelter they could find. Then the roaring gale increased, the mercury plummeted, and the great storm front rumbled northward as a blinding wall of snow. In the fury that followed, heavy anchor cables snapped like thread as vessels of all sizes ran aground, collided, and sank in roiling seas. Conditions on the open ocean were even worse. Ships ran into a raging mix of wind, snow, and churning water. One large yacht that was trying to ride out the gale was swamped by mountainous seas and sank as if slapped by a giant hand.

The two fronts had not gone unnoticed in Washington. The Weather Bureau's head office had called some staff in for Sunday duty and at 10:35 A.M. issued a "cautionary southeast storm warning," adjusted in the evening to a "northwest storm warning." But there had seemed to be no immediate threat.

No one knows if Dunn ever received those advisories, or when telegraph contact with Washington went down. But his own forecast for Monday, issued Sunday evening, was based only on local conditions: "generally fair and colder, preceded by partial cloudiness near the coast. Tomorrow [Tuesday] it promises to be slightly warmer and generally fair."

Even as that report was going out to the newspapers, the Great White Hurricane was roaring up the eastern coast of the United States, traveling at express-train speed on a direct course for New York City.

Those few still up and about late on Sunday evening soon realized something odd indeed was happening. James Algeo and his family were returning to their home in Manhattan when their horse-drawn streetcar jumped its track, probably pushed off by the raging wind and pouring rain. Passengers helped set the car back on the rails, but progress was painfully slow. The wind seemed to howl ever louder as they neared their destination, and a wintry cold began to set in. "It was raining and blowing a perfect hurricane," Algeo recalled. "With me carrying a four-year-old boy and my wife holding on by my coat tail, we reached home about 11:30. What a night!"

Sometime after midnight the rain turned to snow. One New Yorker, Arthur Bier, recoiled in astonishment when he peered out his window Monday morning and saw snow piled high on the ground, with more still falling. "The air looked as though some people were throwing buckets full of flour from all the roof tops," he exclaimed.

What had begun as an unexpected snowfall was turning into something much more dangerous.

Heavy snowfall was no novelty, and New Yorkers bundled up in winter gear and headed for work as usual. Those starting off early enough found the elevated trains still running, if slowly, and at least some of the horse-drawn streetcars in operation. But with every passing hour, conditions worsened. By midmorning the wind was gusting to 85 miles per hour, and the snow showed no sign of letting up.

At the 76th Street station of the Third Avenue Elevated, hundreds of passengers crowded onto a train—then waited nearly half an hour as its engineer tried to get up enough steam to climb the steep grade to 67th Street. Suddenly the sound of a whistle, terribly audible even over the wind, brought everything to a halt: it was the unmistakable call of another train approaching at high speed. Perhaps its engineer didn't look at the track ahead, or was blinded by the "buckets of flour" in the air. Whatever the case, the second train smashed headlong into the back of the stalled train, killing 1 passenger and injuring 14 others.

One by one, trains on all four elevated lines ground to a halt, stranding an estimated 15,000 people high above the streets in cramped, unheated cars. Instant entrepreneurs, producing ladders, charged passengers up to $2 each for an opportunity to clamber down to snow-choked streets.

Intercity rail traffic fared no better. Of 15 scheduled mail trains, only 4 actually arrived. Dozens of other trains were overdue, with no information about their fate, and reports of wrecks came in steadily. "Trains!" thundered Chauncey M. Depew, president of the New York Central Railroad, when asked whether he could maintain service throughout the storm. "Why, we don't even know whether we've got a railroad left!"

Workers in Manhattan arrived hours late to find empty offices and deserted assembly lines—and a storm now so intense that getting home was out of the question. Macy's department store opened as usual—

but closed at noon, the management setting out rows of cots for clerks who were unable or afraid to venture out into the gale.

Farther downtown, on Wall Street, the stock exchange closed when only 30 of 1,100 members showed up for work. Among the many absentees in the financial district that day was George D. Barremore, a 47-year-old malt-and-hops merchant. Leaving his apartment, he found that the elevated railroad he normally rode to work had long since stopped running. So Barremore, a 200-pound six-footer, decided to walk. He never made it: his body was later found in a snowdrift just four blocks from his home.

More resilient was 29-year-old Theodore Roosevelt, who trudged three miles through the storm to keep an appointment, only to find that the person he expected to meet had not come. After plodding back to his house in the East 60's, Roosevelt shot off a terse note: "I presume the blizzard kept you at home."

Equal to the travails of workers and commuters on land were the ordeals of those caught at sea by the "white hurricane." The luxury yacht *Cythera*, bound for Bermuda, vanished without a trace. Men on the freighter *Niagara*, arriving from Havana, Cuba, told of decks knee-deep in snow and ice. And as the schooner *R. H. Heniman* fought doggedly to make port at New London, Connecticut, it grew so cold, one seaman recalled, that "we could not stick it out on deck more than an hour at a time."

So fierce was the storm that the Weather Bureau's own instruments and communications failed.

Back in Manhattan, weatherman Dunn and his co-workers fought their way to the observatory on Monday, beset with anger and frustration. Why hadn't they known? Why hadn't Washington warned them of the storm? The Weather Bureau, when Dunn arrived, was deathly still, with not a sound from telephone or telegraph—just the snow, the cold, and the shrieking wind. And the anemometer, giving all-important data on wind velocity, was dead. Mounted atop a pole 25 feet above the roof, it had been immobilized by a coating of ice.

"There was no one," he added, "who I could get for love or money to climb that pole under such conditions." Except, that is, for his deputy, Francis Long. A veteran Arctic explorer, Long was one of 7 survivors of an 1881 expedition that had been trapped for three years near the North Pole. Calm and determined, he took a hatchet from the office tool chest and headed for the roof. With Dunn and three colleagues straining to steady the pole against 75-mile-an-hour winds, Long shinnied to the top, chipped away the ice around

Despite widespread hardship, *indomitable New Yorkers took the storm in stride and even managed a wry sense of humor, as signs in the snow-clogged street (top) attest. The rugged crew above was one of many that appeared around the city, charging exorbitant fees—and getting them—to dig out buried homes and stores.*

With snow, snow everywhere—making the streets utterly impassable, blocking the Third Avenue El and the city's other elevated rail lines—the Blizzard of '88 for a day or two brought New York to an unaccustomed standstill.

the anemometer, replaced some wiring, and got the instrument spinning again.

By day's end, New York and everything within a 100-mile radius was at a standstill, forcing the thousands of people trapped in the city to find accommodations and amusement where they could. Hotels packed guests two and three to a room, then set out supplementary cots in hallways and even bathrooms. One such visitor was Mark Twain, in from Hartford, Connecticut, who sent word to his wife that he was "Crusoing on a desert hotel." True to the adage that the show must go on, Phineas T. Barnum, whose circus had been scheduled to open that day, played to matinee and evening audiences of 100 at Madison Square Garden. At the same time, bars all over town were doing an exceptionally brisk business; people later recalled that when they ventured outside, there was a distinct smell of rum in the air.

By dawn on Tuesday, the snow had tapered off, and around midday the temperature began to climb. Communication returned, albeit sometimes by circuitous channels. The United Press news agency, for example, established a cable link with Washington, 230 miles away, via a 2,500-mile detour through Pittsburgh and Chicago. Trains, meanwhile, began to run again as locomotives equipped with snowplows cleared the tracks of the elevated railways. Elsewhere,

city officials turned to such critical problems as removing tons of garbage littering snow-covered streets.

From Tuesday on, the weather improved rapidly, and by Friday the city was more or less back to normal. The storm by then belonged to history, its 20.9-inch snowfall a record that would stand for nearly 60 years. More than 400 people had died—half of them in New York City, where frozen bodies were still being discovered weeks later as the mountains of snow melted away. And from Chesapeake Bay to Boston, the "white hurricane" wrecked an estimated 200 boats and ships and killed livestock, birds, and wild animals by the thousands.

But the blizzard also had its positive consequences. Within a quarter of a century, New York's vulnerable aboveground gas and water mains, as well as its overhead tangle of telephone, telegraph, and power lines, had been shifted to safety underground, and the city had its first subway system.

Most significant, perhaps, was the body of legend spawned by the suddenness and fury of the storm. Now firmly entrenched as part of our folklore, the Blizzard of '88 conjures up a time when, despite the odds, the vast majority survived to tell their children and their children's children how, through grit and perseverance, they managed to endure those daunting days of wild weather.

The Johnstown Flood

Broken dam unleashes a torrent of staggering violence

THE LATE EIGHTIES of the 19th century was a time in journalism for freewheeling favoritism and purple prose. Like many other newspapermen, an obliging editor of the Johnstown *Tribune* was happy to place both at the service of his hometown. "Our scenery is grand beyond description," he wrote about the bustling industrial city that had grown up around the intersection of two rivers about 60 miles east of Pittsburgh, in a deep valley of Pennsylvania's heavily wooded Allegheny Mountains. "The atmosphere cool, and invigorating; trout in the neighboring streams large and numerous; drives good; women beautiful and accomplished; men all gentlemen and scholars; hotels as good as the best."

These words were published only a few years before one single, immense sound reverberated through the hills east of Johnstown on a rain-soaked Friday afternoon in May 1889. The sound was that of 20 million tons of water exploding through the South Fork Dam and into the valley, about 14 miles upstream from the city. An hour later Johnstown was hit by a catastrophe that would stop an unbelieving America in its tracks— and send another writer, a young journalist from New York, into his own flight of overwrought prose.

"God looked down from the hills surrounding Johnstown today on an awesome scene of destruction," his report began.

Three hundred miles away in Manhattan, an unim-

pressed editor read the sentence as it came over the wire, then telegraphed back what was probably the only humor to move in or out of Johnstown that day: "Forget flood. Interview God."

The real story had begun at the exclusive South Fork Fishing and Hunting Club, whose members included such titans of industry as Andrew Carnegie, Henry Frick, and Andrew Mellon. Their 700-acre property incorporated Lake Conemaugh, said to be the largest man-made lake in the country, held in check by what was purportedly the country's largest earth dam. Some people worried about the careless way the dam had been built back in the 1840's, years before the club acquired the site, and the lackadasical maintenance it had received since then. On the morning of May 31, 1889, John Parke, a 23-year-old engineer employed by the club, was more worried than most.

It had been raining steadily since the previous afternoon, and Parke noted with alarm that the water line at the dam had risen two feet overnight. At the far end of the lake, away from the dam, the South Fork Creek was tearing off tree limbs three feet above its normal level. On Friday morning, after a night when eight additional inches of rainfall had poured into the lake's mist-covered waters, Parke and a group of the club's workmen struggled vainly to clear the dam's main spillway, now hopelessly clogged with heavy debris from the hills. When he saw water spilling through cracks in the dam, he waited no longer. As fast as his horse could take him over a sodden road, Parke galloped into South Fork, the most northerly of a half dozen hamlets lying along the Little Conemaugh River above Johnstown. There, he shouted to everyone within hearing to head for the high ground before the dam two miles behind him let go.

On his way home, Parke also made a hurried stop— too hurried, as it turned out—at the Pennsylvania Railroad's South Fork signal tower that controlled traffic on the mighty railroad's four-track, New York-to-Chicago main line. Inside the tower, he asked Emma Ehrenfeld, the telegraph operator, to wire Johnstown about the impending collapse. Before the startled woman could tell him that floods had already washed out the telegraph lines into Johnstown, her visitor was out the door and mounting up again.

Parke arrived back at the dam to watch with other alarmed spectators as a newly opened notch in the center of the earthworks grew wider and deeper by the minute. That did it. At 3:10 P.M. the dam, 72 feet high

Roaring over the stone bridge near the heart of town, the torrent created a hideous logjam of crushed buildings, vehicles, trees, and other tangled debris, in which hundreds lost their lives. This 1890 depiction, though melodramatic in style, captures the chaos and sheer horror that made Johnstown a uniquely shocking story.

and 300 yards wide, suddenly disappeared. Like racehorses at the starting gate, 20 million tons of water broke out of the lake with a roar that could be heard for miles and began thundering down toward Johnstown on a 14-mile run of destruction and death.

Reverend G. W. Brown, pastor of the South Fork United Brethren Church, was one of the onlookers who saw the first break in the dam.

"When I witnessed this, I exclaimed, 'God have mercy on the people below,'" he said later. "The dam melted away . . . onward dashed the flood, roaring like a mighty battle, tree-top high."

No one who saw the approaching crest of this flood would ever forget what it looked like.

It took about an hour for the flood to reach Johnstown. The reason for its relatively slow progress was simple and horrible: what was bearing down on the unsuspecting city was not pure lake water at all, but a gigantic mix of people and animals, living and dead, uprooted houses, schools, and factories, parts of heavy, mountain-duty locomotives and their cars, entire bridges and roadbeds, and virtually every tree that lined the gullies and bends of the Little Conemaugh.

Emma Ehrenfeld, the South Fork telegraph operator, had been talking with two trainmen who had come inside the tower to warm themselves before a cheery coal fire. When they heard some shouts, the three looked out the window and saw what one of them later described as a huge hill on the move. Thinking a mountain had torn itself loose, Ehrenfeld wasted not a moment, racing out of the tower "without waiting to get my hat or anything."

In the East Conemaugh yards of the Pennsylvania Railroad, the Day Express to New York was waiting for track clearance when its passengers were suddenly ordered to leave the train. Hurrying out of his car, a new bridegroom from Pittsburgh, Charles Richwood, was terrified by what he later described as "a seething, turbulent wall of water, whose crests seemed mountain-high, filling the entire valley and carrying everything before it as cornstalks before a gale."

Racing back toward his seat, Richwood clutched his bride, Edith, just before water completely filled the interior of the car. Struggling upward through the darkness, Richwood and his wife managed to reach the top of one of the cars. Then after being knocked loose from that refuge, they were plucked from the water by some people on a rooftop going by. But another terror awaited them. Their roof was headed straight for the big Gautier Wire Works of the Cambria Iron Company, and as the Richwoods watched, erupting furnaces began tossing workmen into the air.

147

The power of the press *was potently demonstrated in the days that followed Johnstown's destruction, as the nation was held spellbound by a barrage of bulletins and then mobilized to aid the stricken survivors.*

Grasping a piece of wood drifting by, the couple jumped off the rooftop and managed to steer away from the inferno—and just in time, for the flood ripped loose 200,000 pounds of new barbed wire, which went rolling on with the waters, ready to lacerate anything that blocked its path. Finally, when the Richwoods were still 50 feet from shore, a rescuer plunged into the flood and pushed them to land.

The pleasant little village of Woodvale had no chance at all, surrounded as it was by some of the Little Conemaugh's steepest hills. Almost all of its 250 buildings disappeared, while nearly a third of its 1,000 residents were sucked into the torrent as it headed south—some drowning along the way, others hanging on to anything that bobbed up from the maelstrom churning away beneath them.

Now it was Johnstown's turn.

One of the first in that city to see the approaching terror was a lawyer named Horace Rose, who happened to be home at the time. Some shouts from outside and the sound of a wildly clanging bell summoned him to a window, and then he saw it all—"a great mass of timber, trees, roofs, and debris of every sort, rapidly advancing toward me, wrecking and carrying everything before it."

One of Rose's sons looked up at him.

"Can't we escape?" he asked his father.

"No," Rose answered as gently as he could. "This means death to us all."

But it didn't. Rose, crippled almost instantly as the torrent hit the house, somehow hauled himself onto the roof, but could only watch helplessly as his family floundered in the swirling water. One of his sons also managed to climb onto the roof, however, and almost miraculously a man swimming by was able to help Rose's wife and daughter onto the same fragment of their house. Rose and his family survived the disaster and were all reunited later, riding out the flood until its strength was gone.

Huge locomotive parts were swept up by the torrent and tossed around as if they were playthings.

Accounts of Johnstown's catastrophe held readers across the nation so spellbound that at least one newspaper had to cut its page size to provide enough copies for all. Many of the papers carried photographs of the mess that remained where the big roundhouse serviced the Pennsylvania Railroad's 80-ton locomotives. Out from the witches' brew there catapulted huge sections of boilers, cabs, and wheelbases from 30 engines, rolled downstream toward Johnstown by the charging waters. There, some helped batter into oblivion all of the city's municipal buildings, the fortress-like YMCA headquarters, and Johnstown's newest hotel, Hulbert House, where about 50 people died.

Throughout the city the residents of Johnstown had precious few seconds in which to prepare themselves either to meet death or somehow to avoid it. From her home on Locust Street, Mrs. John Fenn watched her husband swept away while he ran for the front steps. Later, atop her own roof, she endured the agonizing sight of seven of her children being washed loose, one by one, to drown. After a wild three-mile ride astride a tar barrel, Mrs. Fenn was pulled to safety, wailing, "My God, what have I to live for?"

One survivor recognized Mr. Mussante, the town's fresh fruit dealer, careening past with his family on what appeared to be a barn door. As if participating in a surrealistic nightmare, the Mussantes methodically stuffed keepsakes into an old Saratoga trunk that happened to be with them—all working away until the moment when trunk, door, and the entire Mussante family were overturned and vanished.

Little Gertrude Quinn was a terrified eight-year-old who was sharing a floating mattress with a husky workman named Maxwell McAchren. As they neared the shore, McAchren threw the child across 15 feet of water to some waiting arms on the bank. He continued to float on the mattress, traveling at least four miles until a group of men used ropes to reel him in safely to shore. Meanwhile, Gertrude Quinn's rescuers wrapped the little girl in a dry blanket and carried her up to a house on a hill where she was dressed and kept warm. She never saw McAchren again, but some 40 years after the flood, she read his obituary notice in the *Johnstown Tribune*. Her wine-red roses went with Maxwell McAchren to the cemetery.

For days after the disaster, plaster fell, windows shattered, and people were shaken by the roar of dynamiting at the massive stone bridge that spanned the river. The bridge, still standing because the floodwaters had run into a mountain before hitting it, created a barrier against which thousands of tons of debris had piled up—a gruesome mass of bodies, boxcars, houses, animal carcasses, trees, and general rubble that had to be cleared away before it became a menace to the health of survivors and rescue workers. In the end, at least 2,200 people were known dead, with almost 1,000 more missing and never found.

Meanwhile, donations and relief workers poured in. Clara Barton, then in her late 60's, arrived with her newly formed Red Cross. Pittsburgh organized a 20-car relief train only hours after the news reached it. Other trains followed from every direction, bearing lumber, blankets, food, and clothing for the survivors, and with undertakers, embalming fluid, and coffins for the rest. New York, Philadelphia, and Pittsburgh each raised more than half a million dollars in aid. Cincinnati shipped 10 tons of ham. Inmates in one prison baked 1,000 loaves of bread, and every day in Burlingame, California, grade schoolers brought pota-

toes to class to be forwarded to hungry small friends along the Little Conemaugh.

The waters were just receding when a rescue crew heard noises coming from underneath a crushed freight car. Beneath it, a cow was quietly chewing her cud, a small dog was barking at the cow, and five hens were clucking their disapproval of the dog. More than 18 hours after much of Johnstown had disappeared, workers lifting corpses out of the Allegheny River at Pittsburgh, into which the Conemaugh's waters eventually drained, pulled ashore the floor of a wrecked home. On it lay a five-month-old baby who had ridden alone, and unharmed, for some 75 miles on the flood-swollen rivers.

The city of Johnstown was still very much alive.

The numbing aftermath presented tableaus ranging from the tragic to the absurd, as with the shattered buildings (above) deposited in a bizarre heap on a neighbor's doorstep. Nothing illustrated the flood's violence more vividly than John Schultz's house (left), tossed about like a scrap of paper and impaled by an uprooted tree. Incredibly, all six people inside when the torrent hit lived to tell the tale.

Tsunami Terror in Japan

Towering wall of water scours the coast

JUNE 15, 1896, was a gloomy day in the Sanriku district on the northeastern coast of Honshu, the main island of Japan. But even the heavy rains that fell all afternoon could not dampen the spirits of the citizenry: all along the coast, towns and villages were abuzz with activity as people prepared to celebrate a popular Shinto festival. Also crowding the streets were throngs of visitors who had traveled to the coast to join in the parades and pageantry.

By early evening the rain had stopped, the sky had cleared, and all seemed calm. But all was far from well. The first hint of impending danger came at about 7:30 P.M., when a series of undulating, long-lasting shocks began to rumble underfoot. Since seismic activity is common in that part of the world, however, few people took more than passing notice.

Then, about 20 minutes after the first shock, something truly awesome happened: the sea withdrew from the shore, as if sucked in upon itself. Boats at

anchor were torn free of their moorings and swept away by the outgoing tide. Where moments before there had been water, vast numbers of fish were suddenly left high and dry, flapping helplessly on exposed mud flats.

Next came a booming noise from out at sea, its volume increasing rapidly until it sounded like a thousand cannons firing all at once. Before the frightened celebrants could gather their senses, a mountain of water, towering to nearly 100 feet above normal sea levels, came roaring, seething, foaming toward the land at an estimated speed of 500 miles an hour. People tried to run for high ground, but it was too late. The dreaded tsunami had struck.

Widely believed by the ancient Japanese to be expressions of divine wrath, tsunamis, or "tidal waves," as they are loosely known in the West, are massive ocean waves caused by undersea earthquakes, landslides, or volcanic eruptions (not tides). The triggering

Terrified Japanese boatmen *are about to be swamped by a giant sea wave in this 19th-century print.*

disturbances can occur hundreds or even thousands of miles from the places where the waves ultimately hit the land, often with devastating results. A correspondent for *Harper's Weekly* who visited the Sanriku area compared the disaster there with the explosion of the volcanic island of Krakatoa in 1883. The reporter added that the 30 miles of Japanese coastline he had been able to examine after the tsunami were devoid of life. Estimates of the death toll eventually mounted to nearly 30,000 persons.

There were survivors, too. Men who had gone out to sea in fishing boats earlier in the day, for example, for the most part escaped injury. Indeed, many were totally unaware that anything unusual had happened until they returned to their home ports and found the harbors filled with bodies and debris. Their blissful ignorance can be explained by one of the curious facts about tsunamis: out at sea, they can move through the water as waves no more than two feet high from crest to trough, scarcely detectable in a bobbing boat. They become terrifying waves of doom only when they reach shallow water. (Hence the Japanese name, which translates as *tsu*, "harbor," and *nami*, "wave.")

Among those on land who survived the inundation, many owed their lives to strange and capricious strokes of fortune. The only survivors in the town of Hongo, for instance, were a group of elderly men who had skipped the festival to play an ancient Japanese game, Go, high on a hilltop overlooking the sea. In another village only a handful of children escaped. Their parents apparently had raced to high ground with their terrified tots, then rushed downhill again to hurry their older children along. Instead, they were swept out to sea, leaving the huddle of crying orphans.

There were stories, too, of people enduring wild rides at sea aboard pieces of flotsam. One small group found itself washed up, unscathed, on a nearby island, and a baby survived by resting comfortably aboard a floating mat in the midst of all the destruction.

Most of the dead perished by drowning, including one old soldier who reportedly had mistaken the roar of the approaching tsunami for the sound of foreign invaders coming ashore. Grabbing his sword, he rushed outside to fight off the invaders. When his body was later found, tossed high above his native village, his hand was still clenching his trusty sword.

A French missionary was the only Westerner killed by the wave. Two of his confreres searched among the ruins for more than a week, hoping to find his body and give him a proper Christian burial. But they ultimately had to give up because of the frightful conditions they encountered everywhere. Indeed, coping with the thousands of human and animal bodies that lay about on every hand was a formidable task. "It was necessary to build fires to destroy the evidence of putrefaction," noted the correspondent for *Harper's Weekly*, "because there were no disinfectants procur-

Propelled by the earth's movements, speeding waves crest higher and higher as they near land.

Ways of Seismic Sea Waves

TSUNAMIS ORIGINATE deep beneath the ocean. Among the mechanisms that cause them are volcanic eruptions and submarine landslides, but undersea earthquakes are the principal cause.

In the case of an earthquake, the waves are set in motion by a massive disturbance of the sea bed and travel out from the point of origin in concentric circles, much like the waves formed by a pebble dropped in a puddle. In deep water the tsunami's wave length (the distance from crest to crest) can be scores of miles long. Forward speed is proportional to the depth of the water through which the wave passes; the deeper the water, the faster the wave moves. (Speeds of up to 600 miles per hour are possible.) As the wave approaches the shallow coastal water, it begins to slow down, and vast quantities of water pile up in a huge, fast-moving wave. The highest waves are naturally those in V-shaped inlets and harbors.

Early warning systems that detect underwater disturbances by means of networks of seismic and hydraulic sensors are now in operation. Quake and sea-level data collected throughout the Pacific, where tsunamis are most common, are fed to computers at the International Pacific Tsunami Warning Center near Honolulu, Hawaii, in order to predict potential catastrophic waves.

able." Hanging over the land for days, he added, were "the unconquerable stench of death and the smoke of the funereal fires."

When government officials were finally able to enter the area and make a tally of casualties, they reported 10,617 houses swept away, 2,456 houses damaged, 27,122 persons killed, and 9,247 more injured.

Thirty-seven years later, in 1933, the Sanriku district was struck by another tsunami, this one with waves as high as 75 feet. Thanks to last-minute warnings, many were able to reach safety, and only an estimated 3,000 people lost their lives. But who can guess when the monstrous sea waves may visit this beleaguered coastline once again?

The Plague Comes to the Americas

Infected ships bring an ancient killer to the New World

ON MARCH 6, 1900—the Year of the Rat according to the Chinese calendar—a local shopkeeper was found dead of unknown causes in the basement of the shabby Globe Hotel in San Francisco's Chinatown. An autopsy revealed that the man had died of one of the world's oldest and most dreaded scourges: bubonic plague. Twice before in human history the plague bacillus had gone on a rampage: in the 6th-century Plague of Justinian and the 14th-century Black Death. Now a third plague pandemic had reached the shores of the United States.

San Francisco's teeming Chinatown, *shown here in the 1890's, provided ideal conditions for the plague.*

This latest breakout originated in central Asia in the mid-19th century. Moving slowly at first, the plague was reported in the Chinese port of Canton in January 1894; seven months later some 100,000 of the city's poorest residents had died of the disease. Refugees from Canton carried the plague to neighboring Hong Kong, where another 100,000 succumbed. Since both cities were major international shipping centers, the stage was set for the rapid dissemination of the disease worldwide. The Indian port of Bombay was hit in the late summer of 1896; by 1905, the number of plague deaths in India had soared to more than a million a year. Traveling east on rat-infested steamers, the disease infected Hawaii several times before making a New World debut in Paraguay, in April 1899; within a decade or so most of South America had been tainted.

On June 27, 1899, the S.S. *Nippon Maru*, sailing out of Hong Kong by way of Honolulu, docked in San Francisco with 11 Japanese stowaways and, possibly, a shipload of diseased rats on board. The next day, two of the stowaways turned up dead in San Francisco Bay, their bodies (as an autopsy later revealed) infected with the plague bacillus. Whether or not it was actually the *Nippon Maru* that brought the plague to San Francisco is not clear. Still, barely eight months after the ship reached the city, the body of the first U.S. plague victim was dragged out of the Globe Hotel.

Acting with dispatch, the San Francisco Board of Health had the 12 square blocks of Chinatown placed under quarantine and ordered a house-to-house search for more victims. But scarcely had the board begun its work when powerful business interests, supported by most of the local press, rose up in opposition. According to these civic leaders, talk of plague was bad for business and should be suppressed.

There was no plague in California and never had been, insisted the governor.

Others in San Francisco argued that only Asians were susceptible to the disease; Caucasians had nothing to worry about. The Chinese, for their part, were loath to support measures that singled them out as pariahs or threatened them with removal to detention camps.

While the squabbling increased, so did the death toll, and neighboring states began issuing quarantine orders against people and goods from California. Finally, on March 6, 1901—a full year after the discovery of

A plague-infected house in San Francisco is about to be fumigated in this l908 photograph (right). By this time, the role of the rat (above) in spreading plague had been recognized.

the city's first plague death—a federally appointed commission ruled that the plague did exist in San Francisco; one month later a rigorous sanitation drive was launched in Chinatown. Nearly 1,200 houses and some 14,000 rooms were washed from top to bottom with caustic, after which a mercury solution was sprayed on all surfaces and a whitewash often applied for good measure. Household goods were steamed, fumigated, or doused with disinfectant. Despite such steps, however, the epidemic lingered on until early 1904. Of the 127 people who contracted the disease, only 5 survived.

The sanitation measures undertaken in San Francisco reflected the belief that the plague was an infectious disease like smallpox or typhoid, spread directly from person to person. The role of the rat and its fleas in transmitting the disease to man was poorly understood, if at all. But the veil of mystery surrounding the cause and transmission of the plague was gradually beginning to lift. In 1894 Dr. Alexandre Yersin of France and Dr. Shibasaburo Kitasato of Japan, working independently in plague-ravaged Hong Kong, had discovered the bacillus, now known as *Yersinia pestis,* that causes the disease. Four years later, another French researcher, Dr. Paul-Louis Simond, identified the Oriental rat flea, *Xenopsylla cheopsis,* as the agent that carried the plague bacillus from rat to rat and from rat to man. Although ridiculed at first, Simond's discoveries provided the key to plague control during San Francisco's next bout with the killer disease.

On May 26, 1907, some 13 months after earthquake and fire had leveled San Francisco, a sailor died of the plague in the city's U.S. Marine Hospital. By early September, San Francisco was once again on the verge of an epidemic. This time, however, local officials took prompt action. Under the leadership of Assistant Surgeon General Rupert Blue, a campaign was begun to clean up or eliminate those places most likely to harbor rats. The city's 4,000 stables and countless chicken yards had to be floored with concrete and rat-proofed or else torn down. Every household was required to have a covered garbage can. Unsanitary living quarters were shut down. Cement sidewalks and sewers replaced open drains. Rat catchers were paid $2.50 per day plus 10 cents for each rodent they trapped. Rat-poisoning squads roamed the city armed with bits of bread spread with poison. More than 700,000 rats took the bait.

San Francisco's last case of human plague was detected just two months after the sanitation campaign began; eight months later no more plague-infected rats turned up among the small remaining rat population. During this second outbreak, a total of 205 bay area residents contracted the plague, and 103 of them died. Although the disease affected more people this time around, the fact that it was brought under control so swiftly was cause enough for celebration.

The worldwide plague pandemic is believed to have ended sometime in the late 1950's. In the century or so that it lasted, it killed between 10 and 13 million people, the majority of them in India. It also created two new regions of chronic plague infection, one in South America, the other in the western United States. Today the disease is relatively rare in humans. But individual cases—usually traceable to wild rodents rather than to urban rats—still occur year after year, and the threat of a widespread breakout has by no means been eliminated.

153

AGE-OLD PERILS IN A MODERN WORLD

Galveston's Killer Hurricane

Storm leaves glittering Texas port a "city of the dead"

I N HINDSIGHT, it is easy to see that Galveston, Texas, in the year 1900 was a disaster waiting to happen. A popular resort as well as the state's largest port and wealthiest city, Galveston was built on a low-lying barrier island off the Texas mainland in the Gulf of Mexico. Nowhere in the city did the elevation of the land exceed nine feet; in many areas, the terrain rose barely five feet above mean high tide.

Turn-of-the-century Galvestonians, however, were not given to worrying much about their situation. The city had what one native called a "lotus-eater charm" that beguiled people into ignoring the existence of danger. And indeed, for a city built on sand and in the path of hurricanes, Galveston had been very lucky. "Overflows," as locals called storm-driven floods, often struck the 30-mile-long island, but none had ever caused great loss of life or property damage. As protection against flooding, most houses were elevated several feet above ground level. When an overflow did occur, the city frequently went on holiday.

So, when a terse report of a "tropical storm disturbance moving northward over Cuba" reached the Galveston office of the U.S. Weather Bureau on Tuesday, September 4, 1900, it caused no great alarm. Such reports were common this time of year, and in any case, this storm seemed destined for Florida. Over the next three days, Isaac Cline, director of the Galveston weather station, and his brother, Joseph, its chief clerk, routinely monitored the storm on the basis of advisories from Washington. But after inundating parts of Florida as predicted, the "disturbance" suddenly abandoned its northerly trajectory on Thursday afternoon and veered west across open Gulf waters.

It was business as usual in Galveston as the deadly storm fixed its sights on the vulnerable city.

At 10:30 A.M. on Friday, Isaac Cline received instructions from Washington to hoist storm-warning flags. With the wind blowing at a brisk 17 miles an hour, Isaac climbed to the roof of the weather station and raised two pennants: a white triangle indicating "northwesterly direction" and a red and black square signaling a storm of "marked violence." Most Galvestonians, however, remained unconcerned. Summer vacationers, who were still crowding the beaches, may even have welcomed the refreshing winds as a respite from the unseasonably hot weather of the last few days.

As Friday wore on, the Cline brothers watched the rising surf and increasingly cloudy skies. The barometer had been falling all day, too—a clear sign that a severe weather system was approaching. On a positive note, however, the "brick dust sky," a reddish glow that often preceded hurricanes, did not appear that evening. By midnight, the heavens had even cleared somewhat, and the moon shone down on the island. Perhaps, as a reporter for the Galveston *News* speculated in the paper's Saturday morning edition, the storm had "changed its course or spent its force before reaching Texas." As it turned out, the reporter could not have been more wrong.

At around 1 A.M., Saturday, September 8, Joseph Cline finished his work at the weather station and went home to his room at his brother's house, four blocks from the beach. Joseph slept poorly that night, awaking at 4 A.M. with what he later described as a "sense of impending disaster." Going to the window, he discovered that the waters of the Gulf were washing across the backyard, which meant that the tide had risen at least five feet above normal. After hurried consultation with his brother, Joseph returned to the weather station, while Isaac harnessed his horse to a cart and rode off to rouse residents along the shore.

Isaac Cline's mission on the beach met with limited success. Some residents took his advice and moved to higher ground at the center of town, but most stayed put, convinced that this was just another overflow. Many Galvestonians actually set out for the beach to watch the mounting spectacle.

A light rain began to fall at 8:45 A.M. Shortly after 10, Joseph Cline received word from Washington to change the northwest storm warning to northeast. He hoisted a new flag atop the station, but the wind gained strength as it changed direction and soon tore the pennant apart; a few hours later the storm brought down the flagstaff as well.

By noon, the rain and wind had become frighteningly powerful, and several thousand Galvestonians were struggling, belatedly, to reach higher ground. But the wind-driven rain was enough to knock a man down, and floating debris, including wooden paving blocks pried from the streets, made movement even more difficult. By midafternoon, half the city was flooded and the causeways to the mainland had washed away.

Around 2:30 P.M., Joseph Cline returned to the weather station roof to check his instruments only to find that the rain gauge had blown away. The last

The Strand, *a busy commercial street in Galveston, is shown here at the height of the storm. In this nightmare of howling winds and churning water, people and animals alike struggle to stay afloat.*

reading had been 1.27 inches, but before it was over, the storm would pour some 10 inches of rain on the city. The wind at the time was blowing at about 35 miles per hour with gusts of up to 42 miles per hour; the barometric pressure was 29.31 inches and falling.

After having spent most of the morning and early afternoon along the shore trying to convince people of the danger they were in, Isaac Cline went home at midafternoon to see to the safety of his wife and three daughters. Joseph set off for the Western Union office to try to wire a report to Washington, but both the Western Union and the Postal Telegraph offices' lines were down. Luckily, he was able to put a call through to Houston and finish delivering his message just before that connection snapped too. Galveston was

now completely cut off from the outside world. Having done all he could at the weather station, Joseph headed for his brother's house at around 5 P.M.

By now many streets were neck-deep in churning water. Slate roof tiles were flying off buildings and slicing through the air with enough force to decapitate anyone in their way. Despite the obstacles, Joseph made it home in about half an hour. Confident that the Clines' well-built house would withstand the storm, nearly 50 neighbors had taken refuge there.

By 5:30 the barometer had dropped to 28.95 inches, and the weather station's wind gauge was gone— blown to bits after registering a wind velocity of 84 miles per hour with gusts of up to 100 miles per hour. Within the next several hours, as the storm reached

The Red Cross shared its Galveston headquarters with the New York World, *which sponsored Barton's trip to the stricken city.*

RED CROSS TO THE RESCUE

To the 78-year-old Clara Barton, founder of the American National Red Cross, news of the Galveston storm came like "the clang of the fire-bell." Accompanied by a small Red Cross staff, she reached Galveston on September 15 to find the city reeking of the "peculiar smell of burning flesh." Although tired and ill, Barton issued an appeal for help and was soon overseeing the distribution of $120,000 worth of donated cash, food, clothes, lumber, and hardware.

Clara Barton's stay in Galveston lasted about two months and marked the end of her direct participation in disaster relief work—a charitable career that began on the battlefields of the Civil War and that led to the establishment of the American National Red Cross in 1881. The following year, Barton succeeded in having Congress ratify the Geneva Convention on the treatment of wartime casualties and prisoners. She also wrote an amendment to the convention that widened the scope of Red Cross activities to include the distribution of relief in peacetime emergencies. Barton served as president of the American Red Cross until 1904, when long-standing dissension with the Red Cross board ended in her resignation. This feisty Angel of the Battlefield died in 1912. She will long be remembered for her tireless efforts on behalf of those touched by disaster.

its destructive climax, the winds in Galveston would blow at an estimated 100 to 120 miles per hour.

As houses were wrecked and debris hurtled through the skies, Galvestonians tried desperately to hold on to a piece of their disappearing sand bar. At the Tremont Hotel, built on one of the highest spots in the city, some 1,000 people had gathered to wait out the storm. Shortly after 5 P.M., water had begun to seep into the hotel rotunda. An hour later the front desk was submerged, and the crowd of anxious refugees fled to the mezzanine. Although the front windows blew in and the roof was torn off, the building and the people in it survived the hurricane's assault.

Not everyone was so lucky. At about 6:30 P.M. a storm surge sent four more feet of water crashing down on Galveston Island ahead of the hurricane's vortex. Many houses that had survived the storm so far were toppled in a matter of minutes, killing the people inside. An hour later, the Cline house, now the only one in the vicinity left standing, found itself in the path of an enormous section of what had been a streetcar trestle. The wreckage hit the house like a battering ram, knocking it on its side. Isaac blacked out for a few moments, but he revived and managed to save himself and his youngest daughter. Joseph grabbed his two other nieces and went crashing through a window. Eventually the surviving Clines reached safety by climbing from one pile of floating debris to another. Isaac's wife, however, and most of the people who had taken refuge with the family died.

After dropping to a record low of 28.44 inches at around 7 P.M., the barometer began to rise again rapidly. By 10 the eye of the storm had hit the Texas mainland a few miles southwest of Galveston, and the winds, now blowing from the south, had lost considerable speed. Around midnight, the flood tide, which had reached a record 15.2 feet above normal in the surge, began falling. But even as they ebbed, the Gulf waters ripped more houses from their moorings.

Its streets choked with corpses and debris, Galveston after the storm was a scene of mind-numbing devastation.

At dawn on Sunday, September 9, Galvestonians were greeted by clear skies, a calm sea, and destruction beyond belief. In some neighborhoods hardly a single building was left standing. Property losses were later estimated at $20 million (and those were noninflated 1900 dollars). Even worse was the death toll, greater than in any other natural disaster in United States history. Some 6,000 people, out of an estimated population of 37,700, were killed in Galveston alone; another 4,000 to 6,000 people living along adjacent stretches of the Texas coastline also perished. Hundreds of

The hurricane's fury turned parts of Galveston into a vast sea of rubble, with few buildings left standing intact (above). Members of a cleanup squad (left) stop their grim work for a moment to pose for a photograph.

people who had sought shelter in churches died as the buildings collapsed on top of them. At one city hospital, more than 100 patients were killed, as were all but 3 of the 90 children at St. Mary's Orphanage. Yet there were many amazing survival stories, too. One woman was reportedly carried out to sea in her wooden bathtub and brought back again, scarcely the worse for wear, on the morning tide. And not far from St. Mary's Orphanage, rescue workers found a baby whose parents in desperation had pinned it to the roof of their house by driving a nail through its wrist. Miraculously, the baby survived its ordeal.

For those lucky enough to be still alive, food, water, and medical supplies were scarce, and getting about in the city was all but impossible. But if Galveston's desolation was great, so was its citizens' will to survive and rebuild. By Sunday afternoon a Central Relief Committee had been formed. Volunteers took over one of the few remaining seaworthy vessels on the island and set out to inform Houston of the disaster and to ask for help. Able-bodied men were drafted into cleanup squads, some to clear away debris, many more to dispose of the bodies that were rapidly befouling the city. On Thursday, September 13, martial law was

declared in Galveston and orders issued for looters to be shot on sight. Of the six men reportedly dispatched in this manner, one was said to have stashed in his pocket 23 severed fingers decked with rings!

Galveston's news stunned the nation and triggered an outpouring of donations. Gifts from individuals and groups all over the world enabled the Relief Commitee to go on dispensing food and aid for months.

Within a year of the hurricane, Galveston's economy had revived, and the government was making plans to build a three-mile-long protective sea wall along the Gulf shore. Finished in 1904, this remarkable feat of engineering has since been extended to 10 miles. After the wall was built, Galveston itself was raised—as much as 17 feet in some places—by pumping millions of cubic yards of sand fill over a 500-block area. Before the land could be elevated, however, some 2,156 structures—including the 3,000-ton St. Patrick's Church—had to be individually jacked up. The extraordinary effort involved in lifting an entire city was well worth it. In this century, Galveston Island has been hit by a half dozen severe hurricanes, but never again has the loss of life and property come close to the terrible devastation of 1900.

159

Sleeping Sickness Invades Uganda

Insect-borne microbe spreads mass death

EARLY IN THIS CENTURY an English doctor and a Ugandan stood one day on a hill overlooking the northern shore of Lake Victoria. Pointing to the ruins of once extensive banana plantations on every side, the Ugandan quietly observed, "Lumbe has eaten up our fairest gardens."

"Lumbe" was the local personification of disease, and he had "eaten" the gardens by killing their gardeners—specifically, by afflicting them with African sleeping sickness. Between 1900, when the disease reached epidemic proportions, and 1907, when the first effective measures were taken against it, as many as 200,000 Africans living along Victoria's shoreline died—some two-thirds of the area's entire population.

Caused by a microscopic parasite, African sleeping sickness, or trypanosomiasis, is entirely unrelated to the American illness (a type of encephalitis caused by a virus) that is also known as sleeping sickness. And it is anything but the gentle killer its name suggests. The disease first erodes victims' lives in subtle ways, sometimes for years, with headaches, lassitude, insomnia, and a marked feeling of oppression. The disabling second stage brings mental disintegration, pain, severe insomnia by night, and a daytime drowsiness so extreme that, when awakened to eat, victims sometimes fall back to sleep even as they chew. Eventually coma comes, then death.

Although the disease occurs only in Africa and apparently has existed there for centuries, it was Europeans who played the pivotal role in its modern history. First, they inadvertently unleashed it from relatively isolated pockets of infection—an action that led in time to the Ugandan epidemic. Then, alarmed at the catastrophe, they found a way to curb it.

The shores of Lake Victoria in the late 1800's provided ideal conditions for the spread of the illness. Thanks to fertile soil and dependable rainfall, the northern and western shores of the lake and the nearby Buvuma Islands supported a dense human population. The same region also offered an ideal habitat for a species of tsetse fly—*Glossina palpalis*—that feeds on the blood of various creatures, man among them.

In a makeshift laboratory in East Africa, a team of European doctors take blood samples to test for sleeping sickness. The photograph was made in 1906, when the disease was rampant in the area.

The fly and man had always lived together in the area with no more detriment to man than the minor annoyance of the tsetse fly's harmless bite. The crucial missing element was the parasite *Trypanosoma gambiense*, which causes sleeping sickness. It lives in humans, in animals, and in tsetse flies, which are its only means of transmission. (It passes from the fly's salivary glands to the blood of any creature the fly bites.)

Before the 19th century, the parasite, or trypanosome, was confined to a few small areas on the west coast of Africa. It didn't spread because its human hosts rarely left the place where they lived. When European adventurers started to hack their way across the continent, however, they unwittingly released the disease by taking along infected men as porters. Occasionally, too, they took with them infected flies, perhaps as hitchhikers riding on their riverboats. As a result, vast new areas were opened to the disease. Uganda, with its dense human population on Lake Victoria, was among the most susceptible.

It took about 20 years for the sickness to become firmly established in Uganda and begin its wholesale destruction. The suffering and death it brought were devastating beyond belief. And, as one British observer put it, "so rapidly did it spread along the shores of the lake and down the Nile that it seemed to threaten Egypt on the north, India to the east, and South Africa to the south." When the infection finally became an epidemic in 1900, the British, who had made Uganda a protectorate in 1894, took action. "The arrest of the disease became a matter of State importance."

Since there was no cure for the illness, missionaries could do little more than set up rude hospitals and camps for the sufferers, trying as best they could to make death less cruel. Colonial administrators, meanwhile, were preparing to isolate victims in a camp on Buvu Island in Lake Victoria. (The island, ironically, was buzzing with tsetse flies, which would only have intensified the spread of sickness.) But the plan had to be put aside when orders came from London to await the arrival of an official investigating commission.

The first Sleeping Sickness Commission reached Uganda in the summer of 1902. By mapping the incidence of the disease, they discovered a distinct pattern of infection: sleeping sickness occurred in lakeshore villages, on islands, and along riverbanks, but it never extended far from the water. Another breakthrough came when one of the commission members, Dr. Aldo Castellani, found trypanosomes in the cerebrospinal fluid of sleeping sickness patients.

A second commission was sent to Uganda in 1903, led by Dr. David Bruce, an army medical officer who by coincidence had recently discovered that an African livestock disease is caused by trypanosomes and transmitted by tsetse flies. Pursuing Castellani's line of investigation, Bruce prepared maps showing that the distribution of the tsetse fly and the distribution of the

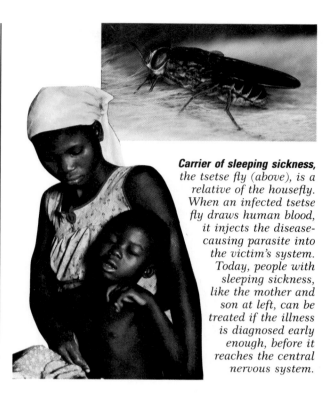

Carrier of sleeping sickness, the tsetse fly (above), is a relative of the housefly. When an infected tsetse fly draws human blood, it injects the disease-causing parasite into the victim's system. Today, people with sleeping sickness, like the mother and son at left, can be treated if the illness is diagnosed early enough, before it reaches the central nervous system.

illness coincided exactly. Collecting flies for examination, and then exposing laboratory monkeys to infected flies, he established once and for all both the cause of sleeping sickness and its means of transmission.

Solving the mystery was an achievement of great importance for the future of all sub-Saharan Africa. But it offered no immediate relief to the dwindling population of Uganda. The fatal grip of the disease was finally broken in 1907, and then not by medicine but by a determined administrator acting in concert with local chiefs who controlled the infested lakeshore.

Hesketh Bell, commissioner of the Protectorate of Uganda, had repeatedly sought permission to relocate the entire population out of fly-infested areas, but he had repeatedly been refused by the Colonial Office in London for fear that such action might cause a native war. Defiant, Bell took matters into his own hands and discussed his plan with the chiefs; together they set it in motion. The relocation was accomplished peacefully. And when man and fly were finally separated, the sickness lost its hold on the people.

But not on the land. Bell had assumed that once the human source of infection was removed, the flies would eventually become disease-free and man could then move back to the bounteous lakeshore. He didn't know that the parasite so recently arrived in the region had taken up permanent residence in various game animals, thereby continuously infecting the tsetse flies that bit them, and so would persist to bedevil the descendants of its first victims to this day.

Mount Pelée: Grim Reaper

Thirty thousand die in a sudden, horrifying convulsion

MARTINIQUE, A CARIBBEAN ISLAND with a romantic history, embracing piracy, luxury, feats of war, and elegantly mannered living, was little known to Americans in 1902. A prized possession of France since the 17th century, it was roughly 40 miles long, 16 miles wide at its broadest point, and extremely mountainous. Along with plantations of sugar cane, tobacco, coffee, and cacao, Martinique was mantled with junglelike forests extending to the tip of the highest peak, Mount Pelée, which rose 4,429 feet above the sea and comprised the entire northern end of the island.

St. Pierre, the island's most populous town, nestled picturesquely at Pelée's southern foot, its houses forming a ribbon of color stretching two miles along a placid bay. Like all Martiniquais, the people of St.

Pierre were intensely religious; the city was the seat of an imposing cathedral and several parish churches. For secular diversion there was a theater, where acting troupes from France performed every winter, as well as clubs, cafes, and balls. And just outside town, Pelée's flattened, cloud-wreathed crest had long been a favorite spot for picnics, with a clear lake on the peak for swimming.

Early in April 1902 some harmless volcanic activity was noted near the summit—the appearance of fumaroles, or smoke holes, that gave off a faintly sulfurous vapor. On April 23 a light rain of cinders fell on the southern and western slopes of the mountain; sharp underground shocks were felt and at first were mistaken for earthquakes. Then on April 25 the mountain awoke, and St. Pierre was enthralled by the wild spectacle of Pelée hurling a vast cloud charged with rocks and ashes straight upward from its summit.

Before long, however, Pelée's brilliant display of pyrotechnics took a new and menacing turn.

On Friday, May 2, half an hour before midnight, the recurring eruptions suddenly assumed a more threatening aspect. Pierrotins were startled out of their sleep by thunderous explosions; at the same time, Mount Pelée shot upward a pillar of dense black smoke laced with brilliant lightning. Dawn disclosed St. Pierre buried under whitish ashes like new-fallen snow. All that day frightful detonations were heard at intervals of five or six hours, and the expediency of leaving the city was discussed publicly.

On Sunday, May 4, the ash rain fell so densely that boats skirting the coast feared to navigate through it. The sea was littered with dead birds. Children of peasant refugees, lost and forlorn, wandered aimlessly through the city with their little donkeys, dazed and adrift. On Monday night the atmospheric disturbances knocked out the city's electrical system, and darkness added to the uncertainty and fear. Toward 2 A.M. Tuesday, mutterings sounded in Pelée's depths, louder than thunder, and people ran out of their houses with lighted lamps and candles, wildly inquiring what had happened. When daybreak disclosed the city undamaged, the tension eased, and the citizens reassured one another.

But on Wednesday, May 7—St. Pierre's last day—

Set ablaze by a superheated volcanic cloud that rolled thousands of feet across the water, more than a dozen ships anchored offshore suffered the same agonizing fate as St. Pierre itself.

162

Ashen and desolate, *the ghastly ruins of St. Pierre bore no resemblance to the stylish, cosmopolitan city that had long been a favorite port of call in the West Indies. Mount Pelée's massive eruption on May 8, 1902, had released a scorching, gaseous avalanche that raced the 5 miles to St. Pierre in less than a minute. Whatever it touched burst into flames, leaving the city a vast brazier of fire, obscured and doomed under a choking pall of smoke and dust.*

there was fresh disquietude. At 4 A.M. Pelée began roaring; vivid lightning flashed continually around the summit, where two fiery craters glowed like blast furnaces. The flight from St. Pierre grew hourly; more and more heads of families sent their womenfolk into the environs or even to the nearby island of Guadeloupe, remaining behind themselves to attend to business affairs. By now the inflow of terrified country folk, bewildered and aimless, more than offset the departures; the population of the city actually increased by several thousand.

It was hot and close all during that night. The air seemed unnaturally still, and Pelée tranquilly emitted its lofty pennant of steam. But at 4 A.M. on Thursday, the rumbling started again, and the volcano began shooting upward a dark ash cloud that drifted west over the sea, pushed by the trade wind; fiery cinders streaked this vertical column of black vapor.

At 6:30 A.M. the passenger steamship *Roraima* dropped anchor in the harbor; her decks were gray with falling ashes, and passengers and crew lined the rail to watch the awesome spectacle of a volcano in full eruption. A short while later another passenger ship, the steamer *Roddam*, anchored close inshore.

Ascension Day dawned clear and sunny, and the air of the city vibrated with the ringing of church bells. On the heights around the city, suburban residents, after a wakeful night, stood viewing the mountain's stupendous display of fireworks. In the St. Pierre post office, the night-shift telegrapher wound up transmission of the latest official reports on the volcano, mentioning no significant new developments. The operator in Martinique's capital, Fort-de-France, 12 miles to the southeast, began his reply. The hands of the clock on the wall of St. Pierre's military hospital pointed to 7:52, when the Fort-de-France telegrapher paused.

"*Allez*," clicked the operator in St. Pierre—the signal to proceed.

The operator in Fort-de-France pressed his key, but the line was dead. In that second St. Pierre died.

A few instants later, a stupendous, roaring explosion rent the air above Fort-de-France, and an enormous column of black smoke was seen to dart up and up with incredible swiftness, mushroom out, and fill the whole sky, eating up the light. The church of Fort-de-France, where the 8 o'clock mass was just beginning, in a twinkling was emptied of everyone but the priests. In sudden, absolute darkness, the people knelt

163

Like a charred sentinel, the blasted hulk of a tree stands amid the lifeless, rubble-strewn landscape that just weeks before had been the bustling, cosmopolitan city of St. Pierre.

in the streets and wailed incoherently. What could be happening at St. Pierre?

The repair ship *Pouyer-Quertier* at 7:52 was working eight miles offshore, with the city in clear view. Suddenly the crew saw the upper flank of the mountain facing south appear to open, and from the gap a dense black vapor shot out like smoke from the muzzle of a cannon. At the same time, they saw a second black cloud—the one visible in Fort-de-France—roiling upward in gigantic whorls, mushrooming out, and quicky covering the entire sky with an umbrella of darkness 50 miles across.

The horizontal cloud sped down the mountain slope, tumbling over and over noiselessly toward the city. It seemed to clutch the ground, falling forward rather than floating, as though composed of some heavy, inert, violently propelled substance. Its leading edge exuded puffs of smoke—"like leaping lions," one witness said—and sometimes it glowed incandescently, while thunderous explosions and scintillations like lightning flashed in its depths.

In less than one minute the cloud reached the northern verge of St. Pierre and unfolded like a sooty blanket, blotting out everything; whatever it touched burst into flames. On the quay, thousands of barrels of rum exploded with a roar.

The ships offshore were anchored broadside to the onrushing cloud and received its full impact; most capsized and sank, their hulls afire. Only the *Roraima* and the *Roddam* remained afloat, but the masts, funnel, and boats of the *Roraima* were carried away, and half a dozen fires broke out on her deck. The *Roddam* heeled until water poured over the lee rail; then her anchor chain snapped, and she slowly righted, scorched and on fire fore and aft. Eight miles distant, the *Pouyer-Quertier* felt the heat, and red-hot stones and ashes rattled on her deck; with difficulty the fearful crew headed the vessel out to sea.

The full horror of the catastrophe remained unknown to the rest of the island for several hours. Officials were stupefied; no word came from the governor; every attempt to communicate with the north proved futile.

Finally, toward noon, the acting governor sent a warship that arrived off the burning town at about half past 12. Examination through powerful glasses revealed no living soul. When the captain came ashore on the Place Bertin, once a tree-shaded square near the center of town, not a tree was standing. The ground was littered with dead. In the center of the square the fountain was still spouting cool, clear water, and the members of the landing party refreshed themselves with a drink. But fire and a suffocating stench prevented any deeper exploration of the ruins.

Of 30,000 trapped in the ill-fated city, only two would be left alive.

Just two survivors were discovered in St. Pierre. One was Léon Compère-Léandre, a shoemaker who lived near enough to the edge of the searing cloud to make his way out afterward, barely clinging to life. The other was a convict named Auguste Ciparis, locked in an underground cell ventilated only by a narrow grating in the door, which faced away from the volcano. Three days after the disaster, his moaning was heard by salvage workers, who dug him out. He was frightfully burned but gave a coherent account of his ordeal.

On the morning of May 8, he said, it had suddenly grown very dark, and hot air, mixed with fine ashes, came in through the door grating and burned him. The excruciating heat lasted only a moment, and he jumped around in agony calling for help. He heard no sound, saw no fire, smelled nothing except what he thought was his own flesh burning. His clothing did not ignite, but his body underneath was seared so deeply that blood oozed from the wounds.

Meanwhile, 30,000 others had perished.

As for the cause, researchers would learn that it was superheated steam, possibly as hot as 1900° F, mixed with lethal gases and explosive dust. Many victims were in casual attitudes, indicating that death had overtaken them without warning; others were contorted in anguish. The clothing had been torn from nearly all the victims struck down outdoors, as would happen in the passage of a cyclone.

The city itself burned for days. Sanitation parties penetrated the ruins bit by bit, to dispose of the dead by cremation. The stench was sickening. Thousands of victims lay under a shroud of ashes, heaped several feet deep, caked by the rains; many were not retrieved for weeks, and few were identifiable.

There was to be no real resurrection. Dead cities are rebuilt by their survivors, and St. Pierre had none.

Miraculously spared, Auguste Ciparis *(also called Ludger Sylbaris) later toured with a circus.*

Luxuriant vegetation soon covered the hideous scars. Up Pelée's slopes the forests crept again, and along the waterfront fishermen built huts in the angles of old basements. But neither these simple homes, nor the occupants of the village that eventually collected there, bore any resemblance to the vanished St. Pierre. A way of life, charming, unique, and irreplaceable, was gone forever, its fate symbolized by a white ossuary standing starkly upon the green hillside, enshrining innumerable bones.

Mount Pelée's Glowing Cloud of Death

THE CLOUD OF DEATH that annihilated Martinique's major city, St. Pierre, in Mount Pelée's lethal 1902 eruption is known as a *nuée ardente*, or "glowing cloud." More like a glowing avalanche, it was a lethal brew of superheated steam and other gases mixed with clouds of incandescent volcanic ash.

Hurtling down the mountainside with terrifying speed, it dealt a triple dose of death and destruction. Its explosive force literally blasted down walls, uprooted trees, and tore the clothing from its victims' bodies. Its searing temperatures of up to 1900°F instantly incinerated buildings and deeply burned the flesh of those in its path. Its gagging combination of poisonous fumes and fiery ash asphyxiated any who might have survived its other horrors.

How did the lethal blast attain such fury? It was in fact the final, convulsive release of long-accumulated pressure. In such an eruption, the volcano's vent is sealed by a plug or dome of solidified magma, much like a cork in a bottle. Below it, a column of molten magma that is exceptionally rich in volatile gases steadily builds up pressure until finally something must give way. Blasting a hole upward through the plug or laterally through the side of the mountain, the gas-charged magma escapes with explosive force. Suddenly released from confinement, the gases expand so rapidly that they shatter the magma into a mushrooming cloud of incandescent ash. Sweeping down the mountainside, this *nuée ardente* destroys everything in its path.

Once the gases have escaped, magma in the volcanic vent begins to solidify and forms a new dome or plug that halts the action until renewed accumulation of gases causes another paroxysm. First analyzed by French scientists studying the 1902 eruptions of Mount Pelée, this type of explosive and uniquely dangerous outburst has been known to geologists ever since as a Peléan eruption.

Exploding sideways instead of upward when a horizontal outlet was opened beneath the volcanic plug, Pelée's scalding cloud raced downhill so fast because the incandescent ash and dust particles rode on a friction-reducing layer of hot gases.

The Frank Slide

Avalanche of rock shatters Canadian mining town

THE LOCAL INDIANS, it was said, refused to camp at the foot of Turtle Mountain. The twin-peaked summit in south central Alberta, Canada, got its name because it was shaped like a turtle's shell, with a mass of limestone jutting out like the head of a turtle 3,000 feet over the Crowsnest River valley below. Perhaps the Indians feared that one day the sleeping turtle would awake and nod its head, and the mountain would come tumbling down.

Whatever fears the Indians harbored about Turtle Mountain were not shared by most of the white men who settled in this remote corner of western Canada in the late 19th century. The Montana banker H. L. Frank, for example, was quick to invest in the vein of coal discovered at the Turtle's foot in October 1900. A year later, Frank's Canadian-American Coal and Coke Company was extracting hundreds of tons of coal a day from the new mine, and he had no difficulty persuading the Canadian Pacific Railway to run a spur line from the CPR tracks to the mine entrance. Down in the valley—in the very shadow of Turtle Mountain—Frank's company began to build the office buildings, miners' cottages, and boarding house that would soon grow into the town of Frank—

named, of course, after its wheeler-dealer founder.

The town was officially incorporated with much hoopla on September 10, 1901, and by the spring of 1903, it had a population of more than 600. Where these new arrivals came from was often a mystery. Many of them preferred not to talk about their pasts or even to give their full names. But shadowy backgrounds did not seem to matter much in Frank as long as the coal kept flowing out of Turtle Mountain.

The young community was a boisterous frontier town straight out of a Hollywood Western. The center of social life was the hotel saloons and gambling casinos, where miners and ranchers would spend their money and free time in the company of "hussies, adventuresses, and parlour sporting ladies," in the words of the weekly Frank *Sentinel*. Tough, raucous, and fatalistic as the people of Frank may have been, nothing could have prepared them for the disaster that struck the town in the early hours of April 29, 1903, and assured it a place in history books.

As it turned out, the Indians had been right all along in avoiding Turtle Mountain. With exceptionally steep eastern slopes and substantial fissures in its limestone top, the mountain was geologically unstable and

Millions of tons of falling rock left a huge scar on the east face of Turtle Mountain and in the valley below. In this aerial photograph of the disaster site, the modern town of Frank, Alberta, appears in the lower right.

primed for a slide. As the miners later recalled, the Turtle had been sending out warnings for months. In the mine tunnels and galleries that ran about a mile into the mountain's heart, timbers would groan at night, and tunnel walls would start and shudder like a ship struck by a wave. On Tuesday night, April 28, Andy Grissack, an old trapper who lived in a tent by the bank of the Crowsnest River, heard a faint rumbling from the mountain. Ned Morgan, who had come to the valley to sell a cow and calf, heard it too, but neither made much of it. Grissack went to sleep, while Morgan headed home about midnight.

At 4:10 Wednesday morning, railroad brakeman Sid Choquette was at the mine siding helping to hook up a string of coal cars to a freight train when he heard a peculiar whistling roar. At that very moment, a mass of limestone half a mile square separated from the east face of Turtle Mountain and came hurtling down toward Frank. Choquette, who had been walking alongside the slow-moving train, leaped for the handrails as the engineer bore down on the throttle. The train managed to cross the bridge over the Crowsnest River just seconds before the wave of rock swept the

bridge away. As the crew looked on helplessly, some 90 million tons of limestone plummeted down the slope of the mountain, crossed the nearly two-mile-wide valley floor, and climbed 400 feet up the opposite slope.

It was all over in 100 seconds, but in that brief interval, the rockslide—and the wall of air it sent racing ahead of it—destroyed nearly everything and everybody in its path. It sealed the entrance to the mine, trapping 17 miners inside. It swept away miners' houses, shacks, and camps; dammed up the Crowsnest River; and buried sections of the CPR tracks under 100 feet of debris. The slide obliterated parts of the south side of Frank and left the whole town choking in a thick white pall of limestone dust.

Jolted awake by a noise that some mistook for a volcanic eruption, others for an earthquake or a mine explosion, the townspeople soon recovered sufficiently to begin sending out search parties. At James Graham's ranch nothing was found alive except the cow he had just bought from Ned Morgan, its horns ripped from its head. Old Andy Grissack seemed to be all right until someone rolled him over and his scalp fell away like a toupee. Alex Leitch, a local merchant, lay crushed in the ruins of his home along with his wife and four sons; two of his daughters, however, came out of the wreckage alive, while a third, the baby Marion, had been thrown clear of the house and was found lying on a bale of hay outside. When rescuers pulled James Warrington from what had been his bedroom, he told them he could feel something soft beneath him. It proved to be his neighbor, Mrs. John Watkins, stuck full of rock fragments but nonetheless still very much alive.

Also alive were the 17 miners sealed inside the mountain. Attempts to blast through the walled-up tunnel from the outside had failed. But 13 hours after the slide, the miners suddenly emerged from the mountainside, dirty but unharmed, having dug their own way out through the rock.

The Frank Slide took at least 70 lives, but because the town's population was constantly shifting and few bodies were ever recovered, the exact death toll remains uncertain. The mine eventually reopened only to be hit by a major fire in 1905. Three years later, H. L. Frank died in a mental institution, his mind unbalanced by the disaster. In 1918 local inspectors finally shut down the mine for good. Today, the town of Frank, slightly relocated and numbering barely 200 souls, forms part of the Municipality of Crowsnest Pass. And still fresh after all these years, the scar on the east face of Turtle Mountain and the mass of debris on the valley floor provide a vivid reminder of one of the greatest landslides ever recorded.

After their miraculous escape from the sealed coal mine at Turtle Mountain, the surviving miners are seen here in the distance walking up the main street of Frank.

The San Francisco Earthquake

Shock waves and wildfires destroy the City by the Bay

JOHN BARRETT, news editor on the San Francisco *Examiner*'s city desk, had been working the Tuesday night shift on April 17–18, 1906. He finished at 5:00 A.M. and was standing on Market Street now, talking with two reporters. The sunlight was coming out of the morning mist, brightening the roofs of the buildings. The city was noiseless except for the clatter of an occasional newspaper wagon or milk cart. One of the men had just told an amusing story, and the others were laughing.

Their laughter was interrupted abruptly. "Of a sudden we found ourselves staggering and reeling," Barrett wrote. "It was as if the earth was slipping gently from under our feet. Then came a sickening swaying of the earth that threw us flat upon our faces. We struggled in the street. We could not get on our feet.

"I looked in a dazed fashion around me. I saw for an instant the big buildings in what looked like a crazy dance. Then it seemed as though my head were split with the roar that crashed into my ears. Big buildings were crumbling as one might crush a biscuit in one's hand. . . . Storms of masonry rained into the street. Wild, high jangles of smashing glass cut a sharp note into the frightful roaring. Ahead of me a great cornice crushed a man as if he were a maggot—a laborer in overalls on his way to the Union Iron Works, with a dinner pail on his arm. . . . It seemed a quarter of an hour before it stopped. As a matter of fact, it lasted about three minutes. Footing grew firm again, but hardly were we on our feet before we were sent reeling again by repeated shocks, but they were milder. Clinging to something, one could stand."

It was dark, like twilight, Barrett recalled. He saw trolley tracks uprooted, twisted in fantastic shapes. He saw cracks, "wide wounds" in the street, and a wild tangle of wires. Some of the wires swayed and shot blue sparks. Water flooded out of one crack. A deadly odor of gas rose from a broken main.

"From the south of us, faint, but all too clear, came a horrible chorus of human cries of agony. Down there in a ramshackle section of the city the wretched houses had fallen in upon the sleeping familes. Down there throughout the day the fire burned. . . . That was what came next—the fire. It shot up everywhere. The fierce wave of destruction had carried a flaming torch with it—agony, death and a flaming torch. It was just as if some fire demon was rushing from place to place with such a torch."

The city going up in flames, though barely 60 years old, was already a world-famous metropolis, "the American Paris." San Francisco was the most important city west of the Mississippi River; a financial, commercial, and cultural center, it was second only to New York in foreign and domestic trade. It was the earliest western terminus of the transcontinental railroad. It was America's gateway to the Orient.

"I watched the vast conflagration from out in the bay," wrote author Jack London, who lived 40 miles away and reached the scene by midafternoon on Wednesday. "East, west, north, and south, strong winds were blowing upon the doomed city."

San Francisco was famous, too, for the mixture of nations among its 450,000 residents—melting-pot Americans, Mexicans, Spaniards, Italians, and the largest Chinese colony in America. To some, this was a wicked city—the all-night town with its notorious Barbary Coast, its 1,000 saloons, its posh restaurants that provided "supper bedrooms" on the upper floors.

Yet San Francisco was also a center of newly acquired, culture-conscious wealth. Opera stars were imported from Europe; extravagant balls marked the social season; millionaires built splendid mansions on Nob Hill; the 800-room Palace Hotel on Market Street was world renowned for its luxury and service.

Much of the city's style and prosperity, of course, had to do with geography. San Francisco lay at the north end of a 50-mile-long peninsula. To the west was the Pacific Ocean; to the east, San Francisco Bay and a complex of docks, wharves, and ferry lines. Lofty hills overlooked one of the world's most beautiful harbors. Unfortunately, the city also happened to lie close by one of the great fractures in the earth's surface—the San Andreas Fault, beginning at Cape Mendecino in northern California and running roughly parallel to the state's coastline for some 800 miles.

On the morning of April 18, 1906, the accumulated stresses and strains within the fault broke loose with a fury that surpassed the combined energy of all the explosives used in World War II. Driving into the coast at a point 90 miles north of San Francisco and ripping south at two miles a second, the shock wave hit the city at 5:13 A.M. with unbelievable power.

One of the guests at the Palace Hotel that morning was the famed Italian tenor Enrico Caruso, who had performed the night before at San Francisco's Grand Opera House. When the earthquake struck, he later recalled, "I waked up, feeling my bed rocking as though I am in a ship. From the window I see buildings shaking, big pieces of masonry falling. I run into the street. That night I sleep on the hard ground—my legs ache yet from so rough a bed."

Spellbound by catastrophe, *San Franciscans look on as the heart of their city is engulfed in flames and smoke, seem-* *ingly oblivious to the rubble all around—and to the fact that the inferno is moving steadily toward them.*

The chief of the Postal Telegraph Cable Company, across Market Street from the Palace, sent out the first news to the rest of the country at 6:00 A.M.

> THERE WAS AN EARTHQUAKE AT FIVE FIFTEEN THIS MORNING, WRECKING SEVERAL BUILDINGS AND WRECKING OUR OFFICES. THEY ARE CARTING DEAD FROM THE FALLEN BUILDINGS. FIRE ALL OVER TOWN. THERE IS NO WATER AND WE HAVE LOST OUR POWER. I'M GOING TO GET OUT OF THE OFFICE AS WE HAVE HAD A LITTLE SHAKE EVERY FEW MINUTES.

More than 50 fires had started within half an hour of the earthquake when live wires touched wood, or escaping gas was ignited by a flame, or stoves fell over and spilled their hot coals. The many separate fires soon merged in a general conflagration. By early afternoon, the downtown business section was being consumed. By early evening, the fires had reached Chinatown and were threatening the mansions on Nob Hill. At dawn on Thursday, the Barbary Coast was set

alight. Pillars of smoke could be seen 100 miles out to sea. Steel I-beams melted; silver coins in the banks fused into solid ingots; overheated bank vaults could not be opened for days, since currency and papers would burst into flame when the air rushed in.

Dennis Sullivan, San Francisco's fire chief for the past 13 years, was in command of 80 stations and 585 firemen. His was considered one of the best fire departments in the country, but he was acutely aware of its deficiencies and of the serious dangers the city faced from fire. Ninety percent of the buildings were wood or wood sheathed in brick, and the city's fire-fighting equipment was not in good condition.

On Tuesday evening, April 17, Sullivan and his wife attended a social gathering. He left to supervise the fighting of two fires, then at 3:00 A.M. retired to an apartment at a nearby fire station. Sullivan was awakened at 5:13 by the lurching of his bed and the sound of falling brick. He ran in the dark to the door of an adjacent room, opened it, and plunged down three stories, landing on a fire wagon. Suffering fractures of his skull, ribs, arms, and legs, he died on Sunday without regaining consciousness.

Sullivan's men attempted to contain the early fires in the city, but they could do almost nothing. Their engines and hoses were useless: the underground iron mains and reservoir conduits had buckled and broken during the earthquake, leaving them with no water to pump. The few cisterns near the fires were soon emptied. At 12:45 P.M., on orders from Gen. Frederick Funston, the last and most extreme step was taken—an attempt to stop the spreading fire by demolishing the buildings that stood in its path.

General Funston, one of the highest-ranking army officers in the region, had in the first hours taken command of fighting the fire, of feeding and sheltering refugees, of communicating with President Theodore Roosevelt, and of anything else that needed to be done. He in effect declared martial law, though he had no right to do so, and he managed to call out about 2,000 army troops stationed at the Presidio, the U.S. military post near the Golden Gate, though they were not under his command. He deployed them the length of Market Street, two men to a block, with orders to apprehend or kill looters.

Through the first three days the city was crowded with people on the move, pushing, pulling, or carrying possessions; searching for relatives; seeking food, water, and shelter; streaming to the safety of open parks; making a circuitous seven-mile walk around the north shore to the Ferry House. By every account they were strangely subdued, moving in brooding silence as though stunned or drugged. "Remarkable as it may seem," observed the author Jack London, who described the scene for *Collier's Weekly*, "Wednesday night, while the whole city crashed and roared into ruin, was a quiet night. There was no shouting and yelling. There was no hysteria, no disorder. . . . Before the flames, throughout the night, fled tens of thousands of homeless ones. Some were wrapped in blankets. Others carried bundles of bedding and dear household treasures. Sometimes a whole family was harnessed to a carriage or delivery wagon that was weighted down with their possessions."

At the same time, excited curiosity seekers stood on hills around the city, watching the fire spread, taking pictures, exchanging rumors. Even among the refugees there were some who felt a kind of exhilaration. Another eyewitness, the psychologist William James, was especially impressed by the displays of kindness and composure on all sides. "Not a single whine or plaintive word did I hear from the hundred losers whom I spoke to. Instead of that there was a temper of helpfulness beyond the counting."

Somewhere amid all the confusion was the 24-year-old matinee idol John Barrymore, who had been seen leaving his room at the St. Francis Hotel soon after the quake and for the next two days was listed among the missing. He reappeared with a harrowing account of wandering about the city in a state of shock and then being conscripted into a work brigade for 24 hours. Only years later did Barrymore admit that the entire story had been a fabrication—and that he had actually spent the time at a friend's house, immersed in one of his soon-to-be-legendary drinking binges.

Overnight, streets and parks were filled with an army of homeless, hungry people.

In the meantime, more than a thousand carloads of refugees fled the city on the Southern Pacific Railroad, which charged them no fare. Some 300,000 other homeless, hungry people crowded into the city's parks. They created enormous problems of providing shelter, sustenance, sanitation, care of the sick and injured, and burial of the dead. The army erected tent cities overnight. The first relief train arrived about

The capricious hand of destruction is evident on Union Street, *where the sidewalk, pavement, and cable-car tracks all buckled—while houses and telephone poles remained serenely intact.*

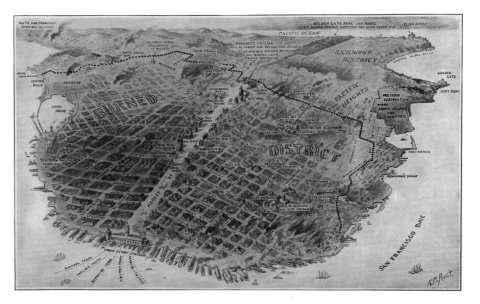

When the smoke cleared, *4.7 square miles in the heart of the city had been blackened by fire and more than 28,000 buildings destroyed. Among the casualties were the opulent Palace Hotel and the $6-million City Hall, whose steel frame survived, but with all its stonework shaken off. Thanks to a rumor that bandits were going to rob the U.S. Mint building of its $200 million in assets, soldiers sent to stand guard were on hand to keep it from burning down.*

midnight on Wednesday, 19 hours after the first quake, and the Red Cross used its supplies to set up round-the-clock food lines. Other supply trains followed; railroads gave them right-of-way on their systems. Soldiers put jailed prisoners to work digging graves. Lost children were taken care of in transit camps set up in Oakland.

General Funston made a crucial decision on the afternoon of Thursday the 19th. Fires were ravaging large areas of the city east of Van Ness Avenue. Now they were spreading westward toward Van Ness itself, which, running north-south, separated the older city from the newer developments, including the Western Addition with its upper-income homes for 150,000 people. If the fire crossed Van Ness, all San Francisco would burn. That street was the widest in the city—

"My Sixty Sleepless Hours" *was the hard-earned title* McClure's Magazine *gave to the dispatch filed by its reporter Henry Lafter from this improvised office.*

125 feet. It was the last possible line of defense, the logical place to make a stand.

With time running short, the inhabitants of all the buildings on the east side of Van Ness Avenue were hastily evacuated. A row of cannon was trained on the condemned dwellings, men went into the houses carrying matches and cans of kerosene, and dynamite was planted in appropriate places. The combined effect of incendiary fires, explosives, and discharge of artillery was spectacular. When the dust settled, many of the finest and newest houses in the city had been leveled for a distance of 16 blocks—one mile—and to a width of 50 yards. But their destruction left a vital corridor 175 feet wide between the advancing fires and the buildings on the west side of Van Ness.

On Friday afternoon the fire came so close to the spared houses on Van Ness Avenue that paint peeled from their siding, but when the wind changed course and began to blow eastward, it appeared that the stand at Van Ness had succeeded. Elsewhere, fires still burned dangerously close to the waterfront, threatening the docks that were San Francisco's economic lifeline. There, however, the city's fire engines had salt water from the bay to pump, and with help from navy fireboats they were able to bring this blaze under control. The last fire anywhere in San Francisco was put out at 7:45 on Saturday morning, April 21.

Now it was time to take the toll, to assess the damage done by the earthquake and by three days and nights of fire. No exact count of the San Francisco dead could ever be made. Estimates varied. Perhaps 500 persons were crushed or were trapped and burned to death; another 350 were missing and never found; and 415 were seriously injured.

The center of the city was in ruins—28,188 buildings destroyed in 512 blocks. The entire business and commercial district was demolished; every retail store of any consequence was burned out. Only one bank building escaped serious damage. Market Street was a footpath through charred timbers, twisted iron, broken glass, and piles of brick. Twenty-nine public school buildings were destroyed and 44 damaged. Nearly three-fourths of the city would have to be rebuilt or extensively repaired. Insurance claims totaled $229 million, close to $3 billion in 1988 dollars. No one knows how much uninsured property was lost.

The steel-frame tall buildings, facing their first test in a major earthquake, did very well; they stood firm, with few casualties and relatively light damage—most of that caused by fire. The worst destruction took place on the "made land," areas that had been built out into the bay by dumping fill into bogs, much of it between the ruined Palace Hotel and the docks. It was there that buildings most readily collapsed.

Though the fires were extinguished, enormous hardships still faced the people of San Francisco.

Meanwhile, thousands of refugees poured back into the city, requiring continued, large-scale relief measures. But there were problems in meeting the most basic needs. Water could not be pumped into the reservoirs because more than 23,000 house faucets were open. Water and sewage were mixed in the mains. No fires could be lit in any house until its chimney was certified as safe, nor could gas and electricity be turned on until the house had been inspected. All cooking had to be done out of doors. There was a persistent shortage of cooking utensils.

Recovery and reconstruction, nonetheless, started at once. Nothing became San Francisco so much as the spirit its people showed in rebuilding it. Crews began to work 24 hours a day, seven days a week, clearing the debris. Most of it was dumped into the shallows of the bay, where in time it served as a foundation for houses pushed farther and farther off the original shoreline. Business was resumed within a week. Shops and offices were installed in many of the large Van Ness Avenue houses that had been saved. In two months, more than 8,000 "refugee houses"— long wooden barracks—were put up, each holding six to eight family units.

The army was able to end its work on July 1. Saloons were permitted to resume business on July 5. Breadlines ended on August 1. Gifts of more than $9 million from across the country and abroad ($45,000 from the empress of China, $245,000 from the Japanese Red Cross) helped in sustaining relief measures.

By the spring of 1907, almost all the rubble was gone. By the end of the third year, a tremendous construction boom had produced more than 20,000 good new houses. Building-trades factories were working double shifts. Masons were paid as much as

Tiny tremors and once-in-a-century quakes are both caused by the two plates' continual, contrary motion.

The San Andreas Fault

ALL AROUND THE WORLD, the earth's crust is seamed with countless faults—fractures along which movements of the crust have taken place. Most are simply breaks in once continuous rock formations. The San Andreas Fault, in contrast, marks the uneasy meeting place of two of the dozen or so thick, rigid plates that make up the earth's outer shell. To the east of the fault, which angles nearly 800 miles along much of the length of California, lies the North American plate; to the west lies the Pacific plate, on which such cities as Los Angeles and San Diego are located.

Earthquakes occur along the fault because the North American plate is slowly but steadily moving southeast, while the Pacific plate pushes relentlessly northwest. Along parts of the fault, the two plates slip past each other without incident, moving as much as two inches annually. (In the last 15 to 20 million years, scientists estimate that such movement has totaled at least 350 miles.) Elsewhere, though, the edges become locked in place for years or even decades at a time, building up stress until the deadlock breaks with a violent shift in position. This sudden release of tension sets the earth to rumbling in all directions in the fearsome convulsion we know as an earthquake.

$12 for an 8-hour day—more than three times the going rate—and some were working 18 hours.

In 1905 San Francisco had announced that in 10 years it would hold the mammoth Panama–Pacific Exposition. Now, instead of canceling the event as everyone expected, the city held its 1915 world's fair on schedule and with resounding success. A few days after the great earthquake, a New York newspaperman who had lived in San Francisco bitterly lamented its fate. "It may rebuild; it probably will; but those who have known that peculiar city by the Golden Gate and have caught its flavor of the Arabian Nights feel that it can never be the same." His grief was surely heartfelt. Just as surely, it was premature.

Mysterious Fireball Blasts Siberia

Cause remains unknown to this day

SOMETHING ARRIVED FROM outer space on the morning of June 30, 1908, and exploded over the forests of central Siberia in a blinding flash, packing an incredibly destructive wallop. That much is certain. The powerful blast is estimated to have been equal to the detonation of 30 million tons of TNT. But the cause is still a matter of speculation.

The fact that a disaster had even taken place went unnoticed by most of the world. Remote and locked in the icy grip of winter for eight months of the year, the area where the blast occurred was largely uninhabited except for a scattering of the reindeer-herding Tungus people. So, despite the widespread devastation, there were no known human fatalities.

Stories of the cataclysm appeared only in regional newspapers. According to one reporter, "a heavenly body of a fiery appearance cut across the sky. . . . Neither its size nor shape could be made out, owing to its speed and unexpectedness. However, many people in different villages distinctly saw that when the flying object touched the horizon a huge flame shot up that cut the sky in two." Fearful sounds of the explosion

filled the air, and violent tremors shook the land. "One had the impression that the earth was about to gape open and everything would be swallowed up in the abyss," he added, concluding that "the invisibility of the source inspired a kind of superstitious terror."

That very evening saw the onset of a series of strange "bright nights" throughout the Northern Hemisphere. One man in Russia discovered that he could take outdoor photographs at midnight; another reported: "I myself was aroused from sleep at 1:15, and so strong was the light at this hour, that I could read a book by it in my chamber quite comfortably. At 1:45 the whole sky . . . was a delicate salmon pink."

Although the bright nights continued for about two months, no one linked them to the exploding fireball. Some reports speculated that they were unusually brilliant displays of the aurora borealis, although the flickering characteristic of such displays was missing. Only in 1930 did a British meteorologist conclude that the millions of tons of atmospheric dust from the Tunguska blast had acted as a vast solar reflector that illuminated the night skies.

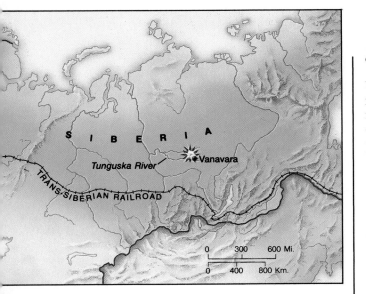

From out of the blue, *an unidentified extraterrestrial object leveled some 25 square miles of forest in remote Siberia (map) early in this century. Giant 30-inch-thick trees were snapped in two like mere matchsticks, creating an unparalleled, eerie scene of desolation shown in the contemporary photograph at left.*

Even that long-delayed connection might not have been made, however, had it not been for a young Russian scientist named Leonid A. Kulik. In 1921 the Russian Academy of Sciences assigned him the job of collecting information about meteorites. Just as he was about to embark on an exploratory trip to Siberia, a colleague handed him a 1908 newspaper clipping about passengers on the Trans-Siberian Railroad who claimed to have witnessed the fall of a large meteor. But Kulik could do little more than plot the presumed location of the impact before an early winter sealed access to the region. Years passed before he was able to arrange a second expedition.

In 1927, however, with a local Tungus man as his guide, Kulik made his way into the area of destruction. "I cannot really take in the whole majestic picture," he wrote in his diary. "From our observation point no sign of forest can be seen, for everything has been devastated and burned."

During the following weeks Kulik penetrated farther into the zone of devastation, expecting to find the remnants of a massive meteorite. What he found, much to his surprise, was an area near the very center of the destruction where the trees were stripped bare of branches but still standing. The explosion evidently had taken place directly above the trees, killing them but leaving them upright.

Extensive exploration on subsequent expeditions convinced Kulik that he would discover neither meteorite nor crater. Although he had not come up with a satisfactory explanation for what had happened, he had succeeded in focusing the attention of other scientists on the mysterious cataclysm in far-off Siberia.

Since his day, an astonishing array of theories has been offered to explain the devastation. Among the most exotic is the suggestion that it was caused by a nuclear explosion aboard an alien spaceship. Two other proposals require equal leaps of the imagination. One holds that a miniature black hole, perhaps no bigger than a speck of dust, struck the earth at Tunguska, passed all the way though the planet, and came out in the North Atlantic. Black holes are formed when aging stars collapse into themselves and their gravity becomes so intense that not even rays of light can escape their pull. Passing through the earth, a black hole theoretically could set off shock waves powerful enough to devastate a forest.

The second theory attributes the damage to an interstellar lump of antimatter that fell to earth. Antimatter is, in effect, the mirror image of ordinary matter and carries an opposite electrical charge. When a particle of antimatter encounters a corresponding particle of matter, both are annihilated in a tremendous burst of energy, such as the explosion that occurred in Siberia.

A more widely accepted explanation says that the culprit was the head of a comet on a collision course with our planet. Plummeting toward the earth, it could have exploded in midair from the incredible heat produced by its friction with the atmosphere. But other scientists prefer a variant of Kulik's original hypothesis: that the Tunguska fireball was caused by a stony meteor or, more likely, an asteroid that exploded two or three miles above the earth, with heat so intense that the entire object was vaporized and the region below it was devastated.

Whatever the cause, whether comet or asteroid or some as yet undreamed-of intergalactic wanderer, the object certainly came from outer space. Recent analysis of microscopic particles apparently left by the explosion has demonstrated, from their content of the heavy metal iridium and other materials, that they are extraterrestrial in origin. Concurrent analysis of ice that was laid down in Antarctica in 1908 and 1909 revealed an exceptional accumulation of cosmic iridium; presumably it fell from the dust thrown into the stratosphere by the Tunguska blast. Based on the amounts of iridium found in Antarctica, the exploding object is estimated to have weighed a staggering 7 million tons.

The mystery of the Siberian fireball may never be resolved. But it does provide some food for thought. What if such an event were to occur again? And what if next time the blast took place not over the trackless wastes of Siberia but over some global trouble spot? Might a nervous nation, believing it was under nuclear attack, react in kind and push the whole world over the brink into the final holocaust? The prospect, to say the least, is sobering.

Earthquake at Messina

Ancient Sicilian city leveled while it sleeps

"**M**ESSINA NON ESISTE PIÙ!" Rosina Calabresi, a terrified survivor of the worst earthquake in Messina's history, cried out in despair at the still-vivid memory of her recent ordeal: "Messina no longer exists!"

Before dawn on the chilly, rainswept morning of December 28, 1908, at the fateful hour of 5:20 A.M., the Sicilian port was hit by the first phase of a violent tremor, which within minutes brought more than 90 percent of the city's buildings hurtling down on a sleeping population of at least 100,000. Days later, in the safety of Rome, Rosina and her son Francesco told their harrowing story to an American writer named Maud Howe. According to Francesco, "there were three long shocks and the earth groaned as it rocked from side to side as if it were in pain. Though the house fell down about us we were not hurt. The door into the street was jammed and would not open. I found a small hole in the wall near it and managed to crawl through it and to help the others out."

Rosina shuddered as she recalled the horrors of that morning. "It was dark, and cold," she told Howe, "and it rained—Oh, God, how it rained!" Francesco and his pregnant wife, Rosina and her husband, and two of the elderly couple's grandchildren spent two days and nights without shelter. Russian sailors—"angels" is how Francesco described them—gave the family food and clothing and eventually safe passage to the mainland aboard their warships.

The earthquake, which measured the equivalent of 7.5 on the Richter scale, originated deep beneath the turbulent waters of the Strait of Messina, between Sicily and the toe of the Italian boot. From there, the radius of destruction extended for miles into Sicily and the mainland.

Nobody knows exactly how many of Messina's citizens died in the cataclysm. Like the Calabresi family, thousands managed to clamber from the ruins, but many of those who did so perished minutes later when a tsunami, a seismic sea wave 26 feet high swept across the city, taking hundreds of victims with it as it re-

A tell-tale clock, stopped by the earthquake at 5:20 A.M., looms over Messina's ruins.

ceded. Others burned to death as ruptured gas mains set the town ablaze. Contemporary estimates of the death toll were as high as 90,000 in Messina and 40,000 in the mainland city of Reggio di Calabria. Another 27,000 people are believed to have died in towns and villages along both coasts of the strait. Recent estimates, however, place the total number of fatalities at about 120,000.

In her account of the disaster, Howe observed that the people saved were mostly from the working class; Rosina's husband, for example, was a retired postman; Francesco, a plumber. These people, wrote Howe, "are up early in the morning and live in small houses. The great palaces of the rich proved fatal deathtraps to most of them."

Indeed, Messina's imposing palaces and public buildings were ill equipped to withstand the shock of the earthquake. (Although earth tremors had hit the Messina region many times in the past—a quake nearly wiped out the city in 1783—quake-resistant measures were not imposed on local architects until the rebuilding of Messina began after 1908.) Walls were often too lofty and too thin for their height, and many of them were constructed of pebbles and rubble, bound with inferior cement and faced with brick or stone. When the earth trembled, the inadequate masonry gave way and the buildings came crashing down into the streets, raising clouds of plaster dust to clog the eyes, noses, and throats of survivors. In many cases, the collapse of the city's grander buildings—the old cathedral, the military hospital, army barracks, and tourist hotels—brought down their humbler neighbors as well, burying hundreds of people in tremendous piles of debris.

Some of the more graphic descriptions of the chaos in Messina came from foreign visitors to the city. Constantine Doresa, a London ship broker staying at the Trinacria Hotel, was rudely jolted awake and immediately "clutched the sides of the bed, which seemed to be falling through space. . . . Then came a series of awful crashes, the roof falling all round me.

I was smothered in brick and plaster. . . . I felt for matches struck a light and was horrified to find my bed on the side of an abyss." Doresa and his traveling companion managed to lower themselves and a Swedish couple from the wreckage by means of knotted sheets. Accompanied by a band of Russian sailors and some crewmen from a Welsh steamer, Doresa later returned to the hotel with ropes and ladders to help rescue other guests.

Newspaper dispatches filed by an eyewitness, the marquis di Ruvolito, paint a grim picture of Messina after the quake. "The spectacle that greets the eye here," he wrote, "is beyond the imagination of Jules Verne." Among other scenes of horror, he describes a half-crazed family huddled under an umbrella on the rubble that had been their home. They refused all aid, preferring, they said, to die among the ruins.

All accounts tell how dazed survivors, many of them injured and most half-naked, stumbled through the wintry, debris-choked streets of the city. Looters, too, roamed the streets, pillaging shops and warehouses and desecrating the bodies of the dead. Even the law-abiding were obliged to forage wherever they could for food, water, and clothing.

The marquis and others wrote about these sad sights in poignant detail, but they also recorded many acts of heroism and charity. British, Italian, and Russian naval vessels were on hand within hours to offer help and protection. The Russians in particular were admired for their bravery in standing up to looters as well as for their rescue efforts. In one of the more amazing of many such rescue stories, the commander of a Russian cruiser managed to pull a pair of babies safe and uninjured from under a heap of rubble. "They were comfortable as possible," he wrote, "and laughing and playing with the buttons on their clothes."

Although no American ships had been sailing in the vicinity of Messina when the quake hit, the American Relief Committee in Rome chartered a German liner, the *Bayern*, which spent about a week in early January distributing supplies and medical assistance among survivors throughout the devastated region.

Relief funds poured in from Europe and the United States and from nearly every city and town in Italy not touched by the disaster. On December 30, King Victor Emmanuel and Queen Elena of Italy arrived in Messina and personally joined in the rescue work. According to Howe, the queen "rolled up her sleeves, put on her apron and went to work" nursing sick and wounded survivors. She became, as Howe noted admiringly, "the most impassioned of all who worked for Italy in the dark hour."

Dazed survivors *struggle over corpse-strewn rubble in this contemporary view of Messina on the day of the quake.*

The Big Blowup in the Northwest

Tri-state terror as millions of acres go up in flames

THREATENING TO SHOOT anyone who tried to pass him, U.S. Forest Ranger Ed Pulaski, tall and covered with grime, resolutely barred the exit of the War Eagle Tunnel, an old abandoned mine. A murmur of protest rose from the lips of the 44 men trapped with him in the damp, dark mine shaft. But Pulaski stood his ground, his bloodshot eyes as unwavering as the loaded pistol he held in his hand.

Just beyond the tunnel's entrance, the forest was engulfed in flames. Pulaski, who in a desperate gamble had herded his crew of fire fighters into the mine, no doubt realized that their rocky haven might well

The entrance to the mine where Ed Pulaski and his fire fighters took refuge from the forest flames.

turn out to be a death trap. But he knew for certain that anyone who ventured into the inferno outside was assured of instant death.

The date was August 20, 1910; the place, the Coeur d'Alene National Forest in northern Idaho. In most years the region's maze of rugged mountain peaks was emerald green with soaring stands of coniferous forest. But in the summer of 1910, the slopes were parched and dusty—the result of a drought that began in early April. The first blaze broke out on April 29, and by June, forests were aflame from Montana all the way across Idaho to eastern Washington.

Throughout May and into June and July, district rangers of the fledgling U.S. Forest Service battled blaze after blaze as the usual spring rains failed to materialize. In July, huge black thunderclouds piled up, sending dry lightning bolts into the tinder-dry trees and igniting still more fires. By midsummer so much of the area was burning that the forest service was forced to hire temporary help—miners and lumbermen who came to work alongside the rangers.

Equipped with the simplest of tools—axes, shovels, saws, and mattocks—the men dug trenches around fires to contain them, cleared underbrush, and cut down trees to make firebreaks. Some 3,000 smaller blazes had been extinguished and 90 large ones brought under control. But at the beginning of August, flames flared anew. On August 8, President William Howard Taft ordered U.S. troops to stand by.

With the air thick with smoke and the sun hanging crimson in the sky, everyone prayed for rain. Instead, on the afternoon of Saturday, August 20, a hurricane-force local wind known as the chinook came roaring out of the southwest at speeds approaching 70 miles an hour. Huge fronts of flame—one estimated to be 18 miles long—rushed across the mountains incinerating everything in their path.

Every available man had been enlisted as a fire fighter, including Ed Pulaski, who was put in charge of a crew of fire fighters battling a blaze in the flaming forests some 10 miles north of Wallace, Idaho. It was there that he spent the night of August 20 seeking safety for his men in the abandoned mine.

In Wallace, the mining and commercial hub of the area, worried residents saw the sky turn an eerie yellow. Smoke and ashes billowed in the distance, blotting out the sun completely so that lamps were needed even in midafternoon. William G. Weigle, the local Forest Service supervisor, recognizing the makings of a major catastrophe, asked the railroad company to keep a train ready for possible evacuation.

The only swift, safe route out of the town was by railroad. And even that route might soon be cut off because the many bridges that spanned plunging canyons were made of wood.

Mayor Walter Hanson agreed with Weigle's assessment of the situation. At 6:00 P.M., as the flames raced into Wallace, he ordered the fire chief to ring the evacuation bell. Although he also ordered all able-bodied men to stay behind and fight the fires, some of the town's most prominent males panicked and fled to the waiting train.

But the cowards were few and the courageous many. Pulaski fought the flames until the intensity of the inferno made such fighting useless. So did thousands of other fire fighters, while their families waited in anguish for their return—or news of their death.

What became of Ed Pulaski? At dawn on August 21, his cook, Frank Foltz, arrived in Wallace half dead, almost naked, his voice seared to an unintelligible croak. He was, nevertheless, able to whisper a plea for help for Pulaski and his crew.

When Emma Pulaski heard the news, she thought she would never see her husband alive. At the War Eagle Tunnel, where Pulaski had holed up with his crew, the smoke finally cleared, revealing five men who lay dead from smoke poisoning. But the rest were safe. One of the living, seeing the wisps of smoke disappearing and the still form of Pulaski on the damp floor of the mine, called to his companions: "Come on outside, boys, the boss is dead."

"Like hell he is," rasped Pulaski, who had regained consciousness just as his death was being announced.

The following day Emma Pulaski glanced from the window of her house, which had escaped the fire, and saw two men staggering toward her. One, being led by the other, was blind. It was Ed, ill but alive. Although his sight returned, he would never fully regain his health. Nor would he lose his place in history as one of the folk heroes of the great forest fire of 1910, which miraculously claimed only 85 known dead, of whom 78 were fire fighters.

The fire finally ended shortly after midnight on August 22. Rains fell, moisture returned to the air, and the wind died down. In the two days that the inferno lasted, it caused incredible damage. Some 3 million acres of forest land were utterly destroyed, along with a staggering total of at least 6 billion board feet of lumber. The nation as a whole was roused to take action against such overwhelming losses. Within a year, Congress passed an act providing federal aid for forest protection. But decades would elapse before Idaho's forests returned to their former glory.

In a report on the tragedy, *The New York Times* noted: "Men have fought the flames to the limit of human endurance." Those who knew Pulaski and his fellow rangers might well have added, "And beyond."

The ramshackle lumber town of South Porcupine before the devastating fire of 1911.

CANADA'S PORCUPINE FIRE

"Fire has taken possession of the town." This was the last telegraph message from the Porcupine region of Ontario, Canada, on July 11, 1911. Only a year earlier, settlers had begun pouring into the thickly forested wilderness to mine one of history's richest gold strikes. Gold fever had created colorful frontier towns such as South Porcupine, Golden City, and Pottsville. Now, in a five-hour firestorm, settlements had been razed to bare, blistered ground.

For two months before the fire, the area suffered the worst, most prolonged drought in memory. On July 10 the dry air rose to 107° F in the shade, and smoke from smoldering brushfires blotted out the sun. Then, at midday on July 11, the settlers heard an incredible roaring sound and saw the sky turn midnight black. Whipped by hurricane-force winds, the fire formed a 20-mile horseshoe-shaped front, rising at times 150 feet in the air and moving at a clip of about 8 miles per hour. Women and children were speedily evacuated from South Porcupine across the lake in every available craft. Those left behind manned a bucket brigade until the temperature rose to 118°, then ran into the turbulent waters for safety, vying for space with bears, moose, and other wild animals.

By nightfall at least 500,000 acres, or 781 square miles, of timberland had been destroyed. Evaporation lowered Porcupine Lake by two feet that day. Official loss of life was put at 73, but residents believe that lone prospectors in the woods brought the total to 200.

Death of the Titanic

Iceberg sinks world's largest ship on maiden voyage

"I CANNOT IMAGINE any condition which would cause a ship to founder. . . . Modern shipbuilding has gone beyond that." So said Edward J. Smith, one of Britain's most distinguished seamen and future captain of the steamship *Titanic,* in 1907. Five years later, as the liner *Bremen* was far out at sea on the North Atlantic, steaming west toward New York, a stroller on the promenade deck called the attention of fellow passengers to a number of objects—it was not clear what they were—floating quietly on the ocean's surface. As the great ship drew closer to the scene, many of those on deck hurried into their staterooms, weeping or unable to speak. Those who remained outside as the ship swept past the silent assemblage far beneath her decks realized what they were seeing. The *Bremen* had come upon many of the lifeless, life-jacketed people who had perished in freezing waters five days earlier, in the predawn hours of April 15, after their ship, the 46,000-ton *Titanic,* began her horrifying 2½-mile descent into the permanent blackness of the ocean floor.

"We saw the body of one woman dressed only in her night dress, and clasping a baby to her breast," one of the *Bremen*'s passengers later reported. "Close by was the body of another woman with her arms tightly clasped round a shaggy dog. . . . We saw the bodies of three men in a group, all clinging to a chair. Floating by just beyond them were the bodies of a dozen men, all wearing life belts and clinging desperately together as though in their last struggle for life."

No such end seemed conceivable when the keel of the *Titanic* was laid in the spring of 1909. The ship was heralded as the biggest object ever set in motion by man; indeed, the statistics that began rolling out of the cavernous shipyards in Belfast seemed larger than life. Every square inch of supporting pavement beneath the new behemoth was holding more than 2 tons of weight. The rudder alone, weighing more than 100 tons, was as big as a full-grown elm tree. Each of the *Titanic*'s four funnels could easily accommodate two locomotives traveling side by side; the vessel's 159 furnaces would eat up 2 tons of coal every mile; and the completed ship would be 11 stories tall and as long as four city blocks. Once this 50,000-horsepower marvel was in motion, a crew of nearly a thousand would be answering the needs and whims of the more than 2,500 passengers she could accommodate when fully booked. Perhaps the most satisfying statistic of all was the 16 watertight compartments, separated by emergency doors that could be dropped in seconds at the flick of an electrical switch from the bridge. If the *Titanic* was not truly "unsinkable," as the tabloids liked to say, she came as close as any vessel ever had.

Passenger comfort, rather than high speed, was the White Star Line's main objective for its newest liner. For top-paying passengers there was a Parisian sidewalk cafe in addition to more standard restaurant accommodations, with three exceptional musicians on hand to serenade the diners. The best suites had sumptuous furnishings and beautifully finished oak paneling that helped justify the peak charge of $4,350 one way (nearly $40,000 in today's dollars). The ship was one of the first to have a swimming pool; a 21-light candelabra illuminated the grand staircase; cigar holders were provided in all the first-class bathrooms; and an electric potato peeler made life a little

The very picture of British seamanship, Captain Edward J. Smith, at 59, planned to retire after the Titanic's gala first voyage. The smoking room (below), like so much else aboard this colossal ship, offered elegance on a scale unmatched in maritime travel.

Westward bound, *the great liner steams away from the Irish coast on April 11, 1912, never to see land again.*

easier for the scullery boys. A gymnasium boasted all the latest exercise machines from Germany, and amateur photographers were delighted to hear that there would be a darkroom on board so that their film could be developed *en voyage.* Even the 1,000 or so steerage passengers on the lower decks would find better living accommodations than many had ever known before.

By any standard—size, design, comfort, or safety—she was without question the greatest ship ever built.

So it was that the new giant of Great Britain approached berth 44 at Southampton on April 3, 1912. As she prepared to cast off on April 10 and head for open seas, "it was clear to everybody on board that we had a ship that was going to create the greatest stir British shipping circles had ever known," wrote Second Officer Charles H. Lightoller. "Each day, as the voyage went on, everybody's admiration of the ship increased; for the way she behaved, for the total absence of vibration, for her steadiness even with the ever-increasing speed, as she warmed up to her work."

Any society columnist who had managed to book passage on the *Titanic*'s first voyage could have filled a notebook in a hurry simply by recording the names and shipboard activities of the rich and famous who were traveling first class. Among them were the mining magnate Benjamin Guggenheim and the recently divorced John Jacob Astor, who had left gossiping celebrity watchers behind to show Europe to his new teenage bride, Madeleine. British nobility was represented by Sir Cosmo and Lady Duff Gordon, and American politics by the dashing Maj. Archibald Butt, formerly an aide to President Theodore Roosevelt and now serving President William Howard Taft. One of the most venerable of all the millionaires was Isidor Straus, head of Macy's department store and a man obviously devoted to Ida Straus, his wife of more than 40 years. Equally notable was Mrs. Margaret Tobin Brown of Denver, Colorado, distinguished by her forthright manner, definite opinions, and fashionably large hats. Known to her friends as Molly, she would soon be celebrated far and wide as the "Unsinkable" Molly Brown. One of the busiest figures aboard was Thomas Andrews, an official of the firm that had built the *Titanic,* who seemed to be spending every waking moment writing down improvements for the ship (too much dark woodwork on the promenade; too many screws in the stateroom hat racks) that could be taken care of when she returned to England.

By Sunday morning, April 14, the *Titanic* had in-

Only minutes from the end, *the stern of the* Titanic *rises dramatically as her bow drops deeper beneath the surface and those still aboard fall or jump into the frigid water. A few days later, a sailor on another ship in the vicinity photographed an iceberg (above) with an unmistakable slash of red paint at the waterline, drifting south toward its own disappearance into the sea.*

creased her daily running speed to nearly 550 miles, and perhaps no one was enjoying the trip more than a young science teacher from London named Lawrence Beesley. With the air growing chilly over the Atlantic, Beesley began a conversation in the ship's library with an especially dedicated English clergyman, Ernest Carter. Carter, who ministered in some of London's dreariest slums, was looking forward to a hymn sing, open to all, that he would be leading at 8:30 P.M. in the second-class dining salon.

The singing that night included a hymn with the refrain "For those in peril on the sea," and Carter added a quiet goodnight by saying that he was sure he spoke for all passengers in expressing the confidence he had in the great new liner because of her exceptional steadiness and size. Shortly afterwards, about 10:45 P.M., Lawrence Beesley turned into his cabin for a bit of bedtime reading.

Things were not quite as relaxed up on the *Titanic*'s bridge, whose windows were providing good protection from a temperature that had fallen sharply and was now holding at 32°F. All through Sunday, the *Titanic*'s officers had been receiving messages from various other liners on the North Atlantic that the Labrador current had apparently carried some tremendous icebergs farther south than usual, well into the shipping lanes. Partly because of a tradition that ships did not slow down until ice could actually be seen, and partly because of poor communication between the radio room and the bridge, the warnings received cursory notice but not much more. At 9:40 P.M., however, a report chattered in on the wireless from a much smaller ship, the *Mesaba*, warning that heavy ice concentrations and "great number large icebergs" lay in the immediate vicinity of the oncoming giant, still steaming hard through the calm, chilly

182

to do in the crow's nest but hold on and wait.

Thirty-seven seconds later a tremor was felt throughout the *Titanic,* and an inky, forbidding shape scraped past the ship on her starboard side. In the controlled inferno of the number 6 boiler room, where heat from the furnaces could drive the temperature up to 101° and keep it there, fireman Frederick Barrett stared unbelievingly at a two-foot-high rush of icy sea water cascading through the *Titanic*'s buckled-in side, just seconds before First Officer William Murdoch activated the electric lever that closed all watertight doors below. With the roar of the sea and the ship's alarm bell in their ears, Barrett and another crewman scrambled into the number 5 boiler room. A moment later the watertight door slammed shut like a guillotine blade behind them. When Barrett climbed the escape ladder and peered down into number 6, he saw that the room was rapidly filling with water.

A hurried inspection belowdecks left no room for doubt: the huge ship had been mortally wounded.

Shipbuilder Thomas Andrews was summoned to the bridge from his cabin. Together, he and a shaken Captain Smith descended into the depths of the ship, doing their best to walk at a pace that would not alarm any passengers who came upon them at an unexpected hour in an unexpected place. In less than 10 minutes, they found that the water was already 14 feet deep in the ship and the bow had started its downward dip. Andrews, wasting no time, did some arithmetic on a sheet of tablet paper and looked up. An hour and a half before she goes down, maybe two, Andrews said; no more than that.

Captain Smith likewise wasted no time. He ordered the radio room to start calling any and all ships for immediate rescue assistance. Then, about 12:05 A.M., he had the *Titanic*'s 16 wooden lifeboats and 4 collapsibles—only half of what was needed—uncovered, and the debarkation into the boats began.

So also began the hundreds of individual episodes of bravery, cowardice, luck, and despair that together made this night one of the most compelling dramas of the century.

Among the throng was Mrs. J. Stuart White, who was not a bit alarmed by the light jolt she noticed ("just as though we went over about a thousand marbles. There was nothing terrifying about it at all"). Within two hours she would be seated in lifeboat number 8, complaining about the discourtesy of smoking on the part of some crew members in the boat, while the stricken liner behind her—all lights still blazing—settled lower into the sea.

Lawrence Beesley, the schoolteacher, had left his

night. The *Titanic*'s hard-pressed chief radio operator, Jack Phillips, was too busy to send the *Mesaba*'s message to the bridge because he was backed up with greetings the *Titanic*'s passengers wanted to send ahead to loved ones in the United States and Canada. So the warning of imminent ice lay unnoticed in the wireless room sometime after two of the liner's lookouts, Frederick Fleet and Reginald Lee, both young Southampton men, made their 50-foot climb to the crow's nest above the forecastle deck and began their watch under a star-studded sky.

At 11:40 P.M., Fleet suddenly saw something dead ahead toward which his ship was moving fast— a something so black that it could scarcely be distinguished from the ocean surface. Fleet got off three strong rings on the lookout bell and followed this up immediately with a terse call to the bridge: "Iceberg right ahead." Then there was nothing else

Shivering but still alive, *survivors in one of the* Titanic's *lifeboats are brought alongside the* Carpathia, *which reached the desolate scene just after 4 A.M.*

cabin to see if he could find out why the *Titanic's* engines had so abruptly fallen silent. When no one could give him a good reason, Beesley went back to his cabin. Later he came out again and noticed "something unusual about the stairs, a curious sense of something out of balance and of not being able to put one's feet down in the right place."

The *Titanic* had already begun her journey to the ocean floor.

Thomas Andrews seemed to be everywhere, helping others to don life jackets, even though he was without one himself. To one of the ship's stewardesses he said that "it is very serious, but keep the bad news quiet, for fear of panic." He was more honest with closer acquaintances. "She is torn to bits below," Andrews told them, warning that the end might be little more than an hour away.

Monsieur Luigi Gatti, manager of the elegant Ritz

Restaurant in the first-class section, was ready for anything: he stood on the boat deck wearing a top hat, carrying a small suitcase, with a traveling blanket over one arm. He would drown sometime during the morning with most of his dining room staff.

The sound most would remember from the vessel's last minutes was that of music coming from the afterdeck.

The metal end pin of Roger Bricoux's cello left a track in the luxurious carpeting of the *Titanic* as he hurried to join his fellow musicians during the lifeboat debarkation. They continued to play until the increasing slant of the deck made it impossible to stand. No member of the orchestra was saved.

John Jacob Astor helped his wife step over a windowsill and into a lifeboat with as much calm as if he were ushering her to a seat on his yacht at Newport. He asked if he might accompany her, was told that he couldn't, and stepped back politely.

Isidor and Ida Straus had made their decision and would not be budged. One survivor heard the old retailing merchant refuse a lifeboat seat, which was offered because of his age, saying, "I do not wish any distinction in my favor which is not granted to others." Ida Straus refused a seat just as emphatically. "No," she said, "I will not be separated from my husband. As we have lived, so we will die." She gave her maid, Ellen Bird, a warm coat to wear in the lifeboat, and then the two went below to accept whatever might happen in the final minutes they had together.

In boiler room number 5, two junior engineers, Herbert Harvey and Jonathan Shepherd, were keeping the pumps going. Then Shepherd fell into a manhole and broke his leg. He was moved to the other end of the room while Harvey and Fred Barrett stayed with the pumps. Suddenly the wall between numbers 5 and 6 caved in, and Barrett made his second miraculous escape of the night. Looking backward and down the escape ladder, he saw Harvey run to Shepherd's aid, and then both were drowned by the incoming flood just before the whole room went dark.

Archie Butt, according to numerous accounts, continued to exhibit the same coolness and courtesy that had made him a favorite in Washington. To a woman screaming with fright, he said gently, "Really, you must not act like that; we are going to see you through this thing." Shortly afterward, he gave Marie Young, music teacher of the Roosevelt children, a special reason to remember him. "Archie put me in the boat; wrapped blankets around me; and tended me as carefully as if we were starting a motor ride. When he had wrapped me up, he stepped upon a gunwale of the boat, and lifting his hat, smiled down at me. 'Goodbye,

Miss Young,' he said. 'Good luck to you and don't forget to remember me to the folks back home.' "

What astonished many who lived through the night was the quiet on board the ship in her final minutes of life. There were only murmurs on the after end of the boat deck where Father Thomas R. Byles heard confessions and gave absolution to a hundred kneeling souls. In the wireless room the only sound was the clatter of the telegraph key as Jack Phillips still transmitted the SOS and the message: "Women and children on boats. Cannot last much longer." Guggenheim and his faithful valet stood quietly side by side; earlier, they had removed their life jackets and changed into full evening dress. "We've dressed up in our best," Guggenheim had told someone who questioned them, "and are prepared to go down like gentlemen."

Now it was the *Titanic*'s turn to give up the effort of staying afloat.

At 2:20 A.M., those in the lifeboats and those already struggling in the water saw the great stern of the ship lift itself clear of the sea and hang suspended for a few seconds, perhaps as long as a minute, before dropping like an elevator into the darkness. In one lifeboat, nine-year-old Frank Goldsmith and his mother both searched the sea for the boy's father just before the *Titanic*'s lights flashed off forever. (Many years later, as a grown man living in Detroit, Goldsmith could not help but remember that moment whenever he heard shouts coming from a ballpark near his house—shouts like those he had heard from frantic people drowning in the open ocean after the *Titanic* disappeared. At his wish, Goldsmith's ashes were taken out to sea after his death and dropped into the same watery expanse where his father had last bid him goodbye.)

Somewhere out beyond the Goldsmith lifeboat, Harold Phillimore, a plucky bath steward, was determined to stay alive somehow until he could find something buoyant that might save him. Suddenly he was pulled up and onto a piece of the ship's paneling by a man he didn't know. As the two sat facing each other, each clutching the slippery wood, Phillimore's companion looked directly at him in the darkness and—in what must have the absolute understatement of the entire disaster—said, "What a night!" and then fell off dead into the sea.

Near dawn, it was almost silent in the boats. Occasionally there was the splash of an oar, or someone weeping, or some hearty words coming out of lifeboat number 6, where Molly Brown had gradually assumed charge of the 28 persons aboard. She was there only by accident: on the *Titanic* she had wrapped herself in her furs, helped another passenger enter number 6, and was turning away to investigate matters elsewhere when she was suddenly lifted up and unceremoniously dropped four feet into the descending lifeboat. Ship's quartermaster Robert Hichens was in such a shivering terror of an iceberg dead ahead that one woman wrapped her steamer robe about his shoulders; Molly Brown used her large sable stole likewise to keep a half-frozen stoker alive, and then got everybody row-

Anxiously awaiting news, *which for days was fragmentary and often inaccurate, crowds gathered outside newspaper offices on both sides of the ocean to read the latest wireless dispatches.*

185

ing to keep their circulation going and their spirits up.

Finally, at about 4 A.M., the most wonderful sight that any of those who had found places in the lifeboats would ever see came steaming toward them at daybreak of a perfect spring morning. The *Carpathia*, a sturdy one-funnel liner owned by the Cunard Line, had picked up the *Titanic*'s last despairing calls for help and with all furnaces blazing had picked her way through the ice fields to make the rescue. After taking aboard all 705 survivors and holding a brief memorial service over the spot where the *Titanic* had gone down, the *Carpathia* headed back for New York, where a crowd of 30,000 gathered for her arrival.

In the months that followed, separate British and U.S. commissions delved into this worst accident in transatlantic shipping history. The statistics alone were appalling: of more than 2,200 passengers and crew, some 1,500 perished. The *Titanic*'s lifeboats, it turned out, could accommodate only about 1,200—a fact even more shocking because it satisfied the legal standards of the day—and in the chaos of the sinking almost 500 of those seats went unfilled. Most cruelly, amid all the headlines about millionaires lost at sea, the fate of those in third class was scarcely mentioned. Some steerage passengers were confined behind metal gates and bulkheads and were not allowed onto the boat deck until many of the lifeboats had been lowered. The consequences were starkest among the young: of the children in first and second class, all but one survived; of those in steerage, two-thirds died.

DISCOVERY OF A STUNNING GRAVEYARD

The drop to the bottom was made at the speed of 100 feet per minute. Inside the odd-looking craft named *Alvin* were an eminent marine geologist, Dr. Robert Ballard, and two associates from the Woods Hole Oceanographic Institution in Massachusetts. Throughout their long journey downward, the three sat hunched inside the cramped research vessel, listening to the harmonies of Vivaldi filtering through the sound system, and looking out through three tiny portholes at the darkness coming up to meet them from the icy depths of the North Atlantic. Somewhere below, hidden in absolute blackness, was the colossus no human eyes had directly seen since it made its own descent to the bottom 74 years earlier.

Finally, hovering just above the ocean floor after a 2½-hour descent, the Ballard team began its search, with *Alvin*'s lights stabbing through a stormlike swarm of waterborne particles as the vessel moved slowly south.

Suddenly, there it was.

"An endless slab of black steel rising out of the bottom," Ballard later wrote about the discovery. "Our journey at long last has reached its goal. *Titanic* is a few inches away. In that brief instant we become the first ever to actually see *Titanic* in her grave."

Already well known for other oceanographic research projects, Ballard had long nurtured a fascination with the lost *Titanic*, and in 1985 he was

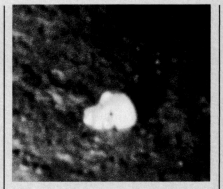

An eerie vision, this doll's head lay in stark solitude on the sea floor.

ready to find her. That summer, he set out aboard the U.S. Navy research ship *Knorr*, which carried two smaller submersible craft—the *Argo*, which could be towed underwater and make videotapes, and the *Angus*, used for still photography. The *Knorr* made a rendezvous with a marine exploration team from France in that same expanse of the North Atlantic where the *Titanic* had last reported her position after colliding with the iceberg. The *Knorr* eventually picked up the search after the French scientists had finished using their own sonar equipment to "plow" 80 percent of the area on the ocean floor where the *Titanic* was believed to be.

On September 1, shortly after midnight, those crew members monitor-ing the *Knorr*'s 20 video screens were suddenly transfixed when the *Argo*'s cameras picked up the image of a huge boiler—a boiler closely resembling those installed at Belfast just before the great liner's first and final voyage. Soon afterward, sonar signals announced the presence nearby of something far larger. The *Titanic* had been found.

Ballard led a brief memorial service on the deck of the *Knorr* in honor of all those who had perished in the *Titanic* or in the freezing waters about her. Then, after additional photographic runs over the wreck, the *Knorr* and her crew returned to a heroes' welcome at Woods Hole.

On the second expedition to the *Titanic* site, made in July 1986, Ballard brought along the 25-foot-long *Alvin*. It was from this dependable little vessel—often perched with its three intent occupants on the deck surfaces of the *Titanic*—that *Jason Jr.*, an even smaller unit described by Ballard as a "swimming eyeball," was sent out on a 250-foot tether to make its way down the same now ghostly staircases up which so many of the *Titanic*'s passengers had climbed to see if there might still be room on the lifeboats.

Contrary to a long-held belief, the *Titanic* had not been sliced open by the iceberg. Instead, the researchers found that the ship's starboard bow plates had buckled under the impact

As has been true of other disasters, the *Titanic*'s tragedy was in some small way redeemed by measures enacted to prevent a recurrence. In the future there would be lifeboat space for everyone aboard a ship, mandatory lifeboat drills on all crossings, and shipping lanes moved farther to the south during iceberg season. But there was something in this disaster that could not be redeemed. Walter Lord, the author of *A Night to Remember*, remarked that "the *Titanic* has come to stand for a world of tranquility and civility that we have somehow lost. . . . In 1912, people had confidence. Now nobody is sure of anything and the more uncertain we become, the more we long for a happier era when we felt we knew the answers."

The *Titanic* brilliantly epitomized that era, and her sudden destruction was an almost incomprehensible blow. One of the survivors was Charles Lightoller, the ship's second officer, who later testified before a congressional inquiry. As the ship plunged, Lightoller had become stuck to a grating directly over the hold. Miraculously, a sudden blast of upcoming air blew him free, and he managed to climb aboard and take charge of an overturned collapsible lifeboat. Balancing himself and about 30 others on that precarious refuge, he had witnessed the death throes of a technological masterpiece and heard the shrieks of others about to meet their own deaths. Describing the experience to committee members, Lightoller delivered a terse and fitting epitaph for the age of assurance: "I don't think I'll ever feel secure of anything ever again."

of the collision, thereby opening up the ship to the sea. Another major discovery was that the stern of the *Titanic* had wrenched itself away from the rest of the ship early in its descent to the bottom.

Before departing, Ballard placed a small memorial marker on the stern. It was on this same stern—rising gradually upward as the bow settled deeper into the sea—that some 1,500 people spent their final moments. There, af-ter the last lifeboat had pulled away, they knew that almost certain death was still some minutes away, and that there was still time, in the silences of mind and heart, to wonder how they would meet it when it came.

The Titanic *was seen by human eyes for the first time since 1912 during* Alvin's *historic exploration.*

Influenza Strikes Worldwide

In the shadow of World War I rages one of the worst catastrophes of all time

IT WAS THE SUMMER of 1918, and Maj. Branch Rickey, who later would gain fame for breaking big league baseball's color line, was sitting on the deck of a World War I troop transport about to leave New York. With him was Charles Sawyer, who would in time become secretary of commerce under President Harry S Truman. Idly chatting, the two men pondered the need for the three coffins lined up on deck.

Soon after they sailed, the need became apparent: a body was placed in each casket and lowered into the sea. Dozens more wrapped bodies followed those first three overboard, until there were no weights left to make the corpses sink. And when the ship arrived at last in Saint-Nazaire, France, after a dreadful, 14-day crossing, many other bodies were laid out on the top deck.

The silent killer that had invaded the ship and inflicted such heavy casualties was a deadly new strain of the influenza virus. In record time the illness raced around the globe and, worldwide, resulted in a minimum of 20 million fatalities.

Caused by a slippery mutant virus, the disease was widely known as Spanish influenza—though for no good reason. Although it ravaged Spain, no evidence suggests that it originated there. Indeed, the first clear trail of the infection led backward from American troop transports to ports of embarkation to army camps—most notably to Fort Riley, Kansas. Two divisions had set out from that old cavalry post toward the end of a spring flu epidemic there that had felled more than 1,100 men and killed 46.

This spring outbreak, however, proved to be merely a beginning, spreading infection but not heavy mortality to France and Flanders. The flu's big sweep came in the fall of 1918, just as the Allies were starting their win-the-war offensive on the western front. But even as Gen. John J. Pershing, commander of the American Expeditionary Forces (AEF), was calling for every available soldier, he received word that the October draft call was canceled because of raging flu outbreaks in army camps and ports.

Pershing won his Argonne battle—in part because the German Army was also racked by flu—but at heavy cost to his troops from both disease and enemy action. While 35,000 men of the AEF were killed in battle or died of wounds between September 1 and November 11, some 9,000 more perished from flu and pneumonia in roughly the same period, and 2,000 of their buddies joined them beneath the soil by the spring of 1919. In the meantime, about 22,000 soldiers died in army camps or service ports back in the United States.

Man for man, the navy was hit even harder, losing 5,000 men to the epidemic in a service only one-tenth the size of the army. The captain of the U.S.S. *Pitts-burgh*, a cruiser on patrol in Rio de Janeiro harbor, for example, saw more than half his men disabled, buried 58 of them, and turned for home, taking the *Pittsburgh* out of the war as surely as if she had been sunk by a torpedo.

The epidemic claimed some 550,000 American victims—nearly ten times the number of battle fatalities in the war.

Although the killer flu seemed to prey most greedily on victims between the ages of 20 and 40—the age group dominating the armed forces—it was not prejudiced in favor of men in uniform. From army camps and naval bases, it penetrated into every corner of the United States.

As frightening as the speed of its spread was the speed with which the flu wrenched its victims from vibrant health to gasping death. In Washington, D.C., one distraught young woman telephoned authorities to report that two of her roommates had died, a third was ill, and she alone remained healthy. When the police came to investigate, they found that all four girls were dead. And in Quincy, Massachusetts, three men fell dead on the sidewalks in a single afternoon.

Tragedy was everywhere, with Philadelphia one of the worst-hit cities; by the end of October, it counted 13,000 dead from the epidemic. New York City suffered 851 deaths on a single day—October 23—and averaged 5,500 new cases of flu each day of the following week. And the Midwest was practically paralyzed, with its sickened miners and factory workers unable to keep up with war orders. In that last terrible week of October, a grand total of 21,000 Americans died in the 48 states, the highest seven-day mortality toll in U.S. history.

Flailing desperately against an unseen foe, Americans tried all manner of defenses. A variety of vaccines were concocted and used, on the theory that a bacterium was the villain. Medical researchers did not learn until years later that flu is caused by a virus, nor did they have the antibiotic know-how to combat the pneumonia that frequently finished off its victims.

Strict control measures were taken to stop the spread of infection. Crowds were dispersed. Theaters, schools, saloons, and even churches were closed in many cities. Fines were levied for spitting in public, and New York City posted prominent signs threatening jail sentences and huge fines for anyone caught coughing or sneezing without a handkerchief.

Among the most ubiquitous of preventive steps was the wearing of face masks. From Europe to Australia, people fixed layers of gauze across their mouths and noses in hopes of preventing the transmission of infectious droplets. In fact, the masks did little if any

With gauze masks *stretched over their faces to guard against the flu, doughboys paraded through Seattle in December 1918. Although the Great War in Europe had ended, the battle against the killer virus raged at home. Home remedies such as hot vinegar packs and snuff and even masks and daily gargling proved useless. Since there was no effective antidote for the disease, it simply had to run its course.*

Emergency hospitals, *like this one in Lawrence, Massachusetts, cropped up all over the country as flu cases multiplied.*

good, since the virus passed easily through the gauze. Even so, San Francisco required masks on everyone in public, and "mask-slackers" were given a hard time. While other cities mandated masks only for those in "contact" occupations, such as dentists, barbers, and bank tellers, legions of Americans "took the veil" voluntarily.

Most Americans of 1918 were hardened by casualties in the family and inured to epidemic illness—older people had stoically withstood plagues of yellow fever, typhoid, and typhus in their own lifetimes. But, while there was no widespread public panic when the flu made its deadly appearance, instances of horror and individual terror could be found on every side. In Portland, Oregon, ambulance drivers on emergency calls often found their patients abandoned in their homes; the families had telephoned for help, then fled the contagion.

In Philadelphia a Catholic priest assembled a caravan of six wagons and a truck and set out with a task force to search back alleys and tenements for victims. Forcing locked doors when necessary, the team collected more than 200 bodies in 24 hours, then carted them to the morgue, which was already stacked with corpses three and four deep.

Dr. James P. Leake, a physician who opened an emergency hospital in Washington, D.C., had his own gruesome tale to tell. The facility

Il conquistatore dell'Europa

The true conqueror *in the war was the flu, according to an Italian cartoon of the time.*

filled so quickly, he later recalled, that "the only way we could find room for the sick was to have undertakers waiting at the door. . . . The living came in one door and the dead went out the other."

Coffins and grave diggers were both in short supply. Many victims went into the ground in plain pine boxes, and in Philadelphia, prisoners were sent to the cemeteries to dig graves. Even when bodies did not pile up, mourning was sometimes restricted. Chicago banned all public funerals for a time, forbade bodies to be taken into church or chapel, and permitted no more than 10 mourners to accompany a coffin to the cemetery.

From a medical point of view, the battle against the flu was essentially a failure. But defeat had its heroes, too, and there were thousands of them among the doctors and nurses who had to stay home and do double duty because the AEF had taken so many of their best and brightest colleagues. While they were able to bring comfort to the stricken, however, they could do little in the way of healing: they were simply powerless to prescribe against a disease for which they knew no cure.

Meantime all manner of "preventions" and "cures" were touted and hustled all across the land: drink scotch, eat lots of garlic, remove tonsils or teeth, inhale chloroform. In October 1918 Surgeon General Rupert Blue felt compelled to issue an official warning. "The Health Ser-

190

vice," he cautioned, "urges the public to remember that there is as yet no specific cure for influenza."

Nor was there any geographical boundary. From its probable starting point at Fort Riley, Kansas, the flu spread like wildfire around the globe. In the first week of November, when the epidemic was loosening its grip on the United States, 14,000 died from it in England. Whole Eskimo villages in the Arctic were wiped out, as were entire settlements in Central Africa. Half a million died in Mexico, while in Canada 44,000 succumbed. French soldiers went down in large numbers, and the disease exploded among French civilians. In order "not to further demoralize the French populace," AEF flu victims in the Paris area were spirited away to cemeteries by night. Flu leapt the Hindenberg Line and ravaged Germany as a companion to defeat and starvation. There also were extraordinarily high death rates in Prague, Bucharest, and Odessa. Russia lost an estimated 450,000 people to the epidemic, Italy 375,000, and Great Britain a final total of 228,000.

And then there was India. As might be expected, the casualties in that teeming country were enormous. In part because innumerable bodies were burned in remote villages before officials could arrive to make an accurate count, death estimates varied wildly. The minimum toll, though, was probably at least 5 million.

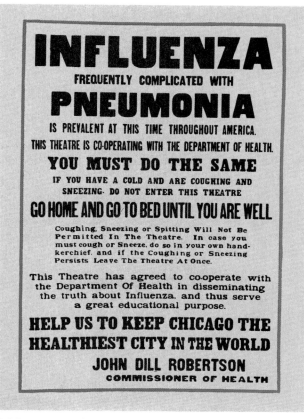

Public warnings *from health officials proved futile against the spreading epidemic. Some cities were simply forced to close their theaters, schools, churches, and other gathering places for months at a time.*

The worst suffering was among the aborigines of the small Pacific islands.

The most vulnerable of all the world's people seemed to be the natives of the South Pacific. Since they had been insulated from all previous flu epidemics, they had not built up defensive immunity. U.S. Navy ships carried the virus to Guam, where 4.5 percent of the population died, and to the Society Islands, where more than 10 percent of all Tahitians perished. Western Samoans suffered the highest per capita devastation of the entire epidemic. A flu-ridden ship from New Zealand put into Apia harbor on the island of Upolu on November 7, 1918, and by the end of the year 7,542 Western Samoans were dead from influenza and its complications—20 percent of the entire population of the territory.

In most parts of the world the monster epidemic had done its worst by the end of 1918. But even then it had not quite completed its carnage. March 1919 saw nearly 4,000 flu-related deaths in London and other British cities. The mortality rate that spring was even higher in Germany. And as late as 1920, a third wave of the epidemic killed 100,000 Americans.

Flu also dogged the 1919 peace conference at Versailles, striking all of the Big Three participants—President Woodrow Wilson of the United States, Prime Minister David Lloyd George of Great Britain, and Premier Georges Clemenceau of France. A great unknown of history is whether Wilson's maladies, including the flu, loosened his grip on the peace process in its crucial stages.

Could a calamity like that of 1918 happen again? Ever since a flu virus in humans was first isolated in 1933, there has been no doubt that some strain of this Type A influenza, as it was called, was the 1918 killer. Along with polio, influenza A thereafter became one of the most studied of all viruses.

Are such extensive research efforts a guarantee against future catastrophe? Not really, or at least not quite. Optimists point to improved vaccines made possible by what has been learned about flu; the less optimistic remind us of the infinite capacity of the flu virus to develop new strains. The viral source of the "Asian" flu epidemic in 1957, for example, was so different from the earlier strain that it was called Type A2. Could yet another mutant encircle the globe before a vaccine could be developed to protect against it? No one knows the answers. The age-old epic of influenza, unreeling its deadliest chapter in 1918, no doubt still has surprises to reveal.

The Great Kanto Earthquake

Tokyo and Yokohama devastated by massive tremors and whirlwinds of fire

FEW EARTHQUAKES in human memory have been more violent or exacted a higher toll. Two minutes before noon on Saturday, September 1, 1923, the earth beneath Sagami Bay, 50 miles south of Tokyo, opened up, unleashing a wave of destruction through the great Kanto Plain, site of Japan's capital city, Tokyo, and its largest seaport, Yokohama. At its epicenter in Sagami Bay, the earthquake registered a lethal 8.3 on the Richter scale. The initial shock lasted nearly five minutes and was followed shortly afterwards by a tsunami, a killer wave that scoured the coast, sweeping people and houses out to sea. A second major tremor blasted the Kanto region 24 hours later, while hundreds of minor aftershocks kept survivors in a state of panic throughout the weekend.

The cataclysm announced itself as "a grinding blow beneath our feet," wrote Roderick Matheson, the *Chicago Tribune*'s Tokyo correspondent. "The earth groaned, buildings began to shift and crack, and then with a roar came the first of a series of tremendous shocks. The ground swayed and swung, making a foothold almost impossible, while from every building rose a fine dust, darkening the air. The groaning of the swaying buildings rose to a roar, and then a deafening sound as the pitching, swaying structures began to crumble and fall.

"A few seconds after the warning tremor the buildings began vomiting the frightened occupants, colliding

with each other and falling as the ground heaved and swung. Tripping over the first litter in the streets, they all ran, staggering and falling, in the direction of the closest open ground. All were pallid with fright, a few fainting and many laughing hysterically."

Although the first tremor brought down many buildings and killed large numbers of people, fire was the principal cause of destruction and death. When the earthquake struck, many families had been cooking their midday meals on the hibachis, or open charcoal braziers, used in every Japanese household.

Hot coals strewn on straw mats in houses built of paper and wood became a formula for instant tragedy.

Within minutes, thousands of homes in Tokyo were ablaze, and because the quake had ruptured the city's water mains, the fires could not be put out. By 4 o'clock, according to Matheson, 21 major fires were raging in the capital, and people were pouring out of

Death came at noon to *downtown Tokyo as the great Kanto earthquake ripped apart the Japanese capital, transforming it into a landscape of horror and desolation.*

the burning districts in search of a safe haven, carrying with them what possessions they could.

But safe havens proved hard to find. Fanned by sharp winds and fed by the debris of wrecked houses, the fires developed into all-consuming whirlwinds of flame that raced through the overcrowded streets and alleys of downtown Tokyo with murderous effect. Bridges and narrow thoroughfares became deathtraps in which refugees could neither press forward nor turn back. On one of the large wooden bridges spanning the Sumida River, for example, hundreds of frantic people were trapped and incinerated by two walls of fire that swept toward the river from either bank.

On the east bank of the Sumida, in the section of Tokyo known as the Low City, police and firemen designated a park, formerly the site of an army clothing depot, as a refugee assembly area. By 4 o'clock Saturday afternoon, some 40,000 people had crammed into the park when suddenly a firestorm descended upon them, killing more than 30,000 in a matter of instants. So tightly packed were the victims, it is said, that they died standing up.

The destruction of Tokyo by fire was "an amazing and terrifying spectacle," according to an eyewitness report published in *The New York Times.* "Frequent dynamiting of buildings strengthened the impression of war. The sky over the city all night long was scarlet or orange, and vast clouds of gray, black and white smoke rolled up from the earth. Imagination would have failed to conceive such a sight." On Sunday morning, continued the report, "half of the city had been leveled and in the smoking ruins the workers were collecting bodies, which were piled in heaps and covered with mats until they were removed for burial." (In fact, the corpses were not buried but rather cremated collectively in kerosene fires.)

Of Tokyo's 15 wards only one, in the hilly High City in the western part of the capital, was untouched by fire. Five wards, all of them in the Low City along the Sumida River and Tokyo Bay, were almost completely wiped out. Tokyo, the hub of Japanese politics, business, and culture, lost more than 300,000 buildings, including 300 government buildings, 1,500 schools and libraries, 2,500 churches, 5,000 banks, 20,000 factories and warehouses, and 250 theaters and amusement centers. Also destroyed in the earthquake was the Imperial University Library, one of the world's oldest and greatest collections of rare books, original documents, and priceless art objects.

Eighteen miles south of Tokyo, the smaller city of Yokohama suffered relatively greater damage than the capital. Late Saturday night Roderick Matheson left a still-burning Tokyo and eventually made his way to the port city by car, sampan, and on foot. It was a horrific journey that took the *Chicago Tribune* reporter "through destroyed villages and over roads growing worse, with stretches split with twenty-foot cracks, bridges down and the roadbed churned and scattered.

"Everywhere the living were sleeping in the open Earth, spasms occurred every few minutes, some severe and bringing down shattered walls. All attempts to rent a sampan, bicycle or ricksha failed, the Japanese being dazed and unwilling."

In Yokohama itself some 60,000 buildings were destroyed, along with the city's vital docks and harbor facilities. "The roads were ripped, torn and gashed with cracks sufficient to engulf an automobile," wrote Matheson. "Dead were everywhere, with more beneath the ruins." The city's foreign quarter was "bare of life and habitation. The ground dropped three feet everywhere in the city, leaving steel work, bridges,

and sewer openings sticking up." In the Japanese sectors "many thousands, cut off by the flames, had died in heaps of ghastly, grotesque attitudes. Thousands were kneeling with hands upraised, many crisped arms sheltering blackened bodies of babes, and others clinging to stones and concrete posts and curbs. It appeared that many had been gassed, dying while scaling banks and climbing out of cracks in the earth. Hundreds escaped death by standing to their chins in mud and water in the canals, and others found death by drowning there, the dead and living standing together during the hours of the holocaust."

In the earthquake and its deadly aftermath, a total of more than 100,000 people were known killed (some 43,000 others disappeared without a trace), another 100,000 were seriously injured, and a staggering 1.5 million were left homeless. But mere statistics do not begin to convey the suffering of the Japanese in one of their darkest hours, nor do body counts reveal the countless horrible ways in which people died. For example, at Nebukawa, on Sagami Bay, a mud slide 50 feet deep pushed most of the village into the bay, killing some 300 inhabitants. At Atami, also on Sagami Bay, a 36-foot-high tsunami took the lives of 160 people. At the Yokosuka naval base, south of Yokohama, 200 schoolchildren were buried alive in an excursion train when a high embankment beside the railroad station collapsed on top of them. Oil tanks on a Yokohama hillside burst open, pouring millions of tons of flaming oil on helpless victims below. At the Yokohama Specie Bank, hundreds of people burned to death while trying to reach the presumed safety of the bank's basement vaults, but those who managed to get into those vaults died an even more gruesome death from heat and suffocation.

"Every hour produces stories more harrowing than the last," reported *The New York Times* on September 10. "All day and half the night the streets are trodden by hungry, weary seekers for relatives. These carry small banners bearing the names of their missing friends, parents or children, or they cry out the names until their voices crack, in hope of awakening a response

After the quake, *the gate of a Buddhist temple in Tokyo was turned into a make-shift food stall and information center (top). With most means of transportation paralyzed, refugees took to the streets in search of shelter (bottom).*

The Pacific Ocean's Tempestuous Ring of Fire

THE ISLANDS OF JAPAN have not been alone in suffering the effects of repeated, massive earthquakes over the centuries. Virtually all the land areas that border the Pacific Ocean—from the west coast of South America north to Alaska, through the Aleutians over to Japan, and south to Indonesia and New Zealand—have been the victims of relentless geological violence since the dawn of history. Along this vast arc, more than three-quarters of the world's major earthquakes occur. And here, too, more than half of the planet's 600 active volcanoes are located.

Scientists have long been aware of this "ring of fire," which can readily be outlined by plotting the sites of earthquakes and eruptions on a map. But the forces behind it remained unknown until the theory of plate tectonics, or "continental drift," came to prominence in the 1960's. Studies since then have confirmed that the earth's crust is split into a number of thick rock plates. The plates beneath the Pacific Ocean are in slow but continuous motion, in some places forcing their way under adjacent continental plates. The hellish temperatures generated by this pro-

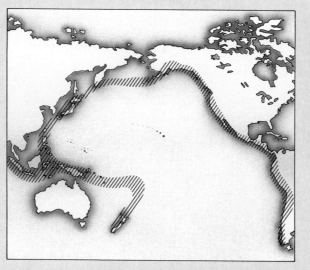

From colossal volcanic eruptions in Indonesia to massive earthquakes in Chile, the rim of the Pacific accounts for most of the earth's mightiest upheavals. This volatile zone—areas of peak seismic intensity are shown at left—includes some 330 active volcanoes and produces more than 3,000 major and minor earthquakes yearly.

cess melt the descending rock, creating a pool of superheated magma that eventually pushes to the surface in a surge of volcanic activity. Elsewhere, the edges of the plates grind relentlessly past one another, building up stress at certain points until the rock finally fractures with the sudden, violent lurch of an earthquake. So it has always been along the Pacific's ring of fire—in Chile, Mexico, California, and Alaska, in Japan, China, and other points to the south and west—and so it will be again.

---

from among the famished multitude." In the darkness of the night, continued the *Times* report, "the endless procession goes on. Every pilgrim carries a Japanese paper lantern and staff, and . . . the moving throng gives the impression of a fantastic drama without words."

At night, rumors spread like wildfire, and terror stalked the streets of Tokyo.

Among the rumors that gained currency in the days following the quake was the notion that Japan's Korean residents were starting fires and poisoning water sources in the stricken areas. Before authorities could re-establish order, vigilantes had embarked on a killing spree that cost many innocent Koreans their lives.

With communication lines down, news from Japan was meager and slow in reaching the rest of the world. At 8:20 P.M., Saturday, September 1, the Radio Corporation of America's San Francisco office received word of the disaster from the company's station at Tomioka, Japan, 144 miles north of Tokyo. The next day *The New York Times* ran a banner headline over its front-page account of the catastrophe. For days afterward this tragic news story dominated the world's attention.

Nearly every country in Europe sent subsistence and medical supplies. France declared a day of mourning for the Japanese dead. Within 48 hours of the earthquake, ships of the U.S. Pacific Fleet arrived in Japanese ports, laden with water, food, and medicine. The American Red Cross set a goal of $5,250,000 for relief supplies. New York City oversubscribed its $1 million quota threefold in three days.

Japan recovered rapidly, thanks to its low foreign debt and good credit rating, the inexhaustible energy of its people, and the lucky circumstance that major industrial centers had survived more or less intact. Reconstruction committees were appointed and plans drawn up to build a splendid and spacious capital city. But the pressing need for shelter and the people's desire to live in houses that were similar in design and construction to what they had lost, standing on the same plot of ground they had occupied before, overrode the planners' dreams. While Yokohama emerged from the disaster a better-designed city (and with a deeper harbor, too, thanks to the effects of the quake on the ocean floor), the new Tokyo turned out to be as cluttered, congested, and flammable as ever. It was also a city that had suffered a stunning blow to its cultural heritage and traditions, a city that now belonged, at least spiritually, to a new, more modern age.

Old Man River on the Loose

Avalanches of water surge across Mississippi Valley

IT IS THE LIFELINE of North America. The mighty Mississippi and its great tributaries drain some 40 percent of the continental United States, a vast wedge of territory comprising 31 states, plus 2 Canadian provinces. Indian tribes, who aptly named it the Great River and the Father of Waters, learned to adapt to the Mississippi's flood cycles. The white man, however, determined to tame the restless river.

In the 18th and early 19th centuries a patchwork of levees, or dikes, was built along the lower Mississippi. But this primitive flood-control system was so disorganized that it was not unheard of for a planter to sabotage his neighbor's dikes in order to safeguard his own fields. In 1879 Congress created the Mississippi River Commission to devise a uniform flood-control plan in cooperation with the U.S. Army Corps of Engineers. Since the corps and the commission were convinced that levees were the best means of flood control, by 1900 a wall of earth stretched for a thousand miles on both sides of the river from Cairo, Illinois, to the Gulf of Mexico—a bulwark broken only where tributaries joined the mainstream.

Yet the Mississippi continued to flood—a fact that failed to dampen the Corps of Engineers' enthusiasm for building ever higher levees. Ironically, the more effectively the river was contained, the more pressure it brought to bear on the levees that contained it and the more likely these were to burst. Between 1858 and 1922, the Mississippi broke through its restraints and seriously flooded the alluvial plain 11 times. But these episodes were mere preludes to the great flood disaster of 1927.

The trouble actually started in August 1926, when heavy rains began falling over much of the Mississippi basin. The widespread downpours persisted throughout most of the following fall and winter. With the soil unable to dry out, excess water had nowhere else to flow but into the Mississippi's tributaries, which began to rise ominously. After a respite in February, the rains came again in March, and by early April people living along the Mississippi were astonished to see the great sternwheeler steamboats—which normally plied waters well below the top of the levees—paddling by in full view, seemingly suspended in air 20 feet above the spectators' heads. Clearly the old monster river, swollen by the excess volume of all its major tributaries at once, was threatening to flood yet again, and in a very bad way indeed.

Serious as the situation was, it was not unmanageable, or so claimed the Corps of Engineers. Maj. Donald Connolly, the officer responsible for flood control on the river from Cairo south to the cotton town of Greenville, Mississippi, declared in Memphis on April 9 that "we are in a condition to hold all the water in sight."

That confidence turned out to be sadly misplaced. At Mound Landing, Mississippi, situated 18 miles north of Greenville on a bend of the river, the levee was exposed to the full pounding force of the flood crest. By April 20 it was obvious that the vulnerable dike was about to give way. All through the night an army of laborers frantically piled 100-pound sandbags onto a levee that was now vibrating under their feet like the lowest pedal note of a huge pipe organ. At about daybreak Gen. Alexander G. Paxton of the Corps of Engineers was on the telephone to Mound Landing from Greenville. A levee worker had just told him that the dike could not possibly hold much longer when Paxton heard three words he would remember for the rest of his life: "There she goes!"

With a volume estimated as equal to

Loaded with refugees, *a wooden barge is pushed along the Sunflower River in western Mississippi, en route to Vicksburg. Tents provide limited shelter on board, and an outhouse has been improvised on the bow.*

Coming to the rescue, *Red Cross steamers bring supplies to homeless Arkansas City residents camped on top of a levee.*

that of Niagara Falls and with a roar that some likened to that of a beast, the Father of Waters burst through the Mound Landing levee and quickly widened the breach to nearly a mile. Water from this single crevasse—as a break in the levee was called—inundated more than 2.3 million acres of land in Mississippi. How many of the luckless levee workers lost their lives in the sudden rush of water will never be known.

As the Mississippi fanned out across the flat delta, refugees fled to whatever high ground they could find.

Over in nearby Scott, Mississippi, Cora Lee Campbell barely escaped alive. Her recollections, still fresh after nearly 50 years, were recorded in *Deep'n as It Come,* Pete Daniel's 1977 history of the flood. After racing over a bridge in Scott just moments before it collapsed, Cora Campbell ran home, "picked this boy, Roosevelt Campbell, Jr., up on my hip . . . and made it to the levee. And when we made it to the levee, chile, them there bubbles was just boiling, boiling, boiling, boiling. That water was deep'n as it come."

Cora Campbell and her family spent three nights and two days on the crowded levee before a boat finally came by to rescue them. "We made little bitty houses," she recalled, "just big enough for a child to get in, and I laid down there on an army blanket that I raised this child in and the water just come up on me and I had to take him and lay him in my breast to keep him dry, from getting chilled. It didn't do me no good."

Early in the evening of April 21, a second crevasse opened up at Pendleton, Arkansas, on the opposite side of the river from Mound Landing. Thirty-two miles to the south, the people of Arkansas City braced themselves for the oncoming flood. When water first began lapping at the outskirts of the town on April 29, 18-year-old Verna Reitzammer was at Sunday school. The flood advanced slowly enough to allow Verna to go home, have dinner, and head over to the family grocery store to help "put the stuff up on the counters." Eventually, however, rising waters forced Verna to climb onto a butcher block in the middle of the street and to wait there for a passing boat to carry her to dry ground. Later, from the upstairs of her home, Verna watched her piano float "out the front door, piece by piece. . . . That's the only thing I cried about in the flood."

197

While Verna Reitzammer mourned the fate of her piano, a vast inland sea some 80 miles wide and 18 feet deep in places was forming over the lower Mississippi Valley. Backwater from the out-of-control river caused the already swollen Arkansas River to breach its levee at a dozen points along the 100-mile stretch between Little Rock and the Mississippi. As other Mississippi tributaries such as the White, Red, and St. Francis rivers tore through their dikes, half of Arkansas and much of Louisiana were inundated. Water from the Mound Landing crevasse re-entered the Mississippi near Vicksburg, but the added pressure caused the levee across the river at Cabin Teele, Louisiana, to break open on May 3, engulfing another 6 million acres. Altogether 120 crevasses—42 of them major ones—released enough water to drown some 16.5 million acres of land in seven states. Mississippi, Arkansas, and Louisiana were the hardest hit.

"One has to see the Mississippi," wrote a *New York Times* correspondent on April 25, "to realize the vastness and awesomeness of the scene. From the bluffs on which Memphis stands, so far as land is concerned, the state of Arkansas is no longer visible. The tops of giant oaks and willows can be seen, but land itself nowhere. Where the trees are thick the picture is, in a way, that of an unmowed lawn on top of the waters."

By mid-May the flood crest began to invade Louisiana's bayou country. In only 48 hours the entire levee system along the Bayou des Glaises in the state's sugar-growing region lay in ruins. On May 17 the Atchafalaya River broke through the massive—some thought impregnable—levee at Melville. "The water leaped through the crevasse with such fury," wrote a reporter for the Memphis *Commercial Appeal*, "that it spread in three distinct currents. One force shot straight west, wrecking houses, barns and fences as it went. Another shot back due north, quickly eating out 50-foot sections of the Texas & Pacific Railroad dump, thus allowing the water to go up into the town proper and completely inundate it. . . . A third current struck out from the south. It swept everything before it."

Washtubs, workbenches, furniture, even chickens and dogs, were seen floating down the raging Atchafalaya.

In New Orleans the authorities had soon realized that piling sandbags on top of the levees would not be enough to save the historic city. The drastic solution they came up with was to blow up the levee at Caernarvon, just below New Orleans. Water from the swollen Mississippi would drain out of this artificially created crevasse and take a shortcut to the Gulf over thinly populated Plaquemines and St. Bernard parishes.

Despite protests from the parishes in question, the levee was blown up on May 3, and within hours the level of the Mississippi above New Orleans began to drop. The blast that saved New Orleans not only tore a hole in the Caernarvon levee, it completely demolished the "levees only" policy of flood control so beloved of the U.S. Army Corps of Engineers.

The waters of the Mississippi and its tributaries did not recede until July, and the economic and social effects of the flood lingered far beyond that. The official death toll was placed at about 250, although as many as 500 people may have drowned or been killed by floating debris. More than 162,000 homes were flooded, and another 41,000 buildings were destroyed.

In a region where cotton was still king, at least 2.5 million acres of cotton land were swamped. Estimated crop losses exceeded $100 million. Some 26,000 head of cattle, 127,000 hogs, 9,000 horses and mules, and 1 million chickens were destroyed. By the time displaced farmers could return to their fields, not only was the planting season long past, but they often lacked the seed and livestock needed to start over.

Almost as impressive as the dimensions of the 1927 flood was the rescue operation mounted in response. Under the joint supervision of Herbert Hoover, then secretary of commerce, and James Fieser of the American Red Cross (nicknamed Calamity Jim for his expertise in disaster relief), some 33,000 people, most of them volunteers, were engaged at one time or another in aiding flood victims. In one of the finest chapters of its distinguished history, the Red Cross sheltered more than 325,000 people in 154 camps, fed another 312,000 in private homes, and helped distribute the $17 million donated by private sources in the United States and abroad, plus another $6 million from railroad and government sources.

Crucial to the rescue efforts were the thousands of boats of all descriptions that volunteered their services. Around Greenville, Mississippi, bootleggers became heroes as they converted their high-powered boats—specially designed to outrun U.S. revenue agents' craft—into rescue vessels. An encouraging sight in battered Vicksburg was that of the great sternwheeler *Sprague*, the largest river steamboat in the world, coming in under full power, her seven coal barges laden with refugees. From Memphis, the daredevil captain of the *Wabash* took his sternwheeler across flooded fields and around half-submerged trees to pick up people huddled on rooftops. But it was men like Herman Caillouet, of Metcalfe, Mississippi, who bore the brunt of the rescue work. In a small launch

From Bessie Smith *to William Faulkner, many artists dealt with the flood in song and story. Faulkner wrote of it in* The Old Man, *and Smith was singing the flood blues even before the waters had ebbed. In the summer of 1927, "Blind Lemon" Jefferson added "Rising High Water Blues" to the list of flood songs.*

powered by a Model T Ford engine, Caillouet scoured the waters of the delta in search of stranded flood victims. During one nearly sleepless 72-hour period, he saved some 200 people but also witnessed his share of tragedy. "There was a house [floating by] with seven people on it," Caillouet recalled. "I presume it was man and wife and five children. . . . And on the way getting to the house, the house was just moving along, you know, all of a sudden it must of hit a stump or something. And the house flew all to pieces. And I searched the boards and things around there for ten minutes, and you know I never saw a soul come up. . . . This man and wife, I imagine, seemed to be about thirty-five years old. Oldest kid was, must have been about sixteen."

If any good can be said to have come from the great Mississippi flood of 1927, it was that federal and local authorities were forced to rethink their flood-control policies. On May 15, 1928, Congress voted $325 million for the building of reservoirs, dams, and spillways to augment and strengthen the existing levee system. America's greatest river has flooded many times since 1927, but never with the devastating consequences of that terrible flood year. Still, anyone who puts full faith in the technology of flood control might well ponder this observation by the old river's most famous pilot, Mark Twain: "One who knows the Mississippi will promptly aver—not aloud, but to himself—that ten thousand River Commissions, with the mines of the world at their back, cannot tame that lawless stream."

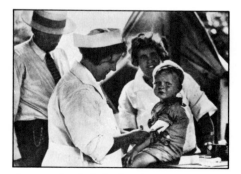

A young flood victim has his arm bandaged by a Red Cross nurse at the shelter set up in the Confederate Cemetery in Vicksburg, Mississippi.

Drought and Despair in Mid-America

Nation's breadbasket becomes its dust bowl

THE SUNDAY SERVICE at the Methodist Episcopal Church in Guymon, Oklahoma, ended on April 14, 1935, as it so often did, with a prayer for rain. All across the state's western panhandle and far into the brown, flat distance beyond, the sun glared down from a cloudless azure sky, heralding yet another hot, dry day. Seemingly endless fields of wheat, the region's economic mainstay, were withering in the heat, and the soil was turning into powder. Unless rain fell—and soon—there would be no harvest. More farms would fail, more banks would foreclose, and the area's desperately hard-pressed residents would sink even deeper into misery and despair.

Toward midafternoon that Sunday, the sky began to darken as a gigantic black cloud rolled in from the northwest. This dense, dark wave of fast-moving tur-bulence, more than a thousand feet high and stretching from horizon to horizon, reminded some people of the smoke from an oil fire; to others it looked more like a roiling mass of muddy, cascading water. The wall of darkness, however, contained not a drop of moisture. What it carried was dust, untold tons of prairie topsoil lifted from bone-dry fields and swept across the region in a choking, blinding storm of destruction.

For nearly four years now, in the windy months of winter and early spring, periodic dust storms had been raging across America's Great Plains. The dusters clogged traffic, derailed trains, buried fence posts, and alternately denuded fields and smothered crops. People had long since learned to stuff rags into window frames and drape wet sheets across doorways to keep the dust out. And they regularly tied damp handker-

chiefs over their nose and mouth in order to breathe.

Even so, most agreed that the "black blizzard" of April 14, 1935, was worse than anything they had ever experienced. The storm had blown up in eastern Wyoming, then gathered momentum as it moved south through Colorado and into Kansas. It blustered into Dodge City at 2:40 in the afternoon, bringing 60-mile-an-hour winds and a 40-minute period of sudden inky darkness. So thick was the gloom in Liberal, Kansas, that a lighted match, held at arm's length, disappeared from view. Said Lila King, age 11, in Liberal, "I was sure I was going to die."

Rolling on southward, the blizzard sped through Guymon, Oklahoma, at more than 80 miles an hour. It then halted a funeral procession near Boise City, Oklahoma, and sent blinded motorists careering off the road in Amarillo, Texas. People huddled in cars, under wagons, in cellars and well houses—wherever they could find shelter—until the worst gusts passed. To one storm victim the gritty darkness seemed to signal "the end of the world." Another declared, "The nightmare is becoming life."

And so it was. The vast open landscape of the Great Plains had always been prone to cycles of rainfall and dusty drought, with the southern sector of the Plains, centered roughly on Guymon, particularly vulnerable to damage. But nothing in anyone's memory approached the punishing conditions that now gripped the region. Recurring crop failures, coupled with falling farm prices and a nationwide financial collapse, had ushered in an era of poverty and disruption that exceeded everyone's worst fears. As an Associated Press report on the April 14 black blizzard declared, the entire region had become a dust bowl.

The area hardest hit by drought was the Dust Bowl proper—a 97-million-acre expanse of prairie and scrubland that encompassed southeastern Colorado and northeastern New Mexico, western Kansas, and the panhandles of Texas and Oklahoma. Government surveyors trekking through the area in the early 19th century had noted its general bleakness; they dubbed it the Great American Desert and declared it unfit for agriculture.

But the cattlemen and farmers of a growing America thought otherwise. Vast herds of cattle grazed the region in the years before the Civil War. Then, begin-

"Black blizzards," such as the one near Boise City, Oklahoma, in 1935 (left), were frequent in the Dust Bowl years. Rolling at speeds as high as 80 miles per hour, they could reduce visibility to zero and make travel impossible, even on foot. Oklahoma was one of the states hardest hit by the flying soil of the great storms that turned farmland into deserts of dust, as shown in this 1937 photo. Thousands of Dust Bowlers abandoned their homesteads and trekked west in search of a new and better life.

ning in the 1870's and 1880's, as the railroads pushed west, homesteaders moved in by the tens of thousands, lured on by government promises of free land and by the introduction of a steel plow that could easily break the stubborn prairie sod. The population of western Kansas increased fourfold during the 1880's; there was a 300-percent increase in the Colorado plains, and a 600-percent rise in the Texas Panhandle.

Hospitals dispensed *masks to reduce respiratory ills.*

The newcomers coped as best they could with the hazards of the climate. When a dry spell in the mid-1890's brought on major crop failures, a number of farmers pulled up stakes and headed back east. But new settlers soon took their place and stayed on to weather new cycles of rainfall and drought.

An unusually moist period began in 1914, coinciding with the outbreak of World War I in Europe and a burgeoning demand for wheat to feed the troops. Area farmers readily filled the need. A new type of mechanized farming was taking hold on the Plains, enabling farmers to increase production dramatically. Vast new fields were carved from virgin prairie; by 1920 more than 17 million acres of Plains land had been brought under cultivation and were producing a giant's share of the nation's wheat crop.

The new mechanized techniques were so fast and efficient that farmers soon faced an unexpected problem: overproduction. Demand dropped after the war, and excess wheat became a glut on the market. Prices fell and to make up for lost income, the farmers opened up still more cropland. When boom times returned in the late 1920's, another 5 million acres had been cut by the plow.

By 1930 most of the nation was skidding into a severe economic depression, triggered by the stock market crash on Wall Street the previous October. But the farmers remained relatively prosperous. The main problem that winter, in fact, was not drought but floods, brought on by heavy rainfall. But soon the rains began to dwindle. And the dust began to fly.

The decade's first dusters blew up in the Texas Panhandle in late winter and early spring of 1932. Limited in extent and causing only minor damage, they proved mere curtain raisers to the coming tragedy. Showers fell in April and May, dampening the soil and temporarily settling the dust. But the weather worsened as the months wore on. Searing winds alternated with sudden cloudbursts and severe local flooding. Hailstorms flattened large sections of the wheat crop; armies of cutworms attacked the rest. Yields that summer plummeted to five bushels per acre. Herds of cattle died of suffocation or starved to death in dust-smothered pastures.

Conditions soon slid from terrible to catastrophic. The worst dust blizzard in years slammed into northern Texas in early 1933, the first of 139 such storms to ravage the panhandle that year. Billows of wind-driven dirt rolled across the fields, piling like snowdrifts against barns and outbuildings.

And the drought was spreading, with the region of dryness extending to Arkansas and north where the Plains were normally moister. In mid-November 1933 the largest black blizzard yet blew up in the Dakotas, darkening the sky for several days and sending a dust cloud thousands of feet into the air, where the prevailing winds carried it all the way to the Great Lakes and the Mississippi Valley.

The farmers' plight grew even worse in 1934. Giant dusters ravaged the Plains all through the spring, climaxing in a four-day mega-blizzard that began on May 9 and rolled across the wheat belt from the Dakotas to Texas. The storm clogged rail lines and disrupted air travel as far east as Chicago.

The wind, howling at speeds of up to 100 miles an hour, scoured the powdery topsoil down to hardpan and carried it east to sprinkle the Atlantic seaboard. The sun grew dim over Baltimore and New York, and in Washington, D.C., a thin film of Great Plains dust settled on President Franklin D. Roosevelt's desk.

As wind and sun continued to pummel the Plains, the human toll began to mount.

While few perished in the storms themselves, the constant inhalation of airborne dust was bringing on an epidemic of respiratory illnesses: bronchitis, strep throat, and, most of all, a catchall ailment known as dust pneumonia. The Red Cross opened six field hospitals in the Dust Bowl states and distributed thousands of dust masks to cope with the emergency.

Even worse than sickness was the drought's economic fallout. As crops failed, farmers were unable to pay off loans they had taken out to expand their holdings or to purchase expensive new equipment during the good times. Banks were compelled to foreclose on mortgages, thus forcing thousands of farm families off the land. Small businesses—from grain stores to pharmacies to tractor dealerships—closed down, their services no longer needed. Finally, the banks themselves went under.

Displaced from their farms, family after family decided to flee the miseries of the Dust Bowl. In battered pickup trucks and Model A Fords piled high with meager possessions, most headed west for California, where the land was still green and opportunity might beckon. By 1936 the migration had swollen to a flood, with one survey reporting that one out of every four farmsteads had been abandoned. All across the Dust Bowl wind-battered buildings stood silent in the empty brown fields, their windows gaping and their doors swinging mournfully on rusty hinges.

In all, half a million people moved west from the Plains during the 1930's. What they found in California was not much better than what they had left behind. The majority could get work only as laborers on huge corporate farms, harvesting lettuce or grapes or whatever else the season dictated, and living in ramshackle packing crate communities without heat or plumbing. To West Coast residents they were Okies, no matter what state they had come from, and they were far from welcome.

The diehards who stuck out the drought in the Dust Bowl fared somewhat better. "I could have left here wealthy, and I'll be damned if I'm going to walk out of here broke now," announced one Guymon farmer. His decision proved to be a wise one, for an array of government agencies swung into action, providing food and clothing; lending money for seed, fodder, and fuel; and setting crop quotas.

Soil conservation specialists moved in to study ways of combating the drought. Destructive practices, such as overgrazing, were singled out for correction. And after the harvest, farmers were encouraged to plow the stubble under (and thus enrich the soil) instead of burning it off. A new method of plowing, with deep furrows cut at right angles to the prevailing wind, helped trap windblown soil. And the Civilian Conservation Corps planted thousands of trees to serve as windbreaks.

The new techniques helped, but recovery was slow. In 1935 alone, at the height of the drought, the Dust Bowl lost a staggering 850 million tons of topsoil; a single storm that year was said to have scooped up twice as much earth as would be needed to fill the Panama Canal. The drought continued through 1936 and into 1937, with the added tragedy of a grasshopper plague that destroyed much of an already scanty crop.

Gradually, however, in county after county, the rains returned. The 1938 harvest was the best in years, and that winter the heavens opened up in a succession of slow, healing downpours that soaked deep into the prairie soil. After eight years of choking dust and weary desperation, the drought was over. "Dust Bowl," the Texhoma *Times* jubilantly proclaimed, "is a term to be discarded and forgotten."

In the worst of times *the wind-driven dust sandblasted leaves from trees and formed 30-foot-high drifts. Farmers were forced to dig out (above) in a futile attempt to restore a semblance of order to their ruined lives. Cattle ranchers, too, suffered as livestock suffocated or starved in barren pastures (left).*

203

The morning after *the killer storm, a mess of wrecked cars and disabled ships choked the piers of New London, Connecticut.*

The New England Hurricane of 1938

Freak storm wipes out lives and property in Northeast

THE FIRST WARNING came on Friday night, September 16, 1938, when the Brazilian freighter *Alegrete* radioed to shore that she had run into a major storm 350 miles northeast of Puerto Rico. For Florida, the *Alegrete*'s report was cause for alarm. The U.S. weather station at Jacksonville determined that the turbulence was moving toward the mainland at a rapid 20 miles per hour and would probably land near Miami on Tuesday evening, September 20. Floridians began barricading their homes and bracing themselves for the worst. By Monday night, however, the storm had changed direction and was traveling due north on a course almost parallel to the eastern seaboard. If it stayed on this familiar track, the hurricane could be expected to veer out to sea somewhere south of Cape Hatteras, North Carolina. On Tuesday night relieved meteorologists at Jacksonville informed the Weather Bureau's headquarters in Washington, D.C., that the storm posed no threat to coastal communities.

All this talk of a hurricane must have seemed remote indeed to those lingering on after Labor Day at the beach resorts of southern Long Island. Major hurricanes were rare in the Northeast, and besides,

the weather hardly seemed menacing. There had been thunderstorms over Long Island on Tuesday night, but on Wednesday morning, September 21, the sun managed at least occasionally to break through the prevailing fog and clouds.

According to Ernest Clowes, a newspaper editor in Bridgehampton, Long Island, it was business as usual on Wednesday in the resort communities he covered. "People made plans for the day; went on to carry them out," he wrote. "Some went to the city, leaving their children with servants; the usual run of small social gatherings, luncheons, picnics, got under way; at Montauk several fishing boats went out to sea." Things were much the same farther north in the resort towns along the Rhode Island coast. Home movies taken that morning show vacationers at their ease, enjoying the still-warm September weather.

But Clowes also noted that the ocean "had been making a big noise all night" and that many local residents drove out to the beach on Wednesday morning to watch the unusually large, white-capped breakers marching along the horizon. When the sun broke through, it "shone with a watery glare in which was a tint of green." A West Indian woman, wise in the ways of tropical storms, remarked to her Long Island employer that it looked and felt like hurricane weather.

Over in Falmouth, Massachusetts, on the southwest tip of Cape Cod, Fire Chief Ray D. Wells also sensed trouble. At 1:30 P.M. he drove by the shore, noted the condition of the sea at low tide, and decided to telephone state police headquarters in West Bridgewater. The south shore of the Cape was going to be inundated before day's end, he reported, and he would need all the boats, equipment, and volunteers neighboring communities could spare. The incredulous state police telephoned him right back to make sure the call had not been a hoax. Wells stood his ground: there was no time to lose.

Indeed, by the time Ray Wells picked up the telephone to call West Bridgewater, a storm front packing winds of up to 150 miles per hour was bearing down on the Northeast with a speed and fury that would win it the nickname of "Long Island Express."

Instead of veering off into the Atlantic as predicted, the storm first sighted by the *Alegrete* was sucked into a warm, humid, low-pressure corridor lying between two high-pressure zones and extending from Cape Hatteras across Long Island and into New England. Since high-pressure zones tend to repulse lows (and a hurricane is an extreme low-pressure zone), the errant storm had nowhere to go but into the corridor, picking up tremendous speed as it went. Without modern tracking facilities and with very few ships left in the path of the storm, the U.S. Weather Bureau—which relied on eyewitness reports for its data—had no way of knowing exactly what was happening until it was too late to issue adequate warnings.

In its torpedo-like drive up the Atlantic coast, the hurricane sideswiped New Jersey, driving a 30-foot-high storm swell onto the beaches of Wildwood, Manasquan, and Point Pleasant. In New York City, radio stations were knocked off the air, and a power failure paralyzed parts of the subway system.

But all this was just a passing encounter. Far worse was in store for Long Island. By early afternoon, the eye of the hurricane was speeding toward the center of the Island's South Shore—an exposed stretch of barrier beach and low-lying coast lined with homes ranging from glamorous 30-room mansions to flimsy summer cottages by the thousands.

The wind came first. It arrived in blasts, full of rain, splintering small boats against

Wind and waves *uprooted this house, and many others like it, on the South Shore of Long Island.*

Under the assault *of 90-mile-per-hour gusts, a church in Danielson, Connecticut, lost its steeple. To take this picture in the middle of the storm, the photographer had to be supported by two men.*

Swollen by the storm, the Connecticut River inundated parts of Hartford. In the city's low-lying factory district, firemen in rowboats conduct a search for stranded workers.

their moorings and whirling heavy garden furniture through the air. As heavy black clouds scudded high overhead, roof shingles tore loose, windows blew out, doors slammed open and shut, utility poles came crashing down. By 3 P.M., said editor Clowes, it was clear this was no ordinary September gale. The barometer had fallen "to unprecedented depths" and the wind was quickly building up to hurricane force. Toward 4 o'clock, an eyewitness noticed a "thick and high bank of fog rolling in fast from the ocean. When it came closer we saw that it wasn't fog. It was water."

It was, in fact, the storm surge, a 30-foot wall of water pulled up from the sea by low air pressure and driven ashore by fierce winds. "The sky was darkened and the warm air was thick with a smother of rain, spray and all sorts of small items going by," Clowes wrote. "A barn, a chicken house, would lift from its foundations and collapse or burst into fragments that flew away down the wind. . . . Roofs or parts of them lifted into the murk and disappeared; chimneys were crashing," and through it all was what Clowes called the "voice of the storm," an intense, "organ-like note," which, once heard, would never be forgotten.

The wind lifted strong men and hurled them down violently; great trees went down like weeds.

Amid tales of death and tragedy, of children swept away and wives watching husbands drown, there were also feats of extraordinary heroism and presence of mind; none, perhaps, was more remarkable than that of the Norwegian-born butler Arni Benedictson. Quietly, systematically, he gathered some two dozen frightened Westhampton residents whose beachfront homes had been wrecked by the hurricane and led them through a maelstrom of wind and flying debris to safety farther inland. Some 30 less fortunate Westhamptonites perished in the storm that day.

As badly as Long Island was hit, the hurricane reserved its killer punch for tiny Rhode Island. Moments before the storm surge came crashing in, owners of vacation cottages at Rhode Island's Misquamicut beach were battening down for what looked to be a September gale. "People on the beach were laughing and joking," one survivor recalled, "trying to put up shutters and fasten windows to keep curtains from getting wet. They thought it was lots of fun. Then suddenly . . . their homes were under 20 to 30 feet of water. Some of the houses just blew up." The surge killed 41 people at Misquamicut alone, including 10 women on a church picnic.

Perhaps worst hit of all was Providence, located 30 miles from the ocean at the head of funnel-shaped Narragansett Bay. Trapped by the bay's narrowing sides, the storm surge mounted to an awesome height and intensity as it inundated the Rhode Island capital, flinging aside 20-ton breakwater boulders like pebbles and hurling a 71-foot-high lighthouse into the sea.

Although Long Island served as a barrier protecting most of Connecticut's coast from the direct effects of the storm surge, that state also took a beating. In the heavily populated port of New London, a fire in the downtown district combined with winds and floods to leave the city in ruins. In Massachusetts, the storm caused extensive property damage and some deaths on Cape Cod, but the foresight and fast action of officials like Chief Wells of Falmouth are credited with saving at least 100 lives. As in New York, large sections of Boston were left without power.

The hurricane roared up the Connecticut River valley to central Massachusetts, and from there up across the woodlands and mountains of Vermont and New Hampshire. By 10 P.M., the weakening storm veered northwest over New York's Lake Champlain and on into Canada, where, after taking a parting shot at Montreal, it eventually died out.

On the morning of September 22, the sun shone brightly on a devastated Northeast. "Acres of trees were scattered about like matchsticks," one witness reported after flying over the affected coastal areas. "Automobiles were lying on their sides, half buried in mud. Houses were flattened out as though they had been crushed under steam rollers. At one spot, nearly 15 houses were whirled together as though they had been in the grip of a giant egg-beater."

Statistics tell a grim story: at least 600 people died in the storm, about 250 of them in Rhode Island alone. Total property damage was estimated at $400 million. More than 4,500 homes were destroyed and another 15,000 damaged; 60,000 people were left homeless.

Thousands of cars and boats were damaged or destroyed, and 20,000 miles of telephone, telegraph, and power lines were knocked down. A few enterprising individuals managed to get messages back and forth between Boston and New York via cable links with London, Paris, and other European capitals. Since roads were impassable and trains at a standstill, those who had to travel between Boston and New York flew, giving the young airline business an unexpected boost.

Recovery was a long, often heartbreaking task. The sea had not only washed away thousands of homes but in several places drastically altered the landscape, making rebuilding impossible. The barrier beach at Charlestown, Rhode Island, now had breachways between ocean and tidal ponds. Residents of Hampton Bays, Long Island, had long talked about dredging just such a channel to give small craft easy access to Shinnecock Bay. On the morning of September 22, they discovered that nature had done the work for them.

Even a catastrophe as great as this one is not without its lighter moments. One such story concerned a Long Island man who on the morning of the storm received in the mail an expensive barometer he had ordered from New York City. Upon opening the package, he was dismayed to find the barometer's needle pointing straight down to the section marked "tornadoes and hurricanes." Hurricanes? With the sun shining outside? He banged the instrument with his fist, but the needle stayed put. Angry, he dashed off a letter of complaint, repacked the barometer in the box, and set out for the village post office. By the time he struggled home against wind and rain, his seafront house had been blown away.

The suddenness of it all, the fact that the hand of God seemed to descend without warning and with such anger, made the '38 hurricane something unique in the lives of those who lived through it. The storm's full fury lasted only a few hours, but for an entire generation in this part of America it changed the world.

A tangle of uprooted trees and skewed utility poles transformed this pleasant street in New London, Connecticut, into a cleanup nightmare. In its destructive run through the Northeast, the great hurricane of 1938 knocked down nearly a quarter of a million trees.

Giant Earthquake Shatters Chile

Midnight horror takes dreadful toll

THE FIRST REPORT of an earthquake out of Santiago, Chile's capital, on that Wednesday morning in January was not terribly alarming. Sandwiched between articles on U.S.–Philippine trade and Canadian defense expenditures on a cluttered inside page of *The New York Times*, it summed up the events in a few short paragraphs. But then, the year was 1939, and in a world preoccupied with the specter of war in Europe, word of a series of shocks in the remote South American country was hardly front-page news. Besides, it was not an uncommon occurrence; seismologists estimated that Chile had been hit by at least one damaging earthquake every three years for the past three centuries.

Within 24 hours, however, frantic messages sent by ham radio operators made it clear that the disaster was huge in scale. A strip of land some 200 miles long and 50 miles wide in the rich agricultural region of south-central Chile had been devastated by a wrenching series of tremors at midnight on January 24.

As details of the upheaval became available through fragmentary local reports, the daily news accounts began to convey the magnitude of the ruin and the desperation of the victims. Worst hit was the area some 250 miles south of Santiago, where the provincial capital of Concepción was flattened into rubble and the surrounding countryside was torn up as if by bulldozers run amok. Chillán, a major city of 50,000 located some 50 miles inland from Concepción, was likewise destroyed.

It would be impossible to make an accurate count of the dead and injured for days to come—if ever. On ruined farms and in the towns and cities caught in the upheaval, neighbor was cut off from neighbor, and thousands still clinging to life were so deeply buried that they were beyond hope of rescue.

Outside help, meanwhile, was slow in coming. A train loaded with food, first aid, and doctors—accompanied by Chile's newly elected president, Pedro

The brutal handiwork *of the quake fills this street in Concepción, where more than 2,000 were reported killed.*

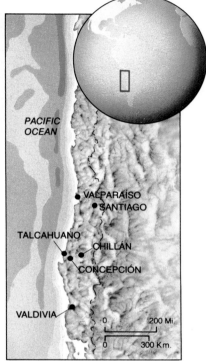

Toppled over like a child's toy, *Chillán's Municipal Theatre was packed with 1,000 moviegoers when the massive jolt ripped it from its foundation. The hardest-hit city in the area, Chillán suffered 10,000 fatalities in a population of 50,000.*

PACIFIC OCEAN

VALPARAÍSO
SANTIAGO

TALCAHUANO
CHILLÁN
CONCEPCIÓN

VALDIVIA

0   200 Mi.

0   300 Km.

Severely damaged *by the violent quake was the 450-mile-long stretch of Chile from Santiago to Valdivia. The tremors, however, were felt all the way to Argentina.*

Aguirre Cerda—set out from Santiago within hours of the first radio reports. But, along with 11 Red Cross convoys, it was stalled by impassable track conditions some 60 miles north of Chillán. Relief planes attempting to land at Concepción, where dazed survivors wandered about aimlessly, could not negotiate the too-short runway and returned to Santiago with tales of appalling destruction.

Throughout that first day the news from local witnesses continued to be nightmarish. For 1,000 people attending a late-night movie at Chillán's Municipal Theater, for example, there had been only a warning rumble when suddenly the entire building collapsed. No one escaped. As *The New York Times* reported, "Indescribable terror was pictured on the faces of the dead when some of the bodies were removed."

The fate of those at home in bed was equally grotesque, as aged mortar and brick gave way and heavy tile roofs fell like lead weights into the ruins. Some people managed to escape into the streets, only to be showered with falling debris. Nearly a century earlier, in 1853, an earthquake had leveled Chillán; now, with the walls of the cathedral crumbling into dust and the Governor's Palace pitching forward onto passing cars in a murderous free-fall, it was happening again.

Seismic stations later reported that the earthquake at its peak had sent needles off seismometers, and residents who had lived through earlier quakes declared this to be the worst in memory. Tremors were felt in distant towns in Argentina and north almost to the border of Peru. But the damage was concentrated in a north–south swath located midway between Santiago and the port of Valdivia and extending inland from the coast to the foothills of the Andes.

In all, some 1.6 million people in six provinces—more than a third of Chile's population—felt the worst of the shocks. In addition to Concepción and Chillán, many smaller cities and towns were destroyed. From Concepción's port of Talcahuano, through which much of the region's harvest was normally shipped, came word of extensive damage to piers, of naval workshops knocked out of commission, and of desperate shortages of food and clothing.

Compounding the horrors of the first long day that followed Chile's overnight chaos was a blazing sun—January is midsummer there—that bore down without mercy on living and dead alike. From relief planes attempting to drop supplies came accounts of "corpses lined up in the blistering sun, evidently awaiting identification by relatives who may never be found." In Chillán, which pilots described as "a vast antheap, with jagged lengths of church towers and other masonry protruding," witnesses spoke of "bodies of victims being tossed into pits in a feverish effort to dispose of them before disease sets in." Aerial observers brought reports of huge crowds roaming aimlessly through the streets of Concepción in search of shelter that could not be found.

Messages from the disaster zone, meanwhile, grew ever more dire. "We must have serums against tetanus and gangrene, also more nurses, and other medical help. Food is very scarce. . . . We must have tents soon." This was the anguished plea from Concepción.

Estimates of casualties were steadily revised upward. In Chillán alone, some 10,000 were believed dead and another 20,000 injured. With rail lines and bridges in ruins, power lines down, and water supplies days or weeks from being restored, life was in chaos. The government had proclaimed martial law through-

out the region, and military authorities had ordered the complete evacuation of Chillán and Concepción. But while local army units were activated to maintain order, the basic necessities of survival—pledged in abundance by the national government, by private charities and individuals, and by friendly foreign governments—remained at the far end of broken rail lines and highways. In the breach, *The New York Times* reported, "a pitifully small army of rescue workers, toiling against heavy odds in almost unbearable heat and with insufficient drinking water, continued feverishly to bury the dead, aid the injured, rescue sufferers imprisoned in ruined buildings and give succor to the homeless."

As relief caravans inched southward, those who could escaped the battered region by car or on foot. By Friday, the third full day following the quake, the first evacuation and relief ships were anchored in Talcahuano. The British cruisers *Ajax* and *Exeter*, placed at the disposal of the Chilean government, dispatched marines to relieve rescue teams and help in the massive cleanup of the port. That evening, the *Exeter* ferried 600 refugees north to Valparaíso, while many other foreign vessels changed plans in order to aid in the evacuation. One hundred doctors and nurses, along with food and medical supplies, were among the first to reach the area.

The rescue effort, however, was erratic. Large areas were still without aid, and in the hardest-hit cities the situation was dire. Reports from several places indicated that even drinking water had become "so scarce that schoolchildren, parched by the intense heat, were receiving it only by the spoonful."

The mounting casualties and the endless catalog of destruction at length became almost unbelievable. Calling the reconstruction of Chillán "out of the question," one city official declared that "like a modern Pompeii, its ruins should be abandoned and another city built elsewhere to take its place."

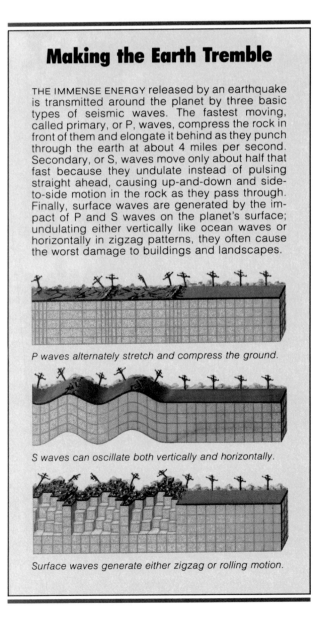

Making the Earth Tremble

THE IMMENSE ENERGY released by an earthquake is transmitted around the planet by three basic types of seismic waves. The fastest moving, called primary, or P, waves, compress the rock in front of them and elongate it behind as they punch through the earth at about 4 miles per second. Secondary, or S, waves move only about half that fast because they undulate instead of pulsing straight ahead, causing up-and-down and side-to-side motion in the rock as they pass through. Finally, surface waves are generated by the impact of P and S waves on the planet's surface; undulating either vertically like ocean waves or horizontally in zigzag patterns, they often cause the worst damage to buildings and landscapes.

P waves alternately stretch and compress the ground.

S waves can oscillate both vertically and horizontally.

Surface waves generate either zigzag or rolling motion.

New tremors, the threat of a volcanic eruption, and heavy rains added to the woes of the survivors.

For a few terrifying hours on Friday, as volcanic peaks overlooking Chillán cast a fearsome reddish glow against the sky, it seemed as if the reference to Pompeii might take on a crueler meaning. But the threatened eruptions did not occur. (Other volcanoes in the earthquake zone, however, did erupt the following week.)

Instead, a new disaster struck on Saturday, when a violent summer tempest broke over the region, soaking thousands of unsheltered, half-naked survivors in a torrential downpour. As night fell, some 100,000 rain-battered refugees from the earthquake zone were, according to *The New York Times*'s dispatch, "trying to push northward ahead of the icy winds from the Andes. Shelter was impossible . . . thousands of injured, insufficiently wrapped in blankets, lay under the trees."

Nor was the nightmare over. Final efforts to free buried survivors from the twisted rubble of Chillán turned up a boy of 12 who had been trapped for four days with his dog. But, as the *Times* reported, "thousands of other voices crazily demanding aid have gradually died away and today they are silent. The survivors have abandoned all hope of again seeing their missing relatives. They no longer shed tears. They do not even talk."

Pushing to evacuate the last of Chillán's survivors—including many thousands of orphans in urgent need of families to care for them—officials debated how best to prevent the spread of disease from the thousands of rotting corpses that lay beyond the reach of burial teams. By nightfall, said one account, it appeared likely that "hundreds of tons of live lime, dynamite and the systematic application of fire might within a few hours put the finishing touches" to the once lovely colonial-style city.

As the slow work of rescue and evacuation continued, officials turned their attention to assessing the social and economic impact of the disaster and its long-term damage to the region. Authoritative sources counted the earthquake's toll at 50,000 dead, 60,000 injured, and more than 700,000 without homes. Although some later estimates revised the death toll down-

Salvaging what was left in the wreckage of Chillán, a man and boy loaded their meager household belongings onto a pair of ox-drawn carts.

The sorrowful toll of Chillán's dead could only partially be gauged by the ubiquitous coffins waiting to be carted away by burial crews. When the coffins ran out, bodies were simply dropped into deep fissures in the ground.

ward, by all accounts the loss of life was overwhelming.

Seventy percent of Concepción was gone and virtually all of Chillán, while the agricultural districts that fed the nation and helped balance the economy had been equally savaged. Barns, warehouses, and grain silos were flattened, irrigation canals destroyed, water supplies contaminated. Planted fields had been sundered from one end to the other, causing widespread destruction of crops just as they were about to be harvested. Overnight, millions of Chile's richest acres were transformed into wasteland; how quickly they could be cleared and made productive again was impossible to predict.

Chaos reigned in other areas of the economy as well. Although the region's coal mines were damaged, the invaluable nitrate and copper mining industries were spared the direct force of the quake. But like so much else in the country, they suffered from the disruption of Chile's vital north–south traffic links. For a nation with Chile's unique dimensions—2,661 miles long but on the average only 125 miles wide— the immobilization of the huge central section had its effects in every quarter.

As the Ministry of Finance prepared to submit a plan for borrowing the equivalent of tens of millions of dollars to aid in reconstruction of the region, the nation was once again paralyzed by nature as a series of aftershocks jolted the ravaged zone. For close to 24 hours on the sixth day following the original quake, terrified survivors waited out tremors that began with a faint rumbling and grew to thunderous volume before fading away. Little damage resulted from the aftershocks—but only because the first quake had done its work so well.

Bomber Blitzes Empire State Building

Towering inferno a grim reality

THE TOLL WAS not dramatic as disasters go: only 14 killed and another 25 injured. Even so, for hosts of New Yorkers, the morning of Saturday, July 28, 1945, was seared forever in their memories as a moment of supreme terror. Before their very eyes, an airplane crashed into the then tallest building in the world—the 1,250-foot Empire State Building—located in the heart of the nation's most populous city.

The aircraft was a twin-engine B-25 bomber, a battle-tested model made famous in 1942 by flying hero Jimmy Doolittle, who led 16 of them in America's first air attack against Japan. Named *Old John Feather Merchant*, the doomed bomber was piloted by Lt. Col. William F. Smith, 27, a decorated veteran with two years of combat service. On board with him when he took off that day for a routine flight from Bedford, Massachusetts, to Newark Airport, New Jersey, were S. Sgt. Christopher Domitrovich and a young sailor hitchhiking a free ride home.

Arriving over New York's La Guardia Airport, Smith was advised by the control tower to land. A deadly combination of surface fog, drizzle, cloud ceiling hovering at a mere 700 feet, and visibility of only three miles or so made for extremely hazardous flying conditions. But Smith was determined to stick to his original flight plan and continue on for the few remaining miles across Manhattan Island to Newark. As he pushed southwest, the control tower warned him that the clouds were so low that the top of the landmark Empire State Building was hidden from view. "Roger, Tower, thank you," was Smith's laconic reply.

Exactly what happened over the next several minutes will never be known. The most likely explanation is that Smith became completely disoriented in the dense fog and mist; while still over Manhattan, he apparently thought he had passed beyond and was preparing to land in New Jersey. Supporting this guess is the fact that he had lowered his landing gear as he began his fatal flight across the metropolis.

As the bomber headed west across midtown Manhattan and then turned south near Fifth Avenue, its fatal flight path was witnessed by scores of horrified spectators. Vincent Galbo spotted the plane no higher than the 22nd floor of the office tower over Grand Central Terminal. Residents or workers in various other skyscrapers on or near Fifth Avenue, drawn to their windows by the ear-shattering roar of an airplane that was clearly flying far too low, stood transfixed as a silver phantom flashed through wisps of cloud. A man on the observation roof of the RCA Building in Rockefeller Center saw the plane 100 feet below him.

Aware at last that he was trapped in a maze of

skyscrapers, Smith made a desperate attempt to gain altitude. His engines whined as the propellers were thrust into their climbing mode, but the landing gear, slow to retract, impeded his ascent.

In the streets below, pedestrians for blocks around sensed impending catastrophe as the rumbling of the errant aircraft reverberated through the midtown canyons. Stan Lomax, a radio sports announcer, glimpsed the plane from Fifth Avenue and shouted, "Climb, you fool, climb!" But it was too late. At 9:55 A.M., *Old John Feather Merchant*—all 12 tons of it—slammed headlong into the 78th and 79th floors of the Empire State Building, about 975 feet above the ground.

Eyewitnesses watching from below reported that they heard the sound of the crash, followed by a moment of eerie silence and then an explosion. With that, an orange curtain of flame shot upward, and fragments of glass, metal, and stone showered down.

For occupants of the 79th floor, most of them em-

In thick morning fog *a low-flying B-25 rammed into the 34th Street side of the Empire State Building, as shown in this artist's view (left). Luckily it was Saturday, so most of the building's 15,000 office workers were at home. Furthermore, the rainy weather had kept away thousands of tourists who normally visited the world's tallest building on weekends.*

The freak accident *left a charred, jagged hole that cut across two floors in the building's side (below). Within three months the hole was patched and the great building had healed its wound without a scar.*

ployees of the National Catholic Welfare Conference, the disaster came without warning. Ten of the office workers, along with the three men in the plane, were crushed or burned to death within moments. Another victim died later of his burns. One of the dead was pitched through a window, his body landing on a ledge seven stories below.

With the plane wedged at an angle in a gaping 18-by 20-foot hole, one of its engines had hurtled across the 79th floor, igniting its own splashed fuel, which in turn touched off an explosion of spilled oxygen tanks. Bursting through to an elevator shaft, the fiery engine plunged to the building's basement, leaving behind 800 gallons of burning gasoline that cascaded down stairwells to the 75th floor.

The other engine and one landing gear tore through the unoccupied 78th floor and split apart. A piece of the engine, along with the 1,100-pound landing gear, hurtled through seven walls, shot out of the building's south face, and bombed through the roof of another building far below, taking no lives but spewing out smoke, flame, and devastation. Back in the Empire State Building, the main chunk of this same engine rocketed through thick walls and snapped the cables suspending an elevator operated by Betty Lou Oliver. She was taking her car down past the 76th floor when suddenly it shuddered and went into a virtual free fall, ending up in the basement.

Covered with debris, her back and legs broken, 20-year-old Mrs. Oliver was pulled to safety through a hole in the cab roof by Donald Molony, a young coast guard medic who happened to be walking past the Empire State Building at the moment of the crash. One of the heroes of the day, Molony then ran up 79 flights in a smoky stairwell and carried Catherine O'Connor to ground level.

O'Connor was one of seven people who had survived the 79th-floor holocaust by fleeing to a room on the south side. As black smoke rolled in under the door, they expected death at any moment—in a fatalistic gesture one young woman had flung her ring out the window—and were astonished when firemen finally broke through to rescue them.

The New York Fire Department did rapid and distinguished duty that day. Its men could reach only the 67th floor by elevator, then had to lug their hoses and other gear up another dozen flights of stairs. Somehow they managed to put out the flames in just 40 minutes. Later, they even found the jettisoned ring and restored it to its owner.

About 1,500 people, including 40 or more in the 86th-floor observatory, reached the ground safely. For weeks after the crash, passers-by stared up in disbelief at the black-rimmed hole where the unimaginable had happened. Thousands of New Yorkers would never forget that dreadful moment when an airplane hit the Empire State Building and made it shudder.

Killer From the Deep

High-speed waves batter Hawaiian Islands

ONE THING WAS CERTAIN, this was no April Fool's joke. At 1:30 A.M., on April 1, 1946, a killer was born 2¼ miles below the forbidding, spray-swept surface of the North Pacific, 90 miles southeast of the Aleutian Island called Unimak. At that moment, the ocean floor on the northern slope of the Aleutian Trench began to slip, triggering a massive undersea earthquake that was recorded within minutes by seismographs around the world.

On Unimak Island, the earthquake rocked the Scotch Cap lighthouse and its five-man coast guard detachment. Twenty-seven minutes later, a second, stronger tremor smashed into the Aleutian Islands, causing the ground at Unimak to heave wildly. For the increasingly nervous crew of the Scotch Cap lighthouse, death at the hands of an even more powerful force of nature was now only 21 minutes away.

The movement of the earth's crust that generated the two massive shocks felt at Unimak created a giant chasm in the Aleutian Trench. As part of the ocean floor disappeared into the center of the earth, water rushed in to fill the yawning gulf. This rapid displace-

ment of water gave rise to huge countersurging waves known as tsunamis. From their point of origin, the killer waves sped out in ever-widening circles to wreak havoc across the Pacific. Located so near the cataclysm's epicenter, Unimak would be its first victim.

In the pitch blackness of that tragic night it is doubtful that the men of Scotch Cap ever saw the 115-foot-high wave crest that came crashing in at a lethal 72 miles per hour. Preceded by an earsplitting roar, the wall of water exploded against the lighthouse, smashing it to bits and sweeping the crew into oblivion. The wave surged onward to engulf a coast guard station located at the edge of a cliff high above Scotch Cap. As the station's personnel scrambled to higher ground, one of their number looked down in the direction of Scotch Cap and saw that the lighthouse beacon was no longer shining.

Throughout the night, while a succession of waves continued to pound the island, the station crew tried vainly to raise a radio response from the lighthouse. At daybreak the beleaguered men peered over the edge of the cliff and beheld a scene of utter devastation. Un-

Moments before death, *a resident of Hilo, Hawaii (left), stares transfixed at the deluge that is about to swallow him up. Elsewhere in the city, people run for their lives before yet another lethal wave (above). The tsunami that was born near the Aleutian Islands off Alaska did its greatest damage in and around Hilo.*

recognizable debris littered the ground where the lighthouse had once stood. Later that morning, a search crew located a piece of a human body; some days later, portions of two other bodies were found. Everything else had been swallowed up by the sea.

While Unimak was undergoing its ordeal by water, the tsunami wave train was racing south toward a larger target, the Hawaiian Islands. Traveling at a fantastic average speed of 490 miles per hour, the first wave covered the nearly 2,300-mile distance to Oahu in slightly over 4½ hours. Oddly enough, ships sailing in that part of the Pacific would not have seen the tsunami coming or felt its passage beneath them, for out in mid-ocean the distance between tsunami wave crests can be as great as 100 miles and the height of the waves only a foot or two above the normal surface of the sea. But as the wave enters shallow coastal waters, its wave length and velocity both decrease, causing huge amounts of water to rear up and sweep ashore with great destructive force. Between 6 and 7 o'clock on the morning of April 1, just such a scenario began to unfold off the shores of the Hawaiian Islands.

In their beachfront cottage at Kawela Bay, a popular resort on Oahu's northern end, the oceanographer Francis P. Shepard and his wife were awakened by a noise that sounded to Shepard "as if dozens of locomotives were blowing off steam directly outside our house." Hurrying to his front window, the young scientist was amazed to see a mass of churning water

"sweeping over the ten-foot top of the beach ridge and coming directly at the house." His scientific curiosity winning out over survival instincts, Shepard grabbed his camera and headed outdoors, where he noted with some regret that instead of advancing farther the giant wave was retreating rapidly, leaving stranded fish flopping about on the newly exposed coral reef.

To the trained eye, the odd behavior of the sea could mean only one thing: tsunami on the way.

While Shepard snapped a pair of photographs, the water began to rise again, forming a second wave that "built higher and higher and then came racing forward with amazing velocity." With little time to spare, Shepard and his wife ran for protection behind their house.

"As I looked back," wrote Shepard in his account of the morning's events, "I saw the water surging over the spot where I had been standing a moment before. Suddenly we heard the terrible smashing of glass at the front of the house. The refrigerator passed us on the left side moving upright out into the [nearby] cane field. On the right came a wall of water sweeping toward us down the road that was our escape route from the area." Of his neighbor's house, continued Shepard, "nothing but kindling was left."

Certain that the full force of the tsunami was still to be felt, the Shepards hurried along the re-emerging beach and through a break in the cane field to the slightly elevated main road. They reached their destination just ahead of a third wave—a "monstrous wall of water," Shepard called it—that flattened the cane field "with a terrifying sound."

In the relative safety of the elevated road, Shepard and his wife commiserated with another couple, who had an amazing story to tell. They had been in their kitchen cooking breakfast when the first wave suddenly lifted their house, carried it several hundred feet, and set it down in the cane field so gently that their breakfast was still in place. "Needless to say," observed Shepard, "they did not stay to enjoy the meal."

After some six waves had come and gone, Shepard decided to return to what was left of his home. Just as he reached the door he became aware that "a very powerful mass of water was bearing down on the place. This time there simply was no island in back of the house during the height of the wave. I rushed to a nearby tree and climbed it as fast as possible and then hung on for dear life." This was the last of the major waves to hit Kawela Bay that day. When it subsided, Shepard found half of his house still standing and his possessions strewn all over the cane fields.

The Shepards' experiences were echoed in many parts of the Hawaiian Islands. Waves 45 feet high crashed into Kauai's north coast. At Haena Bay, two women, one of them with a baby, were standing in front of their homes wondering where to go when the rising water made up their minds for them. Swept off their feet, the women swam to some nearby trees and escaped with their lives. Their houses, however, were lifted off their foundations and wrecked.

The faces of the dead wore a look of incredulity or horror stamped on them by the watery killer from the north.

Hardest hit of all was the northeast coast of the archipelago's "Big Island," the island of Hawaii, which was battered in several places by waves more than 50 feet high (in contrast, Oahu's highest wave was recorded at 36 feet). The worst devastation took place in and around the city of Hilo. Here 96 people drowned or were killed by floating debris. As the corpses piled up, one overwhelmed mortuary began storing them in an icehouse, where they froze so solidly that eventually they had to be chipped apart.

In the tsunami's wake, *pier one of Hilo's Kuhio Wharf, a key loading dock for Hawaii's lucrative sugar crop, lies buried in debris. In the background are the ruins of a sugar warehouse wrecked by the waves.*

For their book *Tsunami!* authors Min Lee and Walter C. Dudley interviewed many survivors of the disaster, and their recollections make grim reading. Frank Kanzaki, a young teacher in the town of Laupahoehoe, northwest of Hilo, was having breakfast at the home of friends when the first wave hit a few minutes after 7 A.M. Kanzaki immediately grabbed two of his friends' daughters, Christine and Stella Nakano, and pushed them to the back of the house just before the tsunami snapped the stilts on which the building stood. After floating for a few seconds, the house began to disintegrate, and Kanzaki found himself struggling to hold on to the girls in churning water. The angry waves soon swept Stella away, but Kanzaki, still clinging to Christine, was deposited on the far side of a neighborhood baseball field amid remnants of smashed houses and other debris.

At her clifftop home overlooking Hilo Bay, Kapua Heuer was getting her family ready for another day when one of her daughters called out, "Mommy, what's wrong with the water?" Looking down at the ocean 30 feet below the edge of her property, Kapua Heuer saw a massive juggernaut of seawater racing inland at incredible speed. As the wave smashed against the cliff and threw spray high over their coconut trees, she and her daughters heard the crash of falling buildings and watched in horror as people struggled for their lives in downtown Hilo.

The April Fool's Day tsunami of 1946 was the most destructive to descend upon the islands since 1819, the year records of such things began to be kept. In all, it took 159 lives, damaged or destroyed some 1,400 homes, and caused extensive crop losses. Many coastal highways, as well as railroads in northern Oahu and in Hilo, were wrecked. So too was a large part of Hilo's protective breakwater. In all, an estimated $26 million worth of property was lost in the disaster.

The fact that Hawaiians had not had to deal with a major tsunami in a very long time accounted in part for the relatively high number of deaths. According to Shepard, most of those who died could have been saved had they run to higher ground at the first signs of trouble. Instead, many people were drawn to the shore "by the strange sight of the reefs being laid bare" and in some cases by the opportunity to catch stranded fish. Those who gave in to their curiosity or greed often paid with their lives. On the other hand, the timing of the disaster may have helped save lives. Had the waves begun arriving two or three hours earlier, the tide would have been higher, fewer people would have been up from their beds and out of their homes, and conceivably many more would have died.

Following the Hawaiian disaster, a Tsunami Warning System was set up, consisting of five seismic stations around the Pacific Rim and an oceanwide network of tide gauges, all under the direction of the International Pacific Tsunami Warning Center at Ho-

Walls of water *more than 25 feet high caused severe damage along the Hilo waterfront, shown here in a photograph taken three days after the disaster.*

nolulu. Thanks to a timely alarm from the center, a powerful tsunami in 1957 killed no one in Hawaii.

The system, however, is no guarantee against disaster. In May 1960 Hawaiians failed to heed warnings of a tsunami associated with the great Chilean earthquake then occurring; as a result, 61 people died in Hilo.

Tsunamis remain an eccentric force of nature. "I can tell you more about what we don't know about a tsunami than what we do know," Gordon Burton, head of the Honolulu warning center, said recently. "By the time it hits a coast, it's an unpredictable critter." Scientists can usually estimate when a tsunami will arrive, but not its intensity. And even some of their arrival predictions have been wrong. On May 7, 1986, thousands of people in Hawaii and along the Pacific coast of North America headed for the hills after an alarm was issued for a tsunami that never came.

One thing is certain about these killer waves: there will be more of them in the foreseeable future. Somewhere beneath one of the earth's great oceans, the sea floor will buckle or a volcano will erupt, giving birth to yet another tsunami. And somewhere along an exposed seacoast, men and women will have to flee to the high ground on whatever will get them there fastest.

RISK AND SURVIVAL ON OUR VIOLENT PLANET

Buried under tons of wet snow, the Swiss town of Airolo begins to recover from the crushing 1951 avalanche.

Winter of Terror

Deadliest avalanches on record scourge the Alps

THE WINTER OF 1950–51 began innocently enough. The month of December, though unusually chilly and overcast in Switzerland and Austria, produced only a scattering of storms and left the peaks and knife-edged valleys of the Alps covered with just half the normal amount of snow. Dismayed by the lack of precipitation, resort owners and skiers feared that the season would be a disastrous one. But unbeknownst to them, fast-changing weather conditions were laying the foundations for disaster of a different kind: a series of intense blizzards that would result in more than 1,300 avalanches in Switzerland alone and stamp the cruel and suffocating mark of "the white death" on the jagged face of the Alps as never before.

Toward mid-January a mass of warm, moist air drifted northeast from the Spanish coast and collided with a wave of Arctic air streaming south. At the same time, a low-pressure system, harried by gale-force winds, moved in from the Baltic area and added fuel to the gathering storm. On January 15 the first heavy snows began to blanket the Alps. After two days there was a brief respite as the sun broke through. But then the great storm roared to life again with a vengeance,

bringing howling, blinding, wind-whipped sheets of snow—at times an incredible four to six inches an hour—and turning day to night.

The people of the Alps have a hard-won knowledge of avalanches, especially of the imperative of quick rescue. Someone caught in an avalanche is most immediately in danger of being injured or knocked unconscious by the impact of ice, rocks, trees, and other debris. There is also a danger posed by snow dust: the natural impulse to gasp for air can result in death by suffocation. By one estimate, 35 percent of those caught in the open by an avalanche die almost immediately from injury or suffocation.

Anyone who survives both of these threats faces yet another: becoming entombed in a mass that has the weight and consistency of hardening cement. Snow under pressure turns to ice; even snow dust, as powdery as it is, can become tightly compressed within a few seconds. If the victim cannot struggle free during the first few moments, his chances for escape rapidly dwindle. And if rescuers cannot reach the scene soon enough—and locate him beneath a huge pile of featureless snow—any oxygen will soon give out.

The people of the Alps also knew perfectly well what these extraordinary snowfalls and high winds meant. Thus when Burtel Gross, an elderly road worker, failed to come home for lunch on January 19 after a morning spent clearing the Ofen Pass road in eastern Switzerland, his neighbors wasted no time in organizing a rescue effort. By 2:45 P.M. a crew was probing an avalanche lying across the Ofen Pass road at Val Barcli, in the neck of Swiss territory jutting southeast into Italy from the Inn Valley.

A detail of five men with a trained rescue dog found Gross's body in a steep gulley after about 45 minutes, and they made preparations to remove it. Suddenly a roar was heard and a cloud of powder snow thundered down Val Barcli, throwing the five men and the dog deeper into the valley and covering them with a pall of icy snow.

This happened at 3:40 P.M.

A search was then begun for the original victim, his five rescuers, and the dog, but by nightfall, even though new help had arrived, nothing had been found. Despite blizzard and darkness, a rescue team continued to work through the debris until about 11 P.M.—when a third avalanche screamed down the valley at high speed. Equipped only with flashlights, and having had no warning, the rescuers knew the thing only by its peripheral effects—by the blast wave and by its sucking one man, Ernest Thut, back from a position of safety into the maelstrom, where he was buried alive.

A dog found Thut 90 minutes later, but it was too late. The decision was made to risk no more lives, and the survivors withdrew, leaving seven men entombed in Val Barcli—six of them heads of families.

The ill-fated rescue attempt at Val Barcli had consequences that proved to be doubly tragic.

Not only did the rescuers become the victims, but one crew, from the village of Zuoz, was urgently needed at home. Through bad luck or bad organization, the crew included the members of the Zuoz Avalanche Committee, which was responsible for taking preventive measures against avalanches that for centuries had threatened the town.

Its main defense was a mortar, fired to bring the slides down while they were still small and harmless. But only the Avalanche Committee could order use of the mortar, and so during the critical afternoon hours of the 19th the villagers couldn't get the authorization they felt they needed to fire it. As snow continued to accumulate on the cornices above the town, neither the crew chief nor the president of the commune would take responsibility for firing the mortar—and

SWEPT AWAY

Among the survivors of an avalanche that bombarded Jackson Hole, Wyoming, in 1967 was ski patroller Richard Porter, who later described his harrowing experience:

"I looked uphill, and saw the snow hurtling toward me. There was no chance to outski the slide; I was knocked down almost immediately. I dropped my poles and began swimming with it in an effort to stay on top of the snow. I finally came to a stop lying on my side, twisted round so that my feet were higher than my head.

"As the snow from above buried me, I managed to move my head around enough to form a small air pocket. The avalanche ended as quickly as it had begun. I could hear the muffled crunch above as the snow settled around me. It was solid, like being in a bag of wet cement. I couldn't move at all."

Thanks to the swift response of rescue teams, however, Porter's story ended happily. He was located and dug out after 65 minutes—gray, unconscious, but alive.

Probing for avalanche victims, *members of a ski patrol form a chain as they gingerly advance down the side of a mountain.*

possibly bringing down an avalanche mightier than any that would happen naturally.

At 10:00 A.M. on January 20 the villagers sought advice from the Swiss Federal Institute for Snow and Avalanche Research, which they could still reach by telephone. The reply was prompt and unequivocal: "Fire immediately."

But even with that guidance, the commune president was unwilling to make the decision himself. Instead he called a meeting of the town council, which debated into the afternoon while the storm continued depositing its massive weights of snow.

At 3:30 P.M. the village leaders decided to fire. The mortar crew chief, however, had already refused to climb to the usual firing position up the valley, deeming it too dangerous. With some of his friends, he carried the weapon to the edge of the village, made a rough calculation of the elevation, deflection, and charge needed at this new position—and at 4:05 sent the projectile aloft into the swirling blizzard.

Listening for its detonation, the crew could hear only a strange humming sound. With no further warning, they were struck by a thunderous wave of snow. One man was flung into a shed, another was buried to the neck, and the crew chief was buried altogether, to be rescued by his comrades in the nick of time.

Soon a little girl ran to the mortar men and told them that a house had disappeared. Before long it became horribly clear that their belated action had triggered the worst combination of snowslides imaginable. The avalanche overran several houses, demolished a four-story building, and killed five people.

Artificial barriers, *such as the rows of fences above, serve to stop the momentum of an avalanche and render it harmless. Avalanche defenses include forests planted at crucial spots to prevent dangerous buildups and buildings ingeniously designed to deflect a slide. The 17th-century Swiss church at left is shaped like the bow of a ship to split the avalanche.*

In the meantime, similar tragedies were taking place in valley after valley across the paralyzed region.

Scores of other Alpine villages and resorts suffered their own terror as hundreds of thousands of tons of snow and ice raced down, at speeds often exceeding 100 miles per hour. A dairy farmer ignored warnings to evacuate and died because of it, along with his wife and five young children. One woman stayed at home to finish her washing before moving to safety. She too died. A family of five were overrun while walking along a road to what they thought would be a safe place. The mother and two children were dug out alive; the father and one son were found dead.

When the storm finally petered out on January 22, its legacy was awesome to behold—roads and railways blocked, utilities in danger of failing, people and animals trapped everywhere. A rail tunnel between Chur and Arosa was closed off by snowslides at both ends, sealing a passenger train inside. About 25 women and children huddled together through a long night of uncertainty as the men struggled to dig their way out. Less fortunate was the small Austrian village of Heiligenblut, where a nighttime avalanche had struck "like an earthquake," in the words of one witness, crushing houses and burying 15 people. Frantic efforts by other villagers saved three of the victims, but the rest could not be found in time.

Thus by small numbers, five in one place, a dozen or more in the next, did the avalanches take their mounting toll. Slowly, sadly, each recovered body adding to the personal tragedy of the survivors, hundreds of towns across Switzerland, Austria, and northern Italy stripped away the white mantle of disaster and tried to re-establish their normally tranquil lives. What

Profile of a Mountainside

AN AVALANCHE occurs when a mountainside can no longer hold an accumulation of snow, and seldom in nature is so much destructive energy unleashed by such random, even trivial causes. A gust of wind, a vibration, a falling tree, or a skier can start the snow rolling. One type of slide is the soft-slab avalanche (foreground), which usually consists of newly fallen snow that turns into a suffocating cloud of powder as it progresses. A hard-slab avalanche (center) results when heavy, packed snow breaks off in large, lethal chunks. Spring avalanches are usually a mixture of water and snow that oozes slowly but relentlessly down a slope (rear).

The faster avalanches, capable of speeds approaching 200 miles per hour, usually last only minutes. The biggest slides carry a million tons or more of snow, ice, rock, and trees. These monsters can scour as much as 3,000 feet of mountainside in 15 to 20 seconds, with impact pressures of more than 20,000 pounds per square foot. Moreover, they often push a powerful blast of air forward as they fall; this concussion alone can uproot forests, rip bridges from their foundations, and hurl animals and people into the air.

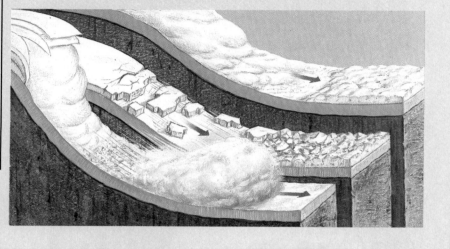

Though some types of avalanches plunge vertically through the air, the most lethal are these ground-hugging slides.

---

they had no way of knowing was that the Winter of Terror was not finished yet.

Early in February another great storm swept down on towns and villages to the south. A near-record 4 feet of snow fell in a single 24-hour period, and in one area, more than 13 feet were deposited in two weeks.

The hissing, thundering sound of avalanches was soon echoing again across the Alps. In the village of Frasco, near the Italian border southeast of Andermatt, Switzerland, a slide of titanic proportions, with a crest some 650 feet in width, raced down 3,700 feet. Miraculously, only four people were killed, but the last of the soldiers sent in to clear away the snow did not depart until July.

Perhaps hardest hit in this second assault was the town of Airolo, located south of Andermatt near the twisting spine of a ravine named Vallascia, or "evil gully" in the local dialect. An estimated 500,000 tons of wet snow, loosened by two savage gusts of wind, swept through the town on February 12, killing 10 people and damaging numerous buildings.

Nor was this the end of it. So much snow had built up that avalanches continued well into April. Complete figures on the damage caused by the Winter of Terror could only be guessed at; 280 people were known dead in Austria, Switzerland, Italy, and France. Adding to the horror, about 1,400 domestic animals perished and, in some areas, perhaps half the wildlife. An estimated 15,000 acres of healthy, avalanche-breaking forest were uprooted as well.

The Alps in winter have always been as treacherous as they are beautiful, and avalanches will continue to claim victims there. But the Winter of Terror is not likely to be repeated. Despite their ferocity, the great blizzards of early 1951 were not solely responsible. Abnormally cold weather in December had slicked earlier snows with a layer of "sugar snow," large granular clusters of ice crystals that can be as slippery as ball bearings. In addition, the early snows were deep enough to cloak natural obstacles that might have served as avalanche breaks later on. In January, when the first storms struck, temperatures dropped sufficiently to keep the fresh snow from settling well. Finally, the fierce mountain wind carved linchpin-like slabs and cornices high on the Alpine peaks, easy triggers for high-speed slides.

Thus the scene was set for disaster by a deadly combination of elements. Inhabitants of the region had experience and certain weapons at hand: explosives designed to trigger avalanches high on the peaks, legally protected stands of trees that prevented dangerous buildups of snow, special wedge-shaped outer walls on vulnerable buildings, trained rescue dogs. But such were the unique dimensions, alignment, and timing of the storms and snowfields that human ingenuity was simply overwhelmed.

One witness of the avalanches of World War I, when Austrian and Italian troops fired howitzers to unleash the white death on one another's columns in the Italian Alps, said simply: "It is a pitiful way to die."

London's Deadly Fog

Poisonous pea souper chokes British capital

MOST LONDONERS, the noted diarist John Evelyn wrote in 1661, "breathe nothing but an impure and thick mist, accompanied by a fuliginous and filthy vapor, corrupting the lungs, so that catarrhs, coughs, and consumptions rage more in this one city, than in the whole Earth." Evelyn was trying to get King Charles II to decree the planting of more trees and shrubs near Whitehall to offset the stench of home coal fires.

But ever more home fires kept burning for another 300 years, and coming on line to darken London's face even more were the coal fires of factories, power plants, locomotives, and steamboats on the Thames. When fog thickened over the city, as it frequently did,

The worst fog in memory made London's streets a commuter's nightmare in December 1952. Armed with a flare, a London Transport bus inspector guides a double-decker through the impenetrable murk.

the smoke of a million or more fires formed a depressing, murky mist. "Stand at the window here," says Sherlock Holmes to Dr. Watson. "Was ever such a dreary, dismal, unprofitable world? See how the yellow fog swirls down the street and drifts across the dun-coloured houses." Yet not even the great fictional detective knew what a devil's brew of lethal pollutants was stirring in that yellow mix.

Britons are not easily given to depression, and Londoners were not only stoical about their fog but rather proud of it. Cockneys in faraway places yearned for a glimpse of "the old smoke." It gave a distinctive ambience to the pages of British literature, especially the novels of Charles Dickens. It was one of his characters who defined the dense brown smoke in the streets as "a London particular." In *Bleak House,* the fog over the heart of the city is emblematic of the "groping and floundering" condition of the law as administered in the Court of Chancery. The novel opens with a powerful evocation of the fog-enshrouded city: "Fog everywhere. Fog up the river, fog down the river. . . . Fog creeping into the cabooses of collier-brigs; fog lying out on the yards, and hovering in the rigging of great ships. . . . Gas looming through the fog in divers places in the streets. . . . Most of the shops lighted two hours before their time—as the gas seems to know, for it has a haggard and unwilling look."

Dickensian villains committed some of their foulest deeds in this foggy milieu. But in late 1952 the literary linkage of fog and death became grim reality.

This time the London fog was not just a screen for criminals but a mass killer in its own right.

On Thursday, December 4, warm air from the Atlantic moved over the city and stayed put, trapping below it cool, moist air in what meteorologists call a temperature "inversion." Unusual for Britain, there was no wind to disperse the dense fog that was forming at ground level. By Friday morning the city was smothered in a thick yellow smog that did not begin to lift until the following Tuesday. Suspended in the murk were tiny particles of soot, sulfur dioxide, and other pollutants that penetrated into the tiniest air passages of the lungs. Soon, as many as 4,000 Londoners were choking their way to a premature death.

At first this fog seemed to nearly all of those who

***A filthy haze cloaks** London's Tower Bridge in 1937. For centuries, polluted fog poisoned the air Londoners breathed.*

endured it just one more bad pea souper. There were no official warnings by press or radio of any special danger. Yes, hospitals noted higher admission rates than normal. Yes, coroners, pathologists, and registrars of death were aware that mortality had soared. But few of London's 8.25 million inhabitants knew, until after it had passed, that they had been visited by one of the worst air pollution disasters of modern times.

News editors apparently told their reporters to round up the usual fog stories. The incidents and accidents they recorded were familiar and often good for a laugh. But as the stories piled up over the weekend, their tone began to sound ominous even to a blitz-hardened generation.

With London all but immobilized by the densest, dirtiest fog in memory, surface trains rolled slowly, if at all, and some of them collided. After one train accident, passengers climbed out of the cars and formed a hand-to-hand chain to safety. Ambulances and fire engines could proceed only when crew members walked in front of them as guides. Motorists by the hundreds abandoned their cars, only to find them layered with soot after the air cleared. The underground trains kept running, but they were jammed with stranded bus riders; at rush hour on Monday evening, some 3,000 commuters lined up for tickets at Stratford Station on the Central Line.

Aircraft, with a few exceptions, were grounded.

Thus there was no repetition of an incident a year earlier when an Air France plane, landing in fog at London's Heathrow Airport, was so completely obscured that five separate search parties groped around the runways for more than an hour before the plane was found and its 33 passengers cautiously bused to the terminal.

As the fog lingered over the weekend, Londoners in their millions gathered around their firesides, heaping more coal on the grates to ward off the chill, thus adding to the pollution that had penned them in. Those who were obliged or determined to walk outside could get lost after only a few steps. Visibility was about one foot in some places, and down by the Thames docks it was reported that "one couldn't see one's feet." A physician got the bright idea of hiring a blind patient to guide him on his rounds, an arrangement that worked splendidly. Only criminals found conditions to their liking; Scotland Yard reported a surge in attacks, burglaries, and robberies under cover of the fog.

The smoky mist seeped indoors, speeding bronchial and cardiac patients to their deaths. In other homes the fog was less deadly but pervasively annoying. Housewives, for example, had to cope with sticky grime on kitchen tables and no milk deliveries.

Ray—London Daily Telegraph
"Honest, guv, it's a smog-mask"

In the thickening murk, this warning was posted in a movie house lobby: "Screen visibility nil."

Humans were not the only sufferers. Livestock assembled for the Smithfield Club's traditional cattle show began rasping on the first day of the fog. Sixty of them required major veterinary treatment. One animal died, 12 had to be slaughtered, and only 2 of these prime carcasses could be salvaged for food. Masks improvised from grain sacks soaked in whiskey saved a number of the beasts. The pigs and sheep in London markets, however, appeared untroubled by the smog.

Altogether it seemed that stoic Londoners had another good clutch of tales to add to their pea souper lore. But the mortality statistics, when gathered and fully comprehended, told an ugly story. Not only were some 4,000 persons added to the normal death list for December, but another 8,000 or so were estimated to have perished later from the long-term effects of the four-day smog. Most of these victims were ailing and elderly people for whom, in former times, the deadly fog would have been accepted as a coup de grace. The

fog that took thousands of English lives in 1873, for example, barely disturbed Victorian complacency. This time, however, the terrible toll among the elderly sparked public concern.

In the aftermath of the disaster, Parliament set up a commission to study London's pollution problem, and in 1956 a Clean Air Act was passed. The new law set strict standards for smoke emission and offered government aid to homeowners and industries that switched from coal to low-sulfur fuels, such as oil and natural gas. Opposition to this measure may well have been smothered by another fog that claimed about 1,000 lives in January 1956.

The fog of December 1952 was decisive in bringing about action to clean London's air, but credit should be given to the fitful but persistent antismoke movement that had helped to build up public awareness of the air pollution problem. Attempts to legislate against the fouling of London's air go back to the 13th century, long before John Evelyn uttered his complaint to King Charles. All such efforts were stifled, however, by the march of industrial progress, especially during the 19th century. As the Industrial Revolution took off, smokestacks multiplied and London became a world leader in bronchitis. Yet pollution was accepted, along with slums and industrial accidents, as the price to be paid for the rapid increase of wealth. The phrase "muck is money" expressed the predominant attitude of the time.

There were always scientists and public servants who fought this consensus, pointing out the dangers of pollution and offering perceptive solutions. In 1887 the general secretary of the British Association for the Advancement of Science gave an address in which he argued that Londoners should "give up burning crude fuel such as ordinary coal in our fires. We must cook by gas and we must sacrifice open fireplaces." A member of the London City Council warned in 1901 that "the combination of smoke and fog had disastrous effects on human life," and "when the people of London knew what the cost in life and money was they would be willing to do everything possible to stop the smoke nuisance."

Such warnings went unheeded for another half century, despite the periodic alarms sent out by London and other smog centers throughout the industrialized world. The most urgent of these alarms had come from Donora, Pennsylvania, a mill town 30 miles down the Monongahela River from Pittsburgh. Best known for producing the great baseball player Stan Musial, Donora was the site of a steel mill, a zinc-reduction factory, and a sulfuric-acid plant. Smoke and fumes from these works, normally just a nuisance, proved deadly when trapped over the town by an atmospheric inversion that lasted for three days in October 1948. At the end of the third day, 6,000 people—nearly half the population—were ill, and 20 had died. The parallels with the London disaster four years later—the inversion, the sulfur dioxide and carbon particulates in the air—were too striking to escape notice by those studying London's problem.

The "muck is money" school still had its adherents in Britain, some of them high in the government, but the parliamentary commission was able to demonstrate that the cost of air pollution was unacceptable financially as well as medically. Air-borne poisons also exacted a cultural and sentimental toll. Surely many Londoners were affected by expert testimony that corrosive smoke had done more damage to Westminster Abbey in the past 100 years than all the wear and tear of the centuries since King Henry III raised its Gothic towers in 1245.

The Clean Air Act worked. Since its passage there have been no killer fogs in London comparable to that of 1952. Sunshine and visibility in the city have markedly increased. And surprisingly, the incidence of fog, even "clean" fog, has declined—which raises an interesting question about the connection between fog and air pollution. According to one theory, London is less foggy today because of a lucky change in its weather that brought about a decrease in westerly, water-bearing winds. But even proponents of this view acknowledge that less pollution means reduced fog density. Fog droplets form around solid nuclei, be they only dust specks. Remove soot and other particulates from the air, and fog has less chance of taking hold.

Whatever the weather, the prospect is that Londoners will never again have to endure the combination of fog and air pollution that felled so many of them in 1952. Anyone nostalgic for a good London pea souper may well have to turn to the novels of Dickens for a literary evocation of fogs past.

THE ENDANGERED AIR: CRISES AROUND THE GLOBE

In late summer of 1955, southern California sweltered through more than seven days of above 100° F temperatures. In Los Angeles, the intense ultraviolet rays of the sun interacted with automobile exhaust fumes to create a deadly brew of ozone and other noxious chemicals. A blue-black haze hung over the city for days, stinging eyes and making breathing a dangerous business, especially for the elderly and infirm.

As in London nearly three years before, the smog crisis in Los Angeles prompted government action. Laws restricting automobile exhaust levels were passed on both the state and federal level. While such measures have reduced the amount of pollutants new cars can emit, the number of vehicles on the road has increased dramatically. Today, the car is still the main cause of Los Angeles smog.

Mexico City, Denver, Athens, New Delhi, and many other cities around the world are struggling with pollution crises of their own. In many instances, a weather phenomenon known as temperature inversion is the catalyst. Normally, air turns colder the higher it is. In an inversion, however, a layer of warm air traps cooler, tainted air

Spectacular sunsets are a byproduct of Mexico City's air pollution crisis.

beneath it. Unable to disperse, pollutants build up close to the ground until winds or rain breaks up the overlying warm air layer. Geographical features such as surrounding mountains can further entrap polluted air, leading to frequent and prolonged smogs.

Dirty air claims many other victims besides human lungs. Sulfurous clouds may be killing Germany's Black Forest. Ozone helps reduce American crop yields. And from the Acropolis to the Taj Mahal, air-borne poisons are eroding many of man's most glorious creations.

The Night the North Sea Overflowed

Wind, waves, and high tide spell disaster for Holland

THE DIKE MASTER of Colijnsplaat, a small North Sea fishing community in the Dutch province of Zeeland, inspected the town's seawall with greater care than usual on Saturday night, January 31, 1953. The nearly 400-year-old ramparts had been battered for hours by howling, gale-force winds and giant waves—products of a ferocious storm that had swept down the east coast of Scotland earlier that Saturday, driving billions of tons of water into the North Sea channel between southeast England and the southwestern Netherlands. In a rare, perhaps once-in-a-century combination of forces, the storm surge coincided with both a severe atmospheric depression that pulled up the sea even higher and the arrival of the spring tide—the twice-monthly maximum tide caused by the alignment of sun, moon, and earth.

All along the coasts of Zeeland, South Holland, and North Brabant—the three low-lying Dutch provinces situated along the estuaries of the Rhine, Maas, and Scheldt rivers—the great stone dikes that had protected the land for centuries groaned under the assault of the swollen sea. In Colijnsplaat the dike master sent for sandbags and reinforcing beams of wood and steel. He also informed the mayor and councilmen to be prepared for an emergency should the situation worsen during the night.

Mending the dikes *became a top priority for the Dutch nation in the wake of one of the worst floods in its history.*

And worsen it did. Soon after midnight, with winds gusting at more than 90 miles per hour and the sea still rising, the dike master ordered a general alarm sounded. Church bells started tolling, and the town's fishmonger scurried through the streets sounding a warning bell. Able-bodied men tumbled out of bed, grabbed their boots, and ran for the seawall. They got there just in time, too, for the pounding waves had loosened one of the brick buttresses along the rampart's inner face. "She's giving way!" someone shouted. In an instant, those standing nearest the tottering pillar threw their weight against it. Rank upon rank of strong shoulders fell in behind to shore up the wall until reinforcement beams could be brought up and wedged in place. For two terrifying hours, 40 men formed a human barricade between Colijnsplaat and the icy sea. Waves spilled over the top, drenching the resolute fighters in frozen brine, but the wall held.

In the heart of the flood zone, the North Sea killed 300 in the village of Oude Tonge (above) and turned streets into slimy canals.

The salvation of Colijnsplaat was one of the brighter episodes in a night of tragedy for the lands bordering the North Sea. In Britain, the northerly gales generated by the storm were among the worst ever recorded. Pummeled by 113-mile-per-hour winds, the sea ferry *Princess Victoria* capsized off Northern Ireland, killing more than 130 passengers, including all 30 women and children on board. (The storm took a total of 307 lives in Great Britain alone.) Along the east coast of England, wind-driven seas swamped coastal defenses from Yorkshire to Kent, spoiling some 250 square miles of farmland for years to come. Germany, Belgium, and northern France likewise suffered serious damage, but it was Holland, veteran of an age-old war against the North Sea, that bore the brunt of the storm's destructive fury.

All night Saturday, the sea rose until it was level with the top of the dikes. At high tide in the early hours of Sunday morning, an unexpected storm surge sent water crashing through the dikes in scores of places throughout Holland's southwestern delta region.

Hundreds of people died in their beds; others awakened to find water rising at the terrifying rate of a foot a minute.

Within moments a wall of water began to cascade across the land, inundating nearly 500,000 acres of polders—low-lying terrain that the Dutch had laboriously wrested from the sea and meticulously maintained over the centuries. In many towns hapless flood victims never even heard the warning bells over the deafening roar of the storm. Others scrambled to whatever high ground they could find, only to have it washed out beneath their feet.

At the farming and fishing village of 's Gravendeel, some 600 citizens, many of them dressed only in nightclothes, ran for the Mill Dike, a windmill built into the town's network of dikes. As the refugees huddled there in the first light of day, dikes several miles away on either side collapsed, releasing the sea behind them. The two raging torrents crashed into each other at the Mill Dike with a force that shot water 200 feet into the air and hurled all 600 people into the flood. On the island of Overflakkee in South Holland, 51 persons gathered atop a dike—women and children clustered in the center, with the men forming a protective ring around them. As a local schoolmaster led the kneeling crowd in prayer, a giant wave broke over their heads but, amazingly, spared their lives. Still on their knees, the thankful refugees began to sing a favorite Dutch hymn; just then the receding wave undermined the dike and swept them all away.

By daybreak on Sunday, some 300,000 lives were in jeopardy as many of the islands and peninsulas that make up the delta region were swallowed by the sea. In town after town terrified people clutched rooftops, tree branches, and telephone poles or stood in attics waist-deep in water, waiting for the onslaught to pass. In the town of Spijkenisse, near Rotterdam, a couple clung to the roof of their home, the wife holding on to the chimney with one arm, to her husband with the other. For more than 24 hours, swirling currents knocked the man's foot against a metal gutter. By the time the couple was rescued, nothing was left of the mangled foot except a few smashed pieces of bone.

Word of the crisis on the coast reached the rest of Holland early Sunday morning. A yachtsman who had taken his boat into the shelter of Voorne Island north of Overflakkee radioed the mainland to report severe flooding in the Zeeland islands. Within hours hundreds of volunteers had gathered at mobilization points in the large cities and were being sped to the dikes armed with shovels and sandbags. Despite their best efforts, however, new breaches continued to be reported for several days after the initial flood.

The most urgent task facing the Dutch nation in the aftermath of the disaster was to shore up those dikes that had been weakened by the storm but were still standing. The more difficult job of rebuilding broken dikes would take, according to some estimates, a year or more. As the Dutch well knew, until all the walls were closed securely there would be no way to hold back the ever threatening sea, no way to pump out water, and thus no way to reclaim the land. As one observer commented, without their protective ramparts "these people might as well be living in the middle of the ocean."

While workers struggled to limit the damage to the dikes, thousands of survivors had to be evacuated from the flood zone. An international force of 150 planes and 2,000 boats was soon working around the clock to rescue more than 50,000 people marooned in Zeeland and South Holland and to provide food and medical supplies to 250,000 others. American, Belgian, and British military relief helicopters played a crucial role in saving lives. On Wednesday, February 4, seven United States helicopters, flying nonstop from dawn to dusk, picked up 450 flood victims from rooftops and other exposed places on the island of Overflakkee. Some of the rescued people, mostly children and the elderly, had to be transported in litters lashed to the fuselage. "It was a tough job," observed Maj. Jack Ruby of the 34th Engineer Combat Group. "It took a maximum-performance take-off to get the plane up, but we just could not leave these people behind." A Dutch official who had spent the whole day on the devastated island reflected the sentiments of local eyewitnesses when he said, "I have seen many miracles performed here, but the greatest of them is the helicopters." In all, the chopper pilots plucked 2,450 people from almost certain death; for many others, however, the helicopters arrived too late.

With a staggering number of people needing help, many died in the bitter cold before rescuers could reach them.

Days went by before the Dutch nation received a clear accounting of just how painful a blow it had sustained. The flood killed a total of 1,850 people and forced the evacuation of 72,000; more than 47,000 houses were damaged or destroyed. In this region of intensive agriculture, the fact that some 800,000 acres

The North Sea's invasion of the southwestern Netherlands devastated town and country alike. At left, children play amid the debris left behind by retreating floodwaters in the city of Poortvliet. The rotting carcasses of drowned cattle pile up on the island of Schouwen Duiveland, above. Dutch farmers lost thousands of head of cattle in the disaster.

The Haringvliet Dam is a major component of the Delta Project, the Netherland's $5-billion protective barrier against the sea.

pushed their country's shoreline westward.

Such daring acts of engineering, however, carry with them the risk of failure, and time and again the sea has risen up to reclaim the lands that the Dutch have so laboriously created. While the 1953 disaster is generally regarded as the worst flood in modern Dutch history, it pales beside several earlier inundations in terms of loss of life and lasting social disruption. On December 14, 1287, a flood in the Zuider Zee area claimed 50,000 lives. At least 10,000 people were killed and 72 towns destroyed during an inundation in the southwest on November 18, 1421. Another 1,500 Hollanders died when flood waters submerged some 400,000 acres on November 1, 1586. In fact, hardly a century has gone by without a major flood catastrophe in the Netherlands. But each time, the devastation only prompted the Dutch to build stronger and better defenses against the sea, and so it did again in 1953.

Three weeks after the storm, the Dutch government appointed a commission to investigate ways to keep the North Sea out of the southwestern delta once and for all. Two main options were considered: to rebuild the 434 miles of existing dikes, only higher and stronger; or to construct a network of barrier dams that would seal off most of the delta's large inlets, thereby reducing Holland's exposed coastline by more than 400 miles. The Delta Commission and the Dutch Parliament chose the second plan, and in 1958 work began on one of the most ambitious engineering projects of modern times.

of farmland had been submerged for days in salt water would have serious long-term economic consequences, as would the loss of more than a quarter of a million livestock and poultry.

Sympathetic foreigners might suggest abandoning some of the flooded areas permanently, but the Dutch are not an easily discouraged people. After all, battling the sea is the essence of their life and history. There is a saying that "God made the earth, but the Dutch made Holland," and indeed, as early as the 12th century, the inhabitants of the Netherlands had begun the monumental task of wresting new land, bit by bit, from the sea. The windmill, that national emblem introduced in the Netherlands by soldiers returning from the Crusades, made the process more efficient. A section of swampland would be surrounded by dikes and, with the help of windmills, pumped dry to create fertile farmlands at or even below sea level. With each passing century the Netherlands acquired hundreds of additional square miles of territory, as Dutch masters of land reclamation refined their techniques and

The challenge tackled by the Delta Project engineers was a formidable one: to build 18.5 miles of dams on a foundation of shifting sands in fast-moving waters as much as 132 feet deep. In order to learn from their experiences as they went along, the engineers worked in ascending order of difficulty, closing off the smallest of the inlets first, saving the largest and most complicated project for the end. In October 1986, the last link in the network—the monumental storm-surge barrier across the Eastern Scheldt—was inaugurated. Rather than blocking the estuary (and altering its ecology) as a closed dam would have done, the barrier's 62 massive steel gates allow the tide to flow in and out normally, but they can be shut whenever a flood threatens. Today the people of the delta region are as secure as modern science and Dutch ingenuity can make them. The price of such security, however, was very high. The Delta Project cost more than 10 billion guilders (some $5 billion) in all, but the Dutch, who know the terrible toll that floods can exact, deem it well worth every guilder.

New Zealand's Christmas Eve Horror

Freakish floodwaters cause nation's worst rail accident

NOT LONG BEFORE MIDNIGHT on Christmas Eve, 1953, an isolated river crossing in New Zealand suddenly and cruelly lived up to its native Maori name, *Tangiwai:* "Weeping Waters." At about 10:15 P.M., a 27-year-old postal employee named Cyril Ellis was about to drive his truck across the bridge at Tangiwai when he slammed on the brakes and stared ahead in disbelief. The normally gentle Whangaehu River had turned into a raging, swollen torrent, so far above its normal level that the bridge was completely engulfed. Boulders, mud, volcanic ash, and chunks of ice produced a roar that could be heard for miles.

Getting out to look around, Ellis had another shock when he glimpsed the light of an approaching train. Although he couldn't see the railroad bridge that spanned the river about 100 yards upstream, he knew

it would be no more passable than the road bridge. (Had it been visible, the sight would have chilled his blood: the bridge's entire central section had been demolished, leaving only the rails stretched like two threads across the chasm.) Running as hard as he could to the railroad embankment, Ellis waved his flashlight in warning, but seemingly to no avail.

Worst of all, as it roared past he could see that it was not a freight train but the Wellington–Auckland night express, its nine passenger cars packed with happy families on holiday, many eager to see Britain's just-crowned Queen Elizabeth II in Auckland the next day. Moments later Ellis could hear their screams as the locomotive, its tender, and the first five passenger coaches crashed into the floodwaters. Left behind, dangling from the edge at a 45° angle, was the sixth

Plunging headlong into the darkness, the locomotive and five crowded passenger cars were engulfed by raging flood-waters as another car hung precariously over the edge.

car, just barely connected to the three rear passenger cars that remained on the rails. (It may have been Ellis's effort to warn the train that saved them from destruction. The wreckage of the engine later revealed that the engineer had slammed shut the throttle, hit the emergency brake valve, and thrown the reverse lever just before plunging into the flood.)

Frantically, Ellis rushed to the back of the train, found a dazed guard, and hurried forward with him to the car teetering on the brink. Finding it filled with passengers too petrified to move, he began pulling those nearest the rear door to safety. But before anyone had been helped out, the car suddenly lurched, its coupling snapped, and it toppled 35 feet into the swirling torrent below.

For what seemed an eternity, Ellis and all the rest were trapped as the coach pitched and rolled wildly in the darkness, filling up fast with water. At last, after about 60 terrifying yards, it crashed to a halt lying on one side, with the other just above the surface of the flood. Amazingly, Ellis's flashlight was still working, and with it he was able to see that—even more amazingly—the others were still alive. But they wouldn't be for long if they didn't get out: water, mud, and chunks of ice were surging through the car with incredible force. Ellis was able to break a hole through the window above his head, and with help from others arriving on the scene, he struggled for 90 minutes to find everyone in the car and hoist each one to safety.

By midnight it was over. Of 22 people in the car, all had been rescued but one, a young girl who drowned in the murky water under a seat. Elsewhere, though, the outcome was far more grim. Some of the passengers in the forward cars had been miraculously spared—28 in all, including one elderly woman who was found almost 300 yards downstream, buried in silt up to her neck. But most were not so lucky. The search for bodies continued for months—some were eventually found 15 miles downstream—and 20 of

the victims were never accounted for. In the end, the official toll listed 151 men, women, and children killed, out of about 285 who had been aboard.

The nation was dumbstruck. New Zealand's worst railway disaster had occurred at a moment of great national pride, the first state visit there by a British monarch. Compounding the shock was the mystifying nature of the disaster. Early reports blamed a cloudburst or a volcanic eruption for the unpredicted flood, but the truth that emerged was far stranger.

Some 22 miles north of Tangiwai rise the twin volcanic peaks of Mount Ruapehu, at 9,175 feet the tallest mountain on New Zealand's North Island. Except for a series of eruptions in 1945–47, it had not been especially active in recent times. In local lore, it is a sighing, lonely female spirit, victim of a broken heart in the days when mountains romanced each other and had illicit trysts. The name *Ruapehu* may come from a combination of Maori words that mean "two" and "to explode or make a loud noise."

About 1,000 feet below the summit lies Crater Lake, a warm and acidic body of water that contrasts oddly with the perpetually snowy heights above it. Volcanic steam bubbles up from the lake's bottom, churning the yellowish layer of sulfur that sometimes forms on the surface. The overflow normally emptied through a natural tunnel beneath a wall of ice provided by the Whangaehu Glacier. Starting in 1945, though, volcanic activity in the center of the lake caused a great dome of black lava to grow, almost filling the cavity of the crater. When it finally settled, the bowl of the lake had deepened, but the natural outlet had been blocked by debris from several eruptions. A new outlet did break through the barrier below the ice, but it proved insufficient, and as the lake waters rose to 26 feet above normal, the pressure kept mounting. The barrier finally burst—about two hours before the Wellington–Auckland express reached Tangiwai.

The powerful flow of water, mud, ice, and stone that raced downward is called a lahar. Characteristically, such dense mudflows, perhaps as much as 30 percent water with a consistency like fresh concrete, course down existing valleys or streambeds with tremendous strength. This one surged into the Whangaehu River with so much force that parts of the train were carried a mile and a half downstream.

Today a warning system is in place to forestall catastrophe in case of another sudden lahar from Mount Ruapehu, and the scenic region around it has become a popular center for tourism and winter sports. But beneath the apparent calm, the memory of disaster is long. Many New Zealanders still recall the Christmas Day when holiday radio programming was canceled so that the names of survivors could be read on the air. And every Christmas Eve, a train slows down long enough to cast a memorial wreath onto the weeping waters of the Whangaehu.

With water lapping *over her starboard rails, the* Andrea Doria *is about to be swallowed up by the Atlantic Ocean.*

Tragedy on the Andrea Doria

*Collision sinks luxury liner without warning
on fog-shrouded sea*

CROSSING FROM GENOA, Italy, to New York City, the great Italian luxury liner *Andrea Doria* was plowing through a thick fog bank south of Nantucket Island on the night of July 25, 1956. Many passengers had already gone to bed, but others watched, incredulous, as lights from another vessel emerged from the curtain of fog. Seconds later, at 11:10 P.M., the sharp prow of the Swedish liner *Stockholm* rammed head-on into the side of the *Andrea Doria*. Mortally wounded, the sleek passenger ship slipped forever beneath the waters of the Atlantic.

The collision—the first ever between major ocean liners on the high seas—has never been satisfactorily explained. Both ships were thoroughly up to date, equipped with navigational radar and other safety features. The *Andrea Doria*'s hull, moreover, was di-

vided into 11 watertight compartments, built to withstand just such a collision. Like the owners of the *Titanic,* the ship's builders were confident that she was unsinkable.

In the weeks of court testimony that followed the disaster, the two sides offered conflicting versions of the chain of events leading up to the collision. On the westbound *Andrea Doria,* Capt. Piero Calamai was concerned about the thick fog that had engulfed the ship, and he sounded his foghorns regularly. The *Stockholm,* meanwhile, traveling east from New York, was sailing many miles to the north of the customary sea-lane used by eastbound shipping. By chance skirting the fog that hid the *Andrea Doria,* the *Stockholm* was sailing under clear skies.

Each ship noted the approach of the other on her

radar screen while they still were several miles apart, and Calamai veered south to give the other vessel what he thought was more leeway. But when they finally came within sight of each other, it was clear that the two liners were on a collision course. Both sides later claimed that they made desperate last-minute attempts to give the other room to pass. And each claimed the other turned directly into her path.

Whatever the case, there was undeniably a terrifying instant of sparks and shrieking steel as the *Stockholm* smashed into the *Andrea Doria*. The instant of impact jarred passengers all over the Italian liner and set off their night-long struggle to escape. And it sent a torrent of seawater into the gaping hole in the ship's side, initiating the fateful tilting of her hull. (Years later, a salvage expedition discovered that damage to the liner was much more extensive than anyone imagined at the time; hence the failure of the watertight compartments to keep the ship afloat.)

The section of twisted wreckage was a scene of both heartbreaking dramas and stunning miracles.

In the cabins hit by the *Stockholm* there was chaos. Col. Walter Carlin, a New York lawyer, had just left his cabin and gone to the bathroom to brush his teeth while his wife reclined in bed. Knocked down by the jolt of the collision, he struggled back to his cabin only to watch in horror as his wife dropped through a hole to the waves below.

Berthed in two nearby cabins were *New York Times* correspondent Camille Cianfarra and his wife, Jane, their daughter, Joan, and Linda Morgan, Jane's daughter by a previous marriage. Joan simply disappeared into the void, as apparently did Linda. Mangled by the collision, Camille died within minutes. Jane was hurled into an adjacent cabin, occupied by Dr. Thure Peterson and his wife, Martha. There she was pinned, entangled in the wreckage, almost touching the twisted form of Martha Peterson, who, though her legs and back were broken, was still alive.

Thure Peterson, in turn, had been thrown into another cabin. Relatively unhurt, he immediately set to work to save his wife and Jane Cianfarra, but he quickly realized he alone could not extricate them. With the aid of a ship's waiter, he struggled feverishly, never knowing when the listing ship might capsize.

The men finally pulled Jane Cianfarra from the debris. Martha Peterson, however, was so tightly trapped that a heavy jack would be needed to free her. The two men eventually obtained one, but hope was waning. At 4:20 A.M., after five hours of struggle, the jack was finally in position when, suddenly and quietly, Mrs. Peterson murmured to her husband, "Oh, darling,

I think I'm going. I'm going." It was over. Peterson escaped the *Andrea Doria* in the next-to-last lifeboat.

Jane Cianfarra thought she had lost everyone in her family, but—incredibly— this was not so. Her daughter Linda Morgan had been asleep in her cabin when the prow of the *Stockholm* plunged through the wall. As it happened, the crushed bow struck her bed in such a way that it carried her and her mattress away, almost gently, onto the retreating *Stockholm*.

For two days Linda Morgan was listed among the *Andrea Doria*'s dead. Only when she was brought to New York did her father, newscaster Edward P. Morgan, discover that his lost daughter had been found alive. Beside Linda's hospital bed he telephoned Jane Cianfarra in another hospital. "Something's happened that some people call a miracle," he exulted, "and I'm with her now."

Thanks to human bravery and a quick response from nearby ships, however, the *Andrea Doria*'s story stands out as one of the greatest rescue sagas in maritime history. When the *Andrea Doria*'s SOS went out, ships came from all directions to her assistance. The casualties included 46 passengers on the *Andrea Doria* and 5 crewmen who died aboard the *Stockholm*. But for 1,660 others, this was a night to savor the ultimate victory—deliverance from death.

Dawn revealed the sad sight of the beautiful liner abandoned and sinking ever deeper into the waves.

The Swedish liner Stockholm, *built to navigate North Sea ice floes, lost 30 feet of her steel-reinforced bow in the accident. She returned to New York (above) with a large number of rescued passengers from the Italian liner.*

235

Vera: Japan's Super-Typhoon

Raging storm ravages major metropolis

ARLY AUTUMN 1959 was a busy time for the citizens of Nagoya, the capital of Aichi Prefecture and, with a population of some 1.3 million, Japan's third-largest city. Throughout the bustling metropolis, preparations were underway for a week-long festival to celebrate the 70th anniversary of the city's recognition as a municipality. Plans for the gala called for decorated floats, flowers, marching bands, speeches, and fireworks. There was even to be a visiting delegation from Nagoya's sister city, Los Angeles, California.

The residents had good reason to be proud of their town, which lies at the head of Ise Bay, an inlet of the Pacific Ocean on the coast of Honshu, Japan's major island. Although Nagoya was heavily damaged by bombs during World War II, it had rebuilt itself under an enlightened, large-scale program of urban planning, and in 1959 it was a major seaport.

Growing up around Nagoya Castle, a prominent landmark dating back to 1610–12, the city had long been known for its fine ceramics. Later it became a textile center as well, and the manufacture of steel, chemicals, and transportation machinery further bolstered its economy in the 20th century. The industrial

hub for some 30 towns within a 25-mile radius, it was also the political, financial, and cultural center for the Pacific coastal area between Tokyo, about 160 miles to the northeast, and Osaka, 90 miles to the southwest.

The age-old symbol of Nagoya—as well known in the Far East as the lion of St. Mark in Venice is in the West—was a pair of dolphinlike sea creatures that had stood for centuries on the roof of Nagoya Castle. Ten feet tall and covered with golden scales, the figures, along with the castle, were demolished in air raids during World War II. But the castle had been expertly reconstructed, and shining new replicas of the figures had been made. They were to stand proudly on display during the upcoming anniversary celebration.

On Sunday, September 20, even as preparations for the festival were underway, an ominous report was issued by the Japan Meteorological Agency: it announced that a tropical depression had formed some 280 nautical miles southeast of Saipan in the Mariana Islands and was heading north-northwest. The next day the depression reached tropical storm intensity; on Tuesday it was upgraded to a typhoon, and a warning was issued. Named Vera, the storm was

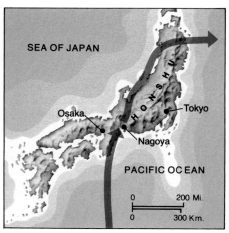

Japan's killer typhoon raged through densely populated Honshu Island (above), leaving thousands dead, injured, or homeless in its wake. At left, rescue workers pluck a young victim of the storm from the wreckage of the apartment building where he lived.

236

Swept along by the flood, *logs from Nagoya's lumberyards crashed through city streets like so many battering rams.*

numbered 5915—that is, it was the 15th typhoon to form in 1959.

For the next three days, through Friday the 25th, the storm moved slowly toward Japan with little change in intensity. Then, on Saturday night, the 26th, Vera went on a rampage, tearing across the Honshu coast with winds of up to 160 miles an hour.

It was business as usual in Nagoya as the worst typhoon in modern Japanese history bore down on the city.

Although plane flights were suspended, there was no panic in Nagoya at the approach of the typhoon. The inhabitants simply put up storm shutters, bought extra supplies, and filled containers with drinking water. Storm warnings were nothing new to the Japanese, particularly in September, which was the bad month. Typhoons, moreover, normally need a week or so to develop, their paths are difficult to predict, and more often than not, they die down to tropical storms or veer harmlessly out to sea.

Typhoons, of course, do strike land three or four times a year, and they do kill people and cause damage—on the average, $100 million each. But to the Japanese they are unavoidable hazards of existence, along with tidal waves, volcanic eruptions, and earthquakes. As Edwin O. Reischauer, former U.S. ambassador to Japan, explains: "Typhoons have accustomed the Japanese to expect natural catastrophes and accept them with stoic resilience. This sort of fatalism might even be called the 'typhoon mentality.'"

Such an attitude is perhaps strengthened by the deep-seated Japanese belief in the typhoon as a good omen. This stems from episodes in 1274 and again in 1281, when Kublai Khan, grandson of Genghis Khan, tried to invade Japan with vast armies of Mongols sailing in huge armadas. Each time, he was thwarted by the intervention of a typhoon—a "divine wind" called *kamikaze*—that scattered and sank his ships.

Some Japanese experts also point out that the storms make an essential contribution to the national economy. Accounting for as much as 8 percent of Japan's annual rainfall, they bring up to 500 billion tons of fresh water to the islands every year.

So it was that for five days Nagoya and the sur-

The people of Nagoya sought refuge wherever they could find it. As floodwaters poured through their living quarters, the victims (below) ran for the roof clutching a few meager possessions. The homeless group at right struggles to safety on a plot of dry ground piled high with clothing, cooking utensils, motorcycles, television sets, furniture, and other rescued valuables.

rounding communities ignored warnings that they lay in the path of a killer and were in mortal danger. But Typhoon Vera did not die down. It did not veer out to sea. And it was anything but benevolent. It proved instead to be the most severe, most destructive weather disaster in the history of modern Japan and one of the worst ever recorded anywhere.

Vera slammed into Nagoya late on Saturday night at the worst possible time—when the tide was full. Sea waves—solid walls of water 17 feet high—hit the city like battering rams, with a force of up to six tons per square foot. Crashing into obstacles, the waves sent tons of seawater shooting 200 feet into the air with an explosive roar. Dams, dikes, sea walls, wharves, bridges, buildings—all were shattered by the dreadful pounding. The relentless waves also leveled lumberyards throughout the city, tearing loose massive heaps of logs and timbers and sending them cascading through the streets.

Winds of up to 138 miles an hour meanwhile tore the roofs off houses and scattered the debris like deadly projectiles. And floodwaters from the bay poured into the city so fast that many people were washed out of their houses and drowned before they could flee; others escaped only by breaking holes through their roofs. One large apartment building collapsed, pinning 84 people in its ruins. In blinding wind and rain, helmeted police officers patrolled the streets, doing their best to guide survivors to safer, higher ground.

The typhoon raged on at peak intensity for three hours before sweeping north past Tokyo, then crossing northern Honshu and heading out to the Pacific, where it died down to a mere tropical storm. In its wake, Vera left an incredible swath of death and destruction. By Sunday morning one-third of Nagoya lay under water; the rest was piled high with rubble, mud, and heaps of lumber strewn about like matchsticks. Bodies littered the streets and floated in Ise Bay. A total of 21 ships were cast ashore on Nagoya's beaches, 7 of them oceangoing vessels.

Throughout the stricken city, people clung desperately to rooftops—fragile havens above the swirling flood.

Lacking both food and drinking water, some flood victims dove into polluted floodwaters to retrieve scraps of food from submerged kitchens or garden plots. (Many were later afflicted with dysentery as a result of such ventures.) Others clutched their most precious possessions—often a television set or a motorcycle—and in some cases refused to be rescued if it meant abandoning their belongings.

Everywhere there were scenes of despair and confusion. Stunned refugees were streaming to places of shelter, many of them carrying pathetic, rain-drenched bundles of bedding and clothing. Others tried to return to their homes to salvage what they could and to protect their valuables from looters. The dead were being gathered up and laid out in long, grim rows on sodden fields near temporary morgues, each body covered with a mat of reeds. Many bodies were beyond identification. The mayor of Nangyo, a suburb of Nagoya, echoed the thoughts of many when he moaned: "I feel as if my arms and legs had been cut off. All I can see is the whole town submerged under a sea and filled with dead."

Wind, rain, high tides, and floodwaters hampered rescue operations. Relief efforts were further delayed because authorities in Tokyo were slow to realize how serious the catastrophe at Nagoya actually was. Concerned with their own storm damage, they assumed that Nagoya could take care of itself. To attract the attention of passing helicopters, 50 school children were positioned on a hillside outside the city in such a way as to form the Japanese word for "Help."

American military forces stationed in Japan joined in the rescue effort. U.S. Navy helicopters dropped food and other supplies on high ground, then circled to lift the ill and the most seriously endangered from the roofs of buildings. Despite the combined operation, some 25,000 hungry people were still marooned on rooftops a week after the typhoon struck.

News from neighboring communities and the outside world gradually trickled into Nagoya. Virtually every town and village along the coast of Ise Bay had been entirely or partially washed out to sea. At Handa, southeast of Nagoya, 300 people were known to be killed, and hundreds of others simply disappeared when gigantic sea waves destroyed 250 houses. In another town, 60 people were buried alive by a landslide that crushed 12 homes. In all, 38 of Japan's 47 prefectures had sustained serious damage.

Some 510,000 acres of cultivated farmland also were devastated. Fruits, rice, vegetables—countless crops were ruined. Herds of domestic animals drowned. Paddy fields that had been reclaimed from the sea over the course of generations were now drenched with salt water; they would remain useless for years to come. Even the oyster beds on farms where cultured pearls were grown suffered irreparable harm.

It was in part because Japan had become a modern industrialized nation with a complex interlocking economy that losses from the storm were so costly. Power lines were downed, as were telephone lines and television and radio towers. Cranes were toppled. Airfield facilities were wrecked. Factories were shut down throughout central Honshu. And the nation's rail system was virtually immobilized, with 22 trains stranded and the tracks broken in countless places.

According to official estimates, Typhoon Vera claimed the lives of more than 5,000 victims, plus hundreds of others who disappeared and were never found. Another 32,285 people suffered injuries. Nearly 40,000 homes were destroyed, with the final bill for property damage totaling between 500 and 600 billion yen—close to $2 billion.

Japan, of course, immediately set about rebuilding. And in a remarkably short time, it recovered from the flailing of the 1959 storm—its super-typhoon—as it had from other disasters of the 20th century. Reischauer, who wrote of the Japanese people's "acceptance of nature's awesome might," also paid tribute to their "great capacity to dig themselves out . . . and after such catastrophes start afresh."

Even Nagoya and its neighbors—the area hardest hit by Typhoon Vera—soon were healing their wounds and getting back to the business of living. Undamaged by wind or flood, the larger-than-life-size golden dolphins still adorned Nagoya's ancient castle, where they continue to endure as a symbol of the city's will to survive.

Searching for loved ones, *an elderly couple peers into a coffin at a makeshift morgue set up in Nagoya.*

A fire-capped sea wave smashes into the oil port of Seward in this rendering from eyewitness accounts.

The Good Friday Earthquake

Shock waves reshape Alaskan coast in the continent's most powerful upheaval

THE MOUNTAINS RISE higher in Alaska than any-where else in North America. Winters are colder, crops grow faster, the salmon catch is richer, the summer nights are brighter and longer. As any resident of the largest state in the United States will gladly point out, Alaska is a land of superlatives—even when it comes to disasters. Late in the afternoon of Good Friday, March 27, 1964, a massive earthquake originating at the northern end of Prince William Sound, 80 miles east of Anchorage, roared through Alaska's south-central coast, breaking almost every existing record for seismic fury.

All along the state's most densely populated region, the earth heaved and buckled. Rock slides and ice falls crashed down the sides of mountains, stripping them of trees and brush. Headlands split open and plunged into the sea. Roadways crumpled, buildings collapsed, entire villages were ravaged. A 30-block section of downtown Anchorage, Alaska's largest city and financial center, fell into ruin. Churned up by the quake, surging ocean waters poured into coastal settlements from Cordova, "clam capital of the world," located on the southeastern extremity of the sound, to Kodiak Island, some 450 miles to the southwest.

As far away as Houston, Texas, the shock caused the ground to lift by as much as four inches. Half a world away, in South Africa, levels of well water jumped abruptly. For two weeks the entire planet vibrated like a giant tuning fork.

Alaskans seldom gave much thought to earthquakes

or their consequences—despite the mild tremors that often ripple through the seismically unstable south-central region. Most citizens tended to shrug off these jostlings as a minor inconvenience of frontier living. And besides, on that Good Friday afternoon people had more pleasant things to think about—such as the upcoming holiday weekend.

All prospects seemed ideal for a fine Easter. In Anchorage, people were at last beginning to unbutton after six harsh months of winter. Temperatures hovered at a comparatively balmy 28° F, and morning snow flurries had come and gone. Schools had let out for the holiday and most offices had already shut their doors when, at 5:36 P.M., disaster struck. First a low-pitched reverberation, like distant cannon fire, rumbled across southern Alaska, and then the earth began to shake. It rolled and surged in great undulating waves for four endless, terrifying minutes. "People were clinging to each other, to lampposts, to buildings," one Anchorage woman reported. A young girl burst into prayer: "Lord, that's enough now. Please stop it."

Long cracks opened up in the frozen ground, gaping wide and then snapping shut like the jaws of bear traps.

Housewife Carol Tucker was browsing through the china section of the new J. C. Penney department store in downtown Anchorage when the whole building began to shake. Mirrors and display cases collapsed, and chunks of ceiling plaster thundered to the floor. As the lights went out, Mrs. Tucker groped her way to a stalled escalator and stumbled down it, holding her hands over her head to protect herself from falling debris. "I knew I had little hope of getting out alive," she said later, "but if I were knocked unconscious I had no hope at all." At the front entrance, by some miraculous instinct, she paused—just as the building's concrete-slab facade broke loose and slid down into the street. One man was crushed to death. A woman driving by in a car was struck and killed. Mrs. Tucker managed to escape out the back door to the relative safety of the store's parking lot.

In the prosperous suburb of Turnagain Heights, set atop a bluff overlooking the sea, the shock set off a landslide. Anchorage *Daily Times* publisher Robert B. Atwood ran outside at the first strong tremor to find a world gone mad. Trees were falling, houses were sliding every which way, and the ground was erupting into frozen, tilted slabs. For a moment Atwood stood watching his own house wrench apart as though "in a giant taffy pull." Suddenly the ground beneath him parted, and he fell into a chasm. Climbing out, Atwood looked down toward the beach, and there was his home—a pile of shattered timbers at the water's edge.

Atwood's neighbor, Tay Thomas, was watching television with her two children in an upstairs bedroom of their home when the shaking started. Instantly Mrs. Thomas gathered up young Anne and David and raced for the front door. Lightly clad and shoeless in the freezing weather, the family rode out the landslide clinging to a disintegrating chunk of their front yard. At one point, Mrs. Thomas recalled, "a crack started to open in the snow between Anne and me." But the terrified mother managed to reach across the chasm and pull the child toward her. When the worst of the rocking was over, Mrs. Thomas and her children found themselves at sea level, along with the ruins of their house. Despite stiffening fingers and toes, they crawled across the frozen, fractured landscape for about 15 agonizing minutes, until rescue workers spotted them and hauled them up by rope to higher ground.

Other neighbors were not so fortunate. Neurosur-

Measuring Earthquakes

IN 1935 American seismologist Charles F. Richter developed a scale for comparing the magnitude of earthquakes. When a quake occurs, seismographs record the earth's movement as a series of zigzag lines on paper wrapped around a revolving cylinder. The Richter scale is a numerical expression of the amplitude of the earthquake waves recorded by seismograph. The weakest quakes are assigned a value of 2.0 or less; those registering over 8.0 are designated "great." (No known shock has ever registered over 8.9.) Each whole number increase on the scale represents a 10-fold increase in measured amplitude and a 31-fold increase in the amount of energy released by the quake.

The Richter scale is based on objective measurements. The Modified Mercalli scale, which supplements the Richter scale, depends on subjective observation of a quake's effects. The Mercalli scale distinguishes 12 levels of intensity, ranging from barely perceptible shaking to near total destruction.

A seismograph's stylus records the "signature" of an earthquake on paper coated with carbon black.

Split open by the quake, *this stretch of Anchorage's Fourth Avenue, and everything on it, plummeted some 20 feet.*

geon Perry Mead had reported for afternoon duty at the local hospital, but his four children remained at home. As the Mead house fell apart, 12-year-old Perry Mead III led his sister and one brother outside to safety. Returning for his baby brother, Merrell, still trapped in the house, young Perry disappeared into a crevasse. Neither body was ever found.

All along the 500-mile arc of destruction created by the earthquake, there were similar episodes of tragedy and miraculous salvation. In the port city of Valdez, 50 miles east of the epicenter, the ground rolled and billowed as though it had been turned into ocean. Cracks opened and shut, squirting jets of water and muck 20 feet into the air. Building foundations gave way, walls collapsed, and live power cables thrashed about like lethal electric snakes. And then the sea moved in. Massive seismic sea waves, set in motion by the violent upheaval of the earth's crust, roared into fjord-like Valdez Inlet at express-train speed and slammed against the coast at 30-minute intervals into the night. Reaching far inland, the tsunamis flooded three-quarters of downtown Valdez. Most residents had time to retreat into the hills, but 32 people lost their lives, and more than $11 million worth of property was destroyed.

A similar devastation hit the oil port of Seward, 120 miles to the west across Prince William Sound. Within

30 seconds of the initial shock, a 4,000-foot stretch of waterfront lurched into the bay, along with piers, warehouses, loading cranes, and a cement plant. A cluster of oil storage tanks exploded into flame, spewing thousands of gallons of burning petroleum across the debris that now littered the harbor. The waterfront slide also generated a harbor wave—a wall of water as high as a three-story house, with a blazing oil slick at its crest. "It was an eerie thing to see," one survivor recalled, "a huge tide of fire washing ashore, setting a high-water mark in flame, and then sucking back."

The lethal combination of quake, flood, and fire just about demolished Seward. Dock yards, rail yards, power plant, oil facilities, boat basin, and nearly half of the city's housing all lay in soggy, blackened ruin. Property damage: $15 million. Death toll: 12 in all, astonishingly light under the circumstances.

Fatalities were also luckily few on Kodiak Island, a local center of the crab and canning industry. While dining in his galley, skipper Bill Cuthbert of the crab boat *Selief* felt his ship being repeatedly buffeted. Staggering onto the deck, he quickly realized what was happening. With tsunami warnings now coming in over the radio, Cuthbert decided to stay on board with two crew members and ride out the crisis. More than an hour after the initial shock, a smooth swell announced the arrival of the first tsunami. Within minutes, a second wave 30 feet high from crest to trough picked up the *Selief* and every other boat in Kodiak Harbor and swept them into town. A third and then a fourth wave carried the *Selief* farther and farther inland. Eventually, Cuthbert was able to snag a telephone pole and tie up his boat, but 77 other fishing boats—nearly half the Kodiak fleet—were sunk or smashed, and two of the island's three fish canneries were carried away. Property losses amounted to $25 million, and 15 people died.

From the Gulf of Alaska, tsunamis raced across the Pacific all the way to Antarctica and Japan.

Traveling at speeds of more than 400 miles an hour, seismic sea waves boiled up on a beach at Depoe, Oregon, and carried away four children who were camping out with their parents. At Crescent City, California, 12 people drowned and 150 stores were smashed. And in far-off Hilo, Hawaii, the waves sent people scurrying for high ground.

Alaska's Good Friday earthquake ranks as the most violent natural cataclysm in the history of North America. Its shock waves sent seismographs off their tracks the world over. The final estimates ranged between 8.3 and 8.6 on the Richter scale—probably twice the force of the San Francisco earthquake of 1906. The energy released equaled about 240 million tons of TNT. More than 100,000 square miles of the earth's surface was wrenched into new configurations.

Yet for all its destructive fury, the quake could have had far worse effects. If schools and offices had been open, or the weather a little colder, many hundreds more people would have died from injury or exposure. The tide happened to be low at zero hour, moderating the effects of the tsunamis. In addition, the local fish canneries had not yet opened for the season, and tourists had not begun their yearly invasion. Without these mitigating factors, the death toll would have been much higher than the final count of 131.

Property losses were another matter. The quake ruined about 75 percent of Alaska's commerce and industry and left thousands homeless. A state with only 250,000 inhabitants now faced a reconstruction bill of at least $300 million. But Alaskans dug themselves out of the ruins with speed and determination, and the state gradually pulled itself together, thanks to generous government and private aid. Corporations, labor unions, and church groups from all over mailed checks to Alaska. And six-year-old Luann Jensen of Eagle Grove, Iowa, sent part of her savings—a nickel and five pennies—along with a note saying, "I'm sorry your house fell down."

All that was left of publisher Robert B. Atwood's suburban Anchorage home after the Good Friday earthquake had done with it was this pile of lumber at the edge of the sea (left). The owner of another ruined home (below) attempts to salvage a few belongings spared by the disaster.

The raging Arno exposed the foundations of buildings and took a great bite out of this two-lane riverfront avenue.

Flood in Florence

Art capital drowns in a torrent of muck and debris

As THE DAWN broke over a rain-soaked Florence, Italy, on November 4, 1966, there emerged a sight that sent chills into the heart of everyone who treasured the art and culture of that splendid city. The lovely Arno River, which normally glides in peaceful silence beneath the Ponte Vecchio, had turned into a raging, frothing menace that refused to be bound by its banks. Swollen by intense rains, the river poured down Florence's narrow streets, filling the basements of workshops, museums, and libraries, climbing walls hung with masterpieces, and banging at the doors of some of the most revered monuments of Western architecture.

All across Florence hundreds of paintings, statues, and other art objects, and millions of books and manuscripts, faced a life-and-death struggle with the Arno. Not only the treasures of the past but also lives and livelihoods of the present were threatened—and in many cases destroyed—as the flood brought down buildings and swept away the tools and materials of hundreds of Florentine artisans.

How did it all happen? The answer is simply rain. Centuries of civilization have stripped the forests from most of the hills and mountains of northern and central Italy. Every year autumn rains create small torrents that rush unimpeded down steep slopes, eroding the soil, swelling the rivers, and often flooding the plains below. But on Thursday, November 3, it seemed that the very windows of heaven had opened. Within 48 hours, 19 inches of rain poured down—four months' worth of precipitation in two days. All northern Italy was caught in the deluge. More than 100 people drowned as water engulfed 750 villages as well as the cities of Venice, Pisa, and Florence. Beleaguered operators of the Arno hydroelectric dams upstream from Florence evidently did not recognize the danger in time; by opening the floodgates too late they actually contributed to the disaster rather than stemming it.

Friday, November 4, was to have been a day of celebration in Florence—the yearly commemoration of the Italian armistice in World War I. In preparation for the event, streets and piazzas had been decked with the colorful flags of Italy and Florence. But Thursday's torrential rains, driven by winds as high as 90 miles per hour, soon left the decorations sodden and torn. By 3 o'clock Friday morning, water was lapping at the top of the arches of the Ponte Vecchio, the venerable Arno River bridge that for centuries had been lined with the shops of goldsmiths and jewelers. Among the first in Florence to realize the imminent danger of flood, the night watchmen on the Ponte Vecchio alerted many of the bridge's shopkeepers, who rushed to save their valuable wares while there was still time.

Most Florentines, however, slept without the least idea of what was happening. Early risers like the American writer Kathrine Taylor, who later published her *Diary of Florence in Flood*, looked out in the morning dumbfounded. The Arno was rapidly rising and had already become thick with flotsam. Taylor recalled how her landlady stood in the doorway "wailing softly *'Quest'Arno, quest'Arno!'* as if reproving a delinquent child," while upstairs a contessa of the old

school refused to believe what was happening. "She has known the Arno all her life, and it never floods."

The contessa, however, had not known the Arno long enough. A marble plaque on a wall in the Via dei Neri shows a finger pointing to a height of 13 feet 10 inches, the high-water mark of the flood that destroyed the Ponte Vecchio on another November 4, in 1333. The river turned deadly once more on September 13, 1557, and on November 3, 1844, it swept through the city at heights of up to seven feet. In fact, hardly a century has gone by without a major flood in Florence. But never had the Arno risen so high or with such violence as on the terrible morning of November 4, 1966. Before the day was out, all former flood records would be surpassed by more than two feet. In some parts of the city the river reached the ceilings of second-story rooms and crushed windows, doors, and floors with the churning pressure of 20 feet of water.

Each building in Florence became a separate island, its residents marooned on upper floors and rooftops.

Raging cataracts smashed into basements and cellars, eroding foundations and flushing out thousands of gallons of thick fuel oil from heating systems. A noxious mixture of oil, mud, and human wastes from ruptured sewers turned the river into a stinking sea of sludge that smeared frescoes, coated statues, and left its unmistakable imprint on all it touched. Before 7:30 A.M., power lines were down; soon the telephones were dead, and gas and water were shut off. The city of Florence was now alone and drowning.

Ever since the disastrous flood of 1333, which toppled the original Ponte Vecchio, the rebuilt span has withstood the periodic assaults of the Arno. But now, as the river hurled trees, automobiles, timbers, and oil drums against it, the shaky bridge became the first focus of concern among the city's leading art custodians. Above the goldsmith shops of the Ponte Vecchio runs a covered gallery built in 1565 at the behest of Grand Duke Cosimo I to provide a protected walkway from his residence in the Pitti Palace, south of the Arno, to the Uffizi, which then served as the government office building, north of the river. In modern times this long and opulent corridor became a part of the world-famous Uffizi Galleries and was filled with portraits, including self-portraits by Raphael, Titian, Rubens, and other masters. All were now in obvious danger.

As the corridor trembled beneath their

Rubble-laden floodwaters *converted the ancient streets of Florence into life-threatening rapids. Here, drenched volunteers hang on to a guideline as they carry a stranded child to safety.*

At the Florence baptistery crowds gather to look at the damage wrought by the flood to the famous *Doors of Paradise*. Fortunately, the missing bronze panels were recovered intact and restored.

feet, Dr. Luisa Becherucci, the director of the Uffizi, joined with Dr. Mazzino Fossi of the Superintendency of Monuments and a few helpers to begin removing the threatened works. The rescue team managed to carry out about 20 paintings when Becherucci, fearing that the bridge was about to collapse, ordered everyone out of the corridor. She did not count, however, on the tenacity of Professor Ugo Procacci, the superintendent of fine art for Florence. When he arrived on the scene after a tortuous journey through nearly impassable streets, nothing could dissuade him from continuing the salvage effort. "We tried to stop him," recalled Fossi, "but he broke out of our grip, furious at us and shouting that he was of age and we had young children." Soon the rest of the team joined Procacci in the corridor, and by 10:30 A.M. its contents had been saved.

Amazingly, the Ponte Vecchio held firm. But that triumph of strength for medieval architecture had serious consequences for the rest of Florence. The rows of arches beneath the old bridge impeded the flow of water, which was now cascading at double its usual volume. Furthermore, a mounting pile of debris was turning the bridge into a dam. Water that might have flowed beneath it swept in cataracts over the embankments east of the bridge and on through the heart of historic Florence.

A few blocks upstream from the Ponte Vecchio, the Piazza dei Cavallegeri leads from the river to Italy's Central National Library, a collection of 3 million volumes comparable to the U.S. Library of Congress. The Arno plunged through the piazza at 40 miles per hour, smashing the windows of the library and sluicing tons of slime and debris directly through its vast stacks in the basement. More than a million books and manuscripts were swallowed up by the flood tide.

It was in the great Franciscan Church of Santa Croce that the flood claimed its most renowned victim.

Located beyond the Central Library, the Gothic Church of Santa Croce is the burial place of Michelangelo, Machiavelli, Galileo, Rossini, and other notables. Its most prized possession by far, however, was the life-size image of Christ on the cross painted about 1280 by the great master Giovanni Cimabue. For centuries, this fountainhead of Renaissance art hung in splendor over the high altar of Santa Croce. In recent times it was displayed in the Uffizi Galleries, but shortly before November 1966 the crucifix was brought back home to Santa Croce and installed in the small museum in the church cloister—where it would be completely at the mercy of the flooding Arno. Shortly before 7 A.M., a torrent of water, mud, and oil crashed through the doors of the church, scarring masterworks of panel and fresco painting and coating the tombs of Florentine heroes with a thick layer of sludge. In the adjacent museum, Cimabue's 700-year-old masterpiece was submerged for 12 hours in water that reached heights of up to 20 feet. By the time it was all over, 75 percent of the painting's pigment had been scoured away. What was left was a part of a face and a broken body, a martyred work of art. Although the painting was later stabilized and to a limited extent restored, no one would ever gaze on its full glory again.

A block away, 14 feet of swirling water buffeted the rich collection of sculpture, paintings, books, and furniture in the Horne Museum. Across the river from the Horne, the Bardini Museum's outstanding collection of early musical instruments was being twisted and cracked as the water disintegrated glues, caused wood to swell, and covered everything with slime.

In the buildings adjacent to the Ponte Vecchio a day-long struggle with the flood was underway. At the Uffizi itself, perhaps the greatest of all Renaissance museums, the main displays were on the upper level, out of the Arno's reach. But the lower level was used for restoration work, and Dr. Umberto Baldini, director of restorations, worked feverishly with Procacci, Fossi, and Becherucci to move about 100 paintings upstairs. Nothing, however, could be done to save the 130,000 photo negatives of artworks that were stored in the basement of the Uffizi. And at the State Archives, housed in basement rooms in another part of the building, 40,000 volumes were drowning in black mud.

Despite the setbacks, love for what they were saving gave energy to the rescue workers. Director Becherucci remembered, "It was a day of great excitement and exhilaration. We worked into the night, and when it was over, we sat down exhausted, and the real meaning of the loss swept over us."

Similar devotion and courage marked many of the stories that emerged from the flood. After working late on Thursday, Dr. Maria Bonelli, the director of the Institute and Museum of the History of Science, spent the night in a ground-floor apartment at the institute. When she awoke the next morning, water was already swirling around her bed and rising fast. Risking her own life, Bonelli struggled to carry the museum's collection—including Galileo's telescopes and other priceless instruments—to the upper floors of the building and across a ledge to the Uffizi. She gave up only when the waist-deep water was about to sweep her away.

What the Uffizi is to painting, the Bargello Museum is to sculpture, and here the Arno went to work with a terrible fury, soaking statues by Michelangelo, Donatello, and other Renaissance masters in 13 feet of water and mire. (In later weeks the same statues would be covered in mounds of talc as restorers tried to draw out moisture from the finely worked stone.)

The blast of water continued to surge down narrow streets toward the Cathedral of Santa Maria del Fiore, Florence's famous Duomo. Within minutes, the piazza in front of the church was transformed from a rain-sodden square to a treacherous whirlpool threatening the beautiful octagonal baptistery at its center. This beloved Florentine landmark is pierced on three sides by bronze-paneled doors. All are exquisite, but those facing east toward the Duomo were deemed worthy by Michelangelo himself of being the Doors of Paradise,

Standing forlornly in the midst of a sea of muck, a statue of the Virgin Mary appears to lament the grim effects of the Arno's rampage through the treasure-filled Church of Santa Croce.

Under David's gaze, rescue workers transport a flood-damaged painting across Florence's main square, the historic Piazza della Signoria, to restoration rooms at the Uffizi Galleries.

so perfect were the Old Testament scenes that Lorenzo Ghiberti had cast in bronze for their adornment. As the Arno rose up against the baptistery, powerful jets of water spurted through cracks between the doors and soon forced them open. As the Doors of Paradise pounded against their stone jamb, five of Ghiberti's panels loosened and then plunged into the muck below. Fortunately, the iron gates around the building kept the panels from being swept away and possibly lost. Recovered and restored, these precious works today bear little, if any, trace of their ordeal.

Spreading north and west, the Arno poured into the cellar of the Archeological Museum and burst through to the main floors above, dragging some 9,000 prized Etruscan artifacts into the slime. In the wake of the flood, the museum resembled an archeological dig as workers struggled to unearth its buried treasures.

Just as the river struck at the art of Florence, it damaged or destroyed the livelihoods of its ordinary citizens. The city center traditionally belonged to the leather workers, weavers, goldsmiths, wool carders, and jewelers, who had long formed the backbone of the Florentine economy. Such artisans and the shops that sold their wares seemed special targets of the flood. Along the commercial Via Cimabue, in the eastern section of the city, stored chemicals mixed with polluted water blew up, destroying warehouses and leaving the street looking as if a bomb had hit it. Some 6,000 small businesses were ruined in the flood, and for many weeks afterwards one of the most typical sights in Florence was that of a shopkeeper or craftsman with a shovel in his hands, trying to dig through the ruins of his shop in order to restore his livelihood.

Despite the flood's destructiveness, the Florentine

RESCUING FLORENCE'S RUINED MASTERPIECES

The Florence flood has been called the worst artistic disaster of modern times. In the days after the Arno River overflowed its banks and deposited a staggering half million tons of mud and wastes on the city, predictions of irreversible artistic losses became commonplace. But such gloom did not take into account the extent to which the disaster itself stimulated the technology needed to overcome its effects.

Hardly a single item that was not destroyed outright by the flood proved beyond the capabilities of the restorers. Art experts, scientists, fund-raisers, and student volunteers from around the world came together in Florence, and from their cooperation sprang art conservation techniques that made the methods used before the flood appear truly antediluvian.

For example, in their search for a

Florence's railroad terminal, like so many facilities in and around the city, was turned into an impromptu book-restoration center in the days after the flood. Like a batch of literary laundry, the unbound pages of books are hung out to dry in the terminal's heating plant. Fortunately, the paper and ink used in ancient bookmaking were of such high quality that they could withstand the rigors of restoration.

safe and effective weapon against the mold that was ruining hundreds of waterlogged frescoes, microbiologists discovered that a common stomach antibiotic called Nystatin fit the bill almost perfectly. Unfortunately, Nystatin comes in pill form—difficult to feed to a wall—but that problem, too, was overcome as chemists from the University of Florence found a practical way to convert the pill into a spray that could be applied over large surfaces. Similar cooperation among experts led to the discovery of a chemical spray that would keep moisture from seeping through to the surface of a fresco, where it could destroy the irreplaceable pigment.

In the course of the Florence art restoration campaign, new solutions were found for perennial art conservation problems not related to the flood. The frescoes at the Monastery of San Marco did not suffer flood damage, but they were being obscured nonetheless by a white veil caused by a chemical change in the frescoes' plaster base. It took a year of research and analysis, but experts eventually found the right chemical agents to reverse the deterioration of the plaster and restore the frescoes to a nearly pristine state of brilliance—without the addition of a single spot of new pigment.

After dealing Florence such a cruel blow, nature reversed herself and people reacted with characteristic courage and patience. Victor and Elizabeth Velen could remember even the worst day of the flood with fondness as they "ate by candlelight with 54 others stranded on the top floor of a 14th-century palazzo." Without telephones, "people shouted messages from house to house, *bocca a bocca,* in relay to the Palazzo Vecchio, where a squad of police was also pinned down by water." As messages were sent back and forth through the night, the Velens felt plunged "back into the Middle Ages, when the alarm must have been given in this fashion during the wars of the Guelphs and Ghibellines."

When the Arno finally returned to its banks, Florence lay under half a million tons of mud, oil, silt, and sewage. At stake now was the city's very identity, which was so closely linked to its art and artisans. But the Florentines rose to the challenge, and so did

admirers of the city the world over. The day after the flood, an international brigade of student volunteers began arriving in Florence to aid in the rescue operation. These "mud angels," as they were called, seemed to delight in slogging through the stench-ridden sludge to retrieve precious artifacts of Western civilization.

On December 21, 1966, Florence reopened all but one of its art galleries and museums. Just short of seven weeks after the flood, only the severely damaged museum at Santa Croce remained closed. "Florence is not destroyed—Florence is not on its knees," declared Mayor Piero Bargellini on the occasion. And indeed, while the flood illustrated clearly the precariousness of any human construction before the ferocity of nature, the recovery of the city and its treasures shows that the Renaissance spirit that produced the art of Florence continues to live in the Florentine people today.

Water, mud, and oil threatened many of the frescoes of Florence. In the Church of Santa Croce, technicians work to save the great 14th-century fresco of the "Last Supper" by Taddeo Gaddi. After much experimentation, art restorers found a chemical that would remove oily mud from the surface of the fresco without harming the pigment.

came to the aid of the art restorers. Continuing cold and damp weather helped preserve many of the water-soaked works of art. Wooden panel paintings, for example, had to dry very slowly so that layers of wood, gesso (the mixture of fine plaster and glue that underlies many paintings), and surface pigment would not separate and flake away. By the time the weather turned dry in December, art restorers had taken over the Limonaia, the vast citrus-tree greenhouses on the grounds of the Pitti Palace. There, the humidity could be controlled and gradually de-

creased to allow safe, even drying.

The most massive task confronting the Florentines after the flood was the rescue of books. But the devotion of restorers and student volunteers made even the arduous work of rescuing hundreds of thousands of sodden books seem manageable. Once again, the ingenious use of existing resources was a key to the success of the restorers. Chains of volunteers were organized to remove books from slimy, mud-drenched library stacks and floors. Other volunteers set to work interleafing each book, page by page,

with blotting paper. Heaters were commandeered and installed in makeshift drying rooms. Tobacco barns, which were already equipped to dry leaves at high temperature, were taken over by the restorers and turned into book-drying centers. At Florence's Belvedere Fortress, experts examined the dried books and supervised their disassembly. At the city's railroad terminal, unbound pages were washed in a bath of water and fungicide, pressed to remove excess moisture, and then hung up to dry for another four to six hours.

Monster Wave in East Pakistan

Watery juggernaut engulfs an ill-fated land

EVERY FEW YEARS the great tropical cyclones roar in, swirling up through the Bay of Bengal and slamming into Bangladesh, the densely populated, desperately poor nation formerly known as East Pakistan. Winds howl with tremendous force, tearing down houses, uprooting palm trees, and driving the seas across the maze of swamps, streams, and low-lying islands that constitute the Ganges River delta. This fertile but fragile land is home to millions of the world's poorest people—mostly subsistence-level fishermen and rice farmers—and the toll of such storms on their lives is mind numbing. More than 20,000 died from a single giant blow in 1963, and nearly 40,000 in a pair of storms two years later. But the cyclone that raged through East Pakistan in the fall of 1970—in the dark early hours of Friday, November 13—reached a level of destructive frenzy beyond all precedent.

It began on the morning of November 10 as an atmospheric depression far down the coast of India—a vortex of high winds and driving rain that lumbered north at about 10 miles an hour. Over the next few days the storm developed into a full tropical cyclone, with gusts of 100 miles an hour or more. As it funneled into the Bay of Bengal, the cyclone generated a massive surge of water that struck East Pakistan, at the head of the bay, with devastating effect.

"At midnight we heard a great roar growing louder from the southeast," reported Kamaluddin Chodhury, a prosperous farmer on Manpura Island. "I looked out. It was pitch black, but in the distance I could see a glow. The glow got nearer and bigger and then I realized it was the crest of a huge wave."

Chodhury quickly gathered his family on the second floor of his house to await the onslaught. As the wave rolled in, Manpura Island simply vanished under an avalanche of water rising 20 feet or more above the high tide mark. The ocean flooded into Chodhury's ground floor and reached up to lap at the second. But his house, more solidly built than the island's usual thatch and bamboo huts, shuddered and held together.

For five hours the family huddled in the darkness, as the winds howled and the rains pelted down. Toward dawn the flood receded, and Chodhury stepped out into a scene of utter desolation. Most familiar objects had been swept away. Whatever remained lay covered in mud. Of the 4,500 bamboo dwellings on Manpura, only 4 still stood. Of the island's 30,000 inhabitants, all but 5,000 had died.

Across a 3,000-square-mile area, houses were flattened and fields stripped bare. Drowned bodies lay heaped upon the beaches or hung where they had caught in the branches of trees. Bhola, the delta's largest island, lost as many as 200,000 residents—one-fifth of its population. On the 13 small islands off the mainland city of Chittagong, not one soul was left alive.

The total death toll ranged, by unofficial estimate, between 300,000 and 500,000. But in this densely packed region, where each square mile of land held as many as 1,000 people, the actual figure was probably much higher. By any count, it was one of the worst natural disasters of the century.

One reason for the extraordinary death rate may have been the absence of an adequate warning. A U.S. weather satellite had tracked the progress of the storm up the Bay of Bengal, and the radio station in Dacca, East Pakistan's capital, had issued

Zeroing in *on the densely populated coast of East Pakistan, the nameless but lethal cyclone of 1970 is shown roaring up the Bay of Bengal in this weather-satellite photograph.*

an alarm. But because of an ambiguity in wording, the storm's true fury had never been made clear. To make matters worse, three weeks earlier a cyclone described in catastrophic terms had fizzled out before it hit the coast, causing little damage. As a result of the false alarm, the new report was not taken very seriously.

Even if they had known what was coming, few people in the Ganges delta had any sure means of escape.

The low earth barriers that surrounded the rice paddies and dwelling areas of the delta region could provide no refuge from a cyclone-driven wave at least 20 feet high. To flee in a small native fishing boat would have been madness. The best recourse was to grab a palm tree and hang on for dear life. For some, this

strategy brought salvation; for many others it did not.

In a moving report for *The New York Times*, correspondent Sydney Schanberg told the story of 40-year-old Munshi Mustansher Billa, a poor rice farmer from Shakuchia Island, who saw the wave carry off each of his three sons and two daughters. Like so many other victims of the storm, Munshi and his wife and children had taken to the trees, catching hold of palm branches as the churning waters lifted the family high above their compound. Clutching his two young sisters, Munshi's oldest son found a handhold on one palm tree, but the force of the wave proved too much for him. "I can't hold them any longer. I have to let go," he yelled, and one after another the girls drowned. When a second wave broke over his head, the young man was dragged under as well. Elsewhere in the compound, Munshi's second son suffered a similar fate.

Meanwhile, Munshi was holding on to a palm tree with one arm and clasping his youngest boy, an infant

Relief arrives in the form of a U.S. military helicopter dropping supply bags into a mob of starving Pakistanis.

A stunned survivor of the cyclone recovers a child's body from its watery grave (above). Other disaster victims pick through the remains of the ruined rice harvest in search of a few precious edible grains (right).

less than a year old, with the other. But in the pounding water and stinging rain the arm holding the baby went numb. Munshi, too, had to let go and, weeping helplessly, watched his child slip away. Soon, another giant surge—the powerful backwash from the initial wave crest—rolled over the island from the north, tearing Munshi from his tree. He grabbed at another, lost it, then caught the last palm tree at the edge of the compound. At almost the same instant he heard his wife cry out from another tree: "My sons are gone, my daughters are gone, and now my husband is gone! I am going too. I don't want to live anymore!" And seconds later she came swirling past him.

Munshi reached for his wife, caught her, and held her tight until the waters receded. Their clothes ripped off and their skin scraped raw, the couple slowly and painfully climbed down from the tree.

"In water still knee deep," wrote Schanberg, "they stumbled—weak, dazed, nearly mad with grief—through floating bodies and animal carcasses toward a neighbor's house hoping to find at least some rags to hide their shame.

"The neighbors were dead, their hut smashed, but a stranger, a boy who had survived, found Munshi and his wife some strips of cloth he had taken from trees and corpses. Sapped of all strength, they fell down on the sodden earth and wept themselves to sleep."

As Munshi's tragedy illustrates, no group suffered as many casualties as the delta's children. Too weak to grasp the palms, they were swept away by the tens of thousands. Yet there were also some amazing escapes. Three days after the storm, a wooden chest washed ashore with six living children inside, ages 3 to 12; they had been placed there by their grandfather, who had then crawled in, too, only to die of exposure.

In one town, corpses clogged the river, and two girls were found floating, alive, on a raft of bloated bodies.

In the aftermath of the storm, survivors roamed about the mud-encrusted landscape, jaws slack and eyes glazed, searching for lost relatives. As the horror mounted, some minds cracked. An old man on Jabbar Island collected the remains of 52 kinsmen, heaped them into a single grave, and sat on top of it, cackling insanely. "Here is my family," he shouted.

So immense was the litter of bodies in the delta that human endeavor seemed unable to reduce it. The survivors wrapped scarves around their heads and noses, against the stench of death, then set to work with shovels. "We have buried 5,000 in mass graves," said one villager after days of digging. "Our hands are aching. We can't dig any more." Some communities heaped the corpses on makeshift rafts and shoved them out to sea, but, often as not, the rafts would wash back to land again with the incoming tide.

As the scope of the disaster became known to the outside world, relief began to trickle in. Less than four days after the cyclone struck, Red Cross shipments of food, clothing, and medicine began arriving at Dacca airport. An international fleet of helicopters started ferrying supplies to the stricken region. A task force of British warships steamed into the bay and set up a secondary airlift. But help could not be brought in fast enough, nor in sufficient quantity, to prevent still further death—from starvation, exposure, and disease.

Beyond the immediate body count, the cyclone wreaked havoc on the delta's fragile economic base. One million head of cattle had perished in the waves, and an untold number of fishing boats had washed out to sea. More than a million acres of rice paddies had been swamped; a full 75 percent of the rice crop, just two weeks away from harvesting, lay blackening in the sun. The destitute villagers, trembling from hunger, picked through the muck in hopes of gleaning a few soggy grains. Fresh water did not exist. Mains had snapped in urban areas, and village springs had turned foul from ocean salt and rotting carcasses. Epidemics of typhoid and cholera, perpetual scourges in the delta, threatened to break out anew.

Compounding the problems of recovery was a foot-dragging response by the Pakistani government. The nation was an uneasy hybrid of two widely diverse and mutually disdainful peoples—the Bengalis of East Pakistan and the dominant Punjabis of West Pakistan. Their principal bond was a shared belief in Islam, but over the past several decades even that tie had begun to unravel. And so the authorities in the capital city of Islamabad, situated in West Pakistan, moved grudgingly at best. Some 40 army helicopters sat idle in West Pakistani airfields; they were never sent to help. Government storehouses close to the delta region held 500,000 tons of grain; days went by before this stockpile was released.

With the help of some $50 million in foreign donations, however, the stricken delta gradually began to pull itself back together. Airdrops of rice helped feed the hungry, and mass inoculations contained the cholera. The wells were cleaned out, new houses were built, and a new rice crop was planted.

But the world of East Pakistan had changed forever. Resentment continued to smoulder against the government in the west, and a local independence movement gained massive support. Demonstrations broke out in the weeks after the cyclone, and by the following March they had mushroomed into full-scale civil war. More death, more devastation for a troubled land. But from the ashes of that conflict there arose a new political entity—Bangladesh, the only nation ever to be spawned by a cyclone.

The Birth of a Killer

TROPICAL CYCLONE is the generic term for some of the world's deadliest storms. Called hurricanes when they occur in the Atlantic Ocean, typhoons in the Pacific, and cyclones in the Indian Ocean, these massive rotating storms originate in the tropics, usually in late summer and autumn, and are characterized by torrential rains and violent winds. No matter where they form, tropical cyclones are all conceived in much the same way. They begin as small areas of low pressure over warm oceans. (Because the surface temperature of the water must be at least 80° F for cyclones to form, their breeding grounds are limited to ocean zones from about 5° to 30° north and south of the equator.) Moist air rises rapidly in such circumstances; as it does so, water vapor in the air cools and condenses, releasing great amounts of heat. This mix of heat and condensed moisture often results in a chaotic cluster of thunderstorms. In most cases, the storms produce a lot of rain and noise, and nothing more. But the right atmospheric conditions, combined with the effects of the earth's rotation, can cause the individual storms in a cluster to merge and begin to rotate (counterclockwise in the Northern Hemisphere, clockwise in the Southern Hemisphere). When this happens, the pressure in the center of the developing cyclone plunges, producing a partial vacuum into which more warm, moist air is sucked. As this air rises, it condenses and produces more heat, adding fuel to the storm. The low-pressure "eye" at the storm's center pulls the rotating air in tighter, causing wind speeds to accelerate, sometimes to more than 180 miles an hour. Torrents of rain fall, and another tropical cyclone has been launched.

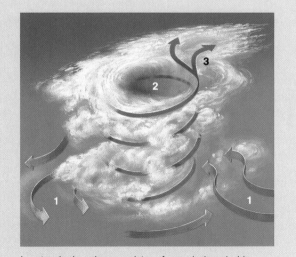

In a tropical cyclone, moist surface winds spiral in from all directions toward the calm eye of the storm (1), then rise rapidly around the eye (2), and finally exit from the storm at high altitudes (3).

Agnes's record-smashing rains *left cattle and vehicles stranded on this farm turned island in Whites Ferry, Virginia.*

A Demon Named Agnes

*Routine tropical storm turns vicious and batters
Mid-Atlantic region*

THEY HAVE SUCH LOVELY NAMES, the rivers of the Mid-Atlantic region: Susquehanna, Genesee, Juniata, Allegheny. Lovely rivers they are, too—except, of course, when they break out of their banks and turn into killers. In the latter half of June 1972, just such a disaster began to unfold as a mammoth rainstorm named Agnes poured some 28 trillion gallons of water—or enough to fill a 67-square-mile lake 2,000 feet deep—into these rivers and their tributaries. In the resulting floods, 122 people died—a relatively small number as such disasters go—but property losses amounted to a breathtaking $3 billion, making Agnes the costliest storm ever to hit the United States.

Born in mid-June as a third-rate tropical storm off Mexico's Yucatán coast, Agnes developed enough punch to be called a hurricane as it crossed the Gulf of Mexico and bruised the Florida panhandle. Losing its

hurricane status over land, Agnes drifted in a northeasterly direction across the southeastern states. But instead of disappearing into the Atlantic as expected, the tropical storm continued north, hugging the coast. Along the way, it picked up massive amounts of moisture and dumped a great deal of it back onto parts of Virginia, Maryland, and New Jersey. Now a swirling cloud mass fully 250 miles in diameter and still sopping wet, Agnes struck New York City on June 22, started up the Hudson River, and then, after shifting erratically to the west, unleashed its worst deluge on both sides of the New York–Pennsylvania border. These two states would bear the brunt of the storm's fury.

The storm gave ample warning of its arrival, burst no great dams on unwary victims, and so was not a killer on the scale of the Johnstown Flood of 1889, which took more than 2,000 lives. The trouble with

As fires burn in the background, *residents of a home for the elderly in flooded Wilkes-Barre, Pennsylvania, are carried to safety from a rescue boat.*

Agnes was that it deposited a tremendous amount of rain on land that had previously been saturated by a week of steady downpours. Agnes's new infusion of water caused already swollen rivers and streams from Virginia to New York to spill over their banks and sweep across country fields and city streets. Storm-driven floods left 330,000 people homeless, ruined crops in much of Pennsylvania and New York, and crippled industries from the Chesapeake Bay fisheries to New York's famous Corning Glass Works. Communities throughout the Mid-Atlantic states were devastated, but none more so than the city of Wilkes-Barre in Pennsylvania's Wyoming Valley.

An industrial city that had known its share of hard times, Wilkes-Barre had been badly inundated in 1936, when the Susquehanna River crested at 33 feet above its normal level. Dikes were subsequently built to contain a rise of 37 feet, but under Agnes's terrible influence, the river would reach heights of more than 40 feet. On Thursday night, June 22, with water nearing the top of the dikes, volunteers rushed to raise a levee of sandbags. Trucks dumped sand and dirt at the foot of the banks, and young men and women filled sacks and slithered up the slippery slopes in the wet, black night. When they ran out of burlap bags, volunteers went from house to house collecting plastic trash bags, pillowcases, anything that would hold sand. The post office even rushed over a truckload of empty mail sacks. But, as one levee worker recalled,

"the river kept coming. We couldn't catch up, and the siren blew and everyone was ordered to evacuate."

The Susquehanna began pouring over its dikes about daybreak on Friday; by nightfall Public Square, the heart of Wilkes-Barre's downtown business district, was under several feet of mud- and debris-laden water. Those who could fled their homes for higher ground; the rest climbed to upper stories or roofs to await rescue. Helicopters buzzed in and out of the stricken area, but the bulk of the rescue work was done by motorboats, whose operators had to be very careful not to snag utility wires, strung 25 feet above ground but now barely above water level.

A terrifying rash of rat attacks added to Wilkes-Barre's growing list of woes.

Electrical short circuits started fires in commercial warehouses containing goods worth millions of dollars. Firemen tried but failed to reach the burning structures, increasingly isolated by the rising flood waters. As the warehouses and their contents went up in flames, a cloud of acrid smoke hung over the desolate, drowning city. Swarms of rats, flushed out of their holes, swam and scuttled to rooftops and proceeded to attack the humans who had also taken refuge there. With three of Wilkes-Barre's hospitals out of service, the worst cases of rat bite, along with other sick and injured people, had to be flown to the state capital of Harrisburg, 122 miles away.

If the scene in Wilkes-Barre was terrifying, at the small northern suburb of Forty Fort it was downright macabre. There, the rushing waters washed coffins out of their graves and sent them floating abroad, some with their skeletal contents sprung loose. When the flood finally subsided, several residents returning to their homes found human skulls and bones among their backyard litter. The local police soon learned to distinguish floating bodies from department store mannequins that were also tumbling down the swollen Susquehanna.

Harrisburg, situated downriver from Wilkes-Barre, was temporarily cut off from the world, its downtown streets inundated. Governor Milton Shapp and his wife had to abandon the new $2 million riverfront executive mansion on June 22. At several points near the city, the Susquehanna sent a current of brown water roaring one-half mile beyond its banks. At a Bethlehem Steel plant south of Harrisburg, only roofs and smokestacks were visible above the water.

South and east of Wilkes-Barre, near Philadelphia, the flooding Schuylkill River poured into Pottstown, driving people onto roofs and treetops. Military helicopters summoned to the embattled town performed heroically, dodging trees and dangerous high-voltage power lines to pluck stranded flood victims from the rainy darkness.

Swollen rivers and creeks also wreaked havoc in the southern-tier counties of New York State, especially in the vicinity of Elmira and Corning. One-half of Elmira's 40,000 residents were evacuated; a telephone operator who stayed behind to take "life-or-death calls" worked her switchboard while furniture bobbed in five feet of water in parts of the office. After the Chemung River went on a rampage through Corning, the town was left without gas, electricity, or drinking water, and 40 percent of its homes were in ruins. At the Corning Glass Works, precious antiques in the company's glass museum were carried off by the flood or lay shattered in mud and debris.

In Virginia, the James River crested at 36 feet, far surpassing the 30-foot record of 1771. While flood waters sloshed through the state capital of Richmond, drinking water there became scarce. Virginia Governor Linwood Holton said his state had suffered damage "the magnitude of which has not been witnessed by the commonwealth in this century." And in both Virginia and Maryland the worst damage was not even visible: the Chesapeake Bay shellfish industry, an employer of thousands, was put out of commission for a year by huge freshets from the Susquehanna, Potomac, Patuxent, and James rivers. Clams, oysters, and crabs, which flourish in salt water, were killed off not only by dilution of their saline habitat but also by an influx of raw sewage, industrial wastes, pesticides, and silt.

Agnes did most of its damage east of the Appalachians, but its clouds reached so far that they deluged streams north and west of the watershed as well. Near Rochester, New York, army engineers watched Genesee River waters swirl to within 50 feet of the top of the 760-foot Mount Morris Dam. When they finally opened the sluice gates to relieve pressure on the dam, 8,500 cubic feet per second of water (a flow equal to that of the American Falls at Niagara) poured into the valley below, forcing thousands of area residents to evacuate their homes and move to higher ground. As far away as downtown Pittsburgh, children swam in parking lots as the flood crest rolled down the Ohio River.

Even before the storm faded on June 24, an army of young volunteers began to converge on the flooded areas, sacrificing their summer

vacations to collect, haul, and distribute relief supplies. One hundred Mennonites, bringing their own tents and tools, showed up at Elmira to rebuild houses, while another contingent worked selflessly in the beleaguered Wyoming Valley. But if the storm brought out the best in some people, it also depressed the spirits and ruined the dreams of thousands. A sort of battle fatigue set in among the stricken population, and recovery was a long, painful process.

Imagine for a moment the ordeal of a typical Wyoming Valley family victimized by the flood. They are on alert all through the night of June 22–23. At 4:30 A.M. the warning comes: evacuate immediately. They snatch up important papers and clothes and head for the highway. If they are lucky, they crowd in with relatives not too far away; otherwise they lay claim to a few square feet of a school gym floor, surrounded by other refugees. Three days later they go back home for a look. Their house is ripped off its foundation. They climb in and haul out the waterlogged sofa and chairs. The ruined refrigerator, washing machine, and television are added to the growing pile of debris in the yard.

Searching for the stranded, *a Red Cross rescue helicopter hovers over downtown Wilkes-Barre, a flood-prone city that endured the full destructive impact of Hurricane Agnes.*

Perhaps some furniture and clothing upstairs can be saved. Eventually army engineers come by, salvage kitchen and bathroom fixtures, and then demolish the house. After inconveniencing their relatives a bit longer, the flood victims find a small mobile home deposited on their lawn, courtesy of the U.S. Department of Housing and Urban Development (HUD). The roof leaks and the heater works poorly, but the trailer is available rent free for a year and the family is back on its property. Now is the time to worry about a great many things. Will loans be available to rebuild the house? Will the shop or factory where the father works reopen? (Some did, but many did not.) Will community life revive? (Months later, many shops, cinemas, and restaurants in the area still stood vacant and caked in mud.)

Even worse than the storm's property damage was the emotional harm Agnes inflicted on so many victims.

Not surprisingly, the number of people seeking psychiatric help in the Wilkes-Barre area doubled in the aftermath of the flood. One man washed down his house, then sat in front of it for three days holding the water hose. Another climbed a tree and refused to come down for 24 hours. A team sent in by the National Institute of Mental Health found claustrophobic reactions to the pressure of living in close quarters, an intense fear of rain, and an attitude of unshakable dependency. Grievances, real or imagined, kindled rage: a politician was stoned by his neighbors when he received a trailer before anyone else. "Nobody trusts anybody," a federal relief officer observed.

People blamed "the government" for not helping more. But in truth, government disaster aid in this election year was generous. Five states—Florida, Maryland, Virginia, Pennsylvania, and New York— were declared disaster areas, thus making them eligible for federal relief funds. On October 30, HUD's Pennsylvania office reported that it had provided temporary dwellings for 14,358 families. By Thanksgiving, the Small Business Administration had disbursed $131 million in home loans—and the first $5,000 of each loan was in reality a gift. In all, federal flood relief programs pumped nearly $2 billion into the Wyoming Valley alone.

Some flood losses were especially poignant, like the ruined encyclopedia set a financially strapped Forty Fort couple had bought for their four children—and then laboriously paid off in $12 installments over three years. Gone, too, for many was the pleasure of recalling the past without pain. While cleaning out what was left of her library, a Wilkes-Barre reporter came across a book called *The Beautiful Susquehanna.* She quickly threw it away.

Hurricane Camille devastated the Mississippi coast (above) in 1969. When a superstorm like Camille strikes land, its name is withdrawn from the rotating lists of hurricane names.

NAMING HURRICANES

Ordinary people, not meteorologists, were the first to name hurricanes, often after the island or town most affected by the storm or after the saint on whose day the disaster occurred.

As systematic weather watching developed in the 20th century, naming storms began to appeal to meteorologists as a sensible alternative to identifying them by latitude and longitude. In 1953, weather services in the United States, following a custom apparently started by an Australian weatherman in the late 19th century, began using women's names to identify storms. The practice was finally abandoned in 1979 when feminists persuaded the World Meteorological Organization (WMO) to alternate men's and women's names when designating tropical storms.

The names used by the National Hurricane Center near Miami are taken in order from an alphabetical list previously agreed upon by the WMO. There are six alphabetical lists at any given time, one for each year in a six-year cycle. At the end of the cycle, the lists are reused. Thus the 1986 list, beginning with Allen and Bonnie comes into play again in 1992. Many Spanish names appear on the lists for North Atlantic, Caribbean, and Gulf of Mexico storms, while names beginning with Q, U, X, Y, and Z are excluded because of their rarity. There are separate lists for Pacific storms, but Asian meteorologists prefer numbers to names.

Death in Managua

Nicaraguan capital leveled by fateful earthquake

CHRISTMAS 1972 promised to be even more festive than usual in Managua, Nicaragua. That year the city was hosting the Twentieth World Amateur Baseball Series. To the intense pride of local fans, Nicaragua's team clinched a second place tie with the United States by winning a crucial game against the reigning champions from Cuba. On the night of the home team triumph, Managuans went wild with excitement, setting off firecrackers and driving around the city honking horns. The victory celebrations were hardly over when it was time to begin the *Gritería de Maria* ("Hurrah for Mary"), a 24-hour round of fireworks, parades, and dancing in the streets that traditionally marks the start of the Christmas holiday.

In the midst of all the merrymaking, two mild tremors shook Managua at 9:30 and 10:15 on the evening of Friday, December 22. As quakes go, these were scarcely worth noting. Although some residents decided to sleep out in the open and others went to bed fully clothed, just in case, there was no panic. After all, Managuans live on top of one of the most active seismic zones in the world. Underground rumblings are often felt here, and many residents could still recall the great quake that destroyed much of the city in 1931. Nothing, however, could have prepared the people of Managua for the tragedy that began to unfold shortly after midnight, Saturday, December 23.

Clocks throughout Managua stopped at 12:29 A.M. as the first in a rapid series of tremors jolted the doomed city.

Nicaraguan strongman Gen. Anastasio "Tachito" Somoza and his American wife, Hope, had just returned from a wedding celebration in the suburbs when their house in Managua's fashionable El Retiro district started to shake. "We were talking," Somoza recalled. "We felt the first tremor and got up and ran to an alley. Something knocked against Hope and bruised her arm and ankle. Then came another tremor and another. The first one oscillated horizontally, and that gave some people time to get out of their homes. The second and third oscillated up and down. That third one was the killer. We thought we were pieces of ice in a cocktail shaker."

Within minutes, at least 70 percent of the city was reduced to rubble. Masonry buildings collapsed on their occupants; wooden structures, tinder-dry after

months of drought, burst into flames. As fires spread everywhere, central Managua began to resemble a scene out of Dante's *Inferno*. Carmela Lacayo, an American teacher visiting Managua, described the "utter chaos" that gripped the ruined city: "people running in the streets screaming, others digging frantically, trying to unearth trapped relatives, still others ripping up their pajamas to use as bandages. One young mother walked in the street clutching her dead baby to her chest while her husband strode zombie-like at her side."

When the first major shock hit, Santos Jimenez, a physician who was also the volunteer chief of Managua's fire department, ran into the street with his family, but then realized that his 14-year-old son had been left behind. Jimenez rushed back into the house and with his bare hands dug the boy from the rubble. Father and son made it outside just before the building collapsed. Although the youngster had stopped breathing by then, Jimenez was able to revive him with artificial respiration.

Having seen to the safety of his family, Jimenez set off for fire department headquarters. When he arrived there, he was stunned by what he saw. With Managua in flames, most of its fire-fighting equipment lay buried under hundreds of tons of masonry. Water, too, became scarce as many of the city's mains burst. Lacking equipment and water, firemen looked on helplessly as entire blocks were consumed.

Throughout Managua, medical personnel coped as best they could with an impossible situation. The 800-bed General Hospital, the city's largest, simply cracked apart during the quake, killing some 75 patients, including 17 babies in the nursery wing. Heroic nurses kept running back into the crumbling building to rescue surviving patients. One especially resourceful nurse bundled eight premature infants into a large carton, commandeered a car and driver, and rode with them to a hospital in León, 50 miles away. Thanks to a portable respirator the nurse brought along, all eight babies survived.

On the ground in front of the wrecked General Hospital, Dr. Agustín Cedeño, chief of the emergency room, set up a makeshift field hospital. Drivers bringing in the wounded by car were asked to keep their headlights on so that the doctors could see. Kneeling in the dust, Cedeño and his staff stopped hemorrhages and set broken bones. Eventually, some 5,000 victims were treated in the outdoor emergency room.

In another part of town, 50 men and women were

Decorations for a holiday cut short *by tragedy hang forlornly over a rubble-strewn street in downtown Managua.*

being held in an ancient prison called *El Hormiguero* ("The Ant Heap") when the quake struck. The surviving male inmates seized the opportunity to flee through holes in the prison walls. Trapped in another part of the jail, the women prisoners screamed for help until a sympathetic guard ran back into the disintegrating building, unlocked the doors, and let them out. An estimated 80 prisoners were crushed to death in the city's three jails; another 400 managed to escape.

Saturday would have been payday in Managua, as well as the day on which Christmas bonuses were handed out. To get a jump on the biggest shopping day of the year, hundreds of sidewalk peddlers had camped for the night around the block-square Central Market building, and unknown numbers of them died when the quake leveled the weak masonry structure.

The full extent of Managua's devastation began to become apparent at daybreak on Saturday. A 320-

block area in the heart of the capital was transformed into a corpse-strewn wasteland cruised by vultures. As fires continued to burn, a pall of smoke and red dust hung over everything. Streets and roads were badly damaged. Water, electricity, and all communication services were nearly wiped out. Normal food distribution channels, already strained by drought, collapsed.

With 20,000 seriously injured people to care for and the four main hospitals destroyed, Managua's medical capabilities were stretched to the breaking point. Government buildings, newspaper plants, and most of the city's schools, colleges, public halls, banks, markets, stores, gas stations, and hotels were in ruins. An estimated 250,000 people, more than half of Managua's population, were left homeless. And lying in the rubble were some 5,000 soon-to-be-festering bodies. After surveying this hellish scene, the commander of Nicaragua's army engineers, Lieut. Col. José Alagret,

Hunger and lawlessness plagued the Nicaraguan capital in the aftermath of the Christmas earthquake disaster. At right, frantic refugees reach out for their share of donated food supplies. Below, a rifle-toting guardsman, masked against the pervasive stench of rotting corpses, keeps a watchful eye out for marauding looters.

observed, "This is a city that was, but is no more."

A series of aftershocks rocked Managua well into Saturday afternoon, but according to a Guatemalan reporter on the scene, "People don't seem to notice them anymore. They just walk along the streets in a daze. Cadavers on the sidewalks go almost unnoticed. All the familiar landmarks—the Casa Presidencial [the president's residence] up on the hill overlooking the city, the Inter-Continental Hotel, the Gran Hotel, the Hotel Balmoral—all are severely damaged."

The tremors that leveled Managua registered at most a modest 6.25 on the Richter scale (only quakes registering 7.0 or higher are considered major). Why, then, did an earthquake that elsewhere might have been barely noticed cause such devastation? As bad luck would have it, the focus of the 1972 quake was located almost directly under Managua at an unusually shallow depth. Even more to the point, Managua is truly a city that should never have been. Volcanoes surround the capital, five faults run beneath it,

and earthquakes are common. Because of repeated volcanic eruptions, Managua sits not on solid rock but on 300 feet of unstable volcanic debris—a dangerous cushion indeed for any city in an active seismic zone.

Another factor contributing to the quake's extreme destructiveness was a local building technique, called *taquezal* construction, commonly used in the poorer sections of the city. Built of wood frames, adobe, and stones, and roofed with unanchored clay tiles, the typical *taquezal* house was a flimsy affair doomed to collapse the moment the earth started heaving.

With the smell of death and the threat of disease hanging over the city, tens of thousands of survivors fled Managua.

Among the first to leave the Nicaraguan capital was the reclusive American billionaire Howard Hughes. Flushed out of his suite in the posh Inter-Continental Hotel by the quake, Hughes was driven to the airport in a limousine and spent the rest of the night there. Early Saturday morning, thanks to General Somoza's intervention, Hughes's private jet was the first plane cleared for takeoff from Managua.

Meanwhile, rescue workers began the grim task of disposing of thousands of unclaimed corpses. Some bodies had to be doused with gasoline and cremated on the spot; others were dumped into hastily dug communal graves. On December 26, the day after the Christmas that never came, a large section of downtown Managua was declared a "contaminated area" to be leveled and covered over with lime.

Despite the horrors all around them, many Managuans balked at leaving the ruins of their homes. In order to force them out, and thereby reduce the possibility of an epidemic, the authorities at first refused to bring food into the city. Profiteers stepped into the breach, however, selling bread for $2 a loaf and soft drinks for $2 a bottle. Looters, too, descended upon Managua, eventually picking it clean of whatever valuables were still to be had.

If Managuans were for the most part too stunned to do much for themselves in the first few days after the quake, the outside world responded quickly and generously. Neighboring Costa Rica flew in a medical team within hours, followed by two more from Cuba. The United States also sent doctors, nurses, supplies, and two fully equipped field hospital tents. Honduras put 200 troops under Somoza's command to help maintain order. More than 20 other countries sent food, clothing, and tools, and countless private individuals took it upon themselves to help out. Among them was baseball superstar Roberto Clemente, who personally organized relief efforts in his native Puerto Rico, then died in the crash of the plane carrying supplies from San Juan to Managua.

As donated goods began to pile up at the Managua airport, rumors spread that General Somoza and his cronies were profiting from the distribution of foreign aid. (Concern that relief supplies were not reaching the needy had in fact prompted Roberto Clemente to accompany the ill-fated plane from San Juan.) Allegations of official corruption persisted throughout the post-quake reconstruction campaign. Proposals to move the capital to a seismically more stable area were rejected by Somoza. "I built my house according to specifications so that it would stand up in quakes," he told a reporter for *Time* magazine. "There's only one crack in my house. Why should I move?" But as his critics were quick to point out, Somoza owned the best property in downtown Managua and thus stood only to gain by expropriating his own land for government projects and then reimbursing himself from the foreign aid funds that were pouring into the country. Such venality wound up offending Nicaraguans of all political persuasions, and the Somoza regime was finally toppled in 1979. Today, downtown Managua remains largely unreconstructed, as political upheavals have succeeded geological ones in this troubled land.

MONSTER LANDSLIDE IN PERU

Managua, Nicaragua, is only one of many seismic hotspots on the Ring of Fire, the belt of geological violence that nearly encircles the Pacific Ocean. All along the ring, quakes and volcanic eruptions are a constant threat. On May 31, 1970, that threat became grim reality for western Peru.

At 3:23 P.M., a fault rupture under the Pacific floor some 15 miles off the Peruvian coast unleashed a quake that registered 7.75 on the Richter scale and killed some 70,000 people.

The shock set off thousands of landslides and avalanches in the Andes, but the worst by far was the cascade of ice, snow, mud, rock, and boulders that plummeted from the north peak of Nevado de Huascarán, Peru's highest mountain. An estimated 90 million cubic yards of debris fell 12,000 feet from Huascarán's summit to the slopes below. Traveling at roughly 200 miles per hour, the lethal mass covered seven miles horizontally before coming to rest in the Rio Santa Valley.

The town of Ranrahirca was buried. Of Yungay, all that was visible were the tops of palm trees and part of the cathedral wall. Throughout the valley, at least 25,000 people lay buried under 10 to 40 feet of debris—victims of the most destructive landslide on record.

At the Monterrico Hippodrome in Lima, Peru, fans run in terror onto the track as the first tremors of the killer quake of May 31, 1970, are felt. The earthquake and the landslides it set off have been termed the worst seismological disaster ever experienced in the Americas.

***Like a nightmare** in broad daylight, a tornado almost 800 feet wide at its base roars across a Kansas field in 1974.*

Terror by Twister

Lethal swarms of tornadoes roar across Midwest

FOR MOST PEOPLE in Xenia, some 15 miles east of Dayton in southwestern Ohio, it had been an uneventful Wednesday afternoon. At the A & W Root Beer stand, manager Betty Marshall was overseeing the preparation of coleslaw and hamburgers for the evening rush, while Diane Hall, her carhop, was outside taking orders. Nearby, a local Choctaw Indian named Thomas Yougen was setting up his tape machine to record what he described simply as Xenia's silence. City Manager Bob Stewart was looking forward to the day's end: he had made dinner reservations for himself and his wife, Yvonne, to celebrate their 20th wedding anniversary.

And over at Xenia High School, 18-year-old Ruth Venuti was waiting for her ride home, as dark clouds hung low on the horizon and daylight seemed already on the wane. The only sounds were coming from the auditorium, where the drama club was rehearsing for an upcoming production.

Something caught Ruth's eye. A mile or two away, above the rooftops to the southwest, a large cloud had begun to form, black and billowing. She watched, fascinated, as it grew into something horizontal, revolving, funnel-shaped, and gigantic.

Ruth Venuti had just witnessed the birth of a tornado, a nightmare that would bring death and wholesale destruction to this quiet city of 27,000.

Despite its business-as-usual atmosphere, this day, April 3, 1974, was far from an ordinary Wednesday. Since early Tuesday, meteorologists across the Midwest had been watching a rare and dangerous weather pattern shaping up. A warm air mass carrying millions of gallons of moisture was headed on a collision course with a fast-moving cold front sweeping east from the Rockies, pushed along by the high-speed, high-altitude winds of the jet stream. At the National Severe Storms Forecast Center in Kansas City, director Allen Pearson watched with deepening anxiety as messages rolled in from points all over the eastern third of the country, as far north as Michigan and as far south as Mississippi.

This was a textbook tornado situation, but on a scale that defied belief.

Tornadoes sweep across the Great American Plains, from Canada to the Gulf of Mexico, at an average rate of about 1,000 a year, a figure far exceeding that of any comparable area on the globe. For good reason, the strip that encompasses Texas, Oklahoma, Kansas, and Missouri is known as Tornado Alley, but no region is immune to this destructive freak of nature.

Even by Tornado Alley standards, the events of April 3, 1974, were extraordinary. Over 18 hours, across a front reaching from Windsor, Ontario, south into Alabama, 148 tornadoes touched down, ravaging towns and farmlands alike. The only thing Ruth Venuti could not have known as she watched the oncoming dark, turbulent cloud was that her quiet little city of Xenia was about to get the very worst of it.

She ran through deserted school corridors, bursting into the auditorium. "Tornado," she gasped. "There's a twister headed this way!"

"I thought she was joking," recalled David Heath, a teacher who was directing the play. "I came very close to telling everyone to forget it and to go through a dance number they were rehearsing again. Instead I jumped off the stage and told everyone to follow me so we could get a view of the tornado."

They couldn't miss it—an angry, seething apparition only 200 yards away and closing in fast. Students and teacher hit the floor, huddling against walls on both sides of the hall as the tornado—making a noise "like the clattering of a thousand sets of venetian blinds, along with tremendous crashing and grating sounds" —slammed into the building.

The air rained rocks and wood, bricks and great clods of earth, millions of deadly daggers of broken glass. Large beams flew in every direction like spears hurled from the

Defeathered but still intact, a chicken surveys the aftermath of an Alabama twister.

hands of giants, all to the eerie accompaniment of a noise remembered by one witness as the "bellowing of a million mad bulls."

The towering black funnel churned its way across Xenia at 40 miles an hour, crushing wood houses to tinder, yanking thick trees out of the ground like weeds, turning cars, trucks—everything up to and including kitchen sinks—into lethal projectiles. Ken and Pam Shields were just sitting down to an early supper with their children when they heard the screen door banging. Ken got up to close it—and summoned his wife. "Have you ever seen a tornado?" he asked almost casually, pointing at the huge thing barreling toward them. They fell to the floor seconds before the tornado hit. It went as quickly as it came, sweeping their house and furniture away with it.

The "insatiable monster," as one observer called it, "seemed to amble along as though out for a leisurely stroll." It killed Virginia Wells as she scrambled out of her bathtub, flattened the A & W Root Beer stand, and reduced the Kroehler furniture factory to a heap of rubble. Carhop Diane Hall died at once, crushed under a refrigerator moments before her fiancé, Ricky Falis, reached her side.

The engineer of a 47-car Cincinnati-bound freight train just rolling into town saw the swaying funnel bearing down on him only moments before it lifted the train's rear cars and flung them across Xenia's main street. It pulverized the red brick post office, crushing postal worker Oscar Robinson on the spot, killed Linda McKibben and Richard Adams as they sat in the Elbow Supper Club, and tore apart the Snediker Museum, Moorehead House, and other landmarks of Xenia's colonial history.

The tornado was remarkably selective in its effects. Shrieking winds slammed the Xenia Hotel, demolishing whole sections of the graceful old building—but leaving intact its centerpiece, a bedroom where President William McKinley had once spent the night. It flattened 123-year-old St. Brigid's Catholic church but left the old Galloway Clock Tower standing and hardly damaged.

Ken Shields crawled out from under the wreckage of his house and one by one found his children. All were safe. But Pam, his wife, lay blood soaked and helpless, a long wooden peg protruding from her neck. He carried her quickly to the family car and started the engine— only to discover that the low pressure inside the tornado had caused all four tires to burst. Undaunted, he started out anyway, pushing ahead as, one by one, the mutilated tires came off their wheels. Every road seemed blocked by wreckage or felled trees, and his feeling of desperation increased when he had to restrain Pam as she tried to pull the wooden peg out of her neck. At last, a police car stopped them—attracted at first by the sight of a car being driven without tires. Immediately recognizing the emergency, the trooper transferred Pam to his car and, siren blaring, drove her to a local hospital, where doctors were working nonstop to treat hundreds of patients. Pam was one of the lucky ones.

It was over as abruptly as it had begun. Estimates of the total elapsed time varied from two minutes to four, but to those in the twister's path, it had seemed an eternity. David Heath picked his way back to the high school auditorium—to find a school bus, upside down, on the stage where only minutes before his fledgling actors and actresses had been rehearsing. The winds had flung it through the building's roof.

As City Manager Bob Stewart stood in front of the town hall, surveying the destruction around him, a distraught assistant exclaimed, "What the *hell* are we going to do?"

Stewart shrugged. "We are going to clean the damn place up," was his reply. "But first we have to keep it from burning up." That meant turning off gas and electricity, two major sources of fire danger, then clearing the streets and organizing rescue squads to hunt for those possibly trapped under collapsed buildings, and finally figuring out a way to get information to as many people as possible.

The havoc wrought in those few frantic minutes was almost inconceivable.

The toll in Xenia was staggering: 33 dead, 1,600 injured; 1,300 buildings destroyed and another 2,000 damaged; hundreds of trees, including Xenia's once proud maples, lay scattered like kindling; 12 churches and six schools were in ruins.

There was at least one unforeseen dividend: Thomas Yougen's tape recorder had picked up the whole thing—the howling and shrieking of the wind and the unforgettable sound of hundreds of nails being pulled out of wood and the walls of the disintegrating

Unlocking the Tornado's Dangerous Secrets

WEATHER RESEARCHERS, aided by satellite photography, specialized radar, and other advanced technology, have learned much in recent years about tornadoes, described by one as "perhaps the ultimate meteorological phenomenon." The headquarters for their research is the National Severe Storms Laboratory in Norman, Oklahoma—in the heart of Tornado Alley, where fronts of cold, dry air moving south from Canada run into northbound masses of warm, wet air from the Gulf of Mexico. Such encounters provide a perfect breeding ground for thunderstorms, whose towering clouds are created by rapid updrafts of the warm air. Given the right conditions—changes in the speed and direction of the wind at different altitudes, downdrafts of colder air from above, the fast-moving winds of the jet stream—those updrafts can begin to rotate, but exactly what extra boost turns a spinning column of air into a full-fledged tornado remains an unsolved riddle.

What meteorologists do know is that the spinning column lengthens at both ends and draws in water vapor, making the funnel visible as it touches down on land. The newborn tornado turns darker as it moves along, sucking up surface dirt, soil, and anything else in its path, which may be a mile wide or a scant 50 feet. Equally variable but far more difficult to measure is a tornado's power. The suddenness with which twisters appear makes on-the-spot observation next to impossible, and the strongest ones simply overwhelm scientific instruments. The fastest wind gust ever recorded was 231 miles an hour, just before the gauge measuring it broke—and that was not even a tornado, which at full force can generate winds close to 300 miles an hour.

Direction of storm

Formed within a spiraling updraft of air in a thunderstorm, the tornado's narrower funnel reaches down to the ground, where its spin pulls in strong wind from all directions.

Kroehler furniture factory. The tape became a sound track for home movie footage shot by 16-year-old Bruce Boyd—as the boy's terrifed mother implored him to take cover. Shown later on national televison, it furnished the best on-the-spot record yet available of a tornado in full destructive spate.

Xenia was not the only community devastated that day. In Sugar Valley, Georgia, tornado winds whirled nine-year-old Randall Goble aloft and dropped him, unharmed, 200 yards away. His parents and two sisters, less lucky, died in the wreckage of their home. A particularly vicious twister flattened the city hall of Jasper in hard-hit northwestern Alabama and leveled surrounding buildings. "We can't talk to the police department," radio announcer Joel Cook panted to listeners over station WARF. "It just blew away."

Little by little, the statistics for Tornado Alley came in: 315 dead, three times the yearly national average and the worst death toll in half a century; nearly 5,500 injured; $500 million in immediate damages, and probably nearly the same amount again to cover reconstruction over a longer period of time. Descriptions from survivors in the various states differed in detail—to housewife Sylvia Humes, the three-funnel tornado that hit her hometown of Hanover, Indiana, sounded "like a big blender"—but all told the same story of chaos, destruction, and loss of life.

The golden arches of a fast-food restaurant (above) in Xenia, Ohio, proved to be no match for the faster winds that tore through the town on April 3, 1974, killing 33 people, injuring 1,600 others, and destroying or damaging more than 3,000 buildings. Nevertheless, as the sign at right attests, the tornado could not destroy the spirit of Xenia's survivors.

In Bear Branch, Indiana, a twister shot Halbert Walston 40 feet through his bathroom wall to land on his back outside. Through blinding pain—an ankle and five ribs were broken and a lung punctured—he struggled to the side of his 15-year-old son, Michael, whose arm had been partially severed at the elbow. Jamming his thumb against an artery in the boy's bicep to stop the bleeding, he sent his wife for help. All survived—but terrifying dreams would haunt Walston's nights during his recovery.

Ultimately, the damage could not be measured solely in terms of shattered buildings, ruined businesses, or even the doleful roll call of the dead. There was another, less tangible dimension to this day of terror. It was exemplified in the fate of tiny Brandenburg, Kentucky, situated west of Louisville on two hills overlooking the Ohio River. Brandenburg was a slow-paced country town like hundreds of others, where all 1,673 of its residents seemed to be first-name friends with one another. Its weekly newspaper, the *Meade County Messenger,* advertised itself proudly as "a long letter from home to those away."

In accountant Larry Allen's words, Brandenburg was "a Mark Twain town . . . Hannibal, Missouri, all over, and I was Tom Sawyer and I loved it."

That idyllic life ended with brutal abruptness on Wednesday afternoon, April 3, 1974. Without warning, a twister roared through and killed 29 people, most of them children playing after school. It took days for grieving parents to identify the remains. It took far longer for the shock to wear off. "My God," murmured country lawyer Ellis Blake as he surveyed the ruins of the community that had been home for 67 years. "What has happened to my good little town?"

Australia's Christmas Cyclone

Furious storm demolishes the city of Darwin

CHRISTMAS, 1974, was etched forever in the memories of the 47,000 inhabitants of Darwin, port city and capital of Australia's remote Northern Territory. Shortly after midnight, Christmas Eve, Cyclone Tracy roared into Darwin and in a single six-hour assault laid waste 90 percent of the metropolis. A pilot flying over the wreckage radioed, "If you've seen pictures of Hiroshima after the atomic bomb, then you know what Darwin looks like."

In Australia no one dreams of a white Christmas, for Christmas comes during the summer rainy season, the time of tropical storms. Cyclone Tracy began on December 21 as a tropical low-pressure system in the Arafura Sea more than 300 miles northeast of the city. The Darwin Tropical Cyclone Warning Centre issued its first alert that afternoon and began tracking the storm. By December 22 the storm was upgraded to a cyclone—elsewhere called a hurricane or typhoon. It was still 130 miles due north of Darwin but moving steadily southwest. It continued on that path, lashing the coast of Melville and Bathurst islands north of Darwin and seemingly heading safely out toward the Timor Sea. But during the early morning of December 24, it made an unexpected 90° turn, picked up wind intensity, and headed straight for Darwin.

Darwinians took the change seriously, but not too seriously. Although warning sirens blared off and on all afternoon, most people had holiday preparations on their minds. No cyclone had damaged Darwin in the past 30 years, and none would, so most believed.

The nonchalant swagger was part of the mystique of Darwin—a frontier boomtown known for informality and intense individualism. Darwin relished its place in the *Guinness Book of World Records* for the greatest per capita beer consumption of any city in the world. Named for the famous naturalist Charles Darwin, it was built around a harbor discovered in 1839 by J. C. Wickham, the captain of H.M.S. *Beagle*. In the 1870's a gold rush and the completion of the Overland Telegraph Line began to attract a colorful array of prospectors, merchants, and adventurers to the settlement.

Darwin's feisty 70-year-old mayor, Harold Brennan, who always wore a pith helmet and insisted that everyone call him "Tiger," embodied the independent spirit of this most isolated of Australia's cities. No rail line connected Darwin to the larger cities to the south, and only a single highway crossed the deserts of the outback. As one man observed, "This is as far from the rest of Australia as you can go and stay dry."

The powerful winds of Cyclone Tracy ripped off roofs, tattered walls, filled the air with flying debris, and even upended a small plane (above).

One of the long-time Darwin residents was Bishop John Patrick O'Loughlin, who had presided over the diocese since 1949. In spite of the cyclone warnings, Bishop O'Loughlin decided to celebrate Midnight Mass at St. Mary's Cathedral. As the Mass began, driving rain had already flooded the church, and the bishop was forced to wade to the altar through ankle-deep water. Soon louvers and large chunks of roof were flying about, and then the electricity went out. "We lit candles," said the bishop, "but they kept blowing out. We wrapped it up pretty fast then. I decided not to take up the collection." The congregation struggled to return home in gale-force winds and torrential rain; the leading edge of Tracy was coming ashore.

The rest of that night was madness. By 1:00 A.M. much of the city was without power, and all police cars had been ordered off the road because driving had become impossible. At 2:30 the most destructive winds, around the center of the storm, knocked the radio station off the air. Shortly after 3:00 the airport anemometer registered gusts of 131 miles per hour—still the wind kept increasing.

The memories of survivors give meaning to the numbers. Elizabeth Burton told how she and her family huddled in their lounge room when the heaviest winds began. Suddenly "the roof was torn off our house with a frightening roar. Seconds later the walls were peeled off the four sides of the building, leaving us shocked and exposed to the tempest." The family then retreated to the bathroom. "I climbed into the bath with the two children," Elizabeth reported, "while mother and my husband huddled under the hand basin. By this time, the walls of the bathroom had gone and we were virtually hanging on to the fittings. When the wind subsided a little we made a dash for shelter under the house wreckage."

Kay Moreland was caught in the city center when the cyclone struck. She and friends tried to take shelter, but the building they were in began to collapse. They escaped to a nearby hotel, where a large group had taken refuge. When it, too, showed signs of collapsing, she watched, transfixed, as four pregnant women were ushered into the hotel's refrigerator room for protection.

At about 4:00 A.M. the winds calmed as the eye of Cyclone Tracy passed over the city. The barometric pressure literally dropped off the scale of the barographs in Darwin. Those who thought the storm was over were caught in the open when wind suddenly resumed with full fury from the opposite direction. Geoff and Barbara James had clung to their front fence for four hours; when the wind shifted, they clambered over and clung to the other side. Many houses that had survived Tracy's initial blast were destroyed when it struck them from behind.

When Christmas Day dawned, "people were crawl-ing out of their wrecked homes like rats out of their holes," Tiger Brennan reported. Nearly everyone was homeless. Most buildings were seriously damaged, many of them beyond repair. Streets were strewn with wrecked cars and buses and uprooted trees, with parts of walls and roofs and broken pieces of furniture mixed in. Heavy-duty iron power poles were curled to the ground. Birds and insects had been blown away and the trees were bare. The terrified citizens of Darwin, however, were more fortunate; only 49 in all had been killed.

Though many had lost everything but the clothes on their backs, the people of Darwin immediately began to deal with the tragedy. An emergency committee began organizing operations to clear the streets, and ambulances began to transport the most seriously injured to the damaged but still-functioning airport for evacuation.

The first report of Darwin's plight reached Canberra, Australia's capital, early Christmas Day. By late evening the first planeload of relief had arrived, including an evacuation team, a surgical team of five doctors and two nurses, and abundant medical supplies.

Since shelter for the survivors was lacking, evacuation operations were put into effect. The first flights on December 26 carried 700, including injured people and pregnant women. Darwin's isolation meant that many had to be flown to Sydney or other southern cities—the equivalent of having a disaster in Chicago and evacuating the injured to Los Angeles. By the 28th, a motley fleet of planes was able to remove more than 8,000 people from the city in a single day. By December 31, 25,000 people had been airlifted from Darwin, and another 10,000 had headed south by road.

Cyclone Tracy taxed every resource and every ability of the independent-minded Darwinians. The vitality of present-day Darwin bears witness to their success. Within three years of the devastation, the pre-Tracy population had almost been regained. By 1985 the city had far surpassed its old size and had grown into a metropolis of 68,500. But to this day Darwin still bears the scars of Cyclone Tracy, and its people must always hope that no Christmas yet to come will bring again that ghost of Christmas past.

"Darwin is gone," lamented a member of the relief team. All that remained after Tracy's passage were flimsy remnants of broken houses like the one at left.

The Great Tangshan Earthquake

Violent tremors rock China's industrial heartland

FOR 23 TERRIFYING SECONDS, at about 3:45 A.M., July 28, 1976, the deadliest earthquake to hit China in four centuries roared through the densely populated city of Tangshan, a coal-mining and electric power center 100 miles southeast of Peking. Moments before, a cascade of flashing, multicolored lights, visible 200 miles away, lit up the skies over the doomed city. Then, in less time than it takes to read this paragraph, the heart of Tangshan—an area of roughly 20 square miles—collapsed into rubble like a house of cards.

Registering between 7.8 and 8.2 on the Richter scale, the powerful quake hurled people six feet into the air. Some Tangshan residents who had managed to cling to trees or posts above the still-vibrating earth were spun about like pinwheels before being thrown clear of their refuges. Thousands of sinkholes dotted the land like so many bomb craters, and in some places the earth split open several feet. Railroad tracks buckled, and fences were displaced as much as 1½ yards out of line. Crops were blown over, trees were uprooted, and bushes were scorched on one side as if by a giant fireball.

Ho Shu-shen, a senior police officer in Tangshan, was awakened by his wife shortly before their world came tumbling down about them. "I looked out and felt a strong wind blowing dust and light rain," Ho later recalled. "Then I saw a quick flash of greenish-blue light in the sky and heard a strange sound from under the ground, like the noise of a freight train.

"The floor began jerking up and down. I jumped out the window, but the earth shook back and forth and threw me to the ground. My house collapsed. For two or three minutes there was no sound. Then I heard people crying everywhere in the darkness in the ruins of their houses."

At the Friendship Guest House in Tientsin, a city 60 miles southwest of Tangshan, Beatrice Steinberg, a New Yorker traveling with her husband, Samuel, on a union-organized tour of China, was awakened by a deep rumbling sound unlike any she had ever heard before. As the room and everything in it began to shake violently, Mrs. Steinberg lurched across the heaving floor toward her husband, now also awake in the other bed.

"I jumped into bed with my husband," Mrs. Steinberg later reported. "I said, 'If we're gonna go, let's go together.'" Clinging tightly to each other in the darkness, the Steinbergs waited for a death that never came. Instead, after a few minutes of silence, they heard calm, polite voices outside their door. "American friends, are you all right?" the voices called out. "Put shoes on. Leave everything. Come with us." Walking hand in hand, the visitors from New York were led outside to their tour bus, which carefully drove them to the center of a city square, well away from any buildings. At dawn, the American tourists, in various states of undress, were amazed to find themselves surrounded by thousands of Chinese sitting in silence, waiting for the danger of aftershocks to pass.

Also staying at the Friendship Guest House were former Australian prime minister Gough Whitlam and his wife, who fled their seventh-floor room still dressed in their pajamas. "Outside, people were digging under the rubble," Mrs. Whitlam later told reporters in Tokyo. "Whole facades of buildings had come down." As for the guest house, said Whitlam, it was "literally split down the middle, with a one-foot gap separating the two parts."

Some of Tientsin's older buildings collapsed completely, but modern structures on the whole held up well, and deaths were few. In Peking, too, a number of older buildings toppled and about 100 people were killed. But although the Chinese capital was badly shaken, most of its citizens escaped with little more

While aftershocks rattle Peking, *a young resident of the Chinese capital waits out the quake emergency in a drainpipe.*

268

Within days of the quake, *an army of workers descended on Tangshan's ruins to begin the massive job of cleaning up.*

than a bad fright and perhaps a showering of plaster dust and broken glass. Amid the torrential rains that began to fall a few hours after the initial shock, many of the capital's 6 million residents abandoned their homes and moved outdoors.

In the still-trembling streets of Peking, millions of people took refuge under makeshift shelters and tents.

For about 24 hours after the first shock struck, China's news media made no mention of the disaster. Unaware of the magnitude of the earthquake or where exactly it was centered, the citizens of Peking relied on the word-of-mouth instructions of police and neighborhood officials to stay outdoors.

Within 48 hours, more than 125 major aftershocks were recorded in northeastern China, the strongest occurring some 16 hours after the initial tremor. None,

however, matched that first killer in sheer destructive power. And nowhere were the effects felt more acutely than in Tangshan. Thanks to the official veil of silence surrounding the disaster, it took years for the outside world to piece together the extent of Tangshan's tragedy. But preliminary reports from foreign survivors evacuated to Peking indicated that the city had been completely leveled. According to later estimates, 95 percent of Tangshan's civil buildings and 80 percent of its industrial plants suffered severe damage. Site of China's third largest coal complex, Tangshan before the earthquake had been a place of giant smokestacks, some of them emblazoned, ironically, with Mao Tse-tung's stern admonition: "Prepare for war and natural disasters." After the earthquake, fleeing foreigners could see only one smokestack still standing over the rubble of Tangshan.

Traditionally reluctant to report disasters, China's Communist leaders were particularly anxious to minimize the impact of the Tangshan earthquake, coming as it did at a time of great political turmoil. At first the

Central Committee of the Chinese Communist Party would concede only that the quake had "caused great losses to people's life and property." But unofficial estimates of the number of people killed in the disaster ranged as high as 750,000 to 1 million—inflated figures given added credence by the party's obsessive concern for secrecy. Three years later an official death toll was finally published, placing the number of fatalities at a lower, but still calamitous, 242,000, the majority in Tangshan. But the death toll tells only part of the story. According to some estimates, the earthquake seriously injured as many as 164,000 people and was responsible for some 1,700 paraplegics and 2,600 orphaned children. And, of course, almost everyone who survived in Tangshan was left to mourn the loss of a relative or friend.

Several factors contributed to the high mortality rate. The earthquake was an extremely powerful one, and its epicenter was located almost directly beneath Tangshan, a city of more than 1 million people. The first shock came at night, when most of the population was asleep, and it came suddenly, with no warning. In fact, the Tangshan earthquake was something of an embarrassment for Chinese science, which over the years had developed a sophisticated system of earthquake prediction based on the observation of strange behavior in animals and sudden changes in the level and temperature of well water. In February 1975, an accurate forecast of a major quake in Liaoning Province had saved thousands of lives. This time, however, no one warned the people of Tangshan.

The Chinese turned down all offers of outside help as they mounted a massive relief effort led by the army.

Within hours of the quake, military reconnaissance aircraft were surveying the damage in Tangshan, and by 5 P.M., food, water canisters, clothing, and medical supplies were being airdropped to the city's beleaguered survivors. The next day, an enormous double convoy was moving rescue workers and emergency

The heart of Tangshan *was leveled in seconds by the deadliest quake to hit this quake-prone land in four centuries.*

supplies from Peking to Tangshan and evacuating thousands of injured people to hospitals in the capital. Within two weeks 100,000 army troops, 30,000 medical personnel, and 30,000 construction workers had come to the aid of Tangshan.

At first, the grim task of burying the dead was undertaken by surviving friends and neighbors, but as the body count and the risk of epidemic grew, the army had to step in. Sealed in plastic bags, corpses were stacked in trucks and driven to a mass burial site outside the city limits.

Many Chinese accounts of the earthquake and the acts of heroism it inspired are colored by Maoist political rhetoric. Among those who took to heart the party directive that all people should "plunge into the anti-quake fight with a firm and indomitable will . . . guided by Chairman Mao's revolutionary line," was Che Cheng-min of Tangshan, whose story, quoted in *The New York Times* on August 30, 1976, made the front page of *The People's Daily* of Peking: "Immediately after the earthquake, Che Cheng-min dragged himself from the ruins of his wrecked house. Seeing him, his 13-year-old daughter and his 16-year-old son cried, 'Quick, Daddy, come and save us.' As he was about to go to their aid, Che Cheng-min heard another call for help coming from [the home of] Chiu Kuang-yu, secretary of the Lu Pei neighborhood party committee."

Heeding the call of duty, Che Cheng-min went to the aid of the party official. "When he returned home," concluded the newspaper account, "Che Cheng-min found his two children dead. But he felt neither remorse nor grief. In the interests of the people of the neighborhood and in the majority interest, he did not hesitate to sacrifice his own children."

The often heavy-handed rhetoric, however, cannot disguise the true courage and dedication displayed by many Chinese in one of their darkest hours. Among the heroes of the earthquake was the Tangshan police official Ho Shu-shen. Ho and his 16-year-old son had escaped from their house just before the quake brought it down. Digging through the rubble, they managed to rescue Ho's wife and two other sons, but failed to reach his 14-year-old daughter in time. Barefoot and clad only in his underwear, Ho grabbed his pistol and ventured into the leveled city. With the help of his sons, the veteran police captain dug 19 of his neighbors out of the ruins of their homes and then organized another rescue team from among the men he had just brought to safety. Working tirelessly, Ho set up a neighborhood police command post to bring a semblance of order to a community in chaos and increasingly plagued by looters. Over the next few

Fear of recurring quakes kept Peking's people outdoors for days after the first tremor hit (above).

Quake sensors (right) were developed in China about A.D. 130. In a quake the pendulum swings toward the source of the shock, causing a ball to drop from dragon to toad.

days, Ho reported, some 70 hard-core looters were arrested and held in makeshift jails.

In China, a land that has endured more than its share of seismic disasters, earthquakes have long been viewed as omens of political upheaval. According to traditional Chinese beliefs, the trembling of the earth could signify that the ruling dynasty had lost its heavenly mandate and was due for an overthrow. China's Communist rulers dismissed such notions as superstitious nonsense, but superstitions die hard in China. And this time, those who held to the ancient theories seem to have been vindicated. Six weeks after the Tangshan earthquake, Mao Tse-tung was dead and a new era for China had begun.

For nearly three years, the Chinese government debated Tangshan's future, with some officials arguing against rebuilding the city in an area prone to earthquakes. In 1979, however, the decision was made to resurrect Tangshan on its original site, and by 1985 some 185,000 families had been rehoused there. Today, although a new, more quake-resistant Tangshan has emerged from the rubble of the old, the city and many of its citizens still bear the physical and psychic scars of those terrible 23 seconds in 1976.

The Fury of Mount St. Helens

Snowcapped peak obliterated in spectacular explosion

TO GENERATIONS OF AMERICANS, volcanic eruptions were exotic spectacles set in distant lands, pouring out rivers of red-hot lava that were fearsome to behold but could be escaped at a walking pace. Such a casual view was understandable, since no known eruption in the 48 contiguous United States had ever claimed a human life. But on May 18, 1980, all that changed. With a small army of scientists, television crews, and curious bystanders on hand, Mount St. Helens in eastern Washington State gave America—and the rest of the world—an unprecedented display of raw volcanic ferocity. The eruption that sunny morning killed all forms of life in a fan-shaped area 17 miles long. It scarred and distorted the landscape, choked lakes and riverbeds, and belched black ash and dust that blanketed parts of three states.

Mount St. Helens, named for an 18th-century British diplomat, is one of 15 volcanoes in the Cascade Range, which dominates the landscape from northern California to British Columbia. Mount Rainier, Mount Hood, Mount Baker (which stirred briefly in 1975), and the rest of these beautiful peaks have all been built up by lava and debris from volcanic eruptions that began millions of years ago. The area around Mount St. Helens was a nature lover's paradise, its streams alive with trout and salmon, its forests populated by elk, black-tailed deer, and mountain lions. The serene, snow-capped peak itself, rising 9,667 feet, was so symmetrical that it was sometimes called the Mount Fuji of America.

But beneath its exquisite surface, Mount St. Helens was up to no good. To predict activity at quiescent volcano sites is nearly impossible—a "prediction" in geological terms means a comparatively precise statement of the time, place, nature, and size of an expected event. But in 1978 two geologists had issued a "forecast," too imprecise to be called a prediction, that an eruption was likely to occur at Mount St. Helens, which had been dormant for more than a century. They could not say when it would happen, but this was clearly a mountain to watch.

The first signal of something brewing was a series of earthquake tremors northwest of the peak, beginning on March 20, 1980, and recurring as often as 40 times an hour. On March 27 came an eruption that shot ash and steam 6,500 feet over the summit. Rumbling noises issued from the belly of the mountain, cracks were noted on its surface, and a second crater, 220 feet in diameter, appeared.

Now the volcano watch was on in earnest. Teams of earth scientists moved in, most from the U.S. Geological Survey (USGS), which set up a command post at its observatory in nearby Vancouver, Washington. Close behind the scientists were reporters and sightseers eager to be on hand for the big bang. A variety of aircraft flew about, photographing surface changes, sampling emitted gases, and peering into the crater, which kept widening and deepening. All manner of monitoring devices—seismographs, tiltmeters, thermal gauges—were implanted at selected sites.

Most ominous of all was a bulge on the north slope that grew larger every day.

Observers were particularly fascinated by a bulge that appeared high on the mountainside and grew at a rate of 5 feet per day, until it stood out 300 feet or more from the slope around it. The bulge pointed menacingly north toward Spirit Lake at the base of the mountain, on the far shore of which were a Boy Scout camp and a number of vacation lodges. The governor of Washington, Dixy Lee Ray, set up a "red zone"

Like a monster breaking loose, Mount St. Helens erupted with an explosive ferocity never before captured on film.

radiating five miles from the peak; she ordered residents out and roads leading in blocked. There was a good deal of grumbling about this from evacuees and the curious, a number of whom slipped around the blockade. One outspoken dissenter was 83-year-old Harry Truman, who adamantly refused to vacate his home on Spirit Lake. As strong-willed and sharp-tongued as his presidential namesake, Truman had lived with his lake and his mountain for 53 years, and no official order or threat of nature was going to budge him. As it turned out, the only thing wrong with the red zone was that it was not big enough.

The morning of Sunday, May 18, dawned clear and beautiful, a fitting day to celebrate the opening of the trout season and renew the joys of spring in the wilderness. But at 8:32 A.M. Mount St. Helens blew out, almost instantly turning a picture-postcard scene into one of unearthly ugliness.

As seismologists would later determine, the catastrophe was kicked off by four nearly simultaneous events. A moderate earthquake shivered not far below the mountain; at once the north slope collapsed into Spirit Lake and the Toutle River in one of the greatest landslides in history. The effect was like the lifting of a pressure valve. Instantaneously, searing gases were released from the magma, groundwater turned to steam, and they combined in a tremendous horizontal explosion through the newly exposed north face— which in turn opened a vertical vent and triggered a second explosive eruption, this one straight up, producing a 12-mile-high column of smoke and ash.

The horizontal blast, following the ground-hugging wave of fluid and fragments from the avalanche, swept 17 miles north at speeds of up to 250 miles an hour. The onslaught scoured more than 200 square miles of terrain, uprooting or knocking down some 6 million mature trees. A few of the 62 people known dead in this area may have been crushed by trees, but most were probably suffocated by ash, as if a cannon had fired wet sand into their mouths and lungs.

One of the dead was 30-year-old David A. Johnston, who had been among the first of the USGS team to reach Mount St. Helens. Johnston had volunteered to descend into the crater for ground samples—"taking the dragon's pulse," as it was called. On the fateful morning he seemed safe enough at his observation post 5½ miles from the summit. He was watching the ominous bulge, and when he saw it move he shouted into his radio, "Vancouver! Vancouver! This is it!" The words marked the last moment of Johnston's life.

The power and heat of the blast defied imagination. Across Spirit Lake, at the spot where Harry Truman had defiantly stood, there was suddenly 40 feet of boiling mud. Boulders more than 60 feet in diameter were blown or carried five miles. A mobile home driven by a couple to a lakeside 11 miles north of Mount St. Helens was hurled 600 feet. All the plastic parts of a truck parked 13 miles north of the mountain melted. Sixteen miles from the blast, fishermen on the Green River were severely burned and survived only by jumping into the water. The lofty, symmetrical peak itself was reduced to a cratered hulk 1,300 feet lower than before.

Gruesome as it was, the death toll could have been worse if the blast had come on a weekday, when some 300 lumberjacks would have been working in the devastated area, thinking they were safely beyond the danger zone. Luckily, too, the resulting floods did not reach their full potential. But the flooding was bad enough, due to "mudflow"—a boiling slurry of water, ash, and fragmented rock that whooshed north under the blast, slammed into a ridge beyond Spirit Lake, and rocketed west into the Toutle River valley. There it formed a hummocky pile 13 miles long, a mile wide, and hundreds of feet deep, squeezing both north and south forks of the Toutle into record-setting floods. Leaking from this deposit, a gritty brown gruel ran on down to clog up the Cowlitz River and shoal up the

great Columbia, so that its navigation channel was reduced from 40 feet to 15, and seagoing ships were isolated in Portland harbor.

Along the way, the mudflow dragged at least three people to their deaths and swept up enough debris and cut timber to form a 20-mile logjam on the Columbia. It also killed millions of Chinook salmon and steelhead trout, some by overheating the Toutle and the Cowlitz, many by clogging their gills with a coating of ash.

The first wave of the crisis passed, but the threat of widespread flooding remained.

The blowdown of trees, the smothering of vegetation, the new ash surface of the slopes, all invited erosion; and Mount St. Helens went on erupting intermittently and throwing out mudflows. With the next spring rains in mind, the U.S. Army Corps of Engineers worked on the battered landscape through summer, fall, and winter, building dams and levees, channeling water into safe courses, and dredging—above all, dredging. By November 1981 they had removed 100 million cubic yards of debris from the Toutle, Cowlitz, and Columbia rivers. After many months and at the cost of $250 million, they had cleared the channels and reopened the Columbia to shipping.

To the devastation on the ground, Mount St. Helens added a colossal nuisance through the sky. Its eruption sent aloft a plume of ash and fragments so huge that it made its own lightning—in long and terrible flashes. The cloud sped east on the wind and came down like an ebony snowfall over eastern Washington, Idaho, and western Montana. Before noon, the sky over Yakima, a city of 51,000 some 85 miles east of the volcano, turned from sunny clear to midnight black—darker than midnight, for headlights could not pierce the shroud of particles.

A week after the first eruption, and again 18 days later, new spouts of ash streamed west, reaching northwest Oregon and spreading a cursed blanket over other regions of Washington. Wherever it fell, dust clogged generators and engines, choked air filters, and otherwise made travel nearly impossible. Governor Ray reported that half the state's patrol cars were immobilized. As breezes or traffic stirred up the deposit, people bought or improvised face masks. The stuff would not melt, and water simply moved it around. Spring

Witness became victim *when a photographer from a local newspaper was trapped in his car and suffocated by volcanic ash.*

Six hundred thousand tons of ash fell on Yakima, Washington (above), in the wake of the eruption. Traffic ground to a halt and streetlights burned all day in the ghostly, dust-filled haze. The greatest challenge was to remove the abrasive fallout (left), much of which ended up in landfills.

crops were damaged, though not fatally; energetic blowing and hosing of trees saved Washington's famous apples. Even more fortunate, the ash proved nontoxic. There was, however, a poisoning of the spirit by frustration, by an awareness that science, which had built up a comfortable civilization, could do nothing to control this destructive outburst of nature.

The aftermath of the disaster, however, provided a reminder of nature's resiliency. Some vegetation had survived after all in the blast area, especially where snow was deep. Soon poking through the gray ash were weedy plants such as fireweed, upright huckleberries, and everlasting lupine—this last important because its roots converted nitrogen into plant food. Avalanche lilies appeared, true symbols of resurrection. Ants and gophers were also survivors and helpfully mixed dead ash with nutrient soil along their underground routes. Migrant spores added to the vegetation; migrant elk began to forage where 5,200 of their kind, along with 6,000 black-tailed deer, had been annihilated. Frogs and salamanders were seen hopping and scurrying along stream banks. Farther

from the epicenter, willows and red alder took root near small ponds.

The public lands surrounding Mount St. Helens are now a 100,000-acre national monument and a tourist attraction. They are also a laboratory in which nature has been allowed to work on its own. Nature has done very well. Within three years of the big eruption, 90 percent of plant species that had originally inhabited the area could again be found.

For scientists, Mount St. Helens offered the chance of a lifetime to develop and improve predictive techniques. After the big blast, the prediction record on continuing activity there was impressive: of 24 eruptions in the next seven years, most were accurately predicted, sometimes within days of their occurrence. It is possible to forecast that other peaks in the Cascades will erupt within the next few centuries. But as one geologist has remarked: "A few centuries is our standard of measurement. It could happen tomorrow." Whenever the next one does come, mankind will learn again that beneath the earth's crust is hellfire, but in it there is also enduring nourishment.

Killer Heat Wave

Hundred-degree-plus weather bedevils the United States

AMERICANS, particularly those living in the Sun Belt, have learned to expect endless days of heat every summer. But the long, hot summer of 1980 punished the nation with one of the costliest heat waves in history. Before the heat ended in early September, it had scorched states from Texas to the Dakotas and all the way up the East Coast to New England. Week after terrible week, the sun beat down through cloudless skies, producing record triple-digit temperatures that

Record temperatures *were set in more than half a dozen states.*

killed crops, dried up reservoirs, felled livestock, buckled hundreds of miles of roads, burned out machinery, set off fires, overloaded city water and electric utilities, and turned many buildings into ovens. Worst of all, the heat wave caused terrible human suffering, claiming 1,265 lives, and accounted for property damage of more than $20 billion.

Meteorologists had no difficulty pinpointing the bizarre combination of atmospheric conditions responsible for the unusual weather. Contrary to its normal summer pattern, the jet stream—the high-altitude river of wind that sweeps from west to east across the continent at 150 miles per hour 7 to 8 miles above the earth—snaked well north of its usual path along the 50th parallel. At the same time, three giant high-pressure systems formed, and without the jet stream to push them along, they stayed in place: one in the Pacific north of Hawaii, a second over the south-central United States, and the third in the Mid-Atlantic states. Together they constituted an enormous dome of stationary, high-pressure air that deflected the usual succession of small-scale, cloud-bearing weather fronts and random storms that give summer weather rain and variability most years. And without clouds to absorb the heat of the sun, the earth baked, growing progressively hotter and drier each day. At the same time, as the land roasted, air trapped beneath the dome of high pressure was continuously being heated by compression as it gradually drifted down through the atmosphere.

For more than a month these deadly climatic conditions remained locked in place over a quarter of the earth's surface. Even Europe was affected by the stationary highs. While Americans baked under a blanket of hot, humid air, people on the other side of the North Atlantic suffered through a miserably cold,

rainy summer. Why? Because the jet stream, flowing so far to the north, was bringing with it cool Canadian air laden with moisture.

The heat wave began in earnest during the third week in June, when temperatures topped 100° in the Dallas–Fort Worth region of Texas. (And they remained there—over 100°—for the next 42 days, peaking at 113° on June 26 and 27.) Texans, who have survived more than their share of adverse weather over the years, tried at first to make light of the situation. "I got to go home and boil some water so I can have a cool drink," one quipped in the Wichita Falls area as the thermometer hit 117° on June 28. Another claimed: "Well, you ain't gonna believe this, but I saw a mockingbird pull a worm out of my wife's flower bed this morning, and the pore little devil had to use a pot holder he found on the clothesline."

By the second week in July, the bizarre weather system was producing uncommonly high temperatures in most of the central third of the nation. On July 13, records were set in Memphis, Tennessee (108°), and in Augusta, Georgia (107°), and Atlanta (105°). One Atlantan, Willie Jones, was brought to the hospital with a body temperature of 115.7°. Packed in cold, wet sheets and ice, he somehow recovered, earning a place in the *Guinness Book of World Records* as having had the highest body temperature ever recorded and the nickname Jones the Human Torch. On July 16 the heat wave reached New York City, sending the mercury up to the 99° mark on the first day, up to 101° four days later.

As officials at the National Oceanic and Atmospheric Administration reported, the intense heat made everyone uncomfortable. But in terms of fatalities, the elderly, the sick, and the poor suffered most, mainly because they lacked access to air conditioners and prompt medical attention when they needed it.

Normally, the body employs a number of defense mechanisms to protect itself against excessive heat. Sweating helps, of course, cooling by the process of evaporation. At the same time, as blood vessels just under the skin enlarge, more blood can circulate closer to the surface, thereby releasing heat. Excessive heat and humidity, however, can stall the process by hindering the evaporation of perspiration. The heart can also become stressed, and an attack may result. In addition, excessive sweating can lead to dehydration. For older people with existing health problems, such as heart disease or circulatory difficulties, the dangers are even greater.

Missouri, which has a disproportionately high population of the elderly, called on the National Guard, the Red Cross, and state and local relief agencies to aid victims. In some neighborhoods, rescuers went door-to-door, distributing free electric fans, checking on the health of occupants, and trying to persuade some to take refuge in air-conditioned auditoriums and armories. Nonetheless, 311 Missourians died of heat-related causes during the emergency, the majority of them in St. Louis and Kansas City, where the poorly ventilated, old brick buildings in which many elderly people lived turned into virtual bake ovens. Small consolation was to be found in the fact that the Kansas City murder rate plummeted, presumably because people were too exhausted to confront one another violently.

The scorching heat also dealt a terrible blow to livestock and farm crops. The poultry farmers of Arkansas, Texas, and Florida were especially hard hit. About 8 million broilers suffocated in one week in Arkansas. Farmers with livestock fared scarcely better. Unable to graze or water their herds, many stockmen chose to slaughter their cattle prematurely rather than risk losing them entirely. Laying hens stopped producing eggs, dairy cows went dry, and pigs literally dropped dead from the heat.

In parts of the Grain Belt, farmers kept a death vigil as thousands of acres of planted crops withered and turned to dust. Long before the summer heat wave, many areas had experienced months of abnormally low precipitation. Now, when irrigation might have helped save some crops, the wells were dry. As the days wore on, more than 80 percent of corn, cotton, soybean, and wheat crops were lost in some areas.

Even zoos and amusement parks suffered from poor attendance as well as overheated animals, and baseball teams unlucky enough to play on artificial grass were subjected to their own private hell: the plastic green turf underfoot could get so hot (146° in one test) that it was painful to walk on. In one midwestern ballpark, a bucket of ice water was stored in the dugout so that players could soak their feet, shoes and all, between innings.

Weathermen watched their instruments day after day, hoping for some sign of a break in the system. Finally, late in July, a dense mass of clouds could be seen forming high over the Atlantic. As it drifted toward the Caribbean, it began to assume the classic pinwheel configuration of a hurricane. Residents along the Gulf Coast began to shore up defenses in preparation for the arrival of the storm named Allen. On August 9, Allen hit the mainland, killing three people and causing $750 million in damages. But the storm had the beneficial effect that meteorologists had hoped for: it broke the back of the heat wave. Temperatures in Texas alone dropped 25 degrees. "We've been blessed," Governor Bill Clements exclaimed gratefully. It took another three weeks before the high temperatures that had been plaguing the East ended.

Believe it or not, a Texas cow makes a meal of a cactus. With mounting feed shortages, ranchers resorted to extreme measures, among them torching the spines of the cacti to make these bristly desert plants edible and rushing their herds to market before the animals died of starvation. In the end, consumers were hit with higher meat prices at the supermarket.

277

Agony in the Mezzogiorno

Earthquake cripples an ill-fated region of Italy

I T HAPPENED in early December 1980, in a densely populated area about half the size of Maryland that lies east and south of Naples. This is perhaps the poorest part of a region with a history of hard times — the land south of Rome known as the Mezzogiorno.

The Italian word *mezzogiorno* means "high noon" — that scorching time of day when the heat of the sun brings most activity to a halt until midafternoon. But then the work begins again, exactly as it has for centuries. The old, eroded ridges of the Apennines,

sunbaked in the summer and battered by merciless rains and snowstorms in winter, are not good for much except the most primitive kind of farming, and everyone who lives there has to toil year-round to scratch out the barest livelihood. In the evenings, those lucky enough to have television sets can see nightly reminders that in many other parts of the world, life just does not have to be that hard.

If the climate and terrain have made life difficult in the Mezzogiorno, so did some of the various rulers who conquered it. The first despots were the Normans in the 12th century. Germans then ruled for a brief time before being ousted by the French, who imposed taxes on livestock and appropriated small farms to merge into huge feudal estates, on which the former owners of the land were the laborers. The Spanish Bourbons took over the Mezzogiorno in the 18th century, but the old feudal patterns remained, and real land reform was not begun until after the end of World War II.

At the same time that improvements in the standard of living were slowly coming to the region, beneath the Mezzogiorno two huge sections of the earth's crust were invisibly grinding toward each other at the speed of only a few centimeters a year. Then, without warning, on a quiet Sunday evening in the late fall of 1980, one or both of the crust plates shifted a few inches and met head-on. Those few inches of movement were enough to trigger the worst earthquake to hit Europe in 65 years. And death descended on the Apennines.

The quake began at 7:35 P.M. on November 23 and was measured at 6.8 on the Richter scale by seismographs around the world. Within seconds, whole towns fell apart into mounds of screaming people, animals, furniture, and building rubble. Throughout that long, terrible night, all of southern Italy continued to lurch and tremble like a giant going insane; then

A stark monument to the destructive force of the quake, one damaged building remains atop a rubble-strewn hillside that had been the village of Calabritto.

__No words are needed__ to read the shock and grief on the face of a dazed survivor. In Avellino (right) and other hard-hit towns, makeshift relief posts were the only source of hot food for many cold weeks to come.

more than 200 cities, towns, and villages were rocked by aftershocks that thundered up from the earth beneath them for a week.

Just outside Salerno, as he drove along the Tyrrhenian seacoast, Luigi Iannone looked through the windshield of his car with astonishment and fear. "I saw the buildings move like the waves of the sea, and the electric cables and trolley lines dropped onto my car," he said later. "It was something terrible."

The hillside town of Laviano, just over a mile from the quake's epicenter, had suddenly ceased to exist.

Thirteen miles southeast of the epicenter, the 15th-century Church of Santa Maria Assunta in Balvano collapsed on a 300-member congregation, many of them mothers with children who were preparing for their first communion. Eighty-one died.

Even before that terrible November day, a quarter of all the buildings in Naples were considered unsafe for human habitation, so when the quake struck, thousands rushed out into the streets to stay there until the shaking stopped. Some 150 miles away from the earthquake's epicenter near Laviano, the big Leonardo da Vinci Airport at Rome ceased operations as air controllers scrambled down from their 195-foot tower while it swayed in the darkness.

The terrible toll of life, however, was taking place inland. In Balvano the village priest, Father Salvatore Pagliuca, said that "it was like the end of the world—enough to drive you mad." One of the first photographs to come out of the stricken area showed the dead of Balvano laid out in a perfect line in one of the few open spaces left in the town—with all feet pointing skyward from the ends of bodies shrouded by whatever bits of blankets and cloth could be found.

That heartrending image was recorded sometime after a visiting missionary, Father Ettore Santoriello, was interrupted in the midst of celebrating Mass and watched in speechless disbelief as the altar of the church shook, just before an entire wall, followed by the roof, collapsed on the screaming congregation.

In the same village, 90-year-old Donata Zarillo was knocked to the floor of her kitchen and pinned there in the darkness as her house fell in on her. Thirty hours later, a rescue worker, Giancarlo Rocchi, heard a faint tapping of wood underneath the mess and, digging down, found the old lady still alive. "She was inside, poor thing," he recalled, "and we had a hard time convincing her it was OK now to come outside." In the town of Avellino, the husband of Alba Corbelli tapped a rescue worker on the arm and asked him to please try to find a photograph of his wife and three children, who had been trapped in the wreckage of their home. "Help me so I won't be left alone without anything to remember my family," he pleaded. Minutes later, his wife, with one leg crushed, was placed alive in Corbelli's arms. But the children were dead.

At Conza della Campania, 80 percent of the town's 2,500 inhabitants were killed by the earthquake. "God should not punish us like this," cried Antonio Piccino. "In 30 seconds everything I worked for for 30 years was gone." Someone finally got through on the telephone to Santomenna. "Do you have supplies of electricity and water?" the official asked, and a shaken voice answered, "We don't have a town here."

In Conza, where bodies were piled up in the streets, nothing of value remained. "The only thing we have found in one piece was an album of classical records," one villager said.

Although hundreds died immediately in this part of the Mezzogiorno, death did not always come swiftly. One 26-year-old woman evoked the horrors of the earthquake for millions of Italians when she recounted her own ordeal on television, telling how she and

The solitary figure of a man cautiously picking his way through the ruins captures the plight of all those trying to function in the aftermath of a disaster, searching instinctively for familiar objects, lost valuables, memories of a loved one—anything that will help them begin the process of putting their shattered lives back together again.

her mother were trapped for 72 hours. "We hugged each other helplessly," she said. "In the darkness, we tried to scrape away the dirt and make a place in which to breathe. Mother prayed and I heard her say, 'Oh God, let me die an hour before my daughter because I could not stand to see her die.' We spoke of many things, important things. When they pulled us out, I felt my mother's face. It was cold. This told me she was near the end, and I burst into tears."

In its toll of lives and property, the 1980 earthquake was devastating enough: more than 3,000 dead, 7,000 injured, 1,500 missing, and 120,000 homeless—just as the first winter storms were due to begin howling down through the passes of the Apennines. But devastation also took another form—shock and anger at the government's sluggish and disorganized response to the disaster. Hundreds died in the hours following the main tremor because authorities in Rome were slow to react, and when they did, the rough terrain of the devastated area made it difficult for medical personnel and vehicles to get through.

Throughout the Mezzogiorno, bitterness ran deep. In Sant'Angelo dei Lombardi, 15 hours after the quake had hit, a health official radioed an angry message. "Eighty percent of the town has been destroyed," he said, "hundreds of people are buried under the rubble, but so far no one has come. . . . The road is open. Why has no one come?"

In Sinerchia, the first relief shipments of food that got through were met with expressions of derision and outright hatred. "There are people under there screaming 'Help, don't let me die like this!' " one furious villager said. "And then they bring us food."

In a nearby village, Mario Vitale was loading a car with supplies for the heavily stricken Sant'Angelo. His comment reflected the opinions of countless others: "The government should have brought barrels of milk by now, but our government doesn't work. It never has, and that's why we're taking these supplies up to Sant'Angelo ourselves."

For hours after the quake, state-run television assured viewers: "There are no reports of damage or loss of life."

Any official uncertainty was dispelled when President Alessandro Pertini flew into the stricken Apennines by helicopter. Few politicians have ever had a more dismal ride. Pertini's chopper flew over fog-covered roads jammed with relatives trying to reach the area and families in villages that had, for all practical purposes, ceased to exist. At Laviano, one man screamed out to him that "the helicopter should have arrived yesterday for the rescue, not today for the spectacle," and at Potenza, the shaken president could hardly speak. "There are no words," he murmured to the silent crowd that stood about him. "They die upon the lips."

Back in the capital city, bitter charges and counter-charges by rival political factions nearly brought the government down. Then, under the experienced leadership of the undersecretary for foreign affairs, Giuseppe Zamberletti, who had led rescue operations after the severe 1976 earthquake in northern Italy, the government started to move. By December 12, it had placed 37,000 of the homeless in tents, 43,000 in trailers, 37,000 in railroad cars, and 53,000 in hotel rooms and ships along the coast. Forty-four thousand relief and rescue workers were now on hand in the Apennines. Some helped to build walkways in emergency campsites that were already ankle-deep in water. Others used bulldozers to flatten out ruined sections of a village or town before spraying formaldehyde over everything to slow the decay of bodies and prevent outbreaks of cholera, typhoid, and other diseases that can breed rapidly in such unsanitary conditions.

Help was also coming in from many parts of the world. In the United States, President Jimmy Carter released $1.5 million for emergency help, and Congress, moving almost as swiftly, voted a total of $50 million in aid, with $40 million earmarked for long-term construction. In the words of Sen. Frank Church of Idaho, chairman of the Senate Foreign Relations Committee, the gift was meant as "an expression of love from one country to another."

The Australian government offered to match every dollar donated privately by its citizens. Sparsely populated Iceland approved $10 million for Italian relief. South Korea and Japan (the latter keenly aware of a major earthquake's power) made donations through the Red Cross. Italy's European neighbors pledged well over a billion dollars in aid.

As people have been doing throughout history after major disasters, the people of the Mezzogiorno reacted in two distinct ways. First, they made valiant attempts to get their lives into some kind of order once again. Second, no matter how devastated their home areas had become, they made it clear that they wanted to remain there.

Three weeks after the quake, for example, survivors in Conza della Campania formed a procession and walked quietly through the tents and trailer homes where they now lived toward a corrugated iron shack in which they could celebrate the birth of Jesus at a makeshift altar. At Balvano, where the rubble in the main square was still dyed red with human blood, villagers put up a Christmas tree where there was still some free space available. At Solofra, in Avellino Province, a visiting priest performed the first marriage ceremony to be held since the earthquake, in a tent put up to give the bride and groom some protection from a driving rainstorm outside. In mountainous Calabritto, the church's regular candlesticks were missing—buried somewhere—so the priest used empty beer bottles to hold the tapers. And in hard-hit Potenza, even as searchers were digging out the dead and injured, a new life had begun when 39-year-old Lucia Pepe gave birth to her sixth child, a girl, in the front seat of a truck.

Although living normally was almost impossible in the makeshift housing, relatively few were willing to accept the government's offer of free hotel rooms and other space in villas along the coast. People were still willing to pile three generations of family into a tempo-

rary shelter 100 feet square; women took their dirty clothes to the outdoor cold-water fountains; in one town, a full year later, 1,300 survivors still waited their turn to use the four outdoor showers, which were kept locked up with a key that always seemed to be disappearing somewhere.

All this while winter winds roared down from the Alps or came whistling north from Sicily.

"We are not going away," said the mayor of Conza della Campania, "even though Rome and Naples seem to have forgotten that we are farmers, and need somewhere to store the hay and animals from our destroyed barns." And in Calitri, a town of 3,400 persons, an old man politely stopped a convoy of vans that had arrived to take villagers out of the storm-battered highlands and into hotels along the Amalfi coast. "You are a good and capable man, but don't come again," the old man said to the young police captain who was in charge of the relocation job. "This is where we lived, and this is where we want to die."

Like a gaping wound, the long trench filled with coffins became a common sight across the bleak landscape of Campania in the days following the quake.

A fireman hoses down *the remains of Flight 759, while police, fire, and medical personnel survey the grim scene.*

The Plane That Fell From the Sky

Explosive downdraft ends vacation flight in tragedy

"**P**OSITIVE CLIMB," observed Capt. Kenneth L. Mc-Cullers as his copilot, First Officer Donald A. Pierce, lifted the three-engine Boeing 727 off Runway 10 at New Orleans International Airport. "Gear up," replied Pierce. It was approximately 4:10 P.M., July 9, 1982, and despite blinding sheets of rain, Pan American Flight 759—a weekend gambler's special originating in Miami and bound for Las Vegas and San Diego—had taken off without apparent incident. For a few more seconds, the flight seemed steady on. Then suddenly the nose of the 105-ton plane, newly loaded with more than 8,000 gallons of highly flammable jet fuel, began to tip downward.

"Come on back," ordered Captain McCullers, urging his copilot to pull back the controls in order to raise the nose. "You're sinking, Don. Come on back." These were the last words recorded on the flight tapes later retrieved from the doomed plane's tail section.

Captain McCullers had barely stopped talking when the plane, which never climbed above 150 feet, clipped the top of a tall tree less than half a mile beyond the runway. Eyewitnesses later reported seeing the plane's left wing tilt toward the ground, as though the pilot was trying to bank north in order to avoid the New Orleans suburb of Kenner and come down instead in nearby Lake Pontchartrain. But McCullers and his crew did not make it. Seconds after hitting the tree, Flight 759 sliced into a power line, veered farther to the left, and then plowed through a four-block section of Kenner, leveling 13 houses and scattering deadly fireballs and chunks of wreckage in all directions.

> **"There was a wall of flame all across the street,"** recalled a Kenner resident. **"I thought I was in hell."**

When Flight 759—or what was left of it—finally came to rest, all 8 crew members, all 138 passengers (including a woman who was seven months pregnant), and 8 Kenner residents were dead. For the victims of the crash, death was surely instantaneous. To judge from the positions of the charred bodies

282

flung over the blasted area, some parents and children aboard the ill-fated craft may have had just enough time to reach out for one another before the flames engulfed them.

As ambulances, firemen, and other rescue workers converged on the still-burning wreckage site, one tiny ray of hope shone through the chaos and despair. Standing right in the path of the out-of-control airliner, the Trahan house had been reduced to a smoldering heap of rubble. Young Mrs. Trahan and her four-year-old daughter were dead, their bodies tossed some distance into the carnage. But two hours later, a sheriff's deputy digging through the wreckage of the house discovered a mattress "moving up and down." Lying underneath was 16-month-old Melissa Trahan, alive and unhurt except for the singed soles of her tiny feet.

Elsewhere, however, the horrors continued, unrelieved by any more miraculous survival stories. In three days of grueling, numbing work, scores of rescue workers filled 316 plastic bags with blackened bodies and parts of bodies. In one debris-choked swimming pool, searchers found 18 arms. In the oppressive summer heat, a sickening stench hung over the wreckage, and the clouds of flies grew so thick that the cleanup operation had to be halted three times so that the area could be sprayed. It took nearly a week to recover and cart off all recognizable bodies, personal property, and pieces of debris. Then, in a deliberate effort to erase the physical scars of the tragedy as quickly as possible, Kenner officials had the site bulldozed, covered with lime, and planted with 135 trees and shrubs.

In the process of identifying the victims of the crash, many poignant ironies came to light. Little things—a sudden change of heart, a car breaking down, a missing loaf of bread—often determined who lived and who died. Donald E. Fitzgerald had driven seven of his relatives to the New Orleans airport so they could fly to his father's funeral in Las Vegas. He, too, had planned to attend, but at the last minute he decided to stay home. As his grandmother and six aunts and uncles boarded Flight 759, Fitzgerald, living up to his long-time nickname, Lucky, drove off alone.

Two sisters and their three children were visiting friends in Florida when they learned of their brother's death in a motorcycle accident in San Diego. Deciding to drive across the country to the funeral, they rented a car and set off. When the vehicle broke down in Louisiana, a helpful family friend allowed the sisters to use her credit card to book seats on Flight 759. A few hours later, the friend had the grim task of telephoning a San Diego funeral home with more bad news for an already bereaved family.

On the ground in Kenner, 61-year-old Ted Weems had sat down to an early supper with his two school-age sons only to discover that they were out of bread and milk. When Weems said he would go to a nearby supermarket, the boys asked to accompany him. Hav-

ing made their purchases, father and sons were about to return home but decided to wait for the rain, now coming down in buckets, to subside. They were still waiting at the supermarket entrance when the exploding airliner demolished their house.

At the time it occurred, the tragedy of Pan Am Flight 759 was the second-worst air disaster in United States history. (It was later demoted to third worst.) It was also one of the most mysterious. For months, experts debated the possible cause of the crash as they sifted through the wreckage and tried to make sense

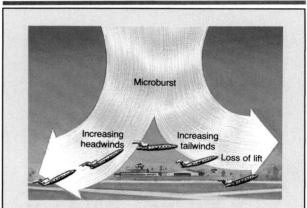

A microburst can cause a low-flying airplane to lose the lift it needs to stay in the air.

The Deadly Wind-Shear Factor

THE ABRUPT CHANGES in wind speed and direction known as wind shears have been blamed for several major airplane crashes, including the wreck of Pan Am Flight 759 near New Orleans. Of the many different types of wind-shear conditions, microbursts are especially dangerous to aircraft. These powerful downdrafts are relatively small (between ¼ and 2½ miles in diameter) and short-lived (2 to 10 minutes). But if they hit an airplane at low altitude, as during takeoff or landing, a pilot may not have sufficient time and space to correct the unexpected dive that results.

Triggered when a mass of air suddenly cools, microbursts usually, but not always, form at the leading edge of a thunderstorm. Because it is denser than the air around it, the cool air mass rapidly sinks. When it hits the ground, the column of air spreads out in all directions, much like water from a garden hose pointed straight down.

A plane entering a microburst first encounters a headwind, which helps lift the craft by increasing airflow around the wings. But as the plane passes the center of the microburst, a tailwind has the opposite effect, cutting airflow around the wings. If the reduction is significant, the aircraft may fall.

Spreading fire and death all around, the Pan Am Boeing 727 airliner crashed into a four-block area of Kenner, Louisiana (above), turning the New Orleans suburb into a little corner of hell. An investigator (left) combs through the wreckage for clues to the cause of the crash. More than eight months later, wind shear was named as the probable culprit.

of the barely audible cockpit conversations preserved by the plane's antiquated and poorly maintained flight recorders. Finally, on March 21, 1983, the National Transportation Safety Board announced that the "probable cause of the accident was the airplane's encounter during the lift-off and initial climb phase of flight with a microburst-induced wind shear, which imposed a downdraft and a decreasing headwind."

In other words, Flight 759 was brought down by an abrupt shift in the speed and direction of the wind—the phenomenon meteorologists call wind shear. Unpredictable and difficult to detect, wind shear is dangerous because in a matter of seconds it can disrupt the normal flow of air over and around an airliner's wings.

(It is this airflow that creates the "lift" needed to raise the plane into the air and keep it there.) For a plane in mid-flight, wind shear may cause only an inconsequential jiggle. Even if the craft starts to lose altitude, the pilot can usually regain control by taking a dive to pick up speed. But during the critical moments of takeoff and landing, when a pilot has no altitude to spare, wind shear can be, and often has been, lethal.

Particularly hazardous is the type of wind shear that felled Flight 759. A microburst is a sudden downdraft of wind that smashes into the ground and spreads out in a starburst pattern. A plane flying at low altitude into a microburst will first encounter strong headwinds, which usually enhance lift, followed by strong tailwinds, which may bring the plane down. It is rather like flying into an upside-down tornado.

Microbursts are often, but not always, associated with thunderstorms. On that fatal July afternoon in New Orleans, bolts of lightning flashed through sheets of driving rain and 20-mile-an-hour gusts of wind. Over the airport a column of thunderclouds reached 35,000 feet into the sky. According to the scenario pieced together by investigators, about 7½ minutes before the crash—while Pan Am Flight 759 was still taxiing toward Runway 10—the airport control tower issued "a low-level wind-shear alert in the Northeast quadrant."

A minute later, Captain McCullers requested a further report on wind conditions and received this reply: "Winds 70° at 17 knots, gusting to 23. Low-level wind-shear alert all quadrants. Frontal passage right now. We're right in the middle of everything." Noting that he had had "quite a few aborts" in the course of his career, McCullers reviewed with his crew the procedures for aborting a takeoff but apparently saw no reason to delay the flight. As the airliner roared down Runway 10, rain began to fall more heavily and the windshield wipers were set at full speed. Still the crew did not sense danger.

Most experts studying the New Orleans disaster did not fault Captain McCullers's decision to take off when he did. Wind shear is an invisible enemy, hard to detect in the best of circumstances. And at the New Orleans airport, circumstances were far from ideal. The five wind monitors then in place around the runways were hardly adequate to scan the entire airport area. To make matters worse, the sensor located in the swampy woods near Kenner was once again out of service, a victim, some thought, of stray hunters' bullets or deliberate vandalism. Thus, there was no way the Pan Am crew could have known the unlikely combination of factors conspiring against them.

For one thing, the microburst struck the airliner while it was still very low in the air and therefore especially vulnerable. Although very powerful, the microburst was relatively small (no more than two nautical miles in diameter). Had the plane been

slightly behind or in front of its actual location, the impact of the downdraft might have been mitigated—or avoided altogether. Then there was the matter of the clipped tree. The evidence seems to indicate that after encountering the downdraft, First Officer Pierce did manage to stop the airliner's descent and get the nose back up—but not enough to avoid the 52-foot-tall tree in its path. According to accident investigators, had the microburst been 25 percent weaker, the plane would have been able to skim safely over all the trees in the vicinity of the airport.

Against astronomical odds, Flight 759 found itself in precisely the wrong place at the wrong time.

If any good can be said to have come from the New Orleans catastrophe, it was that it focused the attention of the public on the dangers of wind shear and the need for vastly improved wind-shear detection systems at airports. At the time of the crash, Low Level Wind Shear Alert Systems were in place at 58 U.S. airports and were scheduled to be installed in more. But this equipment could detect only large-scale wind shear, not the smaller, more lethal microbursts that

brought down Flight 759. In the wake of the crash, federal aviation officials stepped up the development of a much more sophisticated system known as NEXRAD, for "next generation radar." The advanced radar units that are the basis of NEXRAD can detect microbursts, but to do so they must be adapted for airport use and then automated so that their information can be relayed instantly to control tower and cockpit.

Unfortunately, the cost and complexity of the radar system delayed start-up until 1987—too late to save the 133 passengers and crew of Delta Flight 191, brought down by wind shear as it tried to land at the Dallas-Fort Worth airport on August 2, 1985. Full implementation of NEXRAD is not expected to take place until the mid 1990's. Meanwhile, upgraded versions of the Low Level Wind Shear Alert System have been installed at more than 100 U.S. airports.

Also in direct response to the crash of Flight 759, microburst conditions have been programmed into the flight simulators used by professional pilots for retraining. Today commercial airline pilots can rehearse the maneuvers needed to recover lift in a wind-shear emergency. But it is one thing to be able to survive a computer-generated microburst and quite another actually to fly into an upside-down tornado. Efficient detection remains the key to conquering this most baffling and deadly of hazards to safe air travel.

285

Inferno in Australia

Bushfires race out of control across nation's southeast

A wall of fire *lights up the skies over the town of Lorne on the coast of Victoria. When the flames halted a convoy of fire trucks assembled from neighboring towns to aid Lorne, 30 local fire fighters struggled on their own to save their threatened community.*

IT WAS AUSTRALIA's worst natural disaster since Cyclone Tracy ravaged the city of Darwin nearly 10 years earlier, in December 1974, and the worst bushfire the country had known since the Black Friday conflagration of January 13, 1939. On February 16, 1983—Ash Wednesday, as fate would have it—raging fires driven by blast-furnace winds swept across thousands of square miles of southeastern Australia, devastating the states of Victoria and South Australia.

The tragedy had been building all summer. A long and severe drought had left many reservoirs and lakes nearly dry and reduced some stream flows to less than 20 percent of normal. In the bush—the eucalyptus- and scrub-covered lands that so many Australians call home—a lethal combination of heat and drought turned thousands of tons of dead leaves and other ground litter into explosive kindling. During most of the month preceding Ash Wednesday, officials in South Australia and Victoria rated the region's bushfire risk as "very high" to "extreme" and issued several bans against the lighting of bonfires, barbecues, and other unauthorized open fires. In the words of one fire official, southeastern Australia was "a firebomb waiting to go off."

On Ash Wednesday morning, commuters bustling to their jobs in Adelaide and Melbourne braced themselves for another unbearably hot, dry day. Searing winds gusting as high as 70 miles an hour swept south from the desert interior, bringing with them huge clouds of dust that hindered visibility and breathing. By 1:00 P.M. some thermometers topped 110° F, humidity dropped below 10 percent, and official weather reports described conditions as the "worst possible" for the spread of bushfires.

The first fires were reported outside Adelaide about 11:30 A.M. Although local volunteer fire brigades were able to handle many of the early fires, by midafternoon 20 major blazes were raging out of control in a 600-mile arc extending from the Clare Valley wine-growing district, 75 miles north of Adelaide, down through the Adelaide Hills and across the coasts of South Australia and Victoria to the Dandenong Hills, east of Melbourne. The spark that set off an individual fire was often difficult to identify, but two factors were implicated in several cases: arson and collapsed power cables blowing against trees in the fierce winds.

But no matter what its cause, once a bushfire gets going it is almost impossible to put out. In addition to masses of undergrowth, the bush contains another deadly fire hazard—vast stands of lovely eucalyptus

The road to Aireys Inlet, a Victoria community that was blown to bits by a fiery whirlwind, appears eerily peaceful in the wake of the devastating bushfire.

trees. At high temperatures, the oil in eucalyptus leaves breaks down into a flammable gas, causing the tree's crown to explode. Leaping from treetop to treetop, flames sweep through eucalyptus stands at highway speeds, rendering almost all resistance useless.

An army of 20,000 volunteer firemen and 1,200 forestry personnel, supported by 800 fire trucks and tankers, was mobilized to fight the fires. Some 200 bulldozers and excavators were put to work knocking down trees and creating firebreaks. Air-borne observers helped coordinate the fire fighting—that is, until wind and smoke drove the aircraft from the skies. As a fire brigade captain later commented, when a bushfire goes out of control "there is little that a thousand fire trucks and 10,000 fire fighters can do. Fire becomes a cataclysm creating its own wind and weather, a demon with a mind of its own."

As walls of fire advanced on their homes, thousands of people were forced to flee, often with little more than the clothing on their back. Murray Nicoll, a volunteer fire fighter and reporter for an Adelaide radio station, was helping to direct the escaping traffic near his home in the Adelaide Hills, when suddenly the air filled with smoke and ash, and an ominous red glow colored the sky to the west. Shocked at the speed with which the fire was advancing, Nicoll joined a group of about 20 fire fighters, women, and children taking cover behind the rear wall of a nearby farmhouse. While another fire fighter sprayed the children with water, Nicoll reached for a two-way radio transmitter he had brought with him from his station's newsroom and in a broadcast heard around the world described what it was like to be trapped in an inferno: "The sky is red, then it's white! It's going crazy. The fire jumped 100–150 feet high, right over the top of Greenhill Road. There are something like 120 houses at risk up here.... We are in big trouble! We can hardly breathe! The air is white with heat! There are women crying and there are children here. We are in trouble! The flames came up like an express train." The firestorm swept over the 1,000-acre farm in 10 minutes. It destroyed the roof of the farmhouse but miraculously left Nicoll's little group unharmed.

A few minutes later, Nicoll got word that his own house down the road was on fire. "It's in flames," he radioed, "and there's nothing I can do about it. It's exploding still and I just can't bear to look. And the man across the road thinks his wife may be trapped—and his house is burned to the ground."

Compared to many, however, Nicoll was lucky. In the township of Cockatoo, 30 miles east of Melbourne, 12 fire fighters were killed when the wind suddenly shifted and engulfed them in flames. Near Kalangadoo, South Australia, a woman and four children were incinerated when their car stalled and caught fire. Near Timboon, Victoria, Petronella Anderson and her 10-year-old son, Gareth, had just given a ride to a stranded volunteer named Kevin Grigg when fire overtook their car. Mother and son burned to death; Grigg, though also badly burned, survived.

At 9:30 P.M. Ash Wednesday night, about the worst place to be in Australia was outside the Macedon Family Hotel in the hilltop village of Macedon, near Melbourne. A full-fledged firestorm, with winds whirling at 150 miles an hour at its epicenter, was rapidly consuming the town. So intense were the flames that even at some distance, birds fell blazing from the skies. Most residents had already fled the town, but when fire or fallen trees cut off the remaining escape routes, some 250 people gathered in the hotel to wait out the holocaust. Thanks to the valiant efforts of fire fighters, who kept water hoses trained on the hotel, the building and its refugees—if not much else in Macedon—were spared by the flames.

Rain helped to contain most of the major blazes in South Australia by late Wednesday evening. But in Victoria, minor fires continued to burn through Sunday morning. When it was all over, 74 people had lost their lives, and property damage totaled more than $450 million. Fires destroyed more than 2,000 houses and buildings, hundreds of thousands of livestock, and about 1,000 vehicles. Some 2,000 square miles of forest were reduced to scorched earth.

The Ash Wednesday disaster prompted an outpouring of money and volunteers from across Australia. But as the nation came together to help survivors rebuild their lives, it was brutally reminded how dangerous life in the beautiful, untamed bush can be.

Famine in Africa

Specter of mass starvation looms over a continent

THE HOLLOW EYES of a dying child, a mother whose hopeless face is almost beyond suffering—these are the images of tragedy. They and the starving throngs around them haunt the world's imagination, bearing witness to a catastrophe on a scale that defies comprehension.

The particular faces might come from any of a broad band of nations south of the Sahara reaching more than 3,000 miles across the African continent from Senegal on the Atlantic coast to Ethiopia on the Red Sea. That region, known as the Sahel, from the Arabic word for "shore," encompasses some 2.3 million square miles, an area roughly nine times the size of Texas. It was here, where many nations bear names unfamiliar to Western ears—Mali, Mauritania, Burkina Faso, Niger, Chad, Sudan—that a long, ominous series of droughts and crop failures culminated in the mid-1980's in one of this century's worst natural disasters.

Hopelessness *turns to tears for a young Ethiopian boy.*

The devastation came about slowly and inexorably. For generations, the people of the Sahel lived in a harsh but workable balance with the land. The semi-arid region along the border of the world's largest desert could in most years support a modest population. Most were sustained by herding cattle on the natural grasslands or by farming subsistence grains. Herds and crops both depended on the seasonal rains that fall chiefly from June to September.

Traditional life was never easy, and the harsh fact of high infant mortality served to limit the population. It was natural that a premium was placed on large families: children provided valuable labor and, in later years, the only source of support their aging parents could count on. In time, advances in medicine, sanitation, and other areas brought about a gain in life expectancy, but the people of the Sahel continued to have as many children as possible. The result has been enormous population growth in the region, putting equally great pressure on the land. Grasslands that had barely supported migrating herds of cattle and goats were plowed to raise grain, making them more vulnerable to the erosion of precious topsoil. More mouths to feed also meant more cooking, which was almost always done over open wood fires. Whole regions were consequently stripped of soil-preserving trees as families in thousands of villages went out each day to collect the firewood they needed.

Into this difficult situation came the droughts that turned a problem into a catastrophe. They began in 1968, bringing more than half a decade of crop failures and livestock deaths. By the early 1970's, perhaps 250,000 people were dead from the famine, and as many as 3.5 million cattle had been lost.

Steadier rainfall returned after 1974, but seldom was there as much as before the drought. Once again in the early 1980's annual rainfalls began to decline. They reached a new low in 1984, when less than 60 percent of the barely adequate pre-drought average fell. It was then that the disaster took on frightening new dimensions. Rivers declined or dried up entirely. Lake Chad in the heart of the Sahel, with nearly 10,000 square miles of water in the 1960's, had lost almost 90 percent of its area by 1985. Satellite photographs taken the same year revealed that in parts of Senegal the total quantity of plant life had declined by more than 95 percent since 1981.

The impact on the people of the region was staggering. Without crops, without herds—with no resources of any kind—myriads of Africans, especially in remote rural areas, were driven over the line between hunger and true starvation. Village life disintegrated, populations shifted, and families were broken apart. "We do not know where we will go," said a young villager from the parched northern plateau of Burkina Faso, "only that we will go south to look for food." His words voiced the plight of millions of fellow sufferers across the vast expanse of the Sahel.

During the droughts of the early 1970's, one man recalled, it had at least been possible to sell cattle and use the money to buy grain when the crops failed. "But now there is no price for cattle," he lamented. "The markets have disappeared. After the many years of drought, people have nothing left to sell."

In the town of Lere in Mali, where villagers had once come from miles around to an overflowing market, it was reported in 1985 that practically every person who could move had fled the drought to search for food elsewhere. Herders and farmers joined the throngs of the displaced and starving in shantytowns around larger cities. Those who departed, however, were soon replaced in Lere by other drought refugees who had trudged in from even more desperate locations. Everywhere, parched and useless fields were

Empty bowls *tell the story of the famine, as children and adults at a relief camp silently await their one daily meal.*

abandoned; irreplaceable topsoil was lost to blistering dust storms and flowing sand dunes; treeless plains lay naked before the wind's blast.

Media coverage of the 1984–85 famines, especially in Ethiopia, brought images of the starving into the homes of wealthier countries and evoked outpourings of aid from Europe, the United States, and elsewhere. An estimated 2 million people died during that terrible period, half of them in Ethiopia alone. Without doubt, countless others would have perished but for the emergency relief programs.

The fundamental disaster, however, was not eliminated, and even well-intentioned shipments of grain from the West often had unwanted side effects. Much was diverted by corrupt local officials or blocked by civil strife. More important in the long run, the influx of free grain undermined the income of farmers who had managed to survive the drought, making agricultural recovery an even more difficult process. Governments often compounded the problem with policies that ensured artificially low food prices in the cities, where political support was crucial, at the expense of subsistence farmers.

Modest rainfalls returned before the end of 1985, raising crop yields and offering hope that the famine would finally abate. But the rain, welcome as it was,

could not restore lost lives or rebuild shattered economies. The region's political and social institutions remained ill-equipped to deal with the vast proportions of the crisis. National governments, many beset by internal conflicts, still generally failed to support local agriculture, and in some cases—most prominently Ethiopia—government and rebel leaders alike were only too willing to use food as a weapon of war. The result has been a deepening, pervasive pessimism. "In this part of the world," said one relief worker in Burkina Faso, "we do not just think that people will die of hunger. We assume it."

Whether that assumption will continue to be borne out is a question with no easy answer. Meteorologists are unsure if the droughts have been random occurrences or harbingers of a long-term drying of the region. In any event, little can be done about climatic conditions in the Sahel: there is only the hope that those social and political forces that turned drought into disaster can be changed—and changed while there is still something left to save. For in this part of the world, time has become the most precious resource of all. As one Ethiopian man said after walking many miles and selling his last valuable possession—an ox—to buy grain for his ailing family: "We have food for today. I don't know about tomorrow."

Earthquake in Mexico City

Miraculous rescues kindle hope in shattered metropolis

ABEL TORRES CHÁVEZ was attending an early-morning mathematics class at a technical college in downtown Mexico City when the first tremors rattled the six-story building. Within seconds the room was swaying and students were struggling to stay on their feet. Torres Chávez staggered toward the nearest wall, reached out to support himself, and was plunged into darkness as the building collapsed. It was about 7:20 A.M., Thursday, September 19, 1985.

Built on treacherous subsoil, and perhaps in violation of building codes, structures like this one in Mexico City's garment district did not stand a chance when rocked by an earthquake of awesome power.

Two blocks away, at the 367-room Hotel Regis, Danilo Cabrera dove from bed for the bathroom doorway and braced himself inside the door frame as his room rocked. After several long seconds of crunching and grinding, the Regis collapsed, sending Cabrera hurtling down five floors on a cascade of rubble. Unlike many of his fellow guests, Cabrera survived the ordeal with only cuts and broken ribs to show for it.

On the 10th floor of the Maria Isabel Sheraton Hotel, American businessman Les Connolly clung to the walls of his room as the building swayed back and forth. "It would go all the way over one way and you'd think it was going over and you'd be dead," reported Connolly. "Then the next time it would sway all the way the other way and you'd think this time it would crash."

On the streets, traffic came to a halt and people staggered about dazed and crying. Trees and street lights whipped back and forth. Tall buildings swayed with the moving ground. Some structures slumped, their floors collapsing into one another; others keeled over or were knocked down by oscillating neighbors.

Tepito, a raucous slum near the city center, was gone, its adobe tenements toppled by the quake.

Registering a massive 8.1 on the Richter scale, the seismic waves that rocked Mexico City came from a fracture in the earth's crust some 220 miles to the west, 12 miles beneath the Pacific coast. Rippling out in all directions, the first waves took a little longer than two minutes to reach the city, and then kept on coming every two seconds for nearly a full minute—an unusually long time for a quake's period of peak violence to last. Mexico City's downtown district suffered the most because it was built on an ancient lake bed, where deep sediments amplified the shocks.

When the shaking stopped, everything seemed unnaturally still for a moment. Columns of dust and smoke rose into the sky; here and there geysers of flame emanated from broken gas mains. Then the air began to fill with sirens, screams, and faint calls for help from beneath heaps of rubble.

Accustomed to earthquakes, most people in the sprawling, densely populated metropolis of 18 million rode this tremor out and then assumed that nothing terribly serious had happened. Indeed, much of the city escaped unharmed, and even in the heavily dam-

A tomb for many of its guests, the Hotel Regis was one of five Mexico City hotels completely destroyed by the quake.

aged downtown district, the devastation was scattered. Despite its wide yawing, the Maria Isabel Sheraton remained upright. The city's tallest skyscrapers as well as most of its centuries-old, colonial-era buildings still stood. Several hundred thousand passengers emerged unscathed from the subway. Of Mexico City's approximately 1 million buildings, 500 were destroyed and 3,300 damaged—fewer than 1 percent—but at those buildings that did collapse the magnitude of the disaster was staggering. There were as many as 1,000 patients and staff members in the 12-story Juárez Hospital when it toppled; few were left alive. The destruction of the obstetrics wing of General Hospital claimed the lives of 277 mothers, infants, and hospital employees. Perhaps 2,000 men, women, and children were buried under mounds of debris when two of the three wings of the Nuevo León apartment building gave way. In all, and with a stupefying suddenness, more than 9,000 people were dead, 30,000 injured, and 95,000 left homeless.

Even before fire companies and rescue squads began arriving at the disaster sites, volunteers directed by the police were digging through the rubble with their bare hands. By midday, rescue workers were swarming over the fallen buildings, freeing hundreds of survivors and placing hundreds more of the dead in rows along the sidewalks. "The calls for help were the worst during the first day," a volunteer remembered. "There were mountains of rubble. We had no cranes or mechanical shovels, only picks, hand shovels and pliers." Agonized crowds gathered around the piles waiting for relatives or friends to emerge. Those lucky enough still to have electricity watched the tragedy unfold on the single television channel that remained on the air.

At Abel Torres Chávez's school, only his professor and 13 students, including Torres Chávez himself, were still alive. Trapped deep within a hill of broken concrete slabs, Torres Chávez was sitting up, one leg beneath him, his right arm pinned under the body of a dead student. Nearby was another surviving student. At first, the two friends bantered to keep up their spirits, but they soon lapsed into silence as their hopes began to sag. In the distance the sound of passing helicopters and at one point the voices of rescuers could be heard.

A day after the earthquake, hundreds of other victims still lay in heaps of rubble around the city. As

A Mexico City landmark, the Latin American Tower withstood the 1985 earthquake.

"QUAKEPROOF" BUILDINGS

During the Mexico City earthquake of 1985, many buildings designed to resist earthquakes were destroyed as a result of the resonating quality of the city's subsoil combined with certain of the buildings' design characteristics. Engineers studying the disaster found that L-shaped and other asymmetrical structures were especially prone to quake damage. (So were buildings with large, open spaces, such as garages or soaring lobbies, on their lower floors.) In an L-shaped edifice, for example, stress concentrates at the junction of the two wings, causing the building to fly apart.

Every building has what is known as a fundamental frequency—the time it takes the structure to sway back and forth once when subjected to a lateral shock. In the Mexico City earthquake, adjacent buildings of varying heights vibrated at different frequencies and thus tended to knock into—and damage—each other. Buildings between 5 and 20 stories tall, whose frequency of about 2 seconds matched that of the seismic waves, amplified the ground's motion so greatly that many of them simply shook to pieces. On the other hand, skyscrapers such as the 37-story Latin American Tower, whose vibrational frequency exceeded that of the most intense seismic waves, survived intact.

Builders in Mexico City have to abide by some of the world's most advanced codes for quake-resistant design. Why so many buildings toppled anyway remains a topic of concern and study for engineers and architects around the world.

rescue work continued nonstop through Thursday night and Friday, the pace changed from a frantic harvest of easy-to-reach survivors to patient digging, inch by inch, for those trapped deeper beneath compacted floors. Power cutting tools, jackhammers, and heavier equipment were added to the effort, but the job required delicacy so as not to crush survivors in shifting debris. In some places danger from electrical hookups or leaking gas made it necessary to work with wooden mallets and other tools that would not cause sparks. Rescuers frequently turned off their equipment and shouted for quiet around a site so they could listen for faint signs of life. Expert rescue teams with specialized listening and heat-seeking devices and trained rescue dogs began to arrive from Europe and the United States.

Improvised outdoor morgues received a growing number of corpses as well as streams of survivors fearfully seeking lost loved ones. Outside the building where Abel Torres Chávez was trapped, a tearful woman waited for news of her sister-in-law, missing for more than 24 hours. At the Nuevo León housing complex, a woman waved her brother's wedding picture, asking if he had been found. On a public bulletin board a desperate plea was registered: "I am looking for my children Anuar, Anizul, Daniela and Alondra, missing in the tragedy of the Nuevo León building."

On Friday afternoon, rescuers broke through to Torres Chávez's professor and 11 of his fellow students and carried them out, all but one unhurt. Guided by information from the survivors, the rescue crew began working toward the two remaining students. But at 7:38 P.M. an aftershock registering 7.3 on the Richter scale rolled through the city. It caused panic and toppled a handful of damaged buildings, but there was no new destruction. People moved their households into the street, and rescuers pulled back from the mounds of rubble. In the silence Torres Chávez could only tell himself that they would come back.

He woke later to a scratching sound nearby, then heard his name. Rescuers had pushed close enough to pass him some oranges, a flashlight, and a walkie-talkie. They extracted his last living classmate on Saturday morning and then started digging for Torres Chávez, who had to be reached from a different angle.

One of the tunnelers opening the way toward the trapped student was Marcos Efrén Zariñana. Small, wiry, and agile, Zariñana was ideally built for the task at hand, and in the days after the quake he labored tirelessly at various sites, saving many lives. While working at the ruins of the Hotel Regis on Saturday afternoon, the Flea, as Zariñana was being called throughout the city, heard a police officer ask for someone willing to cut a body. Volunteering for the task, Zariñana was sent to the technical school where Torres Chávez was the last student known to be alive. At the end of a tunnel that narrowed to 12 inches, the rescuer found twisted ductwork and a concrete beam crushing the legs of a dead student. Realizing that cutting the duct was the better way through, Zariñana edged back out for shears after calling to Torres Chávez to keep up his spirits.

Zariñana worked until 2:30 A.M., slept for five hours, then crawled back into the rubble at 7:30 Sunday morning. He reached Torres Chávez at 9:00 A.M. and put an arm around his shoulder. Outside the pile, Zariñana's voice crackled from a walkie-talkie: "I am holding Abel."

After another trip in and out of the tunnel, the Flea was too exhausted to continue. Two hours later, he watched as Torres Chávez was finally carried out, a blanket over his head to protect him from the shock of sunlight. People in the crowd began to gather around Zariñana, begging him to save their children.

As the week came to an end, heavy equipment was used to clear sites where no life could be found, but at a few buildings, the rescue work continued. Trained dogs crawled over and burrowed into the rubble, sniffing for life. Using ultrasound equipment, a French team found 35 survivors. At night, when the city quieted, workers would stand silent, listening for any sounds in the wreckage.

On Sunday night rescuers heard a call from near the top of the pile that had been the Labor and Social Ministry building. Trapped under four floors for four days, Rubén Vera Rodríguez had worked his way

slowly to the surface. He was freed in another hour.

Monday morning, medical intern Juan José Hernández Cruz was disinterred, bloodied but alive, from the ruins of Juárez Hospital. The next day, anesthesiologist Martha Torres Granillo was finally freed from beneath a concrete column at the General Hospital site, but only after her gangrenous left leg had been amputated. In all, more than 4,000 people were saved from the ruins in Mexico City, but the most astounding of the rescue stories by far were the very last ones.

From the rubble of General Hospital came the wail of a baby, still alive nearly a week after the quake had buried it.

Early Wednesday morning on September 25, rescue workers at the obstetrics wing of General Hospital freed the unnamed infant daughter of Crisanta Nuñez Ortega, whose own body was never found. Over the next few days, several other infants were pulled from the ruins, alive beyond anyone's expectation.

As the last miracle babies were being saved, Mexican officials had to come to grips with a reconstruction job estimated at $4 billion. The international community quickly mobilized to assist Mexico. But to a nation already deep in the throes of an economic crisis, the quake came as yet one more horror to be endured.

Waiting for the dead, *mourners stand in front of freshly dug graves at a cemetery on the outskirts of Mexico City.*

Laid waste by a tide of mud, *Armero became a graveyard for most of its people. The disaster that engulfed the Andean* *town had been foreseen well in advance, but Colombian authorities did not order an evacuation until it was too late.*

The Wrath of Nevado del Ruiz

Colombia's largest volcano rumbles to life, triggering a deadly tide of mud and melted snow

THE FIRST WARNING NOTES were sounded in late 1984, when mountain climbers scaling Colombia's long-dormant Nevado del Ruiz volcano began reporting minor earthquakes and large plumes of sulfuric gas issuing from its ice-capped peak. One of the string of Pacific Rim volcanoes that make up the deadly Ring of Fire, Nevado del Ruiz had not erupted in a major way since 1595, when a cataclysmic blowout described by Spanish eyewitnesses caused widespread devastation. A more limited eruption in 1845 created mud slides and floods in surrounding valleys and claimed about 1,000 lives. Now, after nearly 400 years of fitful sleep, Nevado del Ruiz was stirring once again.

Throughout the spring and summer of 1985 the 17,822-foot-high summit located 80 miles northwest of Bogotá continued to shake. On September 11, Nevado del Ruiz suddenly spat out a vaporous mixture of steam, rock, and ash. Although no one was hurt, the minor outburst touched off a 15-mile mud slide down

the volcano's northern flank and fueled geologists' fears that the Andean peak was preparing for a major event.

Later that month, the Colombian Institute of Geological Mining Investigations recommended that towns at the base of Nevado del Ruiz be evacuated—advice that Colombian authorities failed to heed until it was too late. On October 7, the institute published a report warning of imminent disaster in the vicinity of Nevado del Ruiz and singling out two sites as particularly vulnerable: the town of Armero, a prosperous farming community 30 miles east of the volcano in the valley of the Lagunilla River, and the village of Chinchiná, located to the west of the summit. A "volcanic hazard map" prepared at this time indicated with remarkable accuracy where the mud slides would occur should Nevado del Ruiz erupt. Although a draft of the map was ready by mid-October, it was not circulated to Colombian authorities until November 8. On October 22 a visiting team of Italian volcanologists urged the Colombian government to begin civil defense preparations at once in the Lagunilla River valley. Nevado del Ruiz had "certainly not finished its activity," the Italians warned. "Actually, the worst may be yet to come."

The worst came on November 13. Shortly after 3:00 P.M. that day, an abrupt explosion of steam heralded one of the most catastrophic volcanic eruptions of the 20th century, a disaster second in destructiveness only to the 1902 eruption of Mount Pelée in Martinique.

By 7:30 P.M. the continuing activity at Nevado del Ruiz had convinced scientists that a major eruption was imminent. Only then was the government persuaded to issue evacuation warnings. Whether or not those warnings ever reached Armero remains a matter of dispute. But even if the message did get through, few if any people in Armero acted upon it. At 9:08 P.M. a pair of spectacular detonations, audible for 20 miles around, followed each other in quick succession. Within the next half hour, a column of steam and ash shot nearly seven miles into the sky. Cruising at an altitude of 24,000 feet, a DC-8 cargo jet enroute from Miami to Bogotá was caught in the volcanic blast. "First came a reddish illumination that shot up to 26,000 feet," the pilot later reported. "Then came a shower of ash that covered us and left me without visibility. The cockpit filled with smoke and heat and the smell of sulfur." Miles below, as the people of Armero and a half dozen neighboring towns slept or prepared for bed, the same ominous odor of sulfur began to fill the Lagunilla Valley.

The Nevado del Ruiz eruption was not accompanied by great outpourings of lava. Instead the superheated magma inside the volcano began to melt the massive cap of ice at its summit. Steaming rivulets of filthy water tumbled down the mountainside in several directions, thickening with volcanic debris and rain-soaked earth to form the deadly, racing mudflows known as lahars.

Moving at speeds of up to 30 miles an hour, and increasing in depth to as much as 50 feet, avalanches of mud raced down the volcano into the channels of rivers flowing away from its base. Two of these churning, viscous lahars converged on the Lagunilla River at a point just above Armero. Already swollen by three days of torrential rains and dammed up by debris from the September eruption, the Lagunilla now burst over

its banks and bore down unchecked on defenseless Armero. At about 11 P.M. the deadly torrent "rolled into town with a moaning sound, like some sort of monster," recalled one survivor. "It seemed like the end of the world."

For most of Armero, it was. Families asleep in their beds were buried in minutes; houses were entombed before their inhabitants ever knew they were in danger. The mudflow cut through the town with horrifying efficiency, swallowing 80 percent of its buildings and killing 90 percent of its 25,000 inhabitants. Those lucky enough to be awakened by the creak of foundations giving way or the terrified cries of neighbors fled before the deadly tide as from a nightmare. Under a night sky putrid with ash, parents and children were torn from one another by sudden surges of the unpredictable flow, one to be hurled to safety on a rising wave, another to be just as inexplicably sucked under. Clothing was ripped away, bones broken, victims dashed against walls or crushed by the weight of careening automobiles.

It was all over in minutes. With most of its people dead, Armero simply did not exist any more. In and around the village of Chinchiná, some 1,000 people lost their lives in the mud. The total death toll throughout the region climbed to more than 25,000. Many thousands more were left homeless, and virtually every survivor lost loved ones.

As word of the tragedy got out, governments and private citizens around the world rallied to Colombia's aid, but the task of rescuing the stranded and caring for survivors often exceeded available resources. While the living were being dug out and the dead mourned, a bitter debate broke out among Colombians over their government's failure to warn of the danger in time and its poor management of relief efforts.

The reawakening of Nevado del Ruiz is by no means over. Rumblings inside the volcano prompted a mass evacuation of the mountainside in June 1986. In March 1988 Nevado del Ruiz began spewing ash once more. Since only 10 percent of its ice cap melted in the 1985 eruption, the threat of mud slides still hangs over those living in the volcano's shadow. With the possible exception of Mount St. Helens in Washington State, no other mountain in the Western Hemisphere is being watched so closely and nervously as the once murderous Nevado del Ruiz.

Life goes on *even in the face of death. A Red Cross worker cradles little baby Consuelo, born just moments before to a survivor of the Armero tragedy.*

Before and after: *The massive gas burst churned up reddish brown iron from the bottom of the once blue Lake Nyos.*

Monster in Lake Nyos

A freak of nature takes a devastating toll in Cameroon

OSSIBLY A THOUSAND years before the West African colony of Cameroon finally achieved independence in 1961, a silent, invisible monster had begun to grow in the 600-foot depths of mile-wide Lake Nyos, about 200 miles north of the new republic's capital city of Yaoundé.

No one really knows the exact moment of the monster's birth. Most scientists, though, are reasonably sure that it was already there, on the lake bottom, in the terrible days of the 18th and early 19th centuries, when Arab traders—driving their slave caravans hard toward the sea—halted now and then along the riverbanks to unload the dead and dying for the crocodiles and vultures to feed upon. It was still growing in the early years of the 20th century, when little steam trains, fueled by ebony and mahogany logs, labored

inland at 10 miles per hour after stationmasters had used their rawhide whips to clear the tracks of natives. More recently, along the shores of Lake Nyos, grandfathers told grandchildren stories about the sultan of Ngaoundere, who commanded his 100-piece orchestra to play from dawn to dusk, and of the court executioner of Garoua, who carried dried parts of beheaded victims in a pouch around his neck.

But all that was long gone by the summer of 1986. The little valley communities around Lake Nyos, a crater lake whose slopes are prime agricultural land, were home to herdsmen and farmers. On the night of August 21 many of these hard-working people were already in bed or finishing up a late evening meal when there came, about 9:00 P.M., a distant rumble somewhere up by the lake that sounded like thunder. No one was surprised, for August is the rainiest month along the ridge of extinct volcanoes that runs along the Cameroonian–Nigerian border.

Then, in a flash, more than 1,700 people were dead. The agent of death? An enormous, invisible bubble of carbon dioxide. The monster had finally broken loose from the lake-bottom sediment and heavy water that had held it in check for centuries. Emerging from the blue surface of the lake like the most frightful genie in the *Arabian Nights*, the bubble killed everything and anything that breathed along the shoreline. Denser than air, the mile-wide gas cloud then flowed down into the adjacent valleys to carry out its deadly mission there. People, cattle, birds, and even ants were asphyxiated almost instantly.

Since there were so few survivors to report on the disaster, the officials in Cameroon were totally unaware of the tragedy. The first word they heard about it came through an unidentified government worker from the village of Wum. The man was traveling the 20 miles from his home to Lake Nyos on his motorcycle when he stopped to pick up a dead antelope on the road; it was a lucky find, for it would provide meat for the family he planned to visit. Shortly afterward, however, he felt dizzy, and then, to his horror, he began seeing dead human bodies sprawled everywhere along the route. Fearing what lay ahead, he turned and fled back the way he had come, but his story was relayed to Bamenda, a provincial headquarters town, and a government official, Gideon Taka, was ordered to check it out. Taka, who reached the Lake Nyos area two days after the deadly cloud had struck, had trouble believing what he saw around him. "Most people were dead. They suffered burns, and those who were still surviving were coughing up blood," Taka later reported. "We saw a lot of corpses in the road; perhaps they thought they could survive by running away."

In the village of Cha, Francis Fang, a farmer, told an interviewer: "My wife dropped to the ground, vomiting blood. The children were burned and screaming. My wife was dead. I picked up my girls and started walking to the hospital. There were dead people everywhere on the road—so many I started stepping on them."

In another village, Nyos, only 4 of its 1,300 people survived. One young mother, Veronica Gmbie, lost five children, including her newest baby, whom she was holding in her arms. Jongi Zong, hurrying over from nearby Sumum, buried his brother and sister-in-law in one grave and their seven children in a second grave beside them. Fred Tenhorn, a Dutch priest, found an eerie scene, with all foliage green and healthy and corpses laid out underneath—"as if a neutron bomb had exploded," he said, killing everyone but leaving the landscape intact.

Even as various countries were channeling the first relief shipments of medicine and food to Cameroon, scientists were flying into the stricken country to study the results of the disaster firsthand. The French volcanologist François Leguern called the massacre at Lake Nyos "the worst volcanic gas disaster ever recorded." He believed that the eruption was the result of deep volcanic activity; but others, including the American experts from the U.S. Office of Foreign Disaster Assistance, thought that an earthquake or landslide had freed the monstrous accumulation of gas from the lake's bottom.

But many of the sorrowing, frightened relatives and survivors were not interested in either theory. They had their own explanation for the exploding waters. Some remembered that three years earlier their tribal chief, on his death bed, had ordered that his finest, fattest cattle be driven off a cliff to drown in Lake Nyos, where the living spirits of the departed resided. But his family had ignored his wishes, and now the chief had had his revenge. Others blamed an angry Mammy Water, a spirit woman of the Cameroonian lakes and rivers, for the explosion.

We may never know what stirred the waters of Lake Nyos and turned the tranquil lake into the lake of death.

Thousands of dead cattle *littered the hillsides north of the lake. No vultures came to feed on the carcasses, since they, too, were dead.*

Horror in Armenia

Quake traps thousands under smoking rubble

Victims' photographs *laid out on the street before the ruins of a Leninakan elementary school offer mute, poignant testimony to the earthquake's fury. A thriving industrial city, Armenia's second largest, Leninakan lay 80 percent destroyed. Shoddy construction techniques were blamed for much of the wreckage.*

IT WAS A MOMENT when it seemed that nothing could go wrong for Soviet President Mikhail S. Gorbachev, who was on a much-publicized two-day visit to New York City. Standing before the United Nations General Assembly, he announced a unilateral cut in Soviet troop strength, a move applauded by Western leaders. As Gorbachev's motorcade sped him through midtown, crowds of New Yorkers gathered at curbside to wave their greetings.

Then came the agonizing news. A catastrophic earthquake had roared through Soviet Armenia, near the Turkish border, ravaging some 4,000 square miles of densely populated land. Schools, factories, hospitals, churches, office buildings, and apartment houses were tumbled into ruin. Three whole cities were practically leveled, and thousands of people were buried under jagged mounds of rubble. Cutting short his triumphant U.S. visit, President Gorbachev boarded a plane for Moscow. His parting words were: "Urgent measures are being taken to help all those affected by this terrible tragedy, and I have to be there."

The tremor, which had hit at 11:41 on the morning of December 7, 1988, was far more destructive than its 6.9 rating on the Richter scale would seem to indicate. The town of Spitak was virtually "erased from the face of the earth," as a Moscow TV commentator put it. Nearby at Kirovakan, a city of some 170,000, the carnage surpassed all imagining. Nearly every building of any size collapsed, entombing its occupants. Block after block of new high-rise apartments gave way, their prefabricated concrete slabs snapping into pieces like so many brittle bones. The same was true at Leninakan, 30 miles to the west. Classes were underway at Elementary School 9 on Gorky Street when the temblor hit, and an instant later the bodies of 50 young children lay crushed. Some 250 people were trapped in the fallout of a Leninakan computer center. Armenia's Seismic Institute went down, destroying valuable equipment inside. A centuries-old cathedral was transformed into a heap of stone and mortar, with only its dome intact.

Survivors wandered the streets, too stunned to speak. Wrapped in coats and blankets against the damp December chill, some huddled around bonfires. Others searched for relatives, clawing through mounds of twisted steel and concrete with their bare hands. "Somewhere here is my brother," lamented a heavily mustached man. "He worked as a factory director. He came home during a break and stayed here. Children are here . . . Oh, the grief is terrible."

All the while, muffled cries for help filtered up through the wreckage from people buried underneath.

Some escaped certain death through the merest flicker of chance. Zhenya Saakyan was at work in her office, she reported, when "suddenly everything collapsed. Then there was complete darkness, and I apparently lost consciousness; there was nothing to breathe." Zhenya was completely buried except for one hand, on which she wore a ring. By a quirk of fate her son spotted the familiar ring and dug her out. Others were not so lucky. As volunteers sifted through the rubble, they laid the corpses in the streets in neatly regimented rows to await identification and burial.

Surveying the devastation at Leninakan, President Gorbachev tried to console the Armenian people, telling the crowds that clustered around him: "All Russia shares your grief." He promised immediate help to feed and shelter survivors, and to rescue the victims still trapped in the debris. Meanwhile, a series of aftershocks continued to rock the disaster area.

Relief was needed on a massive scale. "Every hour of delay means another 20 dead out of every thousand buried," declared a Soviet health official. Vital emergency equipment was sorely lacking—hospital beds and medical supplies, tents and blankets for the many thousands left homeless, construction machinery to dig through the rubble.

To make matters worse, the rescue efforts were crippled by a lack of organization. No one seemed to know where to begin. "Seconds and hours are being lost—that means lives," admonished *Pravda,* the Communist Party daily newspaper. Food shipments were being held up, a party official complained.

Even reaching the disaster area posed major problems. Armenia is a mountainous country, and landslides blocked most of the roadways in and out. The main rail line to Georgia, the neighboring republic to the north, had been uprooted. The airport at Yerevan, the Armenian capital, remained open, but a December fog caused havoc as rescue planes began arriving. A Soviet military transport crashed as it touched down, killing all 79 people aboard. A second plane, bearing medical supplies from Yugoslavia, also went down, bringing death to its crew.

Despite what seemed to be unsurmountable problems, help was pouring in from all quarters. Citizens

A saddened Mikhail Gorbachev looks on as his wife, Raisa, gives comfort to a grieving survivor during the couple's tour of Leninakan.

in Moscow lined up to donate food, clothing, blankets, and blood. The Soviet Army moved in with bulldozers and 6,500 soldiers to help sift through the rubble. Twenty-five brigades of military doctors arrived from Moscow and the republics of Georgia and the Ukraine with bandages, splints, and penicillin.

Another massive infusion of aid poured in from the West. For the first time since World War II, the Soviet Union was willing to accept American aid. Eight U.S. government transport planes crammed with relief gear and supplies headed for Armenia, followed by more than a dozen aircraft supplied by private charities. As Americans opened their wallets, the U.S. relief package reached nearly $14.5 million.

Altogether, 67 nations pitched in with money, supplies, and nearly 2,000 relief workers. A company of 160 French firefighters jetted in with 35 dogs trained to sniff out survivors under the rubble. A British group brought ultrasonic listening devices and fiber-optic cameras. Japan donated $9 million. West Germany offered 16 cranes, and Italy volunteered to build a prefabricated village for homeless Armenians.

As the relief workers set about their task, the forces of nature seemed to conspire against them. Temperatures dropped, and an icy rain began to fall. One volunteer helped pull 48 corpses from a Leninakan classroom, then found one lone survivor. Some victims were pried loose from the wreckage alive, only to expire on the way to the Yerevan hospitals. Each day the moans and whispers from under the rubble grew weaker, until they ceased entirely.

More than one week after the initial shock, 20 more battered, emaciated souls were plucked alive from beneath the remains of Leninakan, and one more from Spitak. They were the last. For weeks rumors persisted of other miraculous rescues, but all proved unfounded.

According to an official count, nearly 25,000 bodies had been recovered, but the precise number of dead will probably never be known. Miraculously, some 15,000 victims had been found alive, and as many as half a million people had been left homeless. One grizzled old man in a tattered winter coat arrived in Yerevan from the quake zone, shaking his head in stunned disbelief "There is nothing left there," he said. "Nothing. Everything must be built from scratch."

The Future of the Earth

Is the worst yet to come?

THE NIGHT of March 23, 1997, was still over much of the North Atlantic Ocean. Beneath a clear sky the container ship *Eldritch III* headed for New York. The single deck officer on watch, Larry Petersen, stared out from the warmth of the bridge. The unusual calm of the deep ocean seemed uncanny, although he had known such periods before.

Suddenly the ship and the sea around it were flooded by an unnatural greenish-white light from the south that rapidly increased in intensity. High up in the southern sky a giant fireball, more than twice the size and brilliance of a full moon, was traveling rapidly towards the north-northwest.

Occasional enormous flashes and sparks of red and blue light illuminated what appeared to be a long, dark trailing tail. It plunged over the horizon directly ahead of the *Eldritch III*. Darkness enveloped the ship for an instant, then a gigantic flash of light occurred where the fireball had disappeared. For some seconds he could see nothing; then, as a weak pink sun rose through the misty eastern horizon, the long, dark, and serpent-like trail of the fireball became clearly visible across the sky.

Capt. Jim Barnes, a tall, stoic New Englander, appeared on the bridge. "Now hear this. This is your captain speaking," he said quietly. "I want all crew members to their emergency stations, all hatches battened down, and everything movable stowed away or lashed down. And I want all this done within 10 minutes. Go!" Larry turned to the captain, his face expressing his puzzlement.

"A giant sea wave may hit us, Mr. Petersen. Alternatively, the very least we can expect is a patch of very bad weather," explained the captain. "Look at those clouds."

Larry turned his eyes to the horizon once more. For a good 30° of arc the distant sky was filled with boiling, billowing cloud, black as ink below, white as ice above, with an enormous anvil-shaped plume rapidly extending far into the stratosphere. Even as he looked, a thin line of black and gray clouds began to slowly spill out across the horizon at the foot of the tall mushroom-like column. At 0720 hours, just as Captain Barnes picked up his microphone to relay another message to the crew, three immense detonations shook the entire ship.

Barnes picked up the telephone. In a few moments he was speaking to the duty manager in the shipping company's New York office. He soon learned that the whole eastern seaboard of the United States from Boston to Norfolk, Virginia, had been illuminated by a brilliant flash of light just before dawn, and that this had been followed by the noise of three tremendous explosions around 7:25 A.M. Nobody knew the cause: there was much speculation on the early morning news programs, but the official attitude in Washington was "No comment." The weather in New York was fine, but visibility was poor to the east because of a thick bank of sea mist behind which heavy storm clouds could be seen building up. Captain Barnes emphasized his belief that a destructive tsunami might strike the coast. The voice from the phone was polite but uninterested as it thanked him for his concern; Barnes then called home.

"Whatever you are doing, drop everything, get everyone in the car, and drive as far inland and onto high ground as quickly as you can," he ordered his wife.

The time was 7:40 A.M. Before she could argue, he slammed the phone down and turned to Larry.

"Your parents in Brooklyn, Mr. Petersen?"

"They live on the tenth floor of a new building, sir. Should be OK."

On the horizon loomed a strange and menacing apparition, unlike anything the captain had ever seen before.

Trying not to let the chilling fear he felt for the safety of his wife and children show, the captain turned to look at the horizon once more; a frightening change had occurred. All the western and northern horizon was now closed in by a cloud with lightning intermittently within it. The sun illuminated a thin band of dancing silver lying directly along the horizon. In 20 minutes the silver band grew into a huge wave over 200 feet high, racing towards them at close on 300 miles an hour.

By 8:10 A.M. the *Eldritch III* had struggled to the crest of the enormous wave and was poised to plunge down into what appeared to be a cauldron of hell. Immediately ahead was a great trough, as deep as the mountainous wave on which the ship floated, and in which the sea had a uniform black bleakness. Behind this, further great waves covered with tumultuous foaming water could be seen approaching.

For the next four hours, the *Eldritch III* was shaken, tossed, lashed with rain and hail, and flooded by great seas in the worst typhoon that any of the crew could remember. Nevertheless, none of the waves that

Like a Titan's hand, *the enormous first wave generated by the meteorite nearly capsizes the* Eldritch III *as it speeds outward in all directions from the point of impact—and aims for North America's defenseless East Coast.*

followed were anything like the first in size. The second-largest was not more than 100 feet in height, the remainder not more than 30 feet. At midday the storm ceased as suddenly as it had begun, and the *Eldritch III* sailed into a relatively calm sea. Before Captain Barnes could speak, however, the radio operator burst onto the bridge, white-faced, his eyes wild.

"The whole of the Atlantic seaboard of the States has been swept away." he shouted. "The tidal wave hit them between 8:30 and 9. New York, Washington, Boston—they've all gone! The vice president was in L.A. He's taken over and declared martial law. It's a national disaster!"

This is the disturbing scenario with which authors Basil Booth and Frank Fitch open their speculative look at our planet's future, *Earthshock*. Fiction, perhaps, but hardly impossible. The solar system is chock-full of astral debris—uncounted billions of stray particles ranging from dust motes to pebbles to asteroids several miles across. Some hurtle through space along paths that will eventually cross the earth's orbit. More than a million tons of extraterrestrial dust drift down upon the earth each year, and every day some 500,000 meteors blaze visible trails across the sky. Virtually all these projectiles burn up in the atmosphere; but sometimes one gets through to the planet's surface. Meteorites large enough to cause large-scale devastation strike the earth only at rare

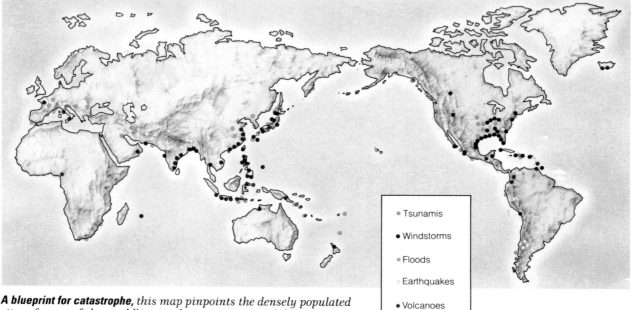

A blueprint for catastrophe, this map pinpoints the densely populated sites of some of the world's most destructive natural disasters.

Legend:
- Tsunamis
- Windstorms
- Floods
- Earthquakes
- Volcanoes

intervals, on average about once every 700 years. But if one were to land in the North Atlantic, the consequences could be truly fearsome. The mammoth wave churned up by the impact would crash against the shores of North America and Europe, surging inland up to 50 miles in places, sweeping away all life and habitation. Many of the world's great cities lie along the Atlantic Coast; most of them would face massive destruction, with a death toll climbing well into the millions.

If the same meteorite were to land on a city, the consequences might be even worse. Not only would countless people die instantly, but a thick shroud of dust would darken the skies and bring on a prolonged winter chill, killing off most of the world's plant and animal life—the same fate that may have befallen the dinosaurs 65 million years ago.

At any moment, primal forces seething above and below the Earth's surface may erupt in unforeseen catastrophe.

Our planet is in a state of perpetual turmoil, never beyond the threat of a sudden unleashing of the immense energies that continually reshape it. Sooner or later, another major hurricane will slam into the eastern seaboard of the United States. The barometer will plunge, winds will pipe up to well above 100 miles an hour, and a crest of ocean anywhere from 10 to 20 feet high will inundate the coast. Ships will sink or run aground, houses will wash away, shorelines will assume new shapes, and thousands of formerly dry acres will lie swamped by salt water. No one knows just when or where the storm will hit. But its arrival is as certain as sunrise.

Should the storm hold off for a year or two, disaster in another form is sure to strike somewhere in the world. Earthquakes, floods, tsunamis, cyclones, wildfires, volcanic eruptions, and other natural shocks take a dreadful toll. Together they have claimed more than 2.8 million lives over the past two decades and cost immeasurable sums in physical damage. Landslides alone obliterate some $5 billion in property each year, tropical cyclones as much as $7 billion. And in the years ahead, as the world's population continues to increase, the threat to life and livelihood multiplies.

By an irony of history, a large percentage of the world's 5 billion people live in regions that are highly disaster-prone—along seacoasts, in flood plains and river deltas, on the fertile slopes of volcanic mountains. Some 700,000 Italians inhabit the flanks of Mount Vesuvius, for example, and 3 million more in nearby Naples. Should Vesuvius blow its top—it has been quiet for four decades, and the longer it remains so, the greater the likelihood of a violent eruption— hundreds of thousands could die.

Earthquakes occur somewhere on the planet about every 30 seconds. But the largest and most devastating—the kind that rip open the landscape, heave down buildings, and snuff out 10,000 to 15,000 lives a year—also tend to strike in densely populated regions. All of Japan's 123 million citizens live atop a geologic Ring of Fire that encircles the Pacific Ocean, subjecting the lands along its margin to periodic convulsions. Both earthquakes and volcanic outbursts happen here with terrifying frequency. The ring cuts through Java and Indonesia, the highlands of Central and South America, and up through Mexico and into California.

A second seismic belt runs east through the Mediterranean and into the cradle of world civilization, striking across Italy and Greece, through Turkey and Central Asia, and as far east as China, with its population of more than a billion souls. As history has shown too many times, no one in this vast expanse is truly safe.

No disaster stirs more apprehension than the massive earthquake expected to roar through Southern California.

One of the most closely watched areas for potential disaster is Los Angeles, which lies dangerously close to the 800-mile-long San Andreas Fault. Major quakes tend to recur along this segment of the fault about once every century and a half, and the last big break was in 1857. Scientific estimates indicate a 60 percent chance that the next one will occur before 2020. Says one of the most knowledgeable experts: "The consensus is, we're coming up on one huge earthquake."

When it arrives, the Los Angeles quake may bring with it more tragedy and mayhem than any other natural disaster in the nation's history. Buildings of unreinforced masonry will tumble into ruin, trapping everyone caught inside under heaps of rubble and shattered glass. Much of the city's freeway system is likely to be impassable, stranding not only thousands of automobiles but rescue workers as well. Sewer mains will break, power lines will snap, and gas-line ruptures will feed a mass outbreak of local fires, just as in the 1906 quake in San Francisco. All emergency services will be strained far beyond capacity. Sections of the city will be without water, and two of its three main aqueducts could be inoperable for months.

Of the city's more than 3 million inhabitants, at least 3,000 will perish in the convulsion, and possibly many more. Should the quake roll through during the Friday afternoon rush hour, according to one estimate, nearly 21,000 people would be killed immediately. With another 80,000 left severely injured, and only 22,000 hospital beds left standing to receive them, the final death count could exceed 45,000.

Many hours would pass before news of the full disaster filtered out to the world at large. Landslides and ground ruptures might well block every exit route, and telephone service could be knocked out for days. But eventually the quake's repercussions would pulse outward far beyond southern California. With as much as $20 billion in property damage, and major disruption of the electronics, defense, and other high-tech industries of the region, the nation's economy would be sent reeling. Computer failures in banks and other institutions would throw financial transactions into chaos, possibly triggering a collapse on Wall Street. The government would have to borrow so much for emergency relief that interest rates would soar. Full recovery would take years.

Nor is Los Angeles the only American metropolis at risk. Cities from Anchorage to Charleston have been struck in the past and could be again. A deep and uneasy fault zone runs beneath southeast Missouri, and if it should stir with the same savage force that it did in 1811, it would shift the course of the Mississippi River, endanger some 12 million lives, and demolish billions of dollars' worth of property.

Even worse than the planet's sudden seizures are the slow, invisible brutalities inflicted on humankind by disease. Typhoid, cholera, and yellow fever rage unabated in many parts of the world, thwarting the advances of modern medicine. Each year some 4 million children die of diphtheria, whooping cough,

The famous freeways of Los Angeles could be twisted into hulking, grotesque pieces of sculpture by the massive earthquake expected within the next few decades.

tetanus, measles, polio, and tuberculosis, simply because they have not been immunized. Malaria alone strikes 200 million people annually and kills about a million; half the deaths in human history may have been caused by this one disease. No vaccine prevents it, and attempts to wipe out the mosquito that carries it have eventually failed, for after repeated sprayings the mosquito becomes immune to the insecticide.

The loss from starvation is equally tragic—and often just as difficult to prevent. More than 400 million people around the world suffer from chronic malnutrition. Improvements in agriculture have boosted crop yields prodigiously since the 1950's, but some 20 million still die each year from lack of food.

Many disasters signal their advent beforehand, and scientists have learned to track the paths of hurricanes, tornadoes, and tsunamis, monitor the gurgling of live volcanoes, and identify sites of some future earthquakes with a degree of accuracy unknown only a generation ago. Those efforts will increase in the 1990's, which have been designated an International Decade for Natural Disaster Reduction.

But there is always the unexpected—the unpredictable. Who would have thought that a strain of bees imported from Africa to Brazil would mingle with local breeds to spawn viciously aggressive insects whose swarming attacks can kill? But such is the case, and now the bees are moving slowly but surely north through Central America toward Texas.

No amount of planning can anticipate the bizarre, the improbable, the unknown.

Who could have expected that rabbits brought to Australia in the 18th century would proliferate in such numbers that they have devoured vast areas of prime grazing land? Or that a tiny organism, previously unknown to science, would attack an American Le-

---

ENDLESS SUMMER IN A GLOBAL GREENHOUSE

The explosion of industrial activity during the last two centuries has wrought profound changes around the world, and from mankind's perspective the benefits have generally outweighed the drawbacks. But one unforeseen effect may yet tip that balance drastically. The machine age has been fueled by coal and petroleum, and their widespread combustion has released great amounts of CO_2—carbon dioxide—into the air. Since the late 1950's there has been a 25 percent increase in atmospheric CO_2, which scientists believe acts like the glass roof in a greenhouse, letting in sunlight to warm the soil, then trapping the heat that would normally radiate back into space.

As it happens, the planet's average annual temperature is climbing at a rate that parallels the increase in CO_2.

The movement seems small enough, from 58°F in the 1880's to 59.3° today, but the current level is the highest on record. If the trend continues—the 1980's have included the four hottest years in a century, and some experts say a rise of up to 9 degrees is possible—the results could be devastating. The world's weather patterns would change, with a sharp upswing in the frequency of droughts, floods, and hurricanes. Enormous sections of productive cropland would be turned into desert or semiarid steppe, among them the vast corn and wheat lands of the American Midwest. As the new dust bowl spread, thousands of farms would fail, sending an army of refugees into the sweltering, overburdened cities. The nation's economic system and those of Western Europe would come under tremendous strain.

Conditions would not be so dire everywhere, of course. There might be an increase of rainfall in Africa's Sahel and other drought-prone regions; forests would creep north toward the Arctic Circle; Canadians and Soviets would have vast areas of newly thawed tundra to farm. But for better or worse, the world we know today would assuredly be changed in ways that can scarcely be imagined.

Prolonged drought could leave America's fertile plains scorched and desolate.

gion convention in Philadelphia in 1976, killing almost 30 Legionnaires and sending 100 more to the hospital? And what could be more unlikely than that the second leading cause of lung cancer in North America and Europe, after cigarette smoking, should be a radioactive gas called radon, which seeps up from bedrock to pollute people's houses?

The deadliest surprise of all was an epidemic that sprang seemingly out of nowhere in the early 1980's and is now sweeping the globe. It first came to notice in a few American cities, where hospitals reported a rising incidence of Kaposi's sarcoma, a rare skin cancer, and other seldom-seen ailments. The victims were mostly young homosexual men, and within a few years they were all dead, their immune systems ravaged in some mysterious way that left them defenseless against diseases of all kinds.

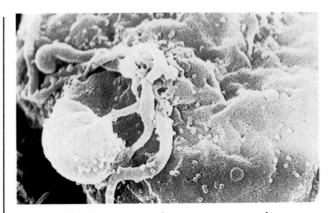

Portrait of a killer: *a research microscope provides an eerie closeup of one of the most mysterious and lethal organisms on earth, the virus that causes AIDS.*

The mysterious, terrifying illness came to be known among doctors as acquired immune deficiency syndrome, or AIDS.

At first AIDS seemed to be a homosexuals' disease, spread through sexual contact. But soon it appeared among other groups—chiefly hemophiliacs, intravenous drug users, and newborn children of infected mothers. Then researchers isolated a virus that causes the immune system to collapse. But no vaccine has yet been found to combat the virus, and once the infection takes hold, no known drug will prevent the long and agonizing death that almost always follows.

The dimensions of the epidemic, in the meantime, have grown at an accelerating rate. By 1983 some 3,000 Americans had contracted the disease, and 1,283 had died. Five years later nearly 70,000 had fallen ill and more than half had died. By 1992 the national death toll is expected to surpass 250,000. And that is just the beginning. AIDS has appeared in more than 130 countries, with nearly 100,000 cases reported and perhaps an equal number of unreported cases. Worldwide, some 10 million men and women are thought to harbor the virus. Based on current trends, at least half will develop the disease itself, and most of those who do will be dead within three years.

Beyond the plagues of nature, man himself could well unleash a virus or bacteria that swarms unexpectedly out of control. In laboratories in the United States and abroad, scientists manipulate the genetic material of living cells to create new and beneficial life forms. By isolating the genes that govern insulin production in human beings, then splicing them into harmless natural bacteria, they build biological factories for turning out abundant supplies of insulin for the world's diabetics. Similar work has produced bacteria that gobble up oil spills, chemicals that keep crops from freezing, artificial viruses that kill insect pests, and super-fat piglets and other new animal breeds. Genetic engineering is still an infant science, however, and some of the organisms in the researchers' test tubes are lethally infectious. A system of government safeguards seeks to keep them imprisoned in the laboratory. But should one escape and rage unchecked through the environment, it could wreak more evil than all the plagues in history.

Other byproducts of human progress are already having an effect on the environment. For the past 200 years, ever since mankind started burning coal and oil to fuel the engines of industrial life, we have poured ever greater amounts of soot, smoke, and gaseous refuse into the atmosphere. Among the worst pollutants are the oxides of sulfur and nitrogen, which waft into the sky and then return to earth as ingredients of a new kind of meteorological event: acid rain.

Downwind from factories and highways, forests die, crops shrivel, and fish life expires in poisoned lakes.

The spruces of Germany's Black Forest are turning a sickly brown; streams in New York's Adirondack Mountains run barren of trout. Periodic red tides—blooms of toxic algae encouraged by acid rain—infest the fishing grounds of the U.S. eastern seaboard, costing fishermen billions of dollars in lost catch.

Sometimes even man's efforts to clean up after himself seem to backfire. Among the most stable industrial chemicals are various compounds of chlorine and fluorine known as CFC's. Used as solvents, refrigerants, in plastic foam packaging, and as spray-can propellants, CFC's are clean, non-toxic, and long lasting. And this is their problem. Released into the air,

305

rate of 1.7 percent annually, our numbers will climb from the present 5 billion to around 8 billion by 2020. In the process of feeding ourselves, we exhaust the fertility of our farmlands; more than three tons of topsoil blow off each acre of U.S cropland in a single year. We deplete our water tables, cut down our rain forests, crowd out the animals that compete with us for living space. About one-third of the earth's land surface now consists of desert, and nearly a quarter of it was added during this century by such activities as excessive timber cutting, overfarming, and overgrazing. The Sahara creeps south at about 15 miles per decade—one reason for the famine in countries along its southern margin.

The Sahara's growth may also be one of the side-effects of the slow but unmistakable rise in temperatures around the world during the past century. If that trend continues, many present centers of world civilization will almost surely plunge into terminal decline. One disastrous consequence of long-term global warming could be a marked rise in sea levels, brought about in part by the melting of the great polar ice sheets. More than 25 million cubic kilometers of water are held there in frozen suspension, most of it in the Greenland and Antarctic ice caps.

Winds of change *will sweep the globe as the next ice age gradually pushes Arctic weather into latitudes that have not known winter in thousands of years.*

they linger for centuries, drifting up into the stratosphere, where they do their damage. A dozen or so miles above the earth's surface, an invisible blanket of ozone gas helps filter out ultraviolet rays from the sun. Large doses of ultraviolet light can be very dangerous, causing skin cancer, blistering sunburn, and freakish mutations in plants and animals of all kinds. And CFC's destroy the ozone layer that shields us from it.

In recent years the concentration of stratospheric ozone has dropped sharply enough to cause genuine alarm among scientists—and spur an international accord restricting the use of CFC's. But that agreement will only slow the decline, not reverse it. Meanwhile, more and more ultraviolet light will reach the earth's surface. Cancer incidence will rise dramatically. Crops may become stunted, leading to episodes of mass starvation. The rich oceanic broth of plankton and other tiny marine forms that larger fish feed on would be endangered. If that happens, one expert warns, "the whole ecosystem will absolutely collapse. We can say good-bye to the whales, the seals, the penguins"—and much else that lives in the sea.

Perhaps it is inevitable that mankind is wearing down the environment as we spew out refuse in our quest for a better life. And each year there are more of us crowding onto an already congested planet. If the world's population increase continues at its present

If the polar masses of ice begin to melt, ocean levels could surge upward by as much as 210 feet.

Even a moderate rise in temperature would put Belgium, Holland, and almost all the world's seaports underwater. Vast sweeps of farmland would disappear from Asia. Parts of Brazil and Australia would be awash. Scandinavia would become an island. The Atlantic would roll across Delaware, Florida, and Louisiana to lap at the foothills of the Appalachians. Pacific breakers would crash against the Sierra Nevada.

Such a wholesale meltdown is unlikely in the decades ahead, but the fact remains that the oceans have already begun to rise—by a foot or more in places during the past 100 years. They may climb another one to three feet in the next, thanks partly to the runoff from melting glaciers and partly to the fact that ocean water expands as the temperature rises.

For the moment, the process is gradual enough that levees, breakwaters, and floodgates can contain the damage. But in a major oceanic upswell, such defenses would be blown away like a pup tent in a tornado. One possible trigger for such a catastrophe would be the sudden collapse of a single ice formation—the West Antarctic ice sheet. The glacier lies frozen in place, but warmer temperatures could cause all 2 million cubic kilometers of it to come crashing into the sea, sending water levels up by 16 to

306

19 feet and swamping many of the world's great cities.

Not all scientists concur with this scenario, to be sure. Some experts feel that today's climbing thermometer is simply a minor fluctuation in the climate cycle. Indeed, from the perspective of the planet's long-term climate shifts, we are heading for a deep and lasting chill.

Over the past 30 to 40 million years, the world has been gripped by a succession of ice ages. These frigid periods, in fact, seem to be the world's normal state, with each cold spell lasting about 100,000 years. The warm times in between—the interglacials—have been mere flickers of time, no more than 10,000 to 12,000 years apiece. We may now be nearing the end of one such sunny era.

The last great ice age ended about 10,000 years ago; could the next be on the way?

Many scientists believe the fundamental cause of ice ages is a series of wobbles and shifts in the earth's orbit that allow less sunlight to reach the poles. As the next such period approaches, events on earth could sharply accelerate the process. A cluster of volcanic eruptions within the span of a few years—something that has happened before—could surround the earth with a shroud of vapor clouds. The sun would barely glimmer, pale and cold in the murky sky. January snows would linger on through spring and summer, their gray-white surfaces reflecting heat back into the sky. Crops would shrivel for lack of warmth, famine would spread, and fuel supplies would dwindle.

As more snows built up in the years that followed, they would form vast sheets of glacial ice. The chill would become even deeper. Ice would blanket much of the world's temperate zones. All Scandanavia would lie buried beneath the ice pack, along with most of Britain, Germany, Poland, and the northern Soviet Union. The ice would swallow up fully a third of the United States. Chicago, Detroit, St. Louis, and New York would all go under. Bleak tundra conditions would prevail throughout the rest of the nation. Miami would reside in a new Siberia.

Lands to the south would fare no better. With the change in climate, the world's deserts would surge toward the equator, obliterating huge tracts of agricultural land. Meanwhile, the oceans would diminish as ever greater percentages of the world's moisture became trapped in the ice sheets. Vast stretches of continental shelf would be laid bare, and savage winds gusting across these desiccated barrens would raise still more clouds of sun-blocking dust. Mankind would survive, to eke out a bitter, chilly existence. But civilization as we know it would disappear.

On the most distant horizon, it will not be ice but fire that writes the last chapter of earth history. Every star has a natural life span, and our sun is no exception. About 5 billion years from now, as the sun's nuclear fuel begins to sputter out, its core will contract and its outer shell will expand in a last fiery burst. Mercury and Venus will be engulfed; the earth's surface will be baked dry. The ultimate fire is a cosmic certainty—though by then our descendants may well have colonized a dozen different solar systems, and who might be here to experience the fireball is anybody's guess. Until that day the world must deal with the crises at hand—and use our creative energies to preserve the planet for future generations to inherit.

Hope springs eternal *in nature as well as in the human spirit. One insistent sprout pushing its way up through the ashen remains of an eruption offers a reminder that our planet's destructive forces have always been balanced by its tireless capacity for healing and renewal.*

CATALOG OF CATASTROPHES

GREAT NATURAL DISASTERS have plagued mankind from time immemorial and will no doubt continue to do so for as long as we walk this planet. Hardly a week goes by without some demonstration somewhere on earth of nature's awesome power to wreak havoc on human life and property. In this book we have recounted some of the most spectacular examples of nature's fury. Following is a selective listing of other natural calamities, past and present, which by their power and destructiveness also deserve to be known as great.

Avalanches & Landslides

The Italian Alps. October 218 B.C. While crossing the Alps to conquer Rome, the Carthaginian army under the great general Hannibal suffered tremendous losses: 18,000 men, 2,000 horses, and several elephants are believed to have perished—many of them victims of Alpine avalanches.

Chiavenna Valley, northern Italy. September 4, 1618. A landslide here destroyed two villages and killed 2,427 people.

Saas, Switzerland. Winter 1689. Avalanches killed more than 300 people in Alpine towns during this terrible winter. With more than 70 dead, the town of Saas, near today's fashionable ski resort of Klosters, was one of the the worst hit.

Goldau Valley, Switzerland. September 2, 1806. The top of the Rossberg, a 5,000-foot peak in central Switzerland, suddenly came loose. The resulting landslide roared into the valley below, wiped out four villages, and killed 457 people.

Wellington, Washington. March 1, 1910. A massive avalanche near this way station in the Cascade Mountains swept a snowbound train and all its passengers into a gorge 150 feet below. As many as 118 people died in the worst snowslide in U.S. history.

Austrian-Italian Alps. 1915–18. During World War I, thousands of soldiers—perhaps as many as 40,000—were killed on the Alpine front by avalanches, many deliberately set off by cannon fire. "The mountains in winter were more dangerous than the Italians," observed an Austrian ski-troop instructor after avalanches killed some 3,000 soldiers in a single 48-hour period.

Kansu Province, China. December 16, 1920. In this mountainous northern region, a quake registering 8.6 on the Richter scale unleashed a series of deadly landslides. Together the tremors and slides may have taken as many as 200,000 lives.

Khait, Tadzhikistan, U.S.S.R. 1949. Triggered by an earthquake, two landslides converged on the Soviet town of Khait in Central Asia, killing 12,000 people.

Blons, Austria. January 12, 1954. At 10:30 A.M. a snowslide crushed the center of Blons, a town of some 367 people. Nine hours later, as survivors were trying to dig out victims, a second avalanche resulted in a death toll of 200.

Nevado de Huascarán, Peru. January 10, 1962. Three tons of snow and ice dropped from the slopes of Huascarán, one of the highest peaks in the Andes, into the valley below. The result: 4,000 fatalities.

Huancavelica Province, Peru. April 16, 1974. Triggered by unusually heavy rains, a landslide in this region about 230 miles southeast of Lima took at least 200 lives and forced the evacuation of 9,000 people.

Lahaul Valley, India. Early March 1979. After nearly a week of heavy snows over the Himalayan foothills in northern India, avalanches buried the Lahaul Valley in up to 20 feet of snow. At least 200 people died.

"No one wept. . . . When the service was over we filed out, one by one. No one said a word but the same thought was on our minds, the thought of the avalanche that might still come. Slowly the people made their way back to their homes through snowdrifts and blizzard. How many of them remembered the old saying in Blons that only five houses were safe in the entire village?"

From an account of the Blons avalanches of 1954

Szechuan Province, China. October 1981. A series of landslides in this southern Chinese province cost 240 people their lives; another 100,000 were left homeless.

Catak, Turkey. June 23–24, 1988. Tons of mud and rock slid down a rain-soaked mountain onto this village near the Black Sea. An estimated 300 people perished.

Droughts & Famines

Central & western Europe. 1315–17. Unusually heavy rains in the spring and summer of 1315 devastated crops and resulted in a famine that killed as much as 10 percent of the population.

Bengal, India. 1769–70. Five of the world's 10 worst famines occurred in India between this date and 1900, killing from 13 million to as many as 26 million people. In each case the cause of the famine was either the failure of the monsoons to bring sufficient rain, or crop damage resulting from too much rain.

U.S.S.R. 1921–22. Drought in southern Russia and the Ukraine, the breadbasket of the Soviet Union, led to a famine in which 5 million people may have died.

China. 1928–29. A drought-caused famine in three central provinces killed 3 million people.

China. 1988. By midsummer, drought had damaged millions of acres of crops in China's central and southern farm belts, while along the east coast, flash floods killed thousands, left tens of thousands homeless, and further damaged crops in the world's most populous nation.

U.S.A. & Canada. 1988. The most severe drought since the Dust Bowl days of the 1930's devastated farms and ranches from California to Georgia and in the Canadian provinces of Manitoba, Saskatchewan, and Alberta. By midsummer the drought had become the costliest in U.S. history.

Earthquakes & Tsunamis

Gulf of Chihli, China. September 27, 1290. Among the ten worst seismic disasters in history, this earthquake in northeastern China left an estimated 100,000 people dead.

Shensi Province, China. January 23, 1556. More than 800,000 people died when a massive earthquake in this northern Chinese region destroyed the artificial caves, carved out of the sides of cliffs, in which millions of peasants lived.

Shemakha, Caucasia. November 1667. An earthquake badly damaged this ancient silk manufacturing town in what is now Soviet Central Asia; 80,000 people died.

Port Royal, Jamaica. June 7, 1692. Thousands were killed as a combination of earthquake and tsunami obliterated this Caribbean seaport and pirate haven.

Quito, Ecuador. February 4, 1797. A massive earthquake altered the landscape around Quito, Ecuador's 9,350-foot-high capital, and killed almost all of its 40,000 inhabitants.

Concepción, Chile. February 20, 1835. A quake witnessed by Charles Darwin killed more than 5,000 people in the Chilean cities of Concepción and Santiago, while a tsunami associated with the tremor ruined the village of Talcahuano.

Charleston, South Carolina. August 31, 1886. The strongest quake ever reported on the East Coast was felt from Boston to New Orleans and as far west as Milwaukee. Worst hit was Charleston, where 100 people died.

Kansu Province, China. December 26, 1932. Another earthquake in this disaster-prone area of northern China claimed some 70,000 lives.

Sanriku, Japan. March 3, 1933. An earthquake-generated tsunami killed 3,000 people, sank 8,000 ships, and destroyed 9,000 dwellings in the Sanriku district of northeastern Honshu, Japan's largest island.

Erzincan, Turkey. December 27, 1939. A quake measuring 8 on the Richter scale virtually wiped out this town in eastern Turkey, killing between 20,000 and 40,000 people.

Assam, India. August 15, 1950. One of the most powerful quakes on record raised the level of the Brahmaputra River and killed some 1,500 people in a sparsely inhabited area near the India-Tibet border.

"A bad earthquake at once destroys our oldest associations: the earth, the very emblem of solidity, has moved beneath our feet like a thin crust over a fluid." *Charles Darwin*

Agadir, Morocco. February 29, 1960. Within 15 seconds, a midnight quake killed 12,000 people in this coastal resort.

South-central Chile. May 21–30, 1960. A series of severe quakes killed more than 5,000 Chileans. On May 22 the worst of the tremors generated tsunamis that raced across the Pacific, adding another 450 deaths to the disaster toll.

Guatemala City, Guatemala. February 4, 1976. A powerful pre-dawn quake buried thousands of Guatemala City residents in the ruins of their adobe houses. The quake and its aftershocks killed 23,000, injured 50,000, and left as many as 1 million people homeless.

Bucharest, Romania. March 4, 1977. Felt from Moscow to Rome, this quake, most likely the strongest to hit Central Europe in modern times, registered 7.2 on the Richter scale and killed some 1,500 people in Romania.

Tabas, Iran. September 16, 1978. A stopover on Marco Polo's journey to China, this ancient Persian market town was leveled by a powerful earthquake that ruined scores of cities and towns and killed more than 16,000 people.

Al Asnam, Algeria. October 10, 1980. Destroyed by earthquake in 1954 and then rebuilt, this city west of Algiers was leveled once again by two tremors that hit shortly after noon on the Muslim sabbath. The result: some 2,600 people dead and another 60,000 injured.

Bihar, India, & Nepal. August 21, 1988. In the worst Himalayan earthquake since the 1950 Assam disaster, a 6.5 Richter scale tremor rocked the India-Nepal border, killing at least 900 and injuring thousands more.

Floods

The Netherlands & England. 1099. Some 100,000 people are believed to have died in this flood caused by a combination of high tides and storm waves. The North Sea has always threatened the lands bordering it, especially Holland. Three of history's 10 most destructive floods—in 1099, 1287, and 1421—have occurred in this low-lying region.

St. Petersburg, Russia. November 19, 1824. Dammed up by ice floes, the Neva River overflowed, drowning 10,000 people in the czarist capital of St. Petersburg (now Leningrad) and nearby Kronstadt.

Dayton, Ohio. March 25–26, 1913. Heavy rains and a sudden spring thaw caused the Ohio River and its tributaries to overflow their banks, killing between 500 and 700 people and nearly wiping out the city of Dayton.

Northern China. 1939. Some 500,000 people died when all the region's rivers overflowed at once; millions more may have perished in the ensuing famine.

Fukien Province, China. Summer 1948. Two months of relentless rain caused the Min River in southeastern China to burst its banks, sending a million refugees fleeing to higher ground. The death toll reached 3,500, and with much of the rice crop wiped out, famine added to the misery of Fukien and its neighboring provinces.

Kansas & Missouri. July 1951. Coming after two months of heavy rains, a four-day storm flooded the Kansas River basin. Forty-one people died, 850,000 acres of cropland were inundated, and property damage surpassed $1 billion, a record at the time for a U.S. natural disaster.

Lynmouth, England. August 15–16, 1952. After receiving nine inches of rain in less than 24 hours, the swollen East and West Lyn rivers sent a wall of water 40 feet high racing into the defenseless town below; 84 people in and around Lynmouth drowned.

Tehran, Iran. August 17, 1954. A flash flood in a normally dry gulch killed more than 1,000 Muslim pilgrims as they worshiped at a shrine near Iran's capital.

Orissa, India. October 7–12, 1955. The deadly monsoons of 1955 flooded the state of Orissa, 200 miles southwest of Calcutta, killing about 1,700 people.

Vaiont Dam, Italy. October 9, 1963. A sudden landslide sent 150 million tons of rock and debris plummeting into the reservoir behind this dam in the Italian Alps. Water poured over the dam face in a 230-foot-high wave that flooded the narrow Piave River valley below, drowning at least 2,500 people.

Mekong Delta, Vietnam. November–December 1964. Typhoons Iris and Joan flooded more than 5 million acres of the delta and left 5,000 dead.

Tunisia. September–October 1968. After 38 days of rain, 80 percent of this normally dry North African country was under water; 542 people drowned, and 1 million head of cattle were lost.

Rapid City, South Dakota. June 9, 1972. A month of heavy rains caused the Canyon Lake Dam above this city to break and spill its contents onto the population below. Floodwaters destroyed 80 blocks in Rapid City and killed 200 people.

Big Thompson Canyon, Colorado. July 31, 1976. A flash flood tore through Thompson Canyon, raising the river's water level by some 20 feet. At least 85 people, most of them vacationers in this resort area, were swept away.

Northern India. September 1978. The worst monsoons in decades led to devastating floods throughout northern India. Nearly 13 million acres of crops were destroyed, and in Calcutta alone some 15,000 people died.

Sudan. August 1988. Coming after a long drought and a serious locust invasion, torrential rains on August 4 and 5 caused one of the worst Nile floods of the 20th century. By mid-August at least 39 flood-related deaths had been reported and about 1.5 million people were homeless.

Bangladesh, September 1988. In the wake of unusually heavy monsoons, most of this impoverished land lay under water. At least 1,000, possibly as many as 2,000, people drowned or died of disease; some 25 million lost their homes.

Hurricanes & Typhoons

Jamestown, Virginia. August 27, 1667. The earliest description of a hurricane in what would be U.S. territory came from the first permanent English colony in North America. According to the London pamphlet *Strange News from Virginia*, "The dreadful Hurry Cane . . . overturned many houses, burying in the ruins much goods and many people."

Bay of Bengal, India. October 7, 1737. Second only to the typhoon that devastated East Pakistan in 1970, this cyclone sank 20,000 ships and took 300,000 lives along the mouth of the Hooghly River near Calcutta. Over the next 2½ centuries, the Bay of Bengal would spawn 7 of the 10 deadliest cyclones on record.

Caribbean. October 10–12, 1780. The worst Atlantic hurricane ever recorded cut a path of destruction from Barbados to Puerto Rico. The Great Hurricane killed between 20,000 and 30,000 people and virtually destroyed the British, Spanish, and French fleets.

New England. September 23, 1815. The Great September Gale struck New England 123 years, almost to the day, before the Great New England Hurricane of 1938. Both storms took the same path, hit with the same intensity, and similarly reshaped the shoreline.

Haiphong, Indochina. 1881. An estimated 300,000 people perished when a typhoon smashed into this city on the Gulf of Tonkin; many more are believed to have died of disease and hunger in the aftermath of the storm.

Bombay, India. June 6, 1882. A cyclone in the Arabian Sea inundated Bombay harbor. The result: more than 100,000 people in the city and its vicinity drowned.

Indianola, Texas. August 19, 1886. This hurricane killed 250 people and razed or damaged nearly every house in the small Gulf Coast town of Indianola. Having suffered two killer storms in 22 years, the people of Indianola decided to abandon their town for good.

Puerto Rico. August 1899. Hurricane San Ciriaco created havoc throughout the Caribbean, especially in Puerto Rico, where 3,000 people died.

Tokyo, Japan. September 30, 1918. In one of the most devastating typhoons ever to hit Tokyo, 1,619 people were killed and 2,400 were left homeless.

Lake Okeechobee, Florida. September 16–17, 1928. After killing nearly 2,000 people in the West Indies, this hurricane—the second worst in U.S. history—hit the south-central section of Florida with tremendous force. As miles of dikes collapsed under the storm's onslaught, the waters of Lake Okeechobee poured into surrounding fields, taking the lives of up to 2,500 people, most of them poor tenant farmers and sharecroppers.

Santo Domingo, Dominican Republic. September 3, 1930. A hurricane packing 200-mile-per-hour winds killed 2,000 Dominicans and nearly destroyed the nation's capital.

Osaka, Japan. September 21, 1934. Some 4,000 people, most of them residents of this bustling, if flimsily built industrial center, were killed when a powerful typhoon tore through the main Japanese island of Honshu.

Hokkaido, Japan. September 26, 1954. With its 100-mile-per-hour winds, this typhoon killed 1,600 people in and around Hakodate Bay in Japan's northern island of Hokkaido. Among the storm's victims were 1,172 passengers of the harbor ferry *Toya Maru*, which capsized under the assault of wind and waves.

Atlantic States (Hurricane Hazel). October 5–18, 1954. The third major storm to hit the eastern seaboard in 1954, Hazel began as a small tropical depression near the Caribbean island of Grenada, but gradually developed into a lethal hurricane. Its passage from the Caribbean to Toronto, Canada, left up to 1,200 people dead.

Louisiana (Hurricane Audrey). June 27, 1957. Despite advance warning, about 500 residents of Louisiana's Gulf Coast lost their lives in this storm, mainly because the warnings were ignored or treated as an excuse for a party.

Caribbean (Hurricane Flora). October 2–7, 1963. The second-deadliest storm ever recorded in the Atlantic, Flora began south of Trinidad and crossed the Caribbean to Cuba, killing more than 7,000 people along the way.

U.S. Gulf Coast (Hurricane Camille). August 14–22, 1969. After roaring through Louisiana, Mississippi, and Alabama with winds gusting up to 200 miles per hour, Camille went on to deposit torrential rains on the Mid-Atlantic States. Property damage amounted to $1.5 billion. Most of the 225 storm-related deaths occurred among residents of the Mississippi Delta region who failed to heed storm warnings.

Honduras (Hurricane Fifi). September 19–20, 1974. When this Caribbean killer was through with Honduras, 5,000 people were dead and about 60,000 had lost their homes.

Caribbean (Hurricane David). August 31–September 4, 1979. Some 1,200 people died during David's passage through the Caribbean. Worst hit were the Dominican Republic and especially Dominica, where little was left standing.

" 'Oh, God,' I thought, 'we're done for sure.' . . . The air had turned into a milky green swirl of mud, water, coconuts, and sheets of galvanized roof, like flying razor blades. Then our own roof went, and I knew we were dead."

From an eyewitness account of Hurricane David's arrival on the Caribbean island of Dominica

Caribbean & Mexico (Hurricane Gilbert). Mid-September, 1988. The fiercest Atlantic storm of the century left up to 300 people dead, 750,000 homeless, and more than $10 billion in damages after a weeklong rampage across Jamaica, the Yucatan Peninsula, and northeast Mexico.

Pestilence

Europe. Syphilis. 1500–50. Whether or not syphilis was brought to Europe from the New World—still a matter of controversy—the disease swept through Europe in the decades following Columbus's voyages of discovery. In the first 15 to 20 years of the epidemic, an estimated 10 million people died of syphilis.

Mexico. Measles. 1530–45. In the wake of the Spanish conquest of the Aztec empire, as many as 1½ million Indians contracted measles and, having no immunity to this foreign disease, quickly died of it.

Boston, Massachusetts. Smallpox. 1721–22. Most likely brought to the city by trading ships from the West Indies, smallpox afflicted some 6,000 Boston residents and killed about 950 of them. A concurrent epidemic in French Canada claimed thousands of lives.

Russia. Ergotism. 1722. This infection of the nervous system is caused by a fungus that grows on rotting rye grain. When tainted grain is baked into bread and eaten, it can lead to violent convulsions, hallucinations, burning pains, and death. In 1722 ergotism killed an estimated 20,000 Russians, among them so many of Peter the Great's soldiers that the czar had to abandon his planned invasion of the West.

New England. Diphtheria. 1735–40. A severe infection of the upper respiratory system, diphtheria took a terrible toll of New England's children over this five-year period. Some New Hampshire towns, for example, reported nearly an 80 percent mortality rate for children under 10.

Philadelphia, Pennsylvania. Yellow fever. 1793. A recurrent New World scourge since the 17th century, yellow fever killed up to 5,000 Philadelphians during this outbreak.

Russia. Typhus. Autumn 1812. Spread from person to person by infected lice, typhus decimated Napoleon's army during his Russian campaign. In one week, nearly 10,000 soldiers, out of a force numbering some 100,000 men, died of the disease. Another group of 300,000 soldiers lost 70 percent of its men to typhus.

Fiji Islands. Measles. 1875. Having contracted measles while on a visit to Sydney, Australia, the son of a local chieftain introduced the disease among the nonimmune population of the islands. Nearly all Fijians caught the disease, and about 20 percent died of it.

Memphis, Tennessee. Yellow fever. August–September 1878. In another of its periodic visitations, yellow fever claimed some 5,000 victims in Memphis. People fleeing the city carried the disease to other parts of the South: 4,000 perished in New Orleans, 2,000 in Greenville, Mississippi, and thousands more succumbed in communities throughout the Mississippi basin.

Eastern Europe. Typhus. 1914-23. A disease of wartime and crowded, filthy conditions, typhus broke out in a Serbian prisoner of war camp during the first year of World War I, spread into the civilian population, and claimed 150,000 lives in six months. Typhus eventually spread to Russia, where in the chaos of the war and the revolution that followed it, some 3 million people died of the disease.

"The streets [of Philadelphia] everywhere discovered marks of the distress that pervaded the city. More than one half the houses were shut up, although not more than one third of the inhabitants had fled into the country. Walking for many hundred yards few persons were met."

Dr. Benjamin Rush, on the yellow fever epidemic of 1793

U.S.S.R. Malaria. 1923. Another result of revolutionary upheaval, malaria struck more than 18 million Soviet citizens; in some places, 40 percent of the victims died.

U.S.A. Polio. Summer 1946. In the worst outbreak in 30 years, this crippling disease struck more than 25,000 people, most of them children, in 23 states. It was the last major polio epidemic before the development of effective polio vaccines.

India. Malaria. 1947. A parasitic disease transmitted by mosquitoes, malaria has been endemic on the subcontinent for centuries. The worst epidemic on record, however, took place in the chaotic first year of India's independence, when 75 million people contracted the disease and an estimated 1 million died of it.

India & Pakistan. Smallpox. 1967. In the last major epidemic of smallpox before its worldwide eradication, this age-old killer attacked 2.5 million people and killed 5,000.

New Delhi, India. Cholera. Summer 1988. The eagerly awaited monsoon rains that brought an end to more than two years of drought in northern India also washed sewage into New Delhi's water supplies. By midsummer, thousands of New Delhi residents had contracted cholera or gastroenteritis, and more than 200 had died of these water-borne diseases. Typhoid and hepatitis, which thrive in the same filthy conditions, threatened to increase the death toll.

Snow & Hail

Moradabad, India. April 20, 1888. The worst hailstorm on record left 246 people dead in this north Indian city.

Rostov, U.S.S.R. July 10, 1923. Hailstones weighing two pounds apiece killed 23 people as well as many head of cattle in this agricultural district northeast of Moscow.

Hyderabad, India. March 10, 1939. This hailstorm killed 200 cattle and 1,000 sheep and damaged crops over a 30-square-mile area in south-central India. Some of the hailstones reputedly weighed up to 7½ pounds, which would make them the heaviest ever recorded.

New York, New York. December 26, 1947. The worst snowstorm to hit New York City since 1888 deposited 25.8 inches of snow on Manhattan streets. The storm caused 77 deaths throughout the Northeast.

Buffalo, New York. January–February 1977. After 40 days of snowfall, the Buffalo area was buried in 35 inches of snow by January 28. Then came a storm from Canada, which packed 70-mile-per-hour winds and dumped masses of additional snow on the city. The four-day blizzard trapped 17,000 people at work and killed 29.

Boston, Massachusetts. February 6, 1978. A record 27.1 inches of snow fell on Boston in 32 hours. The blizzard roared through Massachusetts with hurricane-force winds that toppled houses and caused millions of dollars' worth of property damage. Twenty-nine people died in the storm, and 100,000 were left homeless.

Tornadoes

Natchez, Mississippi. May 7, 1840. The worst U.S. storm disaster of the pre–Civil War period, this deadly tornado hit Natchez at 2:00 P.M. and within 5 minutes wiped out a large part of the city's residential district and killed more than 300 people.

South-central U.S.A. February 9–19, 1884. For 10 horrifying days, tornadoes tore through the U.S. heartland from the Gulf of Mexico all the way to Illinois. The result: some 600 people lost their lives.

St. Louis, Missouri. May 27, 1896. In a 20-minute rampage, this tornado, the first major twister to hit a large U.S. urban center, killed at least 300 people in and around St. Louis, injured about 2,500, and damaged an estimated $12 million worth of property.

Midwest U.S.A. March 23–27, 1917. This series of twisters covered a record 293 miles in four days, killing 211 people in Tennessee, Kentucky, Indiana, and Illinois.

Southern U.S.A. March 21, 1932. Tornadoes cut a swath of destruction through six states, with central Alabama bearing the brunt of the disaster. Affecting mainly rural areas, the twisters killed 268 people, injured at least 1,000, and leveled hundreds of farm dwellings.

"There was a frightening rush of wind. Glass, dust, dirt, sticks—everything seemed to crash into the room and the hall. . . . Then the roof was either sucked off or blew off. . . . The rain came down on us and we huddled together screaming and crying . . . but you couldn't hear the crying and screaming for the wind and rain."

A seventh-grader from the Lake View School in San Angelo, Texas, on the tornado of May 11, 1953

Southern U.S.A. April 2–6, 1936. In one of the worst storm disasters ever to hit the South, violent tornadoes touched down in six states, from Arkansas to South Carolina. Of the more than 400 storm-related fatalities and 1,800 injuries, the majority occurred in just two towns: Tupelo, Mississippi, and Gainesville, Georgia. (Defying the odds, Gainesville would be hit by killer tornadoes three times in the 20th century: in 1903, 1936, and again in 1944.)

South-central U.S.A. March 21–22, 1952. Thirty-one storms ravaged six states from Alabama to Missouri. The death toll rose to 343, and 1,400 were injured.

U.S.A. May–June, 1953. This was a bad month in a bad year for tornadoes in the U.S.A., with devastating twisters hitting three widely scattered parts of the country. On May 11 a single tornado wiped out downtown Waco, Texas, killing 114 people. On June 8 a cluster of six tornadoes swept through southeastern Michigan and northern Ohio; hardest hit of the affected communities was Flint, Michigan, where 113 people died. On June 9 the most destructive twister ever to hit New England killed 94 people in Worcester, Massachusetts. In all, 250 tornadoes were spawned in the U.S.A. between January 1 and June 1, 1953.

Midwest U.S.A. April 11, 1965. On this Palm Sunday, 40 tornadoes and some 50 thunderstorms wreaked havoc in five midwestern states, with Indiana the most severely affected. When it was over, 271 people were dead, 5,000 were injured, and property damage amounted to more than $200 million.

Volcanic Eruptions

Mount Vesuvius. Naples, Italy. December 16, 1631. After 500 years of inactivity Vesuvius began a monthlong eruption that buried six villages in lava, covered nine others in mud, deposited ash over a wide area, including the city of Naples, and killed some 4,000 people.

Galunggung. Java. October 8 & 12, 1822. In the first of two eruptions, this long-inactive volcano sent streams of boiling mud pouring into the villages around it. Four days later, the volcano literally blew its top. In all, more than 100 villages were destroyed and 4,000 people killed.

La Soufrière. St. Vincent, West Indies. May 7, 1902. Just one day before the Mount Pelée disaster on neighboring Martinique, St. Vincent's La Soufrière erupted, killing as many as 2,000 islanders. Thousands more sought refuge in coastal waters and in underground rum storage rooms.

Mount Katmai. Alaska. June 6, 1912. The largest eruption in North American history occurred in an empty stretch of eastern Alaska and thus killed no one. But Mount Katmai's explosion transformed a green, wooded valley into a 50-square-mile moonscape. Now known as the Valley of 10,000 Smokes, the area is so blighted that it served as a training ground for astronauts.

Mount Kelud. Indonesia. May 1919. This volcano is located on a small island between Java and Sumatra. When Kelud erupted in 1919, its crater lake was transformed into a cauldron of seething water, lava, and ash—a deadly brew that eventually poured down the volcano's slopes, killing more than 5,000 villagers. To prevent a similar disaster in the future, a system of drainage pipes and tunnels was installed beneath the crater in 1926.

Mount Lamington. Papua-New Guinea. January 15, 1951. A 6,000-foot volcano on Papua's north coast, Mount Lamington was thought to be extinct until it began rumbling and ejecting smoke on January 15. Five days later, a huge glowing cloud of steam and dust—similar to Mount Pelée's lethal *nuée ardente*—exploded out of the volcano and killed as many as 5,000 people.

Mount Bezymianny. Kamchatka Peninsula, U.S.S.R. March 30, 1956. Located in the uninhabited northeast corner of Siberia and long considered extinct, Bezymianny began showing signs of life in the fall of 1955. On March 30, 1956, the mountain blew up, in one of the most powerful explosions of historical times.

Helgafell. Heimaey Island, Iceland. January 23, 1973. The eruption of the Helgafell volcano on this small island off Iceland's south coast lasted six months, covered a three-square-mile area in lava to a depth of 200 feet, and buried parts of the fishing town of Vestmannaeyjar in up to 20 feet of ash. The town's 5,500 inhabitants were safely evacuated, and by summer of 1975, some 2,400 of them had returned to dig out and start over.

INDEX

ACKNOWLEDGMENTS

The Editors are grateful to the following individuals for their generous assistance.

Paul Richard Bohr, Minnesota Trade Office,
  St. Paul, Minn.
Steven Brantley, U.S. Department of the Interior,
  David A. Johnston Cascades Volcano Observatory,
  Vancouver, Wash.
Richard Burkert, Johnstown Flood Museum,
  Johnstown, Pa.
Andrew Byers, Reader's Digest Canada,
  Montreal, Quebec, Canada
Linda Cordell, California Academy of Sciences,
  San Francisco, Calif.
Vere Dodds, Reader's Digest Australia, Sydney,
  Australia
Carlo Rossi Fantonetti, Reader's Digest Italy,
  Milan, Italy

Clint Hatchett, American Museum of Natural
  History, New York, N.Y.
M.V. Lee, Reader's Digest Hong Kong,
  Hong Kong
David McIntyre, Sweetgrass Communications,
  Crowsnest Pass, Alberta, Canada
Dr. William Ryan, Lamont-Doherty Observatory
  of Columbia University, Palisades, N.Y.
Haraldur Sigurdsson, University of Rhode Island,
  Kingston, R.I.
Dale Wade, U.S. Department of Agriculture,
  Forest Service, Southeastern Forest Experiment
  Station, Dry Branch, Ga.
Edwin Wengi, Swiss Federal Institute for Snow
  and Avalanche Research, Davos, Switzerland

CREDITS

ART:
George Buctel 28, 136, 174–175.
Howard Friedman 15, 18, 30, 34, 35, 44, 47, 55, 69, 123,
  151, 165, 173, 210, 223, 253, 264, 271, 283.
Joe LeMonnier 98, 106, 111, 141, 195, 209, 236, 302.

Dennis Lyall 212.
Christopher Magadini 4, 116–117, 157, 232–233,
  301, 306.
Ken Marschall 182–183, 187.
Richard Williams 80–81.

PHOTOGRAPHS:
The initials AP stand for AP/Wide World Photos and UPI for UPI/
Bettmann Newsphotos.
2–3 (Kilauea volcano) Ken Sakamoto/Black Star. 6 Photri. 7 Chicago
Historical Society. 8–9 (North Shore, Oahu, Hawaii) Darrell Ray Jones/
The Stock Market. 10–11 © 1975 Peabody Museum of Natural History,
Yale University, New Haven, Conn. 12 U.S. Department of Interior,
National Park Service. 13 top left J.L. Lepore/Photo Researchers; top right
Leonard Lee Rue III/Bruce Coleman Inc.; lower Jane Burton/Bruce

Coleman Inc. 14 top From "The World Book Encyclopedia" © 1988 World
Book, Inc.; bottom David A. Hardy/Science Photo Library/Photo Research-
ers. 16 © Mitchell Beazley Publishers, London. 17 right Roberto
Dei/Marka SRL. 18 top Kevin Fleming/Woodfin Camp & Associates. 19
Deep Sea Drilling Project, Scripps Institution of Oceanography. 20 upper
Art Resource, N.Y.; bottom Cliché des Musées Nationaux, Paris. 21
Harald Sund. 22 Hank Morgan/Rainbow. 23 top Jane Burton & Steve
Kirk/Bruce Coleman Inc.; lower U.S.S.R. Academy of Sciences. 24 Yale
Center for British Art, Paul Mellon Collection. 25 Erich Lessing/Magnum.

26 *left* The British Museum/© Michael Holford; *right* Reproduced by courtesy of the Trustees of the British Museum. **27** Robert Harding Picture Library. **29** *left* Jonathan Morse; *right* Henri Lhote. **31** Robert Harding Picture Library. **32–33** Steve Monti/Bruce Coleman Inc. **35** *bottom* Earth Observation Satellite Company. **36** *left* Art Resource, N.Y.; *right* Nimatallah/Art Resource, N.Y. **38 & 39** The Mansell Collection. **40** The Louvre, Paris. **41** The New York Public Library, Picture Collection. **42** Giraudon/Art Resource, N.Y. **43** The Bettmann Archive. **45** Historical Pictures Service, Chicago. **46** Giraudon/Art Resource, N.Y. **48** The J. Paul Getty Museum/Photography by Julius Shulman. **49** *top* Museo Archeologico Nazionale di Napoli/Pedicini Fotografia; *bottom* Scala/Art Resource, N.Y. **50** *left* Guidotti/Madeline Grimoldi Archives; *right* Scala/Art Resource, N.Y. **51** Werner Forman Archive. **52 & 53** Jonathan Blair/Woodfin Camp & Associates. **54** The Bettmann Archive. **55** *top right* The Granger Collection, New York. **56** The Art Museum, Princeton University, Gift of The American Committee for the Excavation of Antioch and Vicinity. **57** Princeton University, Department of Art and Archaeology. **58** *left* The Bettmann Archive; *right* From the Menologium of Basil II/Biblioteca Vaticana/Madeline Grimoldi Archives. **59** The Metropolitan Museum of Art, The Cloisters Collections, 1950. **60** Bodleian Library, Oxford. **61** Scala/Art Resource, N.Y. **62** The Victoria & Albert Museum. **63** Eliot Elisofon/National Geographic Society. **64** Courtesy of the Freer Gallery of Art, Smithsonian Institution, Washington, D.C. **65** S. Franklin/Sygma. **66** *upper* Jerry Jacka; *bottom* De Witt Jones/Woodfin Camp & Associates. **67** Courtesy Department of Library Services, American Museum of Natural History. **68** © David L. Brill 1982. **70–71** (Prairie fire, Alberta, Canada) Robert Semeniuk/The Stock Market. **72** Scala/Art Resource, N.Y. **74** The Metropolitan Museum of Art, The Cloisters Collection, 1954. **75** *upper* The Granger Collection, New York; *bottom* The New York Public Library, Picture Collection. **76** Germanisches Nationalmuseum, Nürnberg. **77** The Granger Collection, New York. **78** Mary Evans Picture Library. **79** *left* SEF/Art Resource, N.Y.; *right* The Granger Collection, New York. **82** *left* BPCC/Aldus Archive; *right* Courtesy of the University of Utah Press. **83** World Health Organization/Photography by J. Mohr. **84** Historical Pictures Service, Chicago. **85** The Granger Collection, New York. **86** Bridgeman/Art Resource, N.Y. **87** The Granger Collection, New York. **88** Reproduced by gracious permission of Her Majesty the Queen. **89** *left* Susan Elizabeth Cross; *right* British Library. **90** Photography by Carlo Gemmellaro, Catania. **91** Gianni Tortoli. **92** Mary Evans Picture Library. **93** The Mansell Collection. **94–95** The Granger Collection, New York. **96** Camara Municipal de Lisboa. **97** From "Planet Earth/Earthquake" by Bryce Walker and the Editors of Time-Life Books; Photo by Joseph Natanson © 1982 Time–Life Books Inc.; Photographed at the Osservatorio Sismico Andrea Bina, Perugia. **98** *upper & * **99** Sigurdur Thorarinsson, Courtesy of the Science Institute, University of Iceland. **101** *left* BPCC/Aldus Archive; *right* Cliché Ville de Nantes, Musées du Château des Ducs de Bretagne/Photography by Patrick Jean. **102** *left* "Conquerors of Yellow Fever" by Dean Cornwell reproduced with the permission of Wyeth-Ayerst Laboratories; *right* The New York Public Library, Picture Collection. **103** The Granger Collection, New York. **104** © David Muench Photography 1988. **105** The State Historical Society of Missouri. **107** Books for Libraries Press. **108** J.C. Allen & Son, Inc. **109** Elizabeth B. Stommel. **110** Tate Gallery, London. **112** National Library of Medicine. **113** The Bettmann Archive. **114 & 115** The Granger Collection, New York. **117** *bottom* Wendy W. Cortesi. **118** The New York Public Library, Picture Collection. **119** The Museum of the City of New York, The J. Clarence Davies Collection. **121** Historical Pictures Service, Chicago. **122** Courtesy of the New York City Fire Museum. **124** The Philadelphia Print Shop, Ltd. **125, 126, 127, 128–129** Chicago Historical Society. **130** Courtesy of The New-York Historical Society, New York City. **131** Gianni Tortoli. **132** Marc Riboud/Magnum. **133** The Cleveland Museum of Art, John L. Severance Fund. **134** The Bettmann Archive. **135** *top left & right* Historical Pictures Service, Chicago; *bottom* The Mansell Collection. **137** SuperStock International. **138** Jean-Loup Charmet. **139** Mary Evans Picture Library. **140** Frontispiece illustration from the 1888 Royal Society Report reproduced in "Krakatau 1883: The Volcanic Eruption and Its Effects" by Tom Simkin and Richard S. Fiske, published by Smithsonian Institution Press. **141** *left* Maurice Krafft. **142** Courtesy of The New-York Historical Society, New York City. **144** *top* Courtesy of The New-York Historical Society, New York City; *bottom* AP. **145** UPI. **146** The Philadelphia Print Shop, Ltd. **148** Courtesy of the Johnstown Flood Museum. **149** *left* American Red Cross; *right* Courtesy of the Johnstown Flood Museum. **150** The Victoria & Albert Museum. **152** Courtesy of California Historical Society, San Francisco/Photography by Arnold Genthe. **153** *left* Tom McHugh/Photo Researchers; *right* U.S. Department of Health, Education, and Welfare, Public Health Service. **154–155** (Tornado, Wichita, Kansas) E.R. Degginger/Bruce Coleman Inc. **158** American Red Cross. **159** Courtesy of the Rosenberg Library Association. **160** Brown Brothers. **161** Georg Gerster/Photo Researchers. **162** Library of Congress. **163** AP. **164** Courtesy of The New-York Historical Society, New York City. **165** Circus World Museum. **166** David McIntyre. **167** Provincial Archives of Alberta, Pollard Collection. **168–169** Courtesy of Hirschl & Adler Galleries Inc. **170 & 171** The Fine Arts Museums of San Francisco, Achenbach Foundation for Graphic Arts. **172** *top* Courtesy of The New-York Historical Society, New York City; *bottom* Courtesy of California Historical Society, San Francisco. **174** TASS from Sovfoto. **176** The New York Public Library. **177** The New York Public Library, Picture Collection. **178** Oregon Historical Society. **179** Archives of Ontario. **180** *upper* The Illustrated London News Picture Library; *bottom* Ulster Folk and Transport Museum Photographic Archive, Harland & Wolff Collection. **181** Popperfoto. **182** *left* Walter Lord Collection; *right* Ken Marschall, Collection of Joseph Ryan. **184 & 185** Brown Brothers. **186** © 1986 Woods Hole Oceanographic Institution. **188–189** Culver Pictures. **190** *top* Culver Pictures; *bottom* Avanti. **191** Culver Pictures. **192–193** Popperfoto. **194** AP. **196** Library of Congress. **197** Department of the Army, U.S. Army Corps of Engineers, Office of History. **198** *top* Courtesy of the Iberia Parish Library/Photography by I.A. Martin; *lower* The New York Public Library, Picture Collection. **199** *top* John Steiner Collection; *bottom* American Red Cross. **200** AP. **201** UPI. **202** The Bettmann Archive. **203** Library of Congress. **204** AP. **205** *top* UPI; *bottom* Courtesy of the Westfield Congregational Church, Danielson, Connecticut. **206** UPI. **207** Photoworld/FPG. **208** AP. **209** UPI. **211** AP. **213** UPI. **214** University of California, Berkeley. **215** National Oceanic and Atmospheric Administration. **216** Lyman House Memorial Museum, Hilo, Hawaii. **217** AP. **218–219** (Lightning over Lake Powell, Arizona) Gary Ladd. **220** Die Weltwoche, Zurich. **221** David Cupp. **222** *upper* David Cupp/Woodfin Camp & Associates; *bottom* David Cupp. **224 & 225** The Bettmann Archive/BBC Hulton. **226** London Daily Telegraph. **227** P. Robert Garvey/The Stock Market. **228** Popperfoto. **229** AP. **230** *left* UPI; *right* Popperfoto. **231** Adam Woolfitt/Woodfin Camp & Associates. **234** Loomis Dean, *Life* Magazine © 1956 Time Inc. **235** AP. **236** *left* Yomiuri Shimbun, *Life* Magazine © 1959 Time Inc. **237** Mainichi Shimbun, *Life* Magazine © 1959 Time Inc. **238** *left* UPI; *right* The Illustrated London News Picture Library. **239** Popperfoto. **240** Painting by Pierre Mion, © National Geographic Society. **241** U.S. Geological Survey. **242** UPI. **243** *left* Steve McCutcheon/AlaskaPhoto; *right* Dennis Cipnic/Black Star. **244** Vittoriano Rastelli. **245** Publifoto. **246** David Lees. **247** *top* David Lees; *bottom* David Lees, *Life* Magazine © 1966 Time Inc. **248** Balthazar Korab Ltd. **249** David Lees. **250** National Oceanic and Atmospheric Administration. **251** Larry Burrows, *Life* Magazine © 1970 Time Inc. **252** *left* UPI; *right* Larry Burrows, *Life* Magazine © 1970 Time Inc. **254** UPI. **255** AP. **256** American Red Cross. **257** Matt Herron/Black Star. **259 & 260** Eddie Adams/*Time* Magazine. **261** Camera Press Ltd. **262** Kansas State Network/Photography by Robert Dundas. **263** Drew Leviton. **265** *top* Gordon Baer/Black Star; *lower* AP. **266 & 267** Australian Picture Library. **268** AP. **269 & 270** Xinhua News Agency. **271** *top* UPI. **272 & 273** Gary Rosenquist/Earth Images. **274** *left* James Mason/Black Star; *right* © National Geographic Society by Robert Madden. **276** Michael Heller. **277** Herman Kokojan/Black Star. **278** Giansanti/Sygma. **279** *left* Piromallo/Gamma-Liaison; *right* Pierre Vauthey/Sygma. **280 & 281** Eduardo Fornacari/Gamma-Liaison. **282** S. Alost/Sygma. **284** *top* Gilmore Dufresne/*Time* Magazine; *lower* UPI. **285** UPI. **286 & 287** Coo-ee Picture Library. **288** Anthony Suau/Black Star. **289** Abbas/Gamma-Liaison. **290** S. Dorantes/Sygma. **291** David Walters/Black Star. **292** Robert Frerck/Odyssey Productions. **293** Roland Neveu/Gamma-Liaison. **294** Shelly Katz/Black Star. **295** Pierre Villard/Sipa Press. **296** *top* Eric Bouvet/Gamma-Liaison; *inset* Anthony Suau/Black Star. **297** Peter Turnley/Black Star. **298** Novosti/Sygma. **299** TASS from Sovfoto. **302** Based on a map from "Confronting Natural Disasters," 1987, With permission from the National Academy Press, Washington, D.C. **303** John Berkey/© 1986 Discover Publications. **304** Viviane Holbrooke/The Stock Market. **305** Centers for Disease Control, Atlanta. **307** Ralph Perry/Black Star.

Efforts have been made to reach the holder of the copyright for each picture. In several cases, these sources have been untraceable, for which we offer our apologies.

TEXT:

American Heritage. "Fire Makes Wind: Wind Makes Fire" by Stewart Holbrook, copyright © 1956 American Heritage Publishing Company. Reprinted with permission from American Heritage, August 1956.

Fulcrum Inc. *The Avalanche Book* by Betsy Armstrong and Knox Williams, copyright © 1986 Fulcrum Inc. (Western Skier Magazine 1/68.) Reprinted by permission.

The Johns Hopkins University Press. *The Earth Beneath the Sea* by Francis P. Shepard, copyright © 1959, 1967 by The Johns Hopkins Press. Reprinted by permission.

Lescher & Lescher, Ltd. *Prelude to Doomsday* by Lately Thomas, copyright © 1961 by Lately Thomas. Reprinted by permission.

Walker and Company. Condensation of "The Violent Planet" from *Earthshock* by Basil Booth and Frank Fitch, copyright © 1979 by Basil Booth and Frank Fitch. Reprinted by permission of Walker and Company and J.M. Dent & Sons, Ltd.

320